SECOND EDITION

BUSINESS INTELLIGENCE

A MANAGERIAL APPROACH

Efraim Turban
University of Hawaii

Ramesh Sharda
Oklahoma State University

Dursun Delen
Oklahoma State University

David King
JDA Software Group, Inc.

With contributions by

Janine E. Aronson
The University of Georgia

Prentice Hall

Boston   Columbus   Indianapolis   New York   San Francisco   Upper Saddle River
Amsterdam   Cape Town   Dubai   London   Madrid   Milan   Munich   Paris   Montreal   Toronto
Delhi   Mexico City   São Paulo   Sydney   Hong Kong   Seoul   Singapore   Taipei   Tokyo

Editorial Director: Sally Yagan
Editor in Chief: Eric Svendsen
Executive Editor: Bob Horan
Director of Editorial Services:
  Ashley Santora
Editorial Project Manager: Kelly Loftus
Editorial Assistant: Jason Calcaño
Director of Marketing: Patrice Lumumba Jones
Senior Marketing Manager: Anne Fahlgren
Marketing Assistant: Melinda Jensen
Senior Managing Editor: Judy Leale
Production Project Manager: Debbie Ryan
Senior Operations Specialist: Clara Bartunek
Senior Creative Director: Jayne Conte

Cover Designer: Suzanne Duda
Manager, Visual Research: Beth Brenzel
Manager, Rights and Permissions:
  Zina Arabia
Manager, Cover Visual Research & Permissions:
  Karen Sanatar
Cover Art: Fotolia
Lead Media Project Manager: Lisa Rinaldi
Full-Service Project Management: Saraswathi
  Muralidhar, PreMediaGlobal
Composition: PreMediaGlobal
Printer/Binder: Edwards Brothers
Cover Printer: Lehigh-Phoenix Color/Hagerstown
Text Font: Garamond

Credits and acknowledgments borrowed from other sources and reproduced, with permission, in this textbook appear on appropriate page within text.

Library of Congress Cataloging-in-Publication Data

Business intelligence: a managerial approach / Efraim Turban . . . [et al.].—2nd ed.
   p. cm.
   Includes bibliographical references and index.
   ISBN-13: 978-0-13-610066-9
   ISBN-10: 0-13-610066-X
  1. Business intelligence.   2. Industrial management.   I. Turban, Efraim.
   HD38.7.B8714 2011
   658.4'72—dc22   2010018459

10 9 8 7 6 5 4 3 2 1

Prentice Hall
is an imprint of

PEARSON

www.pearsonhighered.com

ISBN 10:   0-13-610066-X
ISBN 13: 978-0-13-610066-9

BUSINESS INTELLIGENCE

A MANAGERIAL APPROACH

Dedicated to our spouses and children with love

—The authors

ABOUT THE AUTHORS

Efraim Turban (M.B.A., Ph.D., University of California, Berkeley) is a visiting scholar at the Pacific Institute for Information System Management, University of Hawaii. Prior to this, he was on the staff of several universities, including City University of Hong Kong; Lehigh University; Florida International University; California State University, Long Beach; Eastern Illinois University; and the University of Southern California. Dr. Turban is the author of more than 100 refereed papers published in leading journals, such as *Management Science, MIS Quarterly*, and *Decision Support Systems*. He is also the author of 20 books, including *Electronic Commerce: A Managerial Perspective* and *Information Technology for Management*. He is also a consultant to major corporations worldwide. Dr. Turban's current areas of interest are Web-based decision support systems, the use of intelligent agents in e-commerce systems, and collaboration issues in global e-commerce.

Ramesh Sharda (M.B.A., Ph.D., University of Wisconsin–Madison) is director of the Institute for Research in Information Systems (IRIS), ConocoPhillips Chair of Management of Technology, and a Regents Professor of Management Science and Information Systems in the Spears School of Business Administration at Oklahoma State University (OSU). More than 100 papers describing his research have been published in major journals, including *Management Science, Information Systems Research, Decision Support Systems, INFORMS Journal on Computing, Production Operations Management, Journal of Management Information Systems, Interfaces,* and many others . He cofounded the AIS SIG on Decision Support Systems and Knowledge Management (SIGDSS). Dr. Sharda serves on several editorial boards, including those of *INFORMS Journal on Computing, Decision Support Systems*, and *ACM Transactions on Management Information Systems*. He also is coeditor of *Annals of Operations Research* and series editor of Integrated Information Systems Series and Operations Research Computer Science Interfaces book series with Springer. His current research interests are in decision support systems, collaborative applications, and technologies for managing information overload. He has consulted with many organizations and has taught in international executive education programs. Dr. Sharda is also a cofounder of **iTradeFair.com**, a company that produces virtual trade fairs.

Dursun Delen (Ph.D., Oklahoma State University) is an associate professor of management science and information systems in the Spears School of Business at Oklahoma State University (OSU). Prior to his appointment as an assistant professor at OSU in 2001, he worked for Knowledge Based Systems, Inc., in College Station, Texas, as a research scientist for five years, during which he led a number of decision support and other information systems–related research projects funded by federal agencies such as DoD, NASA, NIST, and DOE. His research has appeared in major journals including *Decision Support Systems, Communications of the ACM, Computers and Operations Research, Computers in Industry, Journal of Production Operations Management, Artificial Intelligence in Medicine,* and *Expert Systems with Applications,* among others. With Prof. David Olson, he recently published a book on advanced data mining techniques. He is an associate editor for the *International Journal of RF Technologies: Research and Applications*, and he serves on the editorial boards of the *Journal of Information and Knowledge Management, International Journal of Intelligent Information Technologies, Journal of Emerging Technologies in Web Intelligence,* and *International Journal of Service Sciences*. His research and teaching interests are in decision support systems, data and text mining, knowledge management, business intelligence, and enterprise modeling.

Dave King (Ph.D.) has over 25 years of experience leading the development of decision support, performance management, and enterprise system software. Currently, he is the senior vice president of New Product Development at JDA Software, Inc., in Scottsdale, Arizona. He joined JDA in 2004 after serving a number of years as the senior vice president of Product Development and CTO for Comshare, Inc. Dr. King has authored a number of articles and books and is the coauthor of *Electronic Commerce: A Managerial Perspective* (Prentice Hall). He also serves on a variety of industrial advisory and university boards including the MIS Advisory Board at the University of Georgia and the Technopolis Advisory Board at Arizona State University.

BRIEF CONTENTS

CONTENTS

PREFACE

We are experiencing a major growth in the use of computer-based decision support. Major companies such as IBM, Oracle, and Microsoft are creating new organizational units focused on analytics to help businesses get more effectiveness and efficiency out of their operations. As more and more decision makers become computer and Web literate, they are using more computerized tools to support their work. At the same time, consumers and organizations are generating unprecedented quantities of data through their interactions with each other. These data stores can be used to develop and promote appropriate products, services, and promotion to customers, and to optimize operations within an organization.

The purpose of this book is to introduce the reader to technologies called business intelligence. In some circles, *business intelligence* (BI) is also referred to as *business analytics*. We use these terms interchangeably. This book presents the fundamentals of the techniques and the manner in which these systems are constructed and used.

Most of the improvements made in this second edition concentrate on three areas: data mining, text and Web mining, and implementation and emerging technologies. Despite the many changes, we have preserved the comprehensiveness and user-friendliness that have made the text a market leader. Finally, we present accurate and updated material that is not available in any other text.

We will first describe the changes in the second edition and then expand on the objectives and coverage.

WHAT'S NEW IN THE SECOND EDITION?

With the goal of improving the text, this second edition makes several enhancements to the first edition. The new edition has many timely additions, and dated content has been deleted. The following major specific changes have been made:

- *Totally Revised or New Chapters.* Chapter 5, "Text and Web Mining" (a totally revised chapter), explores two of the most popular business analytics tools in a comprehensive yet easy-to-understand way. This chapter provides a wide variety of Application Cases to make the subject interesting and appealing to the intended audience. Chapter 6, "Business Intelligence Implementation, Integration, and Emerging Trends" is a new chapter that examines several new phenomena that are already changing or likely to change BI technologies and practices—Radio Frequency Identification (RFID), cloud computing, social networking, Web 2.0, virtual worlds, and so on. The important topic of BI implementation and the strategy of using on-demand computing have been added to this chapter. It also updates coverage on individual/organizational/societal impacts of computerized decision support.

- *Streamlined Coverage.* We have made the book shorter by deleting the preformatted online content, but we have retained the most commonly used content. We will use a Web site to provide updated content and links on a regular basis. We have reduced the number of references in each chapter. Moreover, we have streamlined the introductory coverage of BI and data mining in Chapter 1. This overview can prepare a student to begin thinking about a term project (should the instructor require it) right from the beginning of the term. We have also deleted the chapter that was available online and incorporated some of its content into this edition.

- *New Author Team.* This edition includes one new author and an expanded role for an author from the last edition. Building on the excellent content prepared by the authors of the previous edition (Turban, Sharda, Aronson, and King), Ramesh Sharda and Dursun Delen primarily revised this edition. Both Ramesh and Dursun have worked extensively in decision support system (DSS) and data mining areas and have industry as well as research experience.

- *New Figures for PowerPoints.* Although the figures in the print edition have been retained from the previous edition and new figures have been added for new content, all the figures have been redrawn in color and are available through the online image library for use in PowerPoint presentations.

- *A Live Update Web Site.* Adopters of this textbook will have access to a Web site that will include links to news stories, software, tutorials, and even YouTube videos related to topics covered in the book.

- *Revised and Updated Content.* All of the chapters have new opening vignettes and closing cases. These are based upon recent real application stories and events. In addition, Application Cases throughout the book have been updated to include recent examples of applications of a specific technique/model. New Web site links have been added throughout the book. We have deleted many older product links and references. Finally, most chapters have new exercises, Internet assignments, and discussion questions.

Other specific changes made to the second edition are summarized below:

- Chapter 1 includes new opening and closing cases as well as new and streamlined material within the chapter.

- Chapter 2 includes new material on data warehousing. It includes greater coverage of online analytical processing (OLAP) and multidimensional data modeling. A hands-on scripted demo of MicroStrategy software has been added. In addition, we have streamlined the sections on architectures and implementation issues. Finally, a section on the future of data warehousing has been included.

- Chapter 3 is a new chapter combining material from multiple chapters in the previous edition. Besides streamlining and updating the coverage through a new opening vignette, a new closing case, and discussions throughout, it includes new sections on key performance indicators (KPIs) and operational metrics, Lean Six Sigma, data visualization, and a section on business process management (BPM) architecture.

- Chapter 4 presents an in-depth, comprehensive coverage of data mining. The presentation of the material in this chapter follows a methodical approach resembling the standardized data mining project process. Compared to the corresponding chapter in the last edition, this chapter has been entirely rewritten to make it an easy-to-use digest of information for data mining. Specifically, it excludes text and Web mining (which are covered in a separate chapter) and significantly expands on the data mining methods and methodologies. It also provides detailed coverage on artificial neural networks and their use in managerial decision making. The most popular artificial neural network (ANN) architectures are described in detail; their differences as well as their uses for different types of decision problems are explained. A new section on the explanation of ANN models via sensitivity analysis has been added to this chapter.

- Chapters 5 and 6, as described earlier, are mostly new chapters.

We have retained many good things from the last edition and updated the content. These are summarized below:

- ***Links to Teradata University Network (TUN).*** Most chapters include links to TUN (**teradatauniversitynetwork.com**). The student side of the Teradata site (Teradata Student Network [TSN]; **teradatastudentnetwork.com**) mainly includes assignments for students. A visit to TSN allows students to read cases, view Web seminars, answer questions, search materials, and more.
- ***Fewer Boxes, Better Organized.*** We have reduced the number of boxes by more than 50 percent. Important material has been incorporated into the text. Now there are two boxes: Application Cases and Technology Insights.
- ***Software Support.*** The TUN Web site provides software support at no charge. It also provides links to free data mining and other software. In addition, the site provides exercises in the use of such software. Our book's Web site includes links for additional software.

OBJECTIVES AND COVERAGE

Organizations can now easily use intranets and the Internet to deliver high-value performance-analysis applications to decision makers around the world. Corporations regularly develop distributed systems, intranets, and extranets that enable easy access to data stored in multiple locations, collaboration, and communication worldwide. Various information systems applications are integrated with one another and/or with other Web-based systems. Some integration even transcends organizational boundaries. Managers can make better decisions because they have more accurate information at their fingertips.

Today's decision support tools utilize the Web for their analysis, and they use graphical user interfaces that allow decision makers to flexibly, efficiently, and easily view and process data and models by using familiar Web browsers. The easy-to-use and readily available capabilities of enterprise information, knowledge, and other advanced systems have migrated to the PC and personal digital assistants (PDAs). Managers communicate with computers and the Web by using a variety of handheld wireless devices, including mobile phones and PDAs. These devices enable managers to access important information and useful tools, communicate, and collaborate. Data warehouses and their analytical tools (e.g., OLAP, data mining) dramatically enhance information access and analysis across organizational boundaries.

This book is designed as a textbook for a BI course as well as a supporting text for courses such as introduction to MIS or business strategy. It may supplement an MBA technology management course as well, or a course in an MS in MIS program that has a managerial focus. Another objective is to provide practicing managers with the foundations and applications of BI, knowledge management, data mining, and other intelligent systems.

The theme of this revised edition is BI and business analytics for enterprise decision support. In addition to traditional BI applications, this edition expands the reader's understanding of the world of the Web by providing examples, products, services, and exercises and by discussing Web-related issues throughout the text. We highlight Web intelligence/Web analytics, which parallel BI/business analytics (BA) for e-commerce and other Web applications. The book is supported by a Web site (**pearsonhighered.com/turban**) that provides some online files. We will also provide links to many software tutorials through a special section of the Web site.

FEATURES

- ***Managerial Orientation.*** Business intelligence can be approached from two major viewpoints: technological and managerial. This text takes the second approach. Most of the presentations are about BI applications and implementation. However, we do recognize the importance of the technology; therefore, we present the essentials of technology in each chapter as applicable. We will also provide some detailed technology material in the tutorials through a blog site linked to the book's Web site.

- ***Real-World Orientation.*** Extensive, vivid examples from large corporations, small businesses, and government and not-for-profit agencies from all over the world make concepts come alive. These examples show students the capabilities of BI, its cost and justification, and the innovative ways real corporations are using BI in their operations.

- ***The Teradata University Network (TUN) Connection.*** The TUN is a free learning portal sponsored by Teradata, a division of NCR, whose objective is to help faculty learn, teach, communicate, and collaborate with others in the field of BI. Several hundred universities and faculty participate in and use TUN. Teradata also supports a student portal (**teradatastudentnetwork.com**) that contains a considerable amount of learning resources, such as cases, Web seminars, tutorials, exercises, and links to sources. Our text is interconnected with TUN mainly via the various assignments in all chapters offered to students through the portal.

- ***Most Current Topics.*** The book presents the most current topics relating to BI, as evidenced by the many 2008 and 2009 citations.

- ***Integrated Systems.*** In contrast to other books that highlight isolated Internet-based BI systems, we emphasize those systems that support the enterprise and its many users.

- ***Global Perspective.*** The importance of global competition, partnerships, and trade is increasing rapidly; therefore, international examples are provided throughout the book.

- ***Online Content.*** Files are available online to supplement text material. These include data files for homework assignments and links to many reports, videos, and software.

- ***User-Friendliness.*** While covering all major BI topics, this book is clear, simple, and well organized. It provides all the basic definitions of terms as well as logical conceptual support. Furthermore, the book is easy to understand and is full of interesting real-world examples that keep readers' interest at a high level. Relevant review questions are provided at the end of each section, so the reader can pause to review and digest the new material.

THE SUPPLEMENT PACKAGE: PEARSONHIGHERED.COM/TURBAN

A comprehensive and flexible technology-support package is available to enhance the teaching and learning experience. The following instructor supplements are available on the book's Web site, **pearsonhighered.com/turban**:

- ***Instructor's Manual.*** The Instructor's Manual includes learning objectives for the entire course and for each chapter, answers to the questions and exercises at the end of each chapter, and teaching suggestions (including instructions for projects).

- ***PowerPoint Slides.*** PowerPoint slides are available that illuminate and build on key concepts in the text.

- ***Test Item File and TestGen Software.*** The Test Item File is a comprehensive collection of true/false, multiple-choice, fill-in-the-blank, and essay questions. The questions are rated by difficulty level, and the answers are referenced by book page number. The Test Item File is available in Microsoft Word format and in the computerized form of Pearson TestGen. TestGen is a comprehensive suite of tools for testing and assessment. It allows instructors to easily create and distribute tests for their courses, either by printing and distributing through traditional methods or by online delivery via a local area network (LAN) server. TestGen features wizards that assist in moving through the program, and the software is backed with full technical support.

- ***Materials for Your Online Course.*** Pearson Prentice Hall supports our adopters using online courses by providing files ready for upload into Blackboard course management systems for testing, quizzing, and other supplements. Please contact your local Pearson representative for further information on your particular course.

ACKNOWLEDGMENTS

Many individuals have helped us create the text and the current revision since the publication of the first edition. First, we appreciate the efforts of those individuals who provided formal reviews of this text and our other DSS book—Decision Support and Business Intelligence Systems, 9th Edition, Prentice Hall, 2011.

Ann Aksut, Central Piedmont Community College
Bay Arinze, Drexel University
Ranjit Bose, University of New Mexico
Kurt Engemann, Iona College
Badie Farah, Eastern Michigan University
Gary Farrar, Columbia College
Jerry Fjermestad, New Jersey Institute of Technology
Martin Grossman, Bridgewater State College
Jahangir Karimi, University of Colorado, Denver
Huei Lee, Eastern Michigan University
Natalie Nazarenko, SUNY Fredonia
Kala Chand Seal, Loyola Marymount University
Roger Wilson, Fairmont State University
Vincent Yu, Missouri University of Science and Technology
Fan Zhao, Florida Gulf Coast University

Second, several individuals contributed material to the text or the supporting material. Barbara Wixom wrote the opening vignette for Chapter 1 to illustrate the special relationship of this book to Teradata University Network. Dan Power (**Dssresources.com** and University of Northern Iowa) permitted us to use information from his column on virtual worlds. Deborrah C. Turban (University of Santo Tomas, Philippines) contributed to Chapter 6. Finally, Haluk Demirkan of Arizona State University contributed the MicroStrategy material.

Third, major contributors to the previous edition include Janine Aronson (University of Georgia), who was our coauthor, contributing to the data warehousing chapter; Mike Goul (Arizona State University), whose contributions were included in Chapter 1; and T. P. Liang (National Sun Yet-Sen University, Taiwan), who contributed material on neural networks.

Fourth, several vendors cooperated by providing development and/or demonstration software: Acxiom (Little Rock, AR), California Scientific Software (Nevada City, CA), Cary Harwin of Catalyst Development (Yucca Valley, CA), Demandtec (San Carlos, CA), DS Group, Inc. (Greenwich, CT), Gregory Piatetsky-Shapiro of **KDNuggets.com**, Gary Lynn of NeuroDimension, Inc. (Gainesville, FL), Promised Land Technologies (New Haven, CT), Salford Systems (La Jolla, CA), Sense Networks (New York, NY), Gary Miner of Statsoft, Inc. (Tulsa, OK), Ward Systems Group, Inc. (Frederick, MD), and Wordtech Systems (Orinda, CA).

Fifth, special thanks to the Teradata University Network and especially to Michael Goul, Executive Director; Barb Wixom, Associate Director, TUN; Hugh Watson, who started TUN; Susan Baxley, Program Director; and Mary Gros, Teradata, a liaison between Teradata and the academic community, for their encouragement to tie this book with TUN and for providing useful material for the book.

Sixth, many individuals helped us with administrative matters and editing, proof-reading, charting, and preparations. These include Subramanian Rama Iyer (Oklahoma State University), Mike Henry (OSU), Angie Jungermann (OSU), Brittany Solomon (OSU), and Ivan C. Seballos II (De La Salle Lipa, Philippines). Judy Lang collaborated with all of us, provided editing, and guided us during the entire production of the first edition.

Finally, the Pearson Prentice Hall team is to be commended: Executive Editor Bob Horan, who orchestrated this project; our editorial project manager Kelly Loftus, who kept us on the timeline; Shanthi Lakshmipathy, who copyedited the manuscript; and the production team at Pearson Prentice Hall and the staff at PreMediaGlobal, who transformed the manuscript into a book.

We would like to thank all these individuals and corporations. Without their help, the creation of this book would not have been possible.

E.T.

R.S.

D.D.

D.K.

Note that Web site URLs are dynamic. As this book went to press, we verified that all the cited Web sites were active and valid. Web sites to which we refer in the text sometimes change or are discontinued because companies change names, are bought or sold, merge, or fail. Sometimes Web sites are down for maintenance, repair, or redesign. Most organizations have dropped the initial "www" designation for their sites, but some still use it. If you have a problem connecting to a Web site that we mention, please be patient and simply run a Web search to try to identify the new site. Most times, the new site can be found quickly. We apologize in advance for this inconvenience.

BUSINESS INTELLIGENCE

A MANAGERIAL APPROACH

This book deals with a collection of computer technologies that support managerial decision making by providing information on internal and external aspects of operations. These technologies have had a profound impact on corporate strategy, performance, and competitiveness. These technologies are collectively known as *business intelligence*.

Introduction to Business Intelligence

LEARNING OBJECTIVES

- Understand today's turbulent business environment and describe how organizations survive and even excel in such an environment (solving problems and exploiting opportunities)
- Understand the need for computerized support of managerial decision making

- Describe the business intelligence (BI) methodology and concepts and relate them to decision support system (DSS)
- Understand the major issues in implementing Business Intelligence

The business environment (climate) is constantly changing, and it is becoming more and more complex. Organizations, private and public, are under pressures that force them to respond quickly to changing conditions and to be innovative in the way they operate. Such activities require organizations to be agile and to make frequent and quick strategic, tactical, and operational decisions, some of which are very complex. Making such decisions may require considerable amounts of relevant **data, information,** and **knowledge**. Processing these, in the framework of the needed decisions, must be done quickly, frequently in real time, and usually requires some computerized support.

This book is about using business intelligence as computerized support for managerial **decision making**. It concentrates both on the theoretical and conceptual foundations of business intelligence for decision support, as well as on the commercial tools and techniques that are available. This introductory chapter provides more details of these topics as well as an overview of the book. This chapter has the following sections:

OPENING VIGNETTE: Norfolk Southern Uses Business Intelligence for Decision Support to Reach Success

There are four large freight railroads in the United States, and Norfolk Southern is one of them. Each day, the company moves approximately 500 freight trains across 21,000 route miles in 22 eastern states, the District of Columbia, and Ontario, Canada. Norfolk Southern manages more than $26 billion in assets and employs over 30,000 people.

For more than a century, the railroad industry was heavily regulated, and Norfolk Southern and its predecessor railroads made money by managing their costs. Managers focused on optimizing the use of railcars to get the most production out of their fixed assets. Then, in 1980, the industry was partially deregulated, which opened up opportunities for mergers and allowed companies to charge rates based on service and enter into contracts with customers. On-time delivery became an important factor in the industry.

Over time, Norfolk Southern responded to these industry changes by becoming a "scheduled railroad." This meant that the company would develop a fixed set of train schedules and a fixed set of connections for cars to go between trains and yards. In this way, managers could predict when they could get a shipment to a customer.

Norfolk Southern has always used a variety of sophisticated systems to run its business. Becoming a scheduled railroad, however, required new systems that would first use statistical models to determine the best routes and connections to optimize railroad performance and then apply the models to create the plan that would actually run the railroad operations. These new systems were called TOP, short for Thoroughbred Operating Plan; TOP was deployed in 2002.

Norfolk Southern realized that it was not enough to run the railroad using TOP, it also had to monitor and measure its performance against the TOP plan. Norfolk Southern's numerous systems generate millions of records about freight records, railcars, train **Global Positioning System (GPS)** information, train fuel levels, revenue information, crew management, and historical tracking records. Unfortunately, the company was not able to simply tap into this data without risking significant impact on the systems' performance.

Back in 1995, the company invested in a 1-terabyte Teradata data warehouse, which is a central repository of historical data. It is organized in such a way that the data are easy to access (using a Web browser) and can be manipulated for decision support. The warehouse data come from the systems that run the company (i.e., source systems), and once the data are moved from the source systems to the warehouse, users can access and use the data without risk of impacting operations.

In 2002, the data warehouse became a critical component of TOP. Norfolk Southern built a TOP dashboard application that pulls data from the data warehouse and then graphically depicts actual performance against the trip plan for both train performance and connection performance. The application uses visualization technology so that field managers can more easily interpret the large volumes of data (e.g., there were 160,000 weekly connections across the network). The number of missed connections has decreased by 60 percent since the application was implemented. And, in the past 5 years, railcar cycle time has decreased by an entire day, which translates into millions of dollars in annual savings.

Norfolk Southern has an enterprise data warehouse (EDW), which means that once data are placed in the warehouse, the data are available across the company, not just for a single application. Although train and connection performance data are used for the TOP application, the company has been able to leverage that data for all kinds of other purposes. For example, the marketing department has developed an application called accessNS, which was built for Norfolk Southern customers who want visibility into Norfolk Southern's extensive transportation network. Customers want to know where their shipments are "right now"—and at times, they want historical information: Where did my shipment come from? How long did it take to arrive? What were the problems along the route?

AccessNS allows more than 14,500 users from 8,000 customer organizations to log in and access predefined and custom reports about their accounts at any time. Users can access current data, which are updated hourly, or they can look at data from the past 3 years. AccessNS provides alerting and Really Simple Syndication (RSS) feed capabilities; in fact, 4,500 reports are pushed to users daily. The self-service nature of accessNS has allowed Norfolk Southern to give customers what they want and also to reduce the number of people needed for customer service. In fact, without accessNS, it would take approximately 47 people to support the current level of customer reporting.

Departments across the company—from engineering and strategic planning to cost and human resources—use the EDW. One interesting internal application was developed by human resources. Recently, the department needed to determine where to locate its field offices in order to best meet the needs of Norfolk Southern's 30,000+ employees. By combining employee demographic data (e.g., zip codes) with geospatial data traditionally used by the engineering group, human resources was able to visually map out the employee population density, making it much easier to optimize services offices locations.

Today, the Norfolk Southern data warehouse has grown to a 6-terabyte system that manages an extensive amount of information about the company's vast network of railroads and shipping services. Norfolk Southern uses the data warehouse to analyze trends, develop forecasting schedules, archive records, and facilitate customer self-service. The data warehouse provides information to over 3,000 employees and over 14,000 external customers and stakeholders.

Norfolk Southern was the first railroad to offer self-service BI, and its innovation is setting an example that other railroads have followed. The company was also one of the first railroads to provide a large variety of historical data to external customers.

QUESTIONS FOR THE OPENING VIGNETTE

1. How are information systems used at Norfolk Southern to support decision making?

2. What type of information is accessible through the visualization applications?

3. What type of information support is provided through accessNS?

4. How does Norfolk Southern use the data warehouse for human resource applications?

5. Can the same data warehouse be used for BI and optimization applications?

WHAT WE CAN LEARN FROM THIS VIGNETTE

This vignette shows that data warehousing technologies can offer a player, even in a mature industry, the ability to attain competitive advantage by squeezing additional efficiency from its operations. Indeed, in many cases, this may be the major frontier to explore. Getting more out of a company's assets requires more timely and detailed understanding of its operations, and the ability to use that information to make better decisions. We will see many examples of such applications throughout this book.

Additional resources about this vignette are available on the Teradata University Network (TUN), which is described later in the chapter. These include other papers and a podcast titled "Norfolk Southern Uses Teradata Warehouse to Support a Scheduled Railroad."

Source: Contributed by Professors Barbara Wixom (University of Virginia), Hugh Watson (University of Georgia; 2005), and Jeff Hoffer (University of Dayton).

1.1 CHANGING BUSINESS ENVIRONMENTS AND COMPUTERIZED DECISION SUPPORT

The opening vignette illustrates how a global company excels in a mature but competitive market. Companies are moving aggressively to computerized support of their operations. To understand why companies are embracing computerized support, including BI, we developed a model called the *Business Pressures–Responses–Support Model*, which is shown in Figure 1.1.

The Business Pressures–Responses–Support Model

The Business Pressures–Responses–Support Model, as its name indicates, has three components: business pressures that result from today's business climate, responses (actions taken) by companies to counter the pressures (or to take advantage of the opportunities available in the environment), and computerized support that facilitates the monitoring of the environment and enhances the response actions taken by organizations.

THE BUSINESS ENVIRONMENT   The environment in which organizations operate today is becoming more and more complex. This **complexity** creates opportunities on the one hand and problems on the other. Take globalization as an example. Today, you can easily find suppliers and customers in many countries, which means you can buy cheaper materials and sell more of your products and services; great opportunities exist. However,

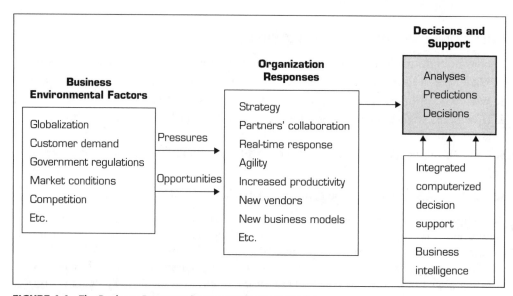

FIGURE 1.1   The Business Pressures-Responses-Support Model.

TABLE 1.1 Business Environment Factors that Create Pressures on Organizations

Factor	Description
Markets	Strong competition
	Expanding global markets
	Booming electronic markets on the Internet
	Innovative marketing methods
	Opportunities for outsourcing with Information Technology (IT) support
	Need for real-time, on-demand transactions
Consumer demands	Desire for customization
	Desire for quality, diversity of products, and speed of delivery
	Customers getting powerful and less loyal
Technology	More innovations, new products, and new services
	Increasing obsolescence rate
	Increasing **information overload**
	Social networking, Web 2.0 and beyond
Societal	Growing government regulations and deregulation
	Workforce more diversified, older, and composed of more women
	Prime concerns of homeland security and terrorist attacks
	Necessity of Sarbanes-Oxley Act and other reporting-related legislation
	Increasing social responsibility of companies
	Greater emphasis on sustainability

globalization also means more and stronger competitors. Business environment factors can be divided into four major categories: *markets, consumer demands, technology,* and *societal.* These categories are summarized in Table 1.1.

Note that the *intensity* of most of these factors increases with time, leading to more pressures, more competition, and so on. In addition, organizations and departments within organizations face decreased budgets and amplified pressures from top managers to increase performance and profit. In this kind of environment, managers must respond quickly, innovate, and be agile. Let's see how they do it.

ORGANIZATIONAL RESPONSES: BE REACTIVE, ANTICIPATIVE, ADAPTIVE, AND PROACTIVE Both private and public organizations are aware of today's business environment and pressures. They use different actions to counter the pressures. Vodafone New Zealand Ltd (Krivda, 2008), for example, turned to BI to improve communication and to support executives in its effort to retain existing customers and increase revenue from these customers (see End of Chapter Application Case). Managers may take other actions, including the following:

Employ strategic planning

Use new and innovative business models

Restructure business processes

Participate in business alliances

Improve corporate information systems

Improve partnership relationships

Encourage innovation and creativity

Improve customer service and relationships

Move to electronic commerce (e-commerce)

Move to make-to-order production and on-demand manufacturing and services

Use new IT to improve communication, data access (discovery of information), and collaboration

Respond quickly to competitors' actions (e.g., in pricing, promotions, new products and services)

Automate many tasks of white-collar employees

Automate certain decision processes, especially those dealing with customers

Improve decision making by employing analytics

Many, if not all, of these actions require some computerized support. These and other response actions are frequently facilitated by computerized DSS.

CLOSING THE STRATEGY GAP　One of the major objectives of computerized decision support is to facilitate closing the gap between the current performance of an organization and its desired performance, as expressed in its mission, objectives, and goals, and the strategy to achieve them. In order to understand why computerized support is needed and how it is provided, let us review the framework for business intelligence and its use in decision support.

SECTION 1.1 REVIEW QUESTIONS

1. List the components of and explain the Business Pressures–Responses–Support Model.
2. What are some of the major factors in today's business environment?
3. What are some of the major response activities that organizations take?

1.2　A FRAMEWORK FOR BUSINESS INTELLIGENCE (BI)

Decision support concepts have been implemented incrementally, under different names, by many vendors who have created tools and methodologies for decision support. As the enterprise-wide systems grew, managers were able to access user-friendly reports that enabled them to make decisions quickly. These systems, which were generally called executive information systems (EIS), then began to offer additional visualization, alerts, and performance measurement capabilities. By 2006, the major *commercial* products and services appeared under the umbrella term *business intelligence* (BI).

Definitions of BI

Business intelligence (BI) is an umbrella term that combines architectures, tools, **databases**, analytical tools, applications, and methodologies. It is a content-free expression, so it means different things to different people. Part of the confusion about BI lies in the flurry of acronyms and buzzwords that are associated with it (e.g., business performance management [BPM]). BI's major objective is to enable interactive access (sometimes in real time) to data, to enable manipulation of data, and to give business managers and analysts the ability to conduct appropriate analysis. By analyzing historical and current data, situations, and performances, decision makers get valuable insights that enable them to make more informed and better decisions. The process of BI is based on the *transformation* of data to information, then to decisions, and finally to actions.

A Brief History of BI

The term *BI* was coined by the Gartner Group in the mid-1990s. However, the concept is much older; it has its roots in the Management Information Systems (MIS) reporting systems of the 1970s. During that period, reporting systems were static and two-dimensional and had no analytical capabilities. In the early 1980s, the concept of *executive information systems* (EIS) emerged. This concept expanded the computerized support to top-level managers and executives. Some of the capabilities introduced were dynamic multidimensional (ad hoc or on-demand) reporting, **forecasting** and prediction, trend analysis, drill down to details, status access, and critical success factors (CSFs). These features appeared in dozens of commercial products until the mid-1990s. Then the same capabilities and some new ones appeared under the name BI. Today, a good BI-based enterprise information system contains all the information executives need. So, the original concept of EIS was transformed into BI. By 2005, BI systems started to include *artificial intelligence* capabilities as well as powerful analytical capabilities. Figure 1.2 illustrates the various tools and techniques that may be included in a BI system. It illustrates the evolution of BI as well. The tools shown in Figure 1.2 provide the capabilities of BI. The most sophisticated BI products include most of these capabilities; others specialize in only some of them. We will study several of these capabilities in more detail in Chapters 2 through 6.

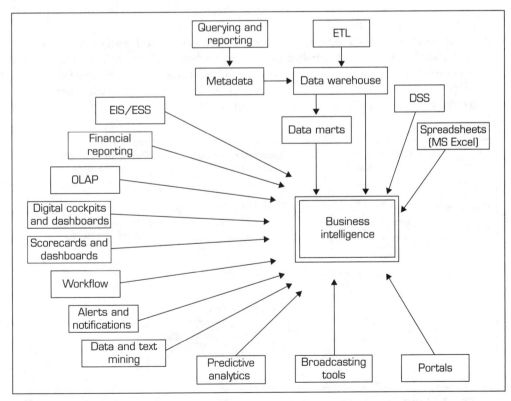

FIGURE 1.2   Evolution of BI.

The Architecture of BI

A BI system has four major components: a *data warehouse*, with its source data; ***business analytics***, a collection of tools for manipulating, mining, and analyzing the data in the data warehouse; *business performance management* (BPM) for monitoring and analyzing performance; and a *user interface* (e.g., a dashboard). The relationship among these components is illustrated in Figure 1.3. We will discuss these in detail in Chapters 2 through 6.

Notice that the data warehousing environment is mainly the responsibility of technical staff, whereas the analytical environment (also known as *business analytics*) is the realm of business users. Any user can connect to the system via the **user interface**, such as a browser. Top managers may also use the BPM component and also a dashboard. Some business analytics and user interface tools are introduced briefly in Section 1.7 and in Chapters 4 and 5.

DATA WAREHOUSING The data warehouse and its variants are the cornerstone of any medium-to-large BI system. Originally, the data warehouse included only historical data that were organized and summarized, so end users could easily view or manipulate data and information. Today, some data warehouses include current data as well, so they can provide real-time decision support (see Chapter 2).

BUSINESS ANALYTICS End users can work with the data and information in a data warehouse by using a variety of tools and techniques. These tools and techniques fit into two major categories:

1. ***Reports and queries.*** Business analytics include static and dynamic reporting, all types of queries, discovery of information, multidimensional view, drill down to details, and so on. These are presented in Chapter 3. These reports are also related to BPM (introduced next).
2. ***Data, text, and Web mining and other sophisticated mathematical and statistical tools.*** **Data mining** (described further in Chapters 2 through 6) is a process of searching for unknown relationships or information in large databases or data warehouses, using intelligent tools such as neural computing, **predictive analytics** techniques, or advanced statistical methods (see Chapter 4). As

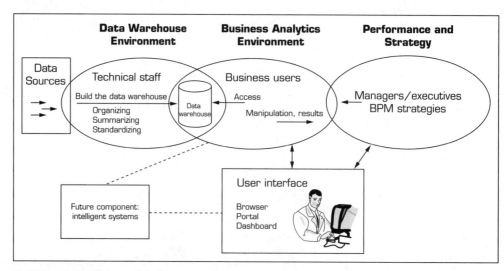

FIGURE 1.3 **A High-Level Architecture of BI.** *Source:* Based on W. Eckerson, *Smart Companies in the 21st Century: The Secrets of Creating Successful Business Intelligent Solutions.* The Data Warehousing Institute, Seattle, WA, 2003, p. 32, Illustration 5.

discussed further in Chapter 5, mining can be done on Web or textual data as well. Two examples of useful applications of data mining follow:

EXAMPLE 1

Forecasting success of new products or services is a challenge for any business. Especially difficult is the problem of estimating revenue from entertainment products such as movies, music, and so on. Epagogix specializes in predicting success of movies based on a detailed analysis of movie scripts. As reported by Davenport and Harris (2009), it predicted a paltry $7 million gross for *Lucky You* in 2007 even though the film included major star power and a major director and cost $50 million to make. The film earned only $6 million. Models based on preferences and recommendations are used by other vendors such as Netflix to predict which movies/music will sell better. (We will see another application of data mining in prediction of box office success of movies, based on our research in Chapter 4.)

EXAMPLE 2

National Australia Bank uses data mining to aid its predictive marketing. The tools are used to extract and analyze data stored in the bank's Oracle database. Specific applications focus on assessing how competitors' initiatives are affecting the bank's bottom line. The data mining tools are used to generate market analysis models from historical data. The bank considers initiatives to be crucial to maintaining an edge in the increasingly competitive financial services marketplace.

Application Case 1.1 describes an application of another BI technique for data mining—cluster analysis.

Application Case 1.1

Location, Location, Location

Hoyt Highland Partners is a marketing intelligence firm that assists health care providers with growing their patient base. The firm also helps determine the best locations for the health care providers' practices. Hoyt Highland was working with an urgent care clinic client. The urgent care clinic faced increased competition from other urgent care operators and convenient care clinics. The clinic needed to decide if it should move its location or change marketing practices to increase its income. To help with this decision, Hoyt Highland identified, using Acxiom's PersonicX system, where the most concentrated areas of the clinic's target audience were located.

Acxiom's PersonicX categorizes every U.S. household into one of 70 segments and 21 life-stage groups. The placement is based on specific consumer behavior as well as demographic characteristics. The information includes consumer surveys outlining behaviors and attitudes and location characteristics for important markets. Hoyt Highland used PersonicX to determine which clusters were well represented in the urgent care clinic database and which clusters provide the operator with the highest return-on-investment (ROI) potential.

Using the software's geospatial analysis capability, Hoyt Highland found that 80 percent of the clinic's patients lived within a 5-mile radius of a clinic location. It also found that young families were well represented, but that singles and seniors were underrepresented. In addition, it found that proximity is a top factor in the choice of an urgent care clinic. This analysis helped the clinic to determine that the best course of action was to change its marketing focus rather than to move its clinics. Today, the clinic focuses its marketing toward patients who live within a 5-mile radius of a clinic location and toward young families.

Source: "Location, Location, Location," Acxiom, **acxiom.com** (accessed March 26, 2009).

BUSINESS PERFORMANCE MANAGEMENT Also referred to as **corporate performance management (CPM)**, **business performance management (BPM)** is an emerging portfolio of applications and methodology that contains evolving BI architecture and tools in its core. BPM extends the monitoring, measuring, and comparing of sales, profit, cost, profitability, and other performance indicators by introducing the concept of management and feedback. It embraces processes such as planning and forecasting as core tenets of a business strategy. In contrast with the traditional DSS, EIS, and BI, which support the bottom-up extraction of information from data, BPM provides a top-down enforcement of corporate-wide strategy. BPM is the topic of Chapter 3 and is usually combined with the *balanced scorecard methodology* and dashboards.

THE USER INTERFACE: DASHBOARDS AND OTHER INFORMATION BROADCASTING TOOLS Dashboards (which resemble automobile dashboards) provide a comprehensive visual view of corporate performance measures (also known as key performance indicators), trends, and exceptions. They integrate information from multiple business areas. Dashboards present graphs that show actual performance compared to desired metrics; thus, a dashboard presents an at-a-glance view of the health of the organization. In addition to dashboards, other tools that broadcast information are **corporate portals**, digital cockpits, and other visualization tools (see Chapter 3). Many visualization tools, ranging from multidimensional cube presentation to virtual reality, are integral parts of BI systems. Recall that BI emerged from EIS, so many visual aids for executives were transformed to BI software. Also, technologies such as **geographical information systems (GIS)** play an increasing role in decision support.

Styles of BI

The architecture of BI depends on its applications. MicroStrategy Corp. distinguishes five styles of BI and offers special tools for each. The five styles are report delivery and alerting; enterprise reporting (using dashboards and scorecards); cube analysis (also known as slice-and-dice analysis); ad hoc queries; and statistics and data mining. We will learn more about MicroStrategy's software in Chapter 2.

The Benefits of BI

As illustrated by the opening vignette, the major benefit of BI to a company is the ability to provide accurate information when needed, including a real-time view of the corporate performance and its parts. Such information is a must for all types of decisions, for strategic planning, and even for survival. Thompson (2004) also noted that the most common application areas of BI are general reporting, sales and marketing analysis, planning and forecasting, financial consolidation, statutory reporting, budgeting, and profitability analysis.

Organizations are being compelled to capture, understand, and harness their data to support decision making in order to improve business operations. Legislation and regulation (e.g., the Sarbanes-Oxley Act of 2002) now require business leaders to document their business processes and to sign off on the legitimacy of the information they rely on and report to stakeholders. Moreover, business cycle times are now extremely compressed; faster, more informed, and better decision making is therefore a competitive imperative. Managers need the *right information* at the *right time* and in the *right place*. Organizations have to work smart. It is no surprise, then, that organizations are increasingly championing BI. The opening vignette discussed a BI success story at Norfolk Southern. You will hear about more BI successes and the fundamentals of those successes in Chapters 2 through 6. Examples of typical applications of BI are provided in Table 1.2. An interesting data mining application using *predictive analytics tools* (discussed further in Chapters 4 through 6) is described in Application Case 1.2.

TABLE 1.2   Business Value of BI Analytical Applications

Analytic Application	Business Question	Business Value
Customer segmentation	What market segments do my customers fall into, and what are their characteristics?	Personalize customer relationships for higher satisfaction and retention.
Propensity to buy	Which customers are most likely to respond to my promotion?	Target customers based on their need to increase their loyalty to your product line.
		Also, increase campaign profitability by focusing on the most likely to buy.
Customer profitability	What is the lifetime profitability of my customer?	Make individual business interaction decisions based on the overall profitability of customers.
Fraud detection	How can I tell which transactions are likely to be fraudulent?	Quickly determine fraud and take immediate action to minimize cost.
Customer attrition	Which customer is at risk of leaving?	Prevent loss of high-value customers and let go of lower-value customers.
Channel optimization	What is the best channel to reach my customer in each segment?	Interact with customers based on their preference and your need to manage cost.

Source: A. Ziama and J. Kasher (2004), *Data Mining Primer for the Data Warehousing Professional.* Dayton, OH: Teradata.

Application Case 1.2

Alltel Wireless: Delivering the Right Message, to the Right Customers, at the Right Time

In April 2006, Alltel Wireless (now merged with Verizon) launched its "My Circle" campaign and revolutionized the cell phone industry. For the first time, customers could have unlimited calling to any 10 numbers, on any network, for free. To solidify the impact of the "My Circle" campaign in a time of rising wireless access rates, Alltel saw a need for a centralized, data-focused solution to increase the number of new customers and to enhance relationships with existing customers.

Through Acxiom's PersonicX segmentation system (**acxiom.com**), Alltel was able to cluster its data on U.S. households based on specific consumer behavior and demographic characteristics. This enriched Alltel's customer and prospect data by providing better insight into buying behavior and customer subscription lifecycle events. With these analytical techniques, Alltel could inform specific customer segments about opportunities that would enhance their wireless experience, such as text messaging bundles and ringtone downloads. Additionally, Alltel could now target new customers who had a greater likelihood to activate a subscription through lower cost Web and call center channels.

By automating its customer lifecycle management with Acxiom's BI software suite, Alltel was able to manage more than 300 direct marketing initiatives per year, increase customer additions by 265 percent, increase ROI by 133 percent, and create ongoing business value of over $30 million.

Source: "Customer Lifecycle Management," Acxiom, **acxiom.com** (accessed March 26, 2009).

AUTOMATED DECISION MAKING   A relatively new approach to supporting decision making is called **automated decision systems (ADS)**, sometimes also known as *decision automation systems* (DAS; see Davenport and Harris, 2005). An ADS is a rule-based system that provides a solution, usually in one functional area (e.g., finance, manufacturing), to a specific repetitive managerial problem, usually in one industry (e.g., to approve or not to approve a request for a loan, to determine the price of an item in a store). Application Case 1.3 shows an example of applying ADS to a problem that every organization faces—how to price its products or services.

ADS initially appeared in the airline industry, where they were called *revenue* (or *yield*) *management* (or revenue optimization) systems. Airlines use these systems to dynamically price tickets based on actual demand. Today, many service industries use similar pricing models. In contrast with **management science** approaches, which provide a model-based solution to generic structured problems (e.g., resource allocation, inventory level determination), ADS provide rule-based solutions. The following are examples of business rules: "If only 70 percent of the seats on a flight from Los Angeles to New York are sold three days prior to departure, offer a discount of x to nonbusiness travelers," "If an applicant owns a house and makes over $100,000 a year, offer a $10,000 credit line," and "If an item costs more than $2,000, and if your company buys it only once a year, the purchasing agent does not need special approval." Such rules, which are based on experience or derived through data mining, can be combined with

Application Case 1.3

Giant Food Stores Prices the Entire Store

Giant Food Stores, LLC, a regional U.S. supermarket chain based in Carlisle, Pennsylvania, had a narrow Every Day Low Price strategy that it applied to most of the products in its stores. The company had a 30-year-old pricing and promotion system that was very labor intensive and that could no longer keep up with the pricing decisions required in the fast-paced grocery market. The system also limited the company's ability to execute more sophisticated pricing strategies.

Giant Foods was interested in executing its pricing strategy more consistently based on a definitive set of pricing rules (pricing rules in retail might include relationships between national brands and private-label brands, relationships between sizes, ending digits such as 9, etc.). In the past, many of the rules were kept on paper, others were kept in people's heads, and some were not documented well enough for others to understand and ensure continuity. The company also had no means of reliably forecasting the impact of rule changes before prices hit the store shelves.

Giant Foods worked with DemandTec to deploy a system for its pricing decisions. The system is able to handle massive amounts of point-of-sale and competitive data to model and forecast consumer demand, as well as automate and streamline complex rules-based pricing schemes. It can handle large numbers of price changes, and it can do so without increasing staff. The system allows Giant Foods to codify pricing rules with "natural language" sentences rather than having to go through a technician. The system also has forecasting capabilities. These capabilities allow Giant Foods to predict the impact of pricing changes and new promotions before they hit the shelves. Giant Foods decided to implement the system for the entire store chain.

The system has allowed Giant Foods to become more agile in its pricing. It is now able to react to competitive pricing changes or vendor cost changes on a weekly basis rather than when resources become available. Giant Foods' productivity has doubled because it no longer has to increase staff for pricing changes. Giant Foods now focuses on "maintaining profitability while satisfying its customer and maintaining its price image."

Source: "Giant Food Stores Prices the Entire Store with DemandTec," DemandTec, **demandtec.com** (accessed March 26, 2009).

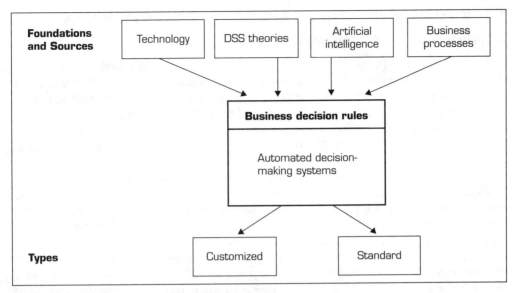

FIGURE 1.4   Automated Decision-Making Framework.

mathematical models to form solutions that can be automatically and instantly applied to problems (e.g., "Based on the information provided and subject to verification, you will be admitted to our university"), or they can be provided to a human, who will make the final decision (see Figure 1.4). ADS attempt to automate highly repetitive decisions (in order to justify the computerization cost), based on business rules. ADS are mostly suitable for frontline employees who can see the customer information online and frequently must make quick decisions. For further information on ADS, see Davenport and Harris (2005).

Event-Driven Alerts

One example of ADS is an event-driven alert, which is a warning or action that is activated when a predefined or unusual event occurs. For example, credit card companies have built extensive **predictive analysis** models to identify cases of possible fraud and automatically alert credit card customers for verification of transactions when unusual activity is noted (e.g. large purchase in an atypical or foreign location when the customer does not have a history of such transactions). If a customer makes a large deposit, the bank may make an offer of a higher interest rate Certificate of Deposit (CD) or investment automatically. Such alerts are also used in generating promotions based on completion of other purchases. Of course, the alerts are also presented through BPM dashboards to appropriate managers responsible for key performance indicators when there are significant deviations from expected results.

SECTION 1.2 REVIEW QUESTIONS

1. Define BI.
2. List and describe the major components of BI.
3. Identify some typical applications of BI.
4. Give examples of ADS.
5. Give examples of event-driven alerts.

1.3   INTELLIGENCE CREATION AND USE AND BI GOVERNANCE

A Cyclical Process of Intelligence Creation and Use

Data warehouse and BI initiatives typically follow a process similar to that used in military intelligence initiatives. In fact, BI practitioners often follow the national security model depicted in Figure 1.5. The process is cyclical with a series of interrelated steps. Analysis is the main step for converting raw data to decision supporting information. However, accurate and/or reliable *analysis* isn't possible unless other steps along the way have been properly addressed. The details of the process and its steps are provided in Krizan (1999) and in Chapter 4.

Once a data warehouse is in place, the general process of *intelligence creation* starts by identifying and prioritizing *specific* BI projects. For each potential BI project in the portfolio, it is important to use return on investments (ROI) and total cost of ownership measures to estimate the cost-benefit ratio. This means that each project must be examined through costing associated with the general process phases as well as costs of maintaining the application for the business user. Additionally, the benefits estimations need to involve end-user examinations of decision-making impacts, including measures reflecting benefits like cashflow acceleration. Some organizations refer to the project prioritization process as a form of **BI governance** (Matney and Larson, 2004). A major governance issue is who should serve as decision makers involved in prioritizing BI projects. The two critical partnerships required for BI governance are: (1) a partnership between functional area heads and/or product/service area leaders (Middles), and (2) a partnership between potential

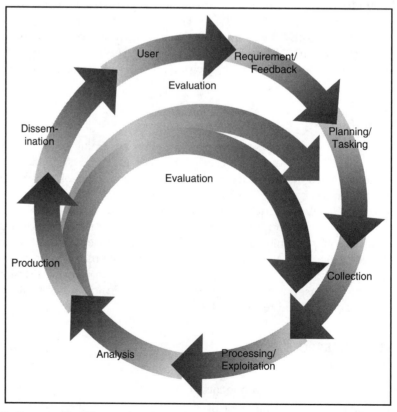

FIGURE 1.5   Process of Intelligence Creation and Use.   *Source:* L. Krizan, *Intelligence Essentials for Everyone.* Washington DC: Joint Military Intelligence College (oocasional paper number six) Department of Defense, p. 6.

Customers and Providers (representatives of the business side and representatives from the IT side). Middles can look across an organization to ensure that project priorities reflect the needs of the entire business; they make sure a project does not just serve to subopti-mize one area over others. Customers can offer insight into the potential usefulness of the **intelligence** generated in a project, and providers are important from the standpoint of reflecting delivery realities. A typical set of issues for the BI governance team is to address: (1) creating categories of projects (investment, business opportunity, strategic, mandatory, etc.); (2) defining criteria for project selection; (3) determining and setting a framework for managing project risk; (4) managing and leveraging project interdependencies; and (5) continually monitoring and adjusting the composition of the portfolio.

Intelligence and Espionage

Although many believe the very term *intelligence* sounds like a cloak-and-dagger acronym for clandestine operations dedicated to stealing corporate secrets, or the gov-ernment's CIA, this couldn't be further from the truth. While such *espionage* does of course occur, we are interested in how modern companies ethically and legally organize themselves to glean as much as they can from their customers, their business environ-ment, their stakeholders, their business processes, their competitors, and other such sources of potentially valuable information. But collecting data is just the beginning. Vast amounts of that data need to be cataloged, tagged, analyzed, sorted, filtered, and must undergo a host of other operations to yield usable information that can impact decision making and improve the bottom line. The importance of these topics increases every day as companies track and accumulate more and more data. For example, exacerbating the exponential growth in the amount of raw data is the emergence of sensor data including *Radio Frequency IDentification* (RFID). Applications based upon sensor and location data will likely be among the most exciting and fastest growing application cat-egories for the next generation of BI specialists. That, coupled with new approaches to synthesize information from text sources through "text mining" and from the Web via Web mining (Chapter 4), suggests that organizations are on the verge of an explosive new era of BI for decision support.

BI has adapted a set of nomenclature, systems, and concepts that clearly distinguish it from its espionage-oriented counterpart of national and international intelligence! That said, there are many analogies between the two, including the fact that major effort must be expended to achieve the collection of reputable sources of intelligence, the processing of that intelligence for purity and reliability, the analysis of raw intelligence to produce usable and actionable information, and the mechanisms for the appropriate dissemination of that information to the right users.

SECTION 1.3 REVIEW QUESTIONS

1. List the steps of intelligence creation and use.
2. What is BI governance?
3. What is intelligence gathering?

1.4 TRANSACTION PROCESSING VERSUS ANALYTIC PROCESSING

To illustrate the major characteristics of BI, first we will show what BI is not—namely, transaction processing. We're all familiar with the information systems that support our transactions, like ATM withdrawals, bank deposits, cash register scans at the grocery store, and so on. These *transaction processing* systems are constantly involved in handling updates to what we might call *operational databases*. For example, in an ATM withdrawal transaction, we need to reduce our bank balance accordingly, a bank deposit adds to an account, and a grocery store purchase is likely reflected in the store's calculation of total sales for the day, and it should reflect an appropriate reduction in the store's inventory for the items we bought, and so on. These **Online Transaction Processing (OLTP)** systems handle a company's routine on-going business. In contrast, a data warehouse is typically a distinct system that provides storage for data that will be made use of in *analysis*. The intent of that analysis is to give management the ability to scour data for information about the business, and it can be used to provide tactical or operational decision support whereby, for example, line personnel can make quicker and/or more informed decisions. We will provide a more technical definition of Data Warehouse (DW) in Chapter 2, but it suffices to say that DWs are intended to work with informational data used for **Online Analytical Processing (OLAP)** systems.

Most operational data in Enterprise Resources Planning (ERP) systems—and in its complementing siblings like *supply chain management* (SCM) or *customer relationship management* (CRM)—are stored in an OLTP system, which is a type of computer processing where the computer responds immediately to user requests. Each request is considered to be a *transaction*, which is a computerized record of a discrete event, such as the receipt of inventory or a customer order. In other words, a transaction requires a set of two or more database updates that must be completed in an all-or-nothing fashion.

The very design that makes an OLTP system efficient for transaction processing makes it inefficient for end-user ad hoc reports, queries, and analysis. In the 1980s, many business users referred to their mainframes as "the black hole," because all the information went into it, but none ever came back. All requests for reports have had to be programmed by the IT staff, whereas only "pre-canned" reports could be generated on a scheduled basis, and ad hoc real-time querying was virtually impossible. While the client/server-based ERP systems of the 1990s were somewhat more report-friendly, it has still been a far cry from a desired usability by regular, nontechnical, end users for things such as operational reporting, interactive analysis, and so on. To resolve these issues, the notions of DW and BI were created.

Data warehouses contain a wide variety of data that present a coherent picture of business conditions at a single point in time. The idea was to create a database infrastructure that is always online and contains all the information from the OLTP systems, including historical data, but reorganized and structured in such a way that it was fast and efficient for querying, analysis, and decision support.

Separating the OLTP from analysis and decision support enables the benefits of BI that were described earlier and provides for competitive intelligence and advantage as described next.

SECTION 1.4 REVIEW QUESTIONS

1. Define OLTP.
2. Define OLAP.

1.5 SUCCESSFUL BI IMPLEMENTATION

Implementing and deploying a BI initiative can be lengthy, expensive, and failure prone. Let's explore some of the issues involved.

The Typical BI User Community

BI may have a larger and more diversified user community. The success of BI depends, in part, on which personnel in the organization would be the most likely to make use of BI. One of the most important aspects of a successful BI is that it must be of benefit to the enterprise as a whole. This implies that there are likely to be a host of users in the

enterprise—many of whom should be involved from the outset of a DW investment decision. Not surprisingly, there are likely to be users who focus at the strategic level and those who are more oriented to the tactical level.

The various classes of BI users who exist in an organization can help to guide how the DW is structured and the types of BI tools and other supporting software that are needed. Members of each group are excellent sources of information on assessing the costs and benefits of specific BI projects once a DW is in place. From the above discussion, it is obvious that one important characteristic of a company that excels in its approach to BI is proper *appreciation* for *different classes* of potential users.

Appropriate Planning and Alignment with the Business Strategy

First and foremost, the fundamental reasons for investing in BI must be aligned with the company's business strategy. BI cannot simply be a technical exercise for the information systems department. It has to serve as a way to change the manner the company conducts business by improving its business processes and transforming decision-making processes to be more data-driven. Many BI consultants and practitioners involved in successful BI initiatives advise that a framework for planning is a necessary precondition. One framework, developed by Gartner, Inc. (2004), decomposes planning and execution into *business, organization, functionality,* and *infrastructure* components. At the business and organizational levels, strategic and operational objectives must be defined while considering the available organizational skills to achieve those objectives. Issues of organizational culture surrounding BI initiatives and building enthusiasm for those initiatives and procedures for the intraorganizational sharing of BI best practices must be considered by upper management—with plans in place to prepare the organization for change. One of the first steps in that process is to assess the IS organization, the skillsets of the potential classes of users, and whether the culture is amenable to change. From this assessment, and assuming there is justification and need to move ahead, a company can prepare a detailed action plan. Another critical issue for BI implementation success is the integration of several BI projects (most enterprises use several BI projects) among themselves and with the other IT systems in the organization and its business partners.

If the company's strategy is properly aligned with the reasons for DW and BI initiatives, and if the company's IS organization is or can be made capable of playing its role in such a project, and if the requisite user community is in place and has the proper motivation, it is wise to start BI and establish a BI Competency Center (BICC) within the company. The center could serve some or all of the following functions (Gartner, 2004).

- The center can demonstrate how BI is clearly linked to strategy and execution of strategy.
- A center can serve to encourage interaction between the potential business user communities and the IS organization.
- The center can serve as a repository and disseminator of best BI practices between and among the different lines of business.
- Standards of excellence in BI practices can be advocated and encouraged throughout the company.
- The IS organization can learn a great deal through interaction with the user communities, such as knowledge about the variety of types of analytical tools that are needed.
- The business user community and IS organization can better understand why the data warehouse platform must be flexible enough to provide for changing business requirements.
- It can help important stakeholders like high-level executives see how BI can play an important role.

Another important success factor of BI is its ability to facilitate a real-time, on-demand agile environment, introduced next.

Real-Time, On-Demand BI Is Attainable

The demand for instant, on-demand access to dispersed information has grown as the need to close the gap between the operational data and strategic objectives has become more pressing. As a result, a category of products called *real-time BI applications* has emerged (see Chapter 3). The introduction of new data-generating technologies, such as *radio-frequency identification* (RFID), is only accelerating this growth and the subsequent need for real-time BI. Traditional BI systems use a large volume of *static* data that has been extracted, cleansed, and loaded into a *data warehouse* to produce reports and analyses. However, the need is not just reporting, since users need business monitoring, performance analysis, and an understanding of why things are happening. These can provide users, who need to know (virtually in real time) about changes in data or the availability of relevant reports, alerts, and notifications regarding events and emerging trends in Web, e-mail, or *instant messaging* (IM) applications. In addition, business applications can be programmed to act on what these real-time BI systems discover. For example, a *supply chain management* (SCM) application might automatically place an order for more "widgets" when real-time inventory falls below a certain threshold or when a *customer relationship management* (CRM) application automatically triggers a customer service representative and credit control clerk to check a customer who has placed an online order larger than $10,000.

One approach to real-time BI uses the DW model of traditional BI systems. In this case, products from innovative BI platform providers (like Ascential or Informatica) provide a service-oriented, near-real-time solution that populates the DW much faster than the typical nightly *extract/transfer/load* (ETL) batch update does (see Chapter 2). A second approach, commonly called *business activity management* (BAM), is adopted by pure play BAM and or hybrid BAM-middleware providers (such as Savvion, Iteration Software, Vitria, webMethods, Quantive, Tibco, or Vineyard Software). It bypasses the DW entirely and uses **Web services** or other monitoring means to discover key business events. These software monitors (or **intelligent agents**) can be placed on a separate server in the network or on the transactional application databases themselves, and they can use event- and process-based approaches to proactively and intelligently measure and monitor operational processes.

Developing or Acquiring BI Systems

Today, many vendors offer diversified tools, some of which are completely preprogrammed (called *shells*); all you have to do is insert your numbers. These tools can be purchased or leased. For a list of products, demos, white papers, and much current product information, see **information-management.com/**. Free user registration is required. Almost all BI applications are constructed with shells provided by vendors who may themselves create a custom solution for a client or work with another outsourcing provider. The issue that companies face is which alternative to select: purchase, lease, or build. Each of these alternatives has several options. One of the major criteria for making the decision is justification and cost–benefit analysis.

Justification and Cost–Benefit Analysis

As the number of potential BI applications increases, the need to justify and prioritize them arises. This is not an easy task due to the large number of intangible benefits. Both direct and intangible benefits need to be identified. Of course, this is where the knowledge of similar applications in other organizations and case studies is extremely useful. For example, the Data Warehousing Institute (**tdwi.org/**) provides a wealth of information about products and innovative applications and implementations. Such information can be useful in estimating direct and indirect benefits.

Security and Protection of Privacy

This is an extremely important issue in the development of any computerized system, especially BI that contain data that may possess strategic value. Also, the privacy of employees and customers needs to be protected.

Integration of Systems and Applications

With the exception of some small applications, all BI applications must be integrated with other systems such as databases, legacy systems, enterprise systems (particularly ERP and CRM), e-commerce (sell side, buy side), and many more. In addition, BI applications are usually connected to the Internet and many times to information systems of business partners.

Furthermore, BI tools sometimes need to be integrated among themselves, creating synergy.

The need for integration pushed software vendors to continuously add capabilities to their products. Customers who buy an all-in-one software package deal with only one vendor and do not have to deal with systems' connectivity. But, they may lose the advantage of creating systems composed from the "best-of-breed" components.

SECTION 1.5 REVIEW QUESTIONS

1. Describe the major types of BI users.
2. List some of the implementation topics addressed by Gartner's report.
3. List some other success factors of BI.
4. Why is it difficult to justify BI applications?

1.6 MAJOR TOOLS AND TECHNIQUES OF BUSINESS INTELLIGENCE

How DSS/BI is implemented depends on which tools are used.

The Tools and Techniques

A large number of tools and techniques have been developed over the years to support managerial decision making. Some of them appear under different names and definitions. The major computerized tool categories are summarized in Table 1.3. Full descriptions are provided in other chapters of this book, as shown in Table 1.3.

Selected BI Vendors

Recently there has been a major surge in BI software and application providers. Some of these company names will become quite familiar after completing this book: Teradata, MicroStrategy, Microsoft, IBM+Cognos+SPSS, SAP+Business Objects, Oracle+Hyperion, SAS, and many others. There has been much consolidation as large software companies acquire others to build a full portfolio of offerings. For example, SAP acquired Business Objects, IBM acquired Cognos in 2008 and SPSS in 2009, and Oracle acquired Hyperion. New enterprises are now emerging in text, Web, and data analysis. Also, companies are collaborating with other companies to build partnerships. For example, SAS and Teradata have entered into a partnership to offer data warehouse and predictive analytic capabilities jointly.

TABLE 1.3 Computerized Tools for Decision Support		
Tool Category	**Tools and Their Acronyms**	**Chapter in the Book**
Data management	Databases and database management system (DBMS)	2
	Extraction, transformation, and load (ETL) systems	2
	Data warehouses (DW), real-time DW, and data marts	2
Reporting status tracking	Online analytical processing (OLAP)	3
	Executive information systems (EIS)	3
Visualization	Geographical information systems (GIS)	3
	Dashboards	3
	Multidimensional presentations	3
Strategy and performance management	Business performance management(BPM)/ Corporate performance management (CPM)	3
	Dashboards and scorecards	3
Business analytics	Data mining	4, 5
	Web mining, and text mining	5
	Web analytics	5
Social networking	Web 2.0	6
New tools for massive data mining	Reality Mining	6

SECTION 1.6 REVIEW QUESTIONS

1. List the six major categories of decision support tools.

2. Identify some companies that are major vendors in BI.

1.7 PLAN OF THE BOOK

The six chapters of this book are organized as follows. BI includes several distinct components. We begin with Chapter 2, which focuses on data warehouses that are necessary for enabling **analytics** and performance measurement. Chapter 3 discusses BPM, dashboards, scorecards, and related topics. We then focus on applications and the process of data mining and analytics in Chapter 4. Chapter 4 also summarizes some of the technical details of the algorithms of data mining, including neural networks. Chapter 5 describes the emerging application of text and Web mining. Chapter 6 attempts to integrate all the material covered here and concludes with a discussion of emerging trends, such as how the ubiquity of cell phones, GPS devices, and wireless personal digital assistants (PDAs) is resulting in the creation of massive new databases. A new breed of data mining and BI companies is emerging to analyze these new databases and create a much better and deeper understanding of customers' behaviors and movements. This has even been given a new name—reality mining. Application Case 1.4 highlights one such example. We will learn about this application and several others in Chapter 6.

Application Case 1.4

The Next Net

Sense Networks is one of many companies developing applications to better understand customers' movements. One of its applications analyzes data on the movements of almost 4 million cell phone users. The data come from GPS, cell phone towers, and local Wi-Fi hotspots. The data are anonymized, but are still linked together. This linkage enables data miners to see clusters of customers getting together at specific locations (bars, restaurants) at specific hours. Clustering techniques can be used to identify what types of "tribes" these customers belong to—business travelers, "young travelers," and so on. By analyzing data at this level of detail, customer profiles can be built with sufficient granularity to permit targeted marketing and promotions.

Besides the conventional use of the information to target customers with better precision and appropriate offers, such systems may someday be helpful in studying crime and the spread of disease. Other companies that are developing techniques for performing similar analyses include Google, Kinetics, and Nokia.

Source: Compiled from S. Baker, "The Next Net," *BusinessWeek,* March 2009, pp. 42–46, Greene, K., "Mapping a City's Rhythm," *Technology Review,* March 2009, at **technologyreview.com/ communications/22286/page1/** (accessed January 2010), and Sheridan, B., "A Trillion Points of Data," *Newsweek,* March 9, 2009, pp. 34–37.

1.8 RESOURCES, LINKS, AND THE TERADATA UNIVERSITY NETWORK CONNECTION

The use of this chapter and most other chapters in this book can be enhanced by the tools described in the following sections.

Resources and Links[1]

We recommend the following major resources and links:

- The Data Warehousing Institute (**tdwi.org**)
- Information Management (**information-management.com**)
- The OLAP Report (**olapreport.com**)
- DSS Resources (**dssresources.com**)
- Information Technology Toolbox (**businessintelligence.ittoolbox.com**)
- Business Intelligence Network (**b-eye-network.com**)
- AIS World (**isworld.org**)
- Microsoft Enterprise Consortium (**enterprise.waltoncollege.uark.edu/mec**)

Cases

All major BI vendors (e.g., MicroStrategy, Microsoft, Oracle, IBM, Hyperion, Cognos, Exsys, SAS, FICO, Business Objects, SAP, and Information Builders) provide interesting customer success stories. Academic-oriented cases are available at Harvard Business School Case Collection (**hbsp.harvard.edu/b01/en/academic/edu_home.jhtml**),

---

[1]As this book went to press, we verified that all the cited Web sites were active and valid. However, URLs are dynamic. Web sites to which we refer in the text sometimes change or are discontinued because companies change names, are bought or sold, merge, or fail. Sometimes Web sites are down for maintenance, repair, or redesign. Many organizations have dropped the initial "www" designation for their sites, but some still use it. If you have a problem connecting to a Web site that we mention, please be patient and simply run a Web search to try to identify the possible new site. Most times, you can quickly find the new site through one of the popular search engines. We apologize in advance for this inconvenience.

Business Performance Improvement Resource (**bpir.com**), Idea Group Publishing (**idea-group.com**), Ivy League Publishing (**ivylp.com**), KnowledgeStorm (**knowledgestorm.com**), and other sites. Miller's *MIS Cases* (2005) contains simple cases, using spreadsheet and database exercises, that support several of the chapters in this book.

Vendors, Products, and Demos

Most vendors provide software demos of their products and applications. Information about products, architecture, and software is available at **dssresources.com**.

Periodicals

We recommend the following periodicals:

- *Decision Support Systems*
- *CIO Insight* (**cioinsight.com**)
- *Technology Evaluation* (**technologyevaluation.com**)
- *Baseline Magazine* (**baselinemag.com**)
- *Business Intelligence Journal* (**tdwi.org**)

The Teradata University Network Connection

This book is tightly connected with the free resources provided by Teradata University Network (TUN; see **teradatauniversitynetwork.com**).

The TUN portal is divided into two major parts: one for students and one for faculty. This book is connected to the TUN portal via a special section at the end of each chapter. That section includes appropriate links for the specific chapter, pointing to relevant resources. In addition, we provide hands-on exercises, using software and other material (e.g., cases), at TUN.

The Book's Web Site

This book's Web site, **pearsonhighered.com/turban**, contains supplemental material related to the text content.

Chapter Highlights

- The business environment is becoming complex and is rapidly changing, making decision making more difficult.
- Businesses must respond and adapt to the changing environment rapidly by making faster and better decisions.
- The time frame for making decisions is shrinking, whereas the global nature of decision making is expanding, necessitating the development and use of computerized DSS.
- Computerized support for managers is often essential for the survival of an organization.

- **Automated decision support** is provided today in many industries to find solutions to repetitive decisions (such as item pricing) based on business rules.
- BI methods utilize a central repository called a data warehouse that enables efficient data mining, OLAP, BPM, and data visualization.
- BI architecture includes a data warehouse, business analytics tools used by end users, and a user interface (such as a dashboard).
- Many organizations use BPM systems to monitor performance, compare it to standards and goals,

and show it graphically (e.g., using dashboards) to managers and executives.
- Data mining is a tool for discovering information and relationships in a large amount of data.

- Web technology and the Internet, intranets, and extranets play a key role in the development, dissemination, and use of management support systems.

Key Terms

analytics
automated decision systems (ADS)
automated decision support
BI governance
business analytics
business intelligence (BI)
business performance management (BPM)

(or corporate performance management [CPM])
complexity
corporate portal
data
database
data mining
decision making

geographical information system (GIS)
global positioning system (GPS)
information
information overload
intelligence
intelligent agent
knowledge

management science
online analytical processing (OLAP)
Online Transaction Processing (OLTP)
predictive analysis
predictive analytics
user interface
Web service

Questions for Discussion

1. Give examples for the content of each cell in Figure 1.2.
2. Differentiate intelligence gathering from espionage.

3. What is BI governance?
4. Discuss the major issues in implementing BI.

Exercises

Teradata University Network (TUN) and Other Hands-On Exercises

1. Go to **teradatastudentnetwork.com**. Using the registration your instructor provides, log on and learn the content of the site. Prepare a list of all materials available there. You will receive assignments related to this site. Prepare a list of 20 items in the site that you think could be beneficial to you.

2. Enter the TUN site and select "cases, projects, and assignments." Then select the case study: "Harrah's High Payoff from Customer Information." Answer the following questions about this case:
  a. What information does the data mining generate?
  b. How is this information helpful to management in decision making? (Be specific.)
  c. List the types of data that are mined.
  d. Is this a DSS or BI application? Why?

3. Go to **teradatastudentnetwork.com** and find the paper titled "Data Warehousing Supports Corporate Strategy at First American Corporation" (by Watson, Wixom, and Goodhue). Read the paper and answer the following questions:
  a. What were the drivers for the DW/BI project in the company?

  b. What strategic advantages were realized?
  c. What operational and tactical advantages were achieved?
  d. What were the critical success factors (CSF) for the implementation?

Team Assignments and Role-Playing

1. Write a five- to ten-page report describing how your company or a company you are familiar with currently uses computers and information systems, including Web technologies, in decision support. In light of the material in this chapter, describe how a manager could use such support systems if they were readily available. Which ones are available to you and which ones are not?

2. Go to **fico.com**, **ilog.com**, and **pega.com**. View the demos at these sites. Prepare a list of ADS by industry and by functional area. Specify what types of decisions are automated.

Internet Exercises

1. Go to **fico.com**. Use the information there to identify five problems in different industries and five problems in different functional areas that can be supported by ADS.

2. Go to **sap.com** and **oracle.com**. Find information on how ERP software helps decision makers. In addition, examine how these software products use Web technology and the Web itself. Write a report based on your findings.

3. Go to **intelligententerprise.com**. For each topic cited in this chapter, find some interesting developments reported on the site, and prepare a report.

4. Go to **cognos.com** and **businessobjects.com**. Compare the capabilities of the two companies' BI products in a report.

5. Go to **microsoft.com**. Examine its BI offerings.

6. Go to **oracle.com**. Check out its BI offerings. How do Oracle's BI offerings relate to its ERP software?

7. Go to **microstrategy.com**. Find information on the five styles of BI. Prepare a summary table for each style.

8. Go to **oracle.com** and click the Hyperion link under Applications. Determine what the company's major products are. Relate these to the support technologies cited in this chapter.

End of Chapter Application Case

Vodafone Uses Business Intelligence to Improve Customer Growth and Retention Plans

The Problem

Vodafone New Zealand Ltd., a subsidiary of the U.K.-based telecommunications giant, had achieved tremendous success in New Zealand. Starting from a very small base, the company quickly attained more than 50 percent market share. However, as the mobile phone industry began to reach maturity, Vodafone's market share stagnated at about 56 percent and the total number of customers leveled off. To make matters worse, other competitors emerged, the cost of compliance with government regulations began to increase, and the revenue per customer also lagged. The company had to refocus its strategy of retaining and increasing revenue from the current customers. John Stewart, senior manager of customer analytics for Vodafone New Zealand, said "Now that we have all of these customers, we need to answer new questions: How do we increase our profit margins? How do we add revenue streams from these customers? And how do we keep them as customers?" Vodafone needed to make better decisions based on real-time knowledge of its market, customers, and competitors. According to reporter Cheryl Krivda, "Vodafone needed to make a wholesale shift to analytical marketing, using business intelligence (BI) that could rapidly provide fact-based decision support. The goal: to help the company deliver the right message to the appropriate customers when they wanted it, using the preferred channel."

Solution

First, Vodafone formed a customer knowledge and analysis department to conduct analysis, modeling, market research, and competitive intelligence. John Stewart was the manager of this unit. Vodafone implemented an enterprise data warehouse (EDW) to obtain a single view of all of the information in the organization. EDW permits a well-integrated view of all of the organization's information to allow generation of predefined or ad hoc queries and reports, online analytical processing, and predictive analysis (see Chapter 4). The company

also developed its analytical team by hiring modeling specialists. In addition to the Teradata data warehouse platform, many other software tools, such as KXEN, SAS, and SPSS, were also used to build models and generate insights.

With the Teradata EDW platform and all the relevant tools in place, employees from Vodafone's sales and marketing department are now able to perform analyses and achieve better customer-offer optimization, campaign effectiveness analysis, and customer service. Stewart believes that the new tools give Vodafone the ability to develop "holistic insights." He says,

> As a team, we're leaning over one another's shoulders, asking questions and providing support. In the process, we learn from each other, which helps us deliver greater value in the insights we put out to the business. When you bring all of these sources of knowledge and information together, you can uncover the deeper insights about our customers.

One application of the EDW is a trigger-based marketing campaign. In the past, manual intervention was required to initiate a marketing campaign. With the new platform, Vodafone can automatically initiate a marketing offer based on a customer's recent activity.

Results

Perhaps the biggest benefit of the EDW is that the analysts can spend more time generating insights than managing data. "Now we can get campaigns to the customer more efficiently and effectively," says Stewart. "That's not to say we send out wave after wave of campaigns, though. It's increasingly targeted and refined in terms of who we campaign to, and the relevance to the customer is greater, too."

The system also provides better information to decision makers to support the decision-making process. Vodafone is developing an application to optimize both revenue and prioritization of customer offers. The goal is "to get

the best possible return . . . from the process of campaigning and contacting customers." Without divulging specifics, it appears that the company is on its way to achieving these goals.

Source: Compiled from C. D. Krivda, "Dialing up Growth in a Mature Market," *Teradata Magazine,* March 2008, pp. 1–3.

QUESTIONS FOR END OF CHAPTER APPLICATION CASE

1. What were the challenges for Vodafone New Zealand?
2. How did it address these issues?
3. List the tools used by Vodafone's applications.
4. What benefits are being derived from this initiative?
5. What can we learn from this case?

References

Acxiom. "Location, Location, Location." **acxiom.com** (accessed March 26, 2009).

Baker, S. (2009, March 9). "The Next Net." *Business Week,* pp. 42–46.

Davenport, T. H., and J. G. Harris. (2009, Winter). "What People Want (and How to Predict It)." *MIT Sloan Management Review,* Vol. 50, No. 2, pp. 23–31.

Davenport, T. H., and J. G. Harris. (2005, Summer). "Automated Decision Making Comes of Age." *MIT Sloan Management Review,* Vol. 46, No. 4, pp. 83–89.

DemandTec. "Giant Food Stores Prices the Entire Store with DemandTec." **demandtec.com** (accessed March 26, 2009).

Gartner, Inc. (2004). *Using Business Intelligence to Gain a Competitive Edge.* A special report. Stamford, CT: Gartner, Inc. **garnter.com**.

Greene, K. (2009, March). "Mapping a City's Rhythm." *Technology Review,* at **technologyreview.com/communications/22286/page1/** (accessed January 2010).

Imhoff, C., and R. Pettit. (2004). "The Critical Shift to Flexible Business Intelligence." White paper, Intelligent Solutions, Inc.

Krivda, C. D. (2008, March). "Dialing up Growth in a Mature Market." *Teradata Magazine,* pp. 1–3.

Krizan, L. (1999, June). *Intelligence Essentials for Everyone.* Washington DC: Joint Military Intelligence College (occasional paper number six), Department of Defense.

Matney, D., and D. Larson. (2004, Summer). "The Four Components of BI Governance." *Business Intelligence Journal.*

Miller, M. L. (2005). *MIS Cases,* 3rd ed. Upper Saddle River, NJ: Prentice Hall.

Sheridan, B. (2009, March 9). "A Trillion Points of Data." *Newsweek,* pp. 34–37.

Thompson, O. (2004, October). "Business Intelligence Success, Lessons Learned." **technologyevaluation.com** (accessed June 2, 2009).

Watson, H. (2005, Winter). "Sorting Out What's New in Decision Support." *Business Intelligence Journal.*

Ziama, A., and J. Kasher. (2004). *Data Mining Primer for the Data Warehousing Professional.* Teradata, Dayton, OH: Teradata.

2

Data Warehousing

LEARNING OBJECTIVES

- Understand the basic definitions and concepts of data warehouses
- Understand data warehousing architectures
- Describe the processes used in developing and managing data warehouses
- Explain data warehousing operations
- Explain the role of data warehouses in decision support

- Explain data integration and the extraction, transformation, and load (ETL) processes
- Describe real-time (active) data warehousing
- Understand data warehouse administration and security issues

The concept of data warehousing has been around since the late 1980s. This chapter provides the foundation for an important type of database, called a *data warehouse*, which is primarily used for decision support and provides improved analytical capabilities. We discuss data warehousing in the following sections:

OPENING VIGNETTE: DirecTV Thrives with Active Data Warehousing

As an example of how an interactive data warehousing and business intelligence (BI) product can spread across the enterprise, consider the case of DirecTV. Using software solutions from Teradata and GoldenGate, DirecTV developed a product that integrates its data assets in near real time throughout the enterprise. The company's data warehouse director, Jack Gustafson, has said publically that the product has paid for itself over and over again through its continuous use. For DirecTV, a technical decision to install a real-time transactional data management solution has delivered business benefits far beyond the technical ones originally anticipated.

DirecTV, which is known for its direct television broadcast satellite service, has been a regular contributor to the evolution of TV with its advanced HD (high definition) programming, interactive features, digital video recording services, and electronic program guides. Employing more than 13,000 people across the United States and Latin America, DirecTV's 2008 revenues reached $20 billion, with total subscriber numbers approaching 50 million.

PROBLEM

In the midst of a continuing rapid growth, DirecTV faced the challenge of dealing with high transactional data volumes created by an escalating number of daily customer calls. Accommodating such a large data volume, along with rapidly changing market conditions, was one of DirecTV's key challenges. Several years ago, the company began looking for a better solution to providing the business side with daily reports on its call-center activities. Management wanted reports that could be used in many ways, including measuring and maintaining customer service, attracting new customers, and preventing customer churn. Equally important, the technical group at DirecTV wanted to reduce the resource load that its current data management system imposed on its CPUs.

Even though an early implementation of the data warehouse was addressing the company's needs fairly well, as business continued to grow, its limitations became clear. Before the active data warehouse solution, the data were pulled from the server every night in batch mode, a process that was taking too long and straining the system. A daily batch-data upload to the data warehouse had long been (and for many companies, still is) the standard procedure. If the timeliness of the data is not a part of your business competitiveness, such a daily upload procedure may very well work for your organization. Unfortunately, this was not the case for DirecTV. Functioning within a highly dynamic consumer market, with a very high call volume to manage, DirecTV's business users needed to access the data from customer calls in a timely fashion.

SOLUTION

Originally, the goal of the new data warehouse system was to send fresh data to the call center at least daily, but once the capabilities of the integrated solutions became apparent, that goal dropped to fresh data every 15 minutes. "We [then] wanted data latency of less than 15 minutes across the WAN (wide area network) running between different cities," Gustafson explains.

The secondary goal of the project was to simplify changed data capture to reduce the amount of maintenance required from developers. Although data sourcing across multiple platforms was not part of the initial requirement, that changed once DirecTV saw the capabilities of the GoldenGate integration system. GoldenGate allows the integration of a range of data management systems and platforms. At DirecTV, that included Oracle, the HP NonStop platform, an IBM DB2 system, and the Teradata data warehouse. "With GoldenGate, we weren't tied to one system," Gustafson says. "That also appealed to us. We're sourcing out of call logs, but we're also sourcing out of NonStop and other data sources. We thought, if we're going to buy a tool to do this, we want it to work with all the platforms we support."

RESULTS

As the capabilities of the system became increasingly clear, its potential benefits to the business also became apparent. "Once we set it up, a huge business benefit [turned out to be] that it allowed us to measure our churn in real time," Gustafson says. "We said, 'Now that we have all these reports in real time, what can we do with them?'" One answer was to use the data to immediately reduce churn by targeting specific customers. With fresh data at their fingertips, call-center sales personnel were able to contact a customer who had just asked to be disconnected and make a new sales offer to retain the customer only hours later the same day. Once the IT group set up the necessary reporting tools, sales campaigns could target specific customers for retention and prioritize them for special offers. That sort of campaign has clearly worked: "Our churn has actually gone down since we've implemented this program," Gustafson says. "Analysts are just raving about how great we're doing compared to our competitors in this area. A lot of it comes down to using this real-time copy to do analysis on customers, and to [make a fresh] offer to them the same day."

The system has also been set up to log customer service calls, reporting back constantly on technical problems that are reported in the field. That allows management to better evaluate and react to field reports, improving service and saving on dispatching technicians. Real-time call-center reports can also be produced to help manage the center's workload based on daily information on call volumes. Using that data, management can compare daily call volumes with historical averages for exception reporting.

In another business-centric use that was not originally anticipated, the company is using real-time operational reports for both order management and fraud detection. With access to real-time order information on new customers, fraud management experts can examine the data and then use that information to weed out fraudulent orders. "That saves us rolling a truck, which drives [labor] and product costs down," Gustafson points out.

QUESTIONS FOR THE OPENING VIGNETTE

1. Why is it important for DirecTV to have an active data warehouse?
2. What were the challenges DirecTV faced on its way to having an integrated active data warehouse?
3. Identify the major differences between a traditional data warehouse and an active data warehouse such as the one implemented at DirecTV.
4. What strategic advantage can DirecTV derive from the real-time system as opposed to a traditional information system?
5. Why do you think large organizations like DirecTV cannot afford not to have a capable data warehouse?

WHAT WE CAN LEARN FROM THIS VIGNETTE

The opening vignette illustrates the strategic value of implementing an active data warehouse, along with its supporting BI methods. DirecTV was able to leverage its data assets spread throughout the enterprise to be used by knowledge workers wherever and whenever they are needed. The data warehouse integrated various databases throughout the organization into a single, in-house enterprise unit to generate a single version of the truth for the company, putting all employees on the same page. Furthermore, the data were made available in real time to the decision makers who needed it, so they could use it in their decision making, ultimately leading to a strategic competitive advantage in the industry. The key lesson here is that a real-time, enterprise-level active data warehouse combined with a strategy for its use in decision support can result in significant benefits (financial and otherwise) for an organization.

Source: L. L. Briggs, "DirecTV Connects with Data Integration Solution," *Business Intelligence Journal*, Vol. 14, No. 1, 2009, pp. 14–16; "DirecTV Enables Active Data Warehousing with GoldenGate's Real-Time Data Integration Technology," *Information Management Magazine*, January 2008; **directv.com**.

2.1 DATA WAREHOUSING DEFINITIONS AND CONCEPTS

Using real-time data warehousing (RDW) in conjunction with **decision support system (DSS)** and BI tools is an important way to conduct business processes. The opening vignette demonstrates a **scenario** in which a real-time active data warehouse supported decision making by analyzing large amounts of data from various sources to provide rapid results to support critical processes. The single version of the truth stored in the data warehouse and provided in an easily digestible form expands the boundaries of DirecTV's innovative business processes. With real-time data flows, DirecTV can view the current state of its business and quickly identify problems, which is the first and foremost step toward solving them analytically. In addition, customers can obtain real-time information on their subscriptions, TV services, and other account information, so the system also provides a significant competitive advantage over competitors.

Decision makers require concise, dependable information about current operations, trends, and changes. Data are often fragmented in distinct operational systems, so managers often make decisions with partial information, at best. Data warehousing cuts through this obstacle by accessing, integrating, and organizing key operational data in a form that is consistent, reliable, timely, and readily available, wherever and whenever needed.

What Is a Data Warehouse?

In simple terms, a **data warehouse (DW)** is a pool of data produced to support decision making; it is also a repository of current and historical data of potential interest to managers throughout the organization. Data are usually structured to be available in a form ready for analytical processing activities (i.e., online analytical processing [OLAP], data mining, querying, reporting, and other decision support applications). A data warehouse is a subject-oriented, integrated, time-variant, nonvolatile collection of data in support of management's decision-making process.

Characteristics of Data Warehousing

A common way of introducing data warehousing is to refer to its fundamental characteristics (Inmon, 2005):

- *Subject oriented.* Data are organized by detailed subject, such as sales, products, or customers, containing only information relevant for decision support. Subject orientation enables users to determine not only how their business is performing, but why. A data warehouse differs from an operational database in that most operational databases have a product orientation and are tuned to handle transactions that update the database. Subject orientation provides a more comprehensive view of the organization.
- *Integrated.* Integration is closely related to subject orientation. Data warehouses must place data from different sources into a consistent format. To do so, they must deal with naming conflicts and discrepancies among units of measure. A data warehouse is presumed to be totally integrated.

- *Time variant (time series).* A warehouse maintains historical data. The data do not necessarily provide current status (except in real-time systems). They detect trends, deviations, and long-term relationships for forecasting and comparisons, leading to decision making. Every data warehouse has a temporal quality. Time is the one important dimension that all data warehouses must support. Data for analysis from multiple sources contains multiple time points (e.g., daily, weekly, monthly views).
- *Nonvolatile.* After data are entered into a data warehouse, users cannot change or update the data. Obsolete data are discarded, and changes are recorded as new data.

These characteristics enable data warehouses to be tuned almost exclusively for data access. Some additional characteristics may include the following:

- *Web based.* Data warehouses are typically designed to provide an efficient computing environment for Web-based applications.
- *Relational/multidimensional.* A data warehouse uses either a relational structure or a multidimensional structure. A recent survey on multidimensional structures can be found in Romero and Abelló (2009).
- *Client/server.* A data warehouse uses the client/server architecture to provide easy access for end users.
- *Real time.* Newer data warehouses provide real-time, or active, data access and analysis capabilities (Basu, 2003; and Bonde and Kuckuk, 2004).
- *Metadata.* A data warehouse contains metadata (data about data) about how the data are organized and how to effectively use them.

Whereas a data warehouse is a repository of data, data warehousing is literally the entire process (Watson, 2002). Data warehousing is a discipline that results in applications that provide decision support capability, allows ready access to business information, and creates business insight. The three main types of data warehouses are data marts, operational data stores (ODSs), and enterprise data warehouses (EDWs). In addition to discussing these three types of warehouses next, we also discuss metadata.

Data Marts

Whereas a data warehouse combines databases across an entire enterprise, a **data mart** is usually smaller and focuses on a particular subject or department. A data mart is a subset of a data warehouse, typically consisting of a single subject area (e.g., marketing, operations). A data mart can be either dependent or independent. A **dependent data mart** is a subset that is created directly from the data warehouse. It has the advantages of using a consistent data model and providing quality data. Dependent data marts support the concept of a single enterprise-wide data model, but the data warehouse must be constructed first. A dependent data mart ensures that the end user is viewing the same version of the data that is accessed by all other data warehouse users. The high cost of data warehouses limits their use to large companies. As an alternative, many firms use a lower-cost, scaled-down version of a data warehouse referred to as an *independent data mart*. An **independent data mart** is a small warehouse designed for a strategic business unit or a department, but its source is not an EDW.

Operational Data Stores (ODS)

An **operational data store (ODS)** provides a fairly recent form of customer information file. This type of database is often used as an interim staging area for a data warehouse. Unlike the static contents of a data warehouse, the contents of an ODS are updated throughout the course of business operations. An ODS is used for short-term decisions involving mission-critical applications rather than for the medium- and long-term decisions associated with an EDW. An ODS is similar to short-term memory in that it stores only very recent information. In comparison, a data warehouse is like long-term memory because it stores permanent information. An ODS consolidates data from multiple source systems and provides a near-real-time, integrated view of volatile, current data. The ETL processes (discussed later in this chapter) for an ODS are identical to those for a data warehouse. Finally, **oper marts** (Imhoff, 2001) are created when operational data need to be analyzed multidimensionally. The data for an oper mart come from an ODS.

Enterprise Data Warehouses (EDWs)

An **enterprise data warehouse (EDW)** is a large-scale data warehouse that is used across the enterprise for decision support. It is the type of data warehouse that DirecTV developed, as described in the opening vignette. The large-scale nature provides integration of data from many sources into a standard format for effective BI and decision support applications. EDWs are used to provide data for many types of DSS, including customer relationship management (CRM), supply chain management (SCM), business performance management (BPM), business activity monitoring (BAM), product lifecycle management (PLM), revenue management, and sometimes even knowledge management systems (KMS). Application Case 2.1 shows the enormous benefits a large company can benefit from EDW, if it is designed and implemented correctly.

Application Case 2.1

Enterprise Data Warehouse (EDW) Delivers Cost Savings and Process Efficiencies

Founded in 1884 in Dayton, Ohio, the NCR Corporation is now a $5.6 billon NYSE-listed company providing technology solutions worldwide in the retail, financial, insurance, communications, manufacturing, and travel and transportation industries. NCR's technology solutions include store automation and automated teller machines, consulting services, media products, and hardware technology.

When acquired by AT&T in 1991, NCR operated on an autonomous country- and product-centric structure, in which each country made its own decisions about product and service offerings, marketing, and pricing and developed its own processes and reporting norms. Under the country model, dozens of different financial and operational applications were required to capture the total results of the company, by no means an enterprise solution.

In 1997, when NCR was spun off on its own again, company operations were losing substantial amounts of money every day. The spin-off provided NCR with the much-needed funds to engage in the deep process changes required to maintain and strengthen its competitive position in the global market and to undertake the transformation to a truly global enterprise.

The goal was to move from a primarily hardware-focused and country-centric organizational model to an integrated, solution-oriented business structure with a global focus. To do this, NCR needed to globalize, centralize, and integrate its vast store of information resources. Only then could it gain effective control over the necessary business changes. NCR's EDW initiative was critical to the company's successful transformation and would be vital to the successful deployment of a new worldwide, single-instance, enterprise resource planning (ERP) system planned for several years later.

NCR Finance and Worldwide Customer Services (WCS) led the drive for implementation of the EDW. Business teams from NCR Finance and WCS, Financial Information Delivery and Global Information Systems (GIS), respectively, worked closely with the EDW team to ensure that IT understood the business requirements for the new structure. The Teradata system was chosen for its scalability, its flexibility to support unstructured queries and high numbers of concurrent users, and its relatively low maintenance costs.

The enormous potential of the EDW spread throughout the company, driving organizational and process changes in NCR Finance, where the financial close cycle was reduced from 14 days to 6 and worldwide reporting integrity standards were established; in WCS, where individual customer profitability profiles and improvement plans were made possible; and in sales and marketing, operations and inventory management, and human resources. ERP operational standardization and a dramatic improvement in the business of serving its customers mean that NCR is poised for the future. Internally and externally, NCR has become a global solution provider, supported by global business processes.

The returns have already been superb. Not only has the EDW project proved to be more than self-funding at the project-cost level, but revenue generation is around the corner. Some of the benefits include $100 million in annual savings in inventory-carrying costs, a $200 million sustainable reduction in accounts receivable, a $50 million reduction in annual finance costs, and $22 million in cost savings over the first 5 years of the EDW implementation for WCS.

There is still much to be done and significant value to be realized by the project. Beyond cost savings and process efficiencies, the strategy going forward is to use the EDW to drive growth.

Although the EDW project was not undertaken as a profit-producing opportunity, it was self-funding. The cost savings far exceeded the expense of implementation. As the EDW matures, growth-focused goals are developing, and the EDW will drive profits in the future. The quantified benefits of the EDW speak for themselves. There are many more benefits of a qualitative nature. A sampling of both follows.

QUALITATIVE BENEFITS
- Reduced financial close cycle from 14 days to 6
- Heightened reporting integrity to corporate standards
- Created individual customer profitability profiles and improvement plans
- Provided consistent worldwide reporting processes

- Improved on-time delivery
- Decreased obsolescence due to enhanced inventory management

QUANTIFIED BENEFITS
- $50 million reduction in annual finance controllership costs
- $200 million sustainable reduction in accounts receivable, which translates into $20 million per year savings in accounts receivable carrying costs
- $100 million sustainable reduction in finished inventory, which, in turn, equals a $10 million per year savings in inventory carrying costs
- $22 million cost savings over the first 5 years of the EDW implementation for WCS, including automation of the service level agreement (SLA) reporting to customers, headcount savings, and lower customer maintenance costs
- $10 million for improved supply chain management
- $6.1 million net present value (NPV) of cost reductions over 5 years as a result of reducing headcount from the financial and accounting reporting function
- $3.5 million reduction in telecommunications costs
- $3 million in savings through the reduction of ERP transition costs
- $1.7 million saved on report development costs in the rollout from Oracle 10.7 and 11 to 11i, for reports that do not have to be custom written for Oracle

Source: Teradata, "Enterprise Data Warehouse Delivers Cost Savings and Process Efficiencies," **teradata.com/t/resources/case-studies/NCR-Corporation-eb4455/** (accessed June 2009).

Metadata

Metadata are data about data (Sen, 2004; and Zhao, 2005). Metadata describe the structure of and some meaning about data, thereby contributing to their effective or ineffective use. Mehra (2005) indicated that few organizations really understand metadata, and fewer understand how to design and implement a metadata strategy. Metadata are generally defined in terms of usage as technical or business metadata. Pattern is another way to view metadata. According to the pattern view, we can differentiate between syntactic metadata (i.e., data describing the syntax of data), structural metadata (i.e., data describing the structure of the data), and semantic metadata (i.e., data describing the meaning of the data in a specific domain).

We next explain traditional metadata patterns and insights into how to implement an effective metadata strategy via a holistic approach to enterprise metadata integration. The approach includes ontology and metadata registries; enterprise information integration (EII); extraction, transformation, and load (ETL); and service-oriented architectures (SOA).

Effectiveness, extensibility, reusability, interoperability, efficiency and performance, evolution, entitlement, flexibility, segregation, user interface, versioning, versatility, and low maintenance cost are some of the key requirements for building a successful metadata-driven enterprise.

According to Kassam (2002), business metadata comprise information that increases our understanding of traditional (i.e., structured) data. The primary purpose of metadata should be to provide context to the reported data; that is, it should provide enriching information that leads to the creation of knowledge. Business metadata, though difficult to provide efficiently, release more of the potential of structured data. The context need not be the same for all users. In many ways, metadata assist in the conversion of data and information into knowledge. Metadata form a foundation for a metabusiness architecture (Bell, 2001). Tannenbaum (2002) described how to identify metadata requirements. Vaduva and Vetterli (2001) provided an overview of metadata management for data warehousing. Zhao (2005) described five levels of metadata management maturity: (1) ad hoc, (2) discovered, (3) managed, (4) optimized, and (5) automated. These levels help in understanding where an organization is in terms of how and how well it uses its metadata.

The design, creation, and use of metadata—descriptive or summary data about data—and their accompanying standards may involve ethical issues. There are ethical considerations involved in the collection and ownership of the information contained in metadata, including privacy and intellectual property issues that arise in the design, collection, and dissemination stages (for more information, see Brody, 2003).

SECTION 2.1 REVIEW QUESTIONS

1. What is a data warehouse?
2. How does a data warehouse differ from a database?
3. What is an ODS?
4. Differentiate among a data mart, an ODS, and an EDW.
5. Explain the importance of metadata.

2.2 DATA WAREHOUSING PROCESS OVERVIEW

Organizations, private and public, continuously collect data, information, and knowledge at an increasingly accelerated rate and store them in computerized systems. Maintaining and using these data and information becomes extremely complex, especially as scalability issues arise. In addition, the number of users needing to access the information continues to increase as a result of improved reliability and availability of network access, especially the Internet. Working with multiple databases, either integrated in a data warehouse or not, has become an extremely difficult task requiring considerable expertise, but it can provide immense benefits far exceeding its cost (see the opening vignette and Application Case 2.2).

Application Case 2.2

Data Warehousing Supports First American Corporation's Corporate Strategy

First American Corporation changed its corporate strategy from a traditional banking approach to one that was centered on CRM. This enabled First American to transform itself from a company that lost $60 million in 1990 to an innovative financial services leader a decade later. The successful implementation of this strategy would not have been possible without its VISION data warehouse, which stores information about customer behavior such as products used, buying preferences, and client-value positions. VISION provides:

• Identification of the top 20 percent of profitable customers
• Identification of the 40 to 50 percent of unprofitable customers

- Retention strategies
- Lower-cost distribution channels
- Strategies to expand customer relationships
- Redesigned information flows

Access to information through a data warehouse can enable both evolutionary and revolutionary change. First American achieved revolutionary change, moving itself into the "sweet 16" of financial services corporations.

Sources: Based on B. L. Cooper, H. J. Watson, B. H. Wixom, and D. L. Goodhue, "Data Warehousing Supports Corporate Strategy at First American Corporation,"*MIS Quarterly*, Vol. 24, No. 4, 2000, pp. 547–567; and B. L. Cooper, H. J. Watson, B. H. Wixom, and D. L. Goodhue, "Data Warehousing Supports Corporate Strategy at First American Corporation," SIM International Conference, Atlanta, August 15–19, 1999.

Many organizations need to create data warehouses—massive data stores of time-series data for decision support. Data are imported from various external and internal resources and are cleansed and organized in a manner consistent with the organization's needs. After the data are populated in the data warehouse, data marts can be loaded for a specific area or department. Alternatively, data marts can be created first, as needed, and then integrated into an EDW. Often, though, data marts are not developed, but data are simply loaded onto PCs or left in their original state for direct manipulation using BI tools.

In Figure 2.1, we show the data warehouse concept. The following are the major components of the data warehousing process:

- ***Data sources.*** Data are sourced from multiple independent operational "legacy" systems and possibly from external data providers (such as the U.S. Census). Data may also come from an online transaction processing (OLTP) or ERP system. Web data in the form of Web logs may also feed a data warehouse.
- ***Data extraction and transformation.*** Data are extracted and properly transformed using custom-written or commercial software called ETL.
- ***Data loading.*** Data are loaded into a staging area, where they are transformed and cleansed. The data are then ready to load into the data warehouse and/or data marts.
- ***Comprehensive database.*** Essentially, this is the EDW to support all decision analysis by providing relevant summarized and detailed information originating from many different sources.

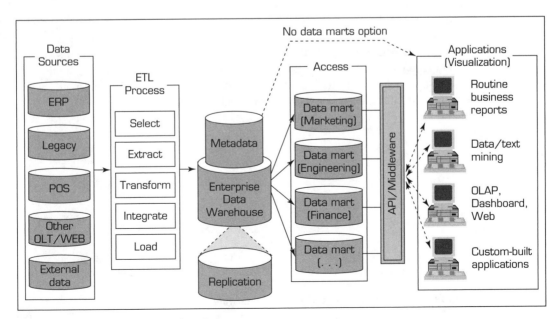

FIGURE 2.1 **A Data Warehouse Framework and Views.**

- ***Metadata.*** Metadata are maintained so that they can be assessed by IT personnel and users. Metadata include software programs about data and rules for organizing data summaries that are easy to index and search, especially with Web tools.
- ***Middleware tools.*** Middleware tools enable access to the data warehouse. Power users such as analysts may write their own **SQL** queries. Others may employ a managed query environment, such as Business Objects, to access data. There are many front-end applications that business users can use to interact with data stored in the data repositories, including data mining, OLAP, reporting tools, and data visualization tools.

SECTION 2.2 REVIEW QUESTIONS

1. Describe the data warehousing process.

2. Describe the major components of a data warehouse.

3. Identify the role of middleware tools.

2.3 DATA WAREHOUSING ARCHITECTURES

There are several basic information system architectures that can be used for data warehousing. Generally speaking, these architectures are commonly called client/server or n-tier architectures, of which two-tier and three-tier architectures are the most common (see Figures 2.2 and 2.3), but sometimes there is simply one tier. These types of multi-tiered architectures are known to be capable of serving the needs of large-scale, performance-demanding information systems such as data warehouses. Referring to the use of n-tiered architectures for data warehousing, Hoffer et al. (2007) distinguished among these architectures by dividing the data warehouse into three parts:

1. The data warehouse itself, which contains the data and associated software.

2. Data acquisition (back-end) software, which extracts data from legacy systems and external sources, consolidates and summarizes them, and loads them into the data warehouse.

3. Client (front-end) software, which allows users to access and analyze data from the warehouse (a DSS/BI/business analytics [BA] engine)

In a three-tier architecture, operational systems contain the data and the software for data acquisition in one tier (i.e., the server), the data warehouse is another tier, and the third tier includes the DSS/BI/BA engine (i.e., the application server) and the client (see Figure 2.2). Data from the warehouse are processed twice and deposited in an additional **multidimensional database**, organized for easy **multidimensional analysis** and presentation, or replicated in data marts. The advantage of the three-tier architecture is its separation of the functions of the data warehouse, which eliminates resource constraints and makes it possible to easily create data marts.

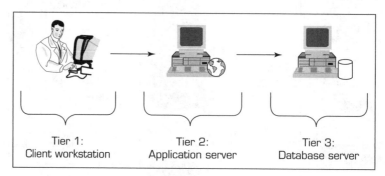

FIGURE 2.2 **Architecture of a Three-Tier Data Warehouse.**

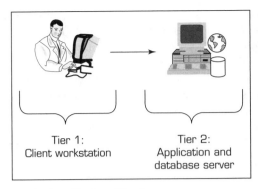

FIGURE 2.3   **Architecture of a Two-Tier Data Warehouse.**

In a two-tier architecture, the DSS engine physically runs on the same hardware platform as the data warehouse (see Figure 2.3). Therefore, it is more economical than the three-tier structure. The two-tier architecture can have performance problems for large data warehouses that work with data-intensive applications for decision support.

Much of the common wisdom assumes an absolutist approach, maintaining that one solution is better than the other, despite the organization's circumstances and unique needs. To further complicate these architectural decisions, many consultants and software vendors focus on one portion of the architecture, therefore limiting their capacity and motivation to assist an organization through the options based on its needs. But these aspects are being questioned and analyzed. For example, Ball (2005) provided decision criteria for organizations that plan to implement a BI application and have already determined their need for multidimensional data marts but need help determining the appropriate tiered architecture. His criteria revolve around forecasting needs for space and speed of access (Ball, 2005).

Data warehousing and the Internet are two key technologies that offer important solutions for managing corporate data. The integration of these two technologies produces Web-based data warehousing. In Figure 2.4, we show the architecture of Web-based data warehousing. The architecture is three tiered and includes the PC client, Web

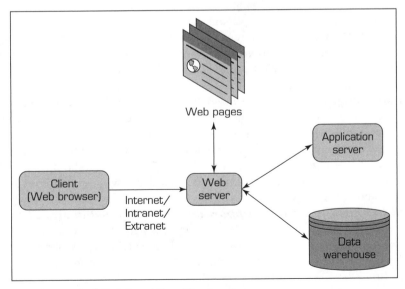

FIGURE 2.4   **Architecture of Web-Based Data Warehousing.**

server, and application server. On the client side, the user needs an Internet connection and a Web browser (preferably Java enabled) through the familiar **graphical user interface (GUI)**. The Internet/intranet/extranet is the communication medium between client and servers. On the server side, a Web server is used to manage the inflow and outflow of information between client and server. It is backed by both a data warehouse and an application server. Web-based data warehousing offers several compelling advantages, including ease of access, platform independence, and lower cost.

The Vanguard Group moved to a Web-based, three-tier architecture for its enterprise architecture to integrate all its data and provide customers with the same views of data as internal users (Dragoon, 2003). Likewise, Hilton Hotels migrated all its independent client/server systems to a three-tier data warehouse, using a Web design enterprise system. This change involved an investment of $3.8 million (excluding labor) and affected 1,500 users. It increased processing efficiency (speed) by a factor of six. When it was deployed, Hilton expected to save $4.5 to $5 million annually. Finally, Hilton experimented with Dell's clustering (i.e., parallel computing) technology to enhance scalability and speed (Anthes, 2003).

Web architectures for data warehousing are similar in structure to other data warehousing architectures, requiring a design choice for housing the Web data warehouse with the transaction server or as a separate server(s). Page-loading speed is an important consideration in designing Web-based applications; therefore, server capacity must be planned carefully.

Several issues must be considered when deciding which architecture to use. Among them are the following:

- *Which database management system (DBMS) should be used?* Most data warehouses are built using relational database management systems (RDBMS). Oracle (Oracle Corporation, **oracle.com**), SQL Server (Microsoft Corporation, **microsoft.com/sql/**), and DB2 (IBM Corporation, **306.ibm.com/software/data/db2/**) are the ones most commonly used. Each of these products supports both client/server and Web-based architectures.

- *Will parallel processing and/or partitioning be used?* **Parallel processing** enables multiple CPUs to process data warehouse query requests simultaneously and provides scalability. Data warehouse designers need to decide whether the database tables will be partitioned (i.e., split into smaller tables) for access efficiency and what the criteria will be. This is an important consideration that is necessitated by the large amounts of data contained in a typical data warehouse. A recent survey on parallel and distributed data warehouses can be found in Furtado (2009). Teradata (**teradata.com**) has successfully adopted and often commented on its novel implementation of this approach.

- *Will data migration tools be used to load the data warehouse?* Moving data from an existing system into a data warehouse is a tedious and laborious task. Depending on the diversity and the location of the data assets, migration may be a relatively simple procedure or (in contrary) a months-long project. The results of a thorough assessment of the existing data assets should be used to determine whether to use migration tools, and if so, what capabilities to seek in those commercial tools.

- *What tools will be used to support data retrieval and analysis?* Often it is necessary to use specialized tools to periodically locate, access, analyze, extract, transform, and load necessary data into a data warehouse. A decision has to be made on (i) developing the migration tools in-house, (ii) purchasing them from a third-party provider, or (iii) using the ones provided with the data warehouse system. Overly complex, real-time migrations warrant specialized third-party ETL tools.

Alternative Data Warehousing Architectures

At the highest level, data warehouse architecture design viewpoints can be categorized into enterprise-wide data warehouse (EDW) design and data mart (DM) design (Golfarelli and Rizzi, 2009). In Figure 2.5 (parts a–e), we show some alternatives to the basic architectural design types that are neither pure EDW nor pure DM, but in between or beyond the traditional architectural structures. Notable new ones include hub-and-spoke and federated

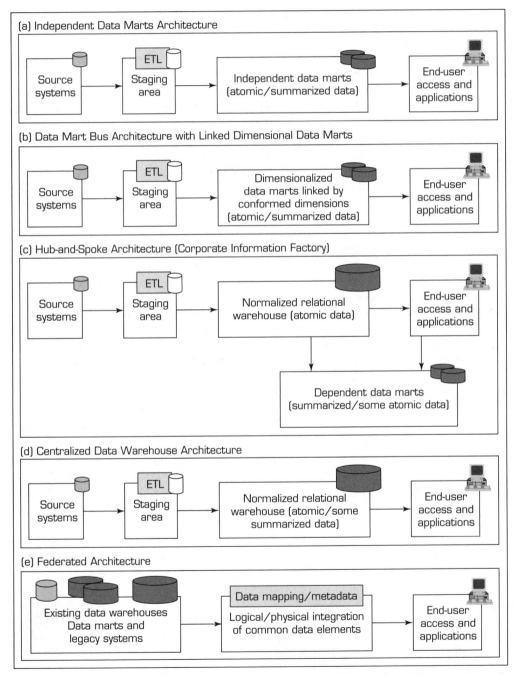

FIGURE 2.5 Alternative Data Warehouse Architectures. *Source:* Adapted from T. Ariyachandra and H. Watson, "Which Data Warehouse Architecture Is Most Successful?" *Business Intelligence Journal*, Vol. 11, No. 1, First Quarter, 2006, pp. 4–6.

architectures. The five architectures shown in Figure 2.5 (parts a–e) are proposed by Ariyachandra and Watson (2005, 2006a, and 2006b). Previously, in an extensive study, Sen and Sinha (2005) identified 15 different data warehousing methodologies. The sources of these methodologies are classified into three broad categories: core-technology vendors, infrastructure vendors, and information-modeling companies.

a. ***Independent data marts.*** This is arguably the simplest and the least costly architecture alternative. The data marts are developed to operate independently of each other to serve for the needs of individual organizational units. Because of the independence, they may have inconsistent data definitions and different dimensions and measures, making it difficult to analyze data across the data marts (i.e., it is difficult, if not impossible, to get to the "one version of the truth").

b. ***Data mart bus architecture.*** This architecture is a viable alternative to the independent data marts where the individual marts are linked to each other via some kind of middleware. Because the data are linked among the individual marts, there is a better chance of maintaining data consistency across the enterprise (at least at the metadata level). Even though it allows for complex data queries across data marts, the performance of these types of analysis may not be at a satisfactory level.

c. ***Hub-and-spoke architecture.*** This is perhaps the most famous data warehousing architecture today. Here the attention is focused on building a scalable and maintainable infrastructure (often developed in an iterative way, subject area by subject area) that includes a centralized data warehouse and several dependent data marts (each for an organizational unit). This architecture allows for easy and customization of user interfaces and reports. On the negative side, this architecture lacks the holistic enterprise view, and may lead to data redundancy and data latency.

d. ***Centralized data warehouse.*** The centralized data warehouse architecture is similar to the hub-and-spoke architecture except that there are no dependent data marts; instead, there is a gigantic enterprise data warehouse that serves for the needs of all organizational units. This centralized approach provides users with access to all data in the data warehouse instead of limiting them to data marts. In addition, it reduces the amount of data the technical team has to transfer or change, therefore simplifying data management and administration. If designed and implemented properly, this architecture provides a timely and holistic view of the enterprise to whomever, whenever, and wherever they may be within the organization. The central data warehouses architecture, which is advocated mainly by Teradata Corp., advises using data warehouses without any data marts (see **Figure 2.6**).

e. ***Federated data warehouse.*** The federated approach is a concession to the natural forces that undermine the best plans for developing a perfect system. It uses all possible means to integrate analytical resources from multiple sources to meet changing needs or business conditions. Essentially, the federated approach involves integrating disparate systems. In a federated architecture, existing decision support structures are left in place, and data are accessed from those sources as needed. The federated approach is supported by middleware vendors that propose distributed query and join capabilities. These eXtensible Markup Language (XML)–based tools offer users a global view of distributed data sources, including data warehouses, data marts, Web sites, documents, and operational systems. When users choose query objects from this view and press the submit button, the tool automatically queries the distributed sources, joins the results, and presents them to the user. Because of performance and **data quality** issues, most **experts** agree that federated approaches work well to supplement data warehouses, not replace them (Eckerson, 2005).

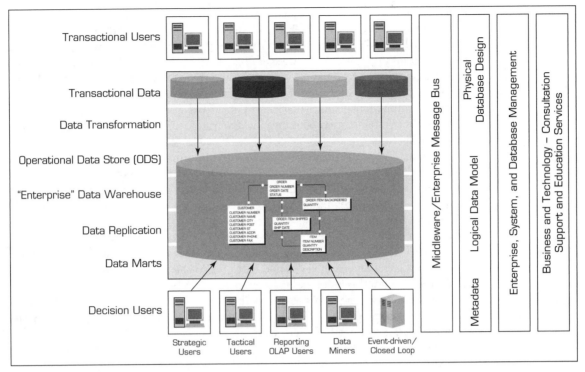

FIGURE 2.6 **Teradata Corporation's Enterprise Data Warehouse.** *Source*: Teradata Corporation (teradata.com). Used with permission.

Ariyachandra and Watson (2005) identified 10 factors that potentially affect the architecture selection decision:

1. Information interdependence between organizational units
2. Upper management's information needs
3. Urgency of need for a data warehouse
4. Nature of end-user tasks
5. Constraints on resources
6. Strategic view of the data warehouse prior to implementation
7. Compatibility with existing systems
8. Perceived ability of the in-house IT staff
9. Technical issues
10. Social/political factors

These factors are similar to many success factors described in the literature for information systems projects and DSS and BI projects. Technical issues, beyond providing technology that is feasibly ready for use, are important, but often not as important as behavioral issues such as meeting upper management's information needs and user involvement in the development process (a social/political factor). Each data warehousing architecture has specific applications for which it is most (and least) effective and thus provides maximal benefits to the organization. However, overall, the data mart structure seems to be the least effective in practice. See Ariyachandra and Watson (2006a) for some additional details.

Which Architecture Is the Best?

Ever since data warehousing became a critical part of modern enterprises, the question of which data warehouse architecture is the best has been a topic of regular discussion. The two gurus of the data warehousing field, Bill Inmon and Ralph Kimball, are at the heart of this discussion. Inmon advocates the hub-and-spoke architecture (e.g., the Corporate Information Factory), whereas Kimball promotes the data mart bus architecture with conformed dimensions. Other architectures are possible, but these two options are fundamentally different approaches, and each has strong advocates. To shed light on this controversial question, Ariyachandra and Watson (2006b) conducted an empirical study. To collect the data, they used a Web-based survey targeted at individuals involved in data warehouse implementations. Their survey included questions about the respondent, the respondent's company, the company's data warehouse, and the success of the data warehouse architecture.

In total, 454 respondents provided usable information. Surveyed companies ranged from small (less than $10 million in revenue) to large (in excess of $10 billion). Most of the companies were located in the United States (60%) and represented a variety of industries, with the financial services industry (15%) providing the most responses. The predominant architecture was the hub-and-spoke architecture (39%), followed by the bus architecture (26%), the centralized architecture (17%), independent data marts (12%), and the federated architecture (4%). The most common platform for hosting the data warehouses was Oracle (41%), followed by Microsoft (19%) and IBM (18%). The average (mean) gross revenue varied from $3.7 billion for independent data marts to $6 billion for the federated architecture.

They used four measures to assess the success of the architectures: (1) information quality, (2) system quality, (3) individual impacts, and (4) organizational impacts. The questions used a seven-point scale, with the higher score indicating a more successful architecture. Table 2.1 shows the average scores for the measures across the architectures.

As the results of the study indicate, independent data marts scored the lowest on all measures. This finding confirms the conventional wisdom that independent data marts are a poor architectural solution. Next lowest on all measures was the federated architecture. Firms sometimes have disparate decision-support platforms resulting from mergers and acquisitions, and they may choose a federated approach, at least in the short run. The findings suggest that the federated architecture is not an optimal long-term solution. What is interesting, however, is the similarity of the averages for the bus, hub-and-spoke, and centralized architectures. The differences are sufficiently small that no claims can be made for a particular architecture's superiority over the others, at least based on a simple comparison of these success measures.

Ariyachandra and Watson also collected data on the domain (e.g., varying from a subunit to company-wide) and the size (i.e., amount of data stored) of the warehouses. They found that the hub-and-spoke architecture is typically used with more enterprise-wide

TABLE 2.1 Average Assessment Scores for the Success of the Architectures

	Independent Data Marts	Bus Architecture	Hub-and Spoke Architecture	Centralized Architecture (No Dependent Data Marts)	Federated Architecture
Information Quality	4.42	5.16	5.35	5.23	4.73
System Quality	4.59	5.60	5.56	5.41	4.69
Individual Impacts	5.08	5.80	5.62	5.64	5.15
Organizational Impacts	4.66	5.34	5.24	5.30	4.77

implementations and larger warehouses. They also investigated the cost and time required to implement the different architectures. Overall, the hub-and-spoke architecture was the most expensive and time-consuming to implement.

SECTION 2.3 REVIEW QUESTIONS

1. What are the key similarities and differences between a two-tiered architecture and a three-tiered architecture?
2. How has the Web influenced data warehouse design?
3. List the alternative data warehousing architectures discussed in this section.
4. What issues should be considered when deciding which architecture to use in developing a data warehouse? List the 10 most important factors.
5. Which data warehousing architecture is the best? Why?

2.4 DATA INTEGRATION AND THE EXTRACTION, TRANSFORMATION, AND LOAD (ETL) PROCESSES

Global competitive pressures, demand for return on investment (ROI), management and investor inquiry, and government regulations are forcing business managers to rethink how they integrate and manage their businesses. A decision maker typically needs access to multiple sources of data that must be integrated. Before data warehouses, data marts, and BI software, providing access to data sources was a major, laborious process. Even with modern Web-based data management tools, recognizing what data to access and providing them to the decision maker is a nontrivial task that requires database specialists. As data warehouses grow in size, the issues of integrating data grow as well.

The business analysis needs continue to evolve. Mergers and acquisitions, regulatory requirements, and the introduction of new channels can drive changes in BI requirements. In addition to historical, cleansed, consolidated, and point-in-time data, business users increasingly demand access to real-time, unstructured, and/or remote data. And everything must be integrated with the contents of an existing data warehouse. Moreover, access via personal digital assistants and through **speech recognition** and synthesis is becoming more commonplace, further complicating integration issues (Edwards, 2003). Many integration projects involve enterprise-wide systems. Orovic (2003) provided a checklist of what works and what does not work when attempting such a project. Properly integrating data from various databases and other disparate sources is difficult. But when it is not done properly, it can lead to disaster in enterprise-wide systems such as CRM, ERP, and supply chain projects (Nash, 2002).

Data Integration

Data integration comprises three major processes that, when correctly implemented, permit data to be accessed and made accessible to an array of ETL and analysis tools and data warehousing environment: data access (i.e., the ability to access and extract data from any data source), data federation (i.e., the integration of business views across multiple data stores), and change capture (based on the identification, capture, and delivery of the changes made to enterprise data sources). See Application Case 2.3 for an example of how BP Lubricants benefits from implementing a data warehouse that integrates data from many sources. Some vendors, such as SAS Institute, Inc., have developed strong data integration tools. The SAS enterprise data integration server includes customer data integration tools that improve data quality in the integration process. The Oracle Business Intelligence Suite assists in integrating data as well.

Application Case 2.3

BP Lubricants Achieves BIGS Success

BP Lubricants established the Business Intelligence and Global Standards (BIGS) program following recent merger activity to deliver globally consistent and transparent management information. As well as timely business intelligence, BIGS provides detailed, consistent views of performance across functions such as finance, marketing, sales, and supply and logistics.

BP Lubricants is one of the world's largest oil and petrochemicals groups. Part of the BP plc group, BP Lubricants is an established leader in the global automotive lubricants market. Perhaps best known for its Castrol brand of oils, the business operates in over 100 countries and employs 10,000 people. Strategically, BP Lubricants is concentrating on further improving its customer focus and increasing its effectiveness in automotive markets. Following recent merger activity, the company is undergoing transformation to become more effective and agile and to seize opportunities for rapid growth.

Challenge

Following recent merger activity, BP Lubricants wanted to improve the consistency, transparency, and accessibility of management information and business intelligence. In order to do so, it needed to integrate data held in disparate source systems, without the delay of introducing a standardized ERP system.

Solution

BP Lubricants implemented the pilot for its BIGS program, a strategic initiative for management information and business intelligence. At the heart of BIGS is Kalido, an adaptive enterprise data warehousing solution for preparing, implementing, operating, and managing data warehouses.

Kalido's federated enterprise data warehousing solution supported the pilot program's complex data integration and diverse reporting requirements. To adapt to the program's evolving reporting requirements, the software also enabled the underlying information architecture to be easily modified at high speed while preserving all information. The system integrates and stores information from multiple source systems to provide consolidated views for:

- ***Marketing.*** Customer proceeds and margins for market segments with **drill down** to invoice-level detail
- ***Sales.*** Sales invoice reporting augmented with both detailed tariff costs and actual payments
- ***Finance.*** Globally standard profit and loss, balance sheet, and cash flow statements—with audit ability; customer debt management supply and logistics; consolidated view of order, and movement processing across multiple ERP platforms

Benefits

By improving the visibility of consistent, timely data, BIGS provides the information needed to assist the business in identifying a multitude of business opportunities to maximize margins and/or manage associated costs. Typical responses to the benefits of consistent data resulting from the BIGS pilot include:

- Improved consistency and transparency of business data
- Easier, faster, and more flexible reporting
- Accommodation of both global and local standards
- Fast, cost-effective, and flexible implementation cycle
- Minimal disruption of existing business processes and the day-to-day business
- Identification of data quality issues and help with their resolution
- Improved ability to respond intelligently to new business opportunities

Source: Kalido, "BP Lubricants Achieves BIGS, Key IT Solutions," **keyitsolutions.com/asp/rptdetails/report/95/cat/1175/** (accessed August 2009); Kalido, "BP Lubricants Achieves BIGS Success," **kalido.com/collateral/Documents/English-US/CS-BP%20BIGS.pdf** (accessed August 2009); and BP Lubricant homepage, **bp.com/lubricanthome.do** (accessed August 2009).

A major purpose of a data warehouse is to integrate data from multiple systems. Various integration technologies enable data and metadata integration:

- Enterprise application integration (EAI)
- Service-oriented architecture (SOA)
- Enterprise information integration (EII)
- Extraction, transformation, and load (ETL)

Enterprise application integration (EAI) provides a vehicle for pushing data from source systems into the data warehouse. It involves integrating application functionality and is focused on sharing functionality (rather than data) across systems, thereby enabling flexibility and reuse. Traditionally, EAI solutions have focused on enabling application reuse at the application programming interface level. Recently, EAI is accomplished by using SOA coarse-grained services (a collection of business processes or functions) that are well defined and documented. Using Web services is a specialized way of implementing an SOA. EAI can be used to facilitate data acquisition directly into a near-real-time data warehouse or to deliver decisions to the OLTP systems. There are many different approaches to and tools for EAI implementation.

Enterprise information integration (EII) is an evolving tool space that promises real-time data integration from a variety of sources such as **relational databases**, Web services, and multidimensional databases. It is a mechanism for pulling data from source systems to satisfy a request for information. EII tools use predefined metadata to populate views that make integrated data appear relational to end users. XML may be the most important aspect of EII because XML allows data to be tagged either at creation time or later. These tags can be extended and modified to accommodate almost any area of knowledge (Kay, 2005).

Physical data integration has conventionally been the main mechanism for creating an integrated view with data warehouses and data marts. With the advent of EII tools (Kay, 2005), new virtual data integration patterns are feasible. Manglik and Mehra (2005) discussed the benefits and constraints of new data integration patterns that can expand traditional physical methodologies to present a comprehensive view for the enterprise.

We next turn to the approach for loading data into the warehouse: ETL.

Extraction, Transformation, and Load (ETL)

At the heart of the technical side of the data warehousing process is **extraction, transformation, and load (ETL)**. ETL technologies, which have existed for some time, are instrumental in the process and use of data warehouses. The ETL process is an integral component in any data-centric project. IT managers are often faced with challenges because the ETL process typically consumes 70 percent of the time in a data-centric project.

The ETL process consists of **extraction** (i.e., reading data from one or more databases), transformation (i.e., converting the extracted data from its previous form into the form in which it needs to be so that it can be placed into a data warehouse or simply another database), and load (i.e., putting the data into the data warehouse). Transformation occurs by using rules or lookup tables or by combining the data with other data. The three database functions are integrated into one tool to pull data out of one or more databases and place them into another, consolidated database or a data warehouse.

ETL tools also transport data between sources and targets, document how data elements (e.g., metadata) change as they move between source and target, exchange metadata with other applications as needed, and administer all runtime processes and operations (e.g., scheduling, error management, audit logs, statistics). ETL is extremely important for data integration as well as for data warehousing. The purpose of the ETL process is to load

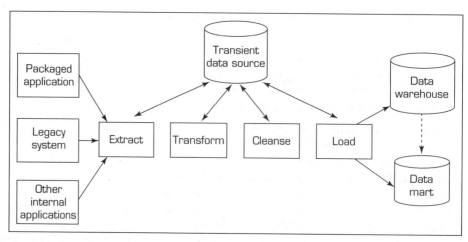

FIGURE 2.7   The ETL Process.

the warehouse with integrated and cleansed data. The data used in ETL processes can come from any source: a mainframe application, an ERP application, a CRM tool, a flat file, an Excel spreadsheet, or even a message queue. In Figure 2.7, we outline the ETL process.

The process of migrating data to a data warehouse involves the extraction of data from all relevant sources. Data sources may consist of files extracted from OLTP databases, spreadsheets, personal databases (e.g., Microsoft Access), or external files. Typically, all the input files are written to a set of staging tables, which are designed to facilitate the load process. A data warehouse contains numerous business rules that define such things as how the data will be used, summarization rules, standardization of encoded attributes, and calculation rules. Any data quality issues pertaining to the source files need to be corrected before the data are loaded into the data warehouse. One of the benefits of a well-designed data warehouse is that these rules can be stored in a metadata repository and applied to the data warehouse centrally. This differs from the OLTP approach, which typically has data and business rules scattered throughout the system. The process of loading data into a data warehouse can be performed either through data transformation tools that provide a GUI to aid in the development and maintenance of business rules or through more traditional methods, such as developing programs or utilities to load the data warehouse, using programming languages such as PL/SQL, C++, or .NET Framework languages. This decision is not easy for organizations. Several issues affect whether an organization will purchase data transformation tools or build the transformation process itself:

- Data transformation tools are expensive.
- Data transformation tools may have a long learning curve.
- It is difficult to measure how the IT organization is doing until it has learned to use the data transformation tools.

In the long run, a transformation-tool approach should simplify the maintenance of an organization's data warehouse. Transformation tools can also be effective in detecting and scrubbing (i.e., removing any anomalies in the data). OLAP and data mining tools rely on how well the data are transformed.

As an example of effective ETL, let us consider Motorola, Inc., which uses ETL to feed its data warehouses. Motorola collects information from 30 different procurement systems and sends them to its global SCM data warehouse for analysis of aggregate company spending (Songini, 2004).

Solomon (2005) classified ETL technologies into four categories: sophisticated, enabler, simple, and rudimentary. It is generally acknowledged that tools in the sophisticated category will result in the ETL process being better documented and more accurately managed as the data warehouse project evolves.

Even though it is possible for programmers to develop software for ETL, it is simpler to use an existing ETL tool. The following are some of the important criteria in selecting an ETL tool (Brown, 2004):

- Ability to read from and write to an unlimited number of data source architectures
- Automatic capturing and delivery of metadata
- A history of conforming to open standards
- An easy-to-use interface for the developer and the functional user

Performing extensive ETL may be a sign of poorly managed data and a fundamental lack of a coherent data management strategy. Karacsony (2006) indicated that there is a direct correlation between the extent of redundant data and the number of ETL processes. When data are managed correctly as an enterprise asset, ETL efforts are significantly reduced, and redundant data are completely eliminated. This leads to huge savings in maintenance and greater efficiency in new development while also improving data quality. Poorly designed ETL processes are costly to maintain, change, and update. Consequently, it is crucial to make the proper choices in terms of technology and tools to use for developing and maintaining the ETL process.

A number of packaged ETL tools are available. Database vendors currently offer ETL capabilities that both enhance and compete with independent ETL tools. SAS acknowledges the importance of data quality and offers the industry's first fully integrated solution that merges ETL and data quality to transform data into strategic valuable assets. Other ETL software providers include Microsoft, Oracle, IBM, Informatica, Embarcadero, and Tibco. For additional information on ETL, see Golfarelli and Rizzi (2009), Karacsony (2006), and Songini (2004).

SECTION 2.4 REVIEW QUESTIONS

1. Describe data integration.
2. Describe the three steps of the ETL process.
3. Why is the ETL process so important for data warehousing efforts?

2.5 DATA WAREHOUSE DEVELOPMENT

A data warehousing project is a major undertaking for any organization and is more complicated than a simple, mainframe selection and implementation project because it comprises and influences many departments and many input and output interfaces and it can be part of a CRM business strategy. A data warehouse provides several benefits that can be classified as direct and indirect. Direct benefits include the following:

- End users can perform extensive analysis in numerous ways.
- A consolidated view of corporate data (i.e., a single version of the truth) is possible.
- Better and more-timely information is possible. A data warehouse permits information processing to be relieved from costly operational systems onto low-cost servers; therefore, many more end-user information requests can be processed more quickly.
- Enhanced system performance can result. A data warehouse frees production processing because some operational system reporting requirements are moved to DSS.
- Data access is simplified.

Indirect benefits result from end users using these direct benefits. On the whole, these benefits enhance business knowledge, present competitive advantage, improve customer service and satisfaction, facilitate decision making, and help in reforming business processes, and therefore, they are the strongest contributions to competitive advantage. (For a discussion of how to create a competitive advantage through data warehousing, see Parzinger and Frolick, 2001.) For a detailed discussion of how organizations can obtain exceptional levels of payoffs, see Watson et al. (2002). Given the potential benefits that a data warehouse can provide and the substantial investments in time and money that such a project requires, it is critical that an organization structure its data warehouse project to maximize the chances of success. In addition, the organization must, obviously, take costs into consideration. Kelly (2001) described a ROI approach that considers benefits in the categories of keepers (i.e., money saved by improving traditional decision support functions); gatherers (i.e., money saved due to automated collection and dissemination of information); and users (i.e., money saved or gained from decisions made using the data warehouse). Costs include those related to hardware, software, network bandwidth, internal development, internal support, training, and external consulting. The net present value (NPV) is calculated over the expected life of the data warehouse. Because the benefits are broken down approximately as 20 percent for keepers, 30 percent for gatherers, and 50 percent for users, Kelly indicated that users should be involved in the development process, a success factor typically mentioned as critical for systems that imply change in an organization.

Application Case 2.4 provides an example of a data warehouse that was developed and delivered intense competitive advantage for the Hokuriku (Japan)

Application Case 2.4

Things Go Better with Coke's Data Warehouse

In the face of competitive pressures and consumer demand, how does a successful bottling company ensure that its vending machines are profitable? The answer for HCCBC is a data warehouse and analytical software implemented by Teradata. HCCBC built the system in response to a data warehousing system developed by its rival, Mikuni American Corporation. The data warehouse collects not only historical data but also near-real-time data from each vending machine (viewed as a store) that could be transmitted via wireless connection to headquarters. The initial phase of the project was deployed in 2001. The data warehouse approach provides detailed product information, such as time and date of each sale, when a product sells out, whether someone was shortchanged, and whether the machine is malfunctioning. In each case, an alert is triggered, and the vending machine immediately reports it to the data center over a wireless transmission system. (Note that Coca-Cola in the United States has used modems to link vending machines to distributors for over a decade.)

In 2002, HCCBC conducted a pilot test and put all its Nagano vending machines on a wireless network to gather near-real-time point-of-sale (POS) data

from each one. The results were astounding because they accurately forecasted demand and identified problems quickly. Total sales immediately increased 10 percent. In addition, due to the more accurate machine servicing, overtime and other costs decreased 46 percent. In addition, each salesperson was able to service up to 42 percent more vending machines.

The test was so successful that planning began to expand it to encompass the entire enterprise (60,000 machines), using an active data warehouse. Eventually, the data warehousing solution will ideally expand across corporate boundaries into the entire Coca-Cola Bottlers network so that the more than 1 million vending machines in Japan will be networked, leading to immense cost savings and higher revenue.

Sources: Adapted from K. D. Schwartz, "Decisions at the Touch of a Button," *Teradata Magazine*, **teradata.com/t/page/117774/index.html** (accessed June 2009); K. D. Schwartz, "Decisions at the Touch of a Button," *DSS Resources*, March 2004, pp. 28–31, **dssresources.com/cases/coca-colajapan/index.html** (accessed April 2006); and Teradata Corp., "Coca-Cola Japan Puts the Fizz Back in Vending Machine Sales," **teradata.com/t/page/118866/index.html** (accessed June 2009).

Coca-Cola Bottling Company (HCCBC). The system was so successful that plans are under way to expand it to encompass the more than 1 million Coca-Cola vending machines in Japan.

Clearly defining the business objective, gathering project support from management end users, setting reasonable time frames and budgets, and managing expectations are critical to a successful data warehousing project. A data warehousing strategy is a blueprint for the successful introduction of the data warehouse. The strategy should describe where the company wants to go, why it wants to go there, and what it will do when it gets there. It needs to take into consideration the organization's vision, structure, and culture. See Matney (2003) for the steps that can help in developing a flexible and efficient support strategy. When the plan and support for a data warehouse are established, the organization needs to examine data warehouse vendors. (See Table 2.2 for a sample list of vendors; also see The Data Warehousing Institute [**twdi.com**] and *DM Review* [**dmreview.com**].) Many vendors provide software demos of their data warehousing and BI products.

TABLE 2.2   Sample List of Data Warehousing Vendors

Vendor	Product Offerings
Computer Associates (**cai.com**)	Comprehensive set of data warehouse (DW) tools and products
DataMirror (**datamirror.com**)	DW administration, management, and performance products
Data Advantage Group (**dataadvantagegroup.com**)	Metadata software
Dell (**dell.com**)	DW servers
Embarcadero Technologies (**embarcadero.com**)	DW administration, management, and performance products
Business Objects (**businessobjects.com**)	Data cleansing software
Harte-Hanks (**harte-hanks.com**)	CRM products and services
HP (**hp.com**)	DW servers
Hummingbird Ltd. (**hummingbird.com**)	DW engines and exploration warehouses
Hyperion Solutions (**hyperion.com**)	Comprehensive set of DW tools, products, and applications
IBM (**ibm.com**)	DW tools, products, and applications
Informatica (**informatica.com**)	DW administration, management, and performance products
Microsoft (**microsoft.com**)	DW tools and products
Oracle (including PeopleSoft and Siebel) (**oracle.com**)	DW, ERP, and CRM tools, products, and applications
SAS Institute (**sas.com**)	DW tools, products, and applications
Siemens (**siemens.com**)	DW servers
Sybase (**sybase.com**)	Comprehensive set of DW tools and applications
Teradata (**teradata.com**)	DW tools, products, and applications

Data Warehouse Vendors

McCloskey (2002) cited six guidelines that need to be considered when developing a vendor list: financial strength, ERP linkages, qualified consultants, market share, industry experience, and established partnerships. Data can be obtained from trade shows and corporate Web sites, as well as by submitting requests for specific product information. Van den Hoven (1998) differentiated three types of data warehousing products. The first type handles functions such as locating, extracting, transforming, cleansing, transporting, and loading the data into the data warehouse. The second type is a data management tool—a database engine that stores and manages the data warehouse as well as the metadata. The third type is a data access tool that provides end users with access to analyze the data in the data warehouse. This may include query generators, visualization, EIS, OLAP, and data mining capabilities.

Data Warehouse Development Approaches

Many organizations need to create the data warehouses used for decision support. Two competing approaches are employed. The first approach is that of Bill Inmon, who is often called "the father of data warehousing." Inmon supports a top-down development approach that adapts traditional relational database tools to the development needs of an enterprise-wide data warehouse, also known as the EDW approach. The second approach is that of Ralph Kimball, who proposes a bottom-up approach that employs dimensional modeling, also known as the data mart approach.

Knowing how these two models are alike and how they differ helps us understand the basic data warehouse concepts (Breslin, 2004). Table 2.3 compares the two approaches. We describe these approaches in detail next.

THE INMON MODEL: THE EDW APPROACH   Inmon's approach emphasizes top-down development, employing established database development methodologies and tools, such as entity-relationship diagrams (ERD), and an adjustment of the spiral development approach. The EDW approach does not preclude the creation of data marts. The EDW is the ideal in this approach because it provides a consistent and comprehensive view of the enterprise. Murtaza (1998) presented a framework for developing EDW.

THE KIMBALL MODEL: THE DATA MART APPROACH   Kimball's data mart strategy is a "plan big, build small" approach. A data mart is a subject-oriented or department-oriented data warehouse. It is a scaled-down version of a data warehouse that focuses on the requests of a specific department such as marketing or sales. This model applies dimensional data modeling, which starts with tables. Kimball advocated a development methodology that entails a bottom-up approach, which in the case of data warehouses means building one data mart at a time.

WHICH MODEL IS BEST?   There is no one-size-fits-all strategy to data warehousing. An enterprise's data warehousing strategy can evolve from a simple data mart to a complex data warehouse in response to user demands, the enterprise's business requirements, and the enterprise's maturity in managing its data resources. For many enterprises, a data mart is frequently a convenient first step to acquiring experience in constructing and managing a data warehouse while presenting business users with the benefits of better access to their data; in addition, a data mart commonly indicates the business value of data warehousing. Ultimately, obtaining an EDW is ideal (see Application Case 2.5). However, the development of individual data marts can often

TABLE 2.3   Contrasts Between the Data Mart and EDW Development Approaches

Effort	Data Mart Approach	EDW Approach
Scope	One subject area	Several subject areas
Development time	Months	Years
Development cost	$10,000 to $100,000+	$1,000,000+
Development difficulty	Low to medium	High
Data prerequisite for sharing	Common (within business area)	Common (across enterprise)
Sources	Only some operational and external systems	Many operational and external systems
Size	Megabytes to several gigabytes	Gigabytes to petabytes
Time horizon	Near-current and historical data	Historical data
Data transformations	Low to medium	High
Update frequency	Hourly, daily, weekly	Weekly, monthly
Technology		
Hardware	Workstations and departmental servers	Enterprise servers and mainframe computers
Operating system	Windows and Linux	Unix, Z/OS, OS/390
Databases	Workgroup or standard database servers	Enterprise database servers
Usage		
Number of simultaneous users	10s	100s to 1,000s
User types	Business area analysts and managers	Enterprise analysts and senior executives
Business spotlight	Optimizing activities within the business area	Cross-functional optimization and decision making

Sources: Based on J. Van den Hoven, "Data Marts: Plan Big, Build Small," in *IS Management Handbook*, 8th ed., CRC Press, Boca Raton, FL, 2003; and T. Ariyachandra and H. Watson, "Which Data Warehouse Architecture Is Most Successful?" *Business Intelligence Journal*, Vol. 11, No. 1, First Quarter 2006, pp. 4–6.

Application Case 2.5

HP Consolidates Hundreds of Data Marts into a Single EDW

In December 2005, Hewlett-Packard planned to consolidate its 762 data marts around the world into a single EDW. HP took this approach to gain a superior sense of its own business and to determine how best to serve its customers. Mark Hurd, HP's president and chief executive, stated that "there was a thirst for analytic data" inside the company that had unfortunately led to the creation of many data marts. Those data silos were very expensive to design and maintain, and they did not produce the enterprise-wide view of internal and customer information that HP wanted. In mid-2006, HP started to consolidate the data in the data marts into the new data warehouse. All the disparate data marts will ultimately be eliminated.

Sources: Based on C. Martins, "HP to Consolidate Data Marts into Single Warehouse," Computerworld, December 13, 2005.

TABLE 2.4 Essential Differences Between Inmon and Kimball's Approaches

Characteristic	Inmon	Kimball
Methodology and Architecture		
Overall approach	Top-down	Bottom-up
Architecture structure	Enterprise-wide (atomic) data warehouse "feeds" departmental databases	Data marts model a single business process, and enterprise consistency is achieved through a data bus and conformed dimensions
Complexity of the method	Quite complex	Fairly simple
Comparison with established development methodologies	Derived from the spiral methodology	Four-step process; a departure from RDBMS methods
Discussion of physical design	Fairly thorough	Fairly light
Data Modeling		
Data orientation	Subject or data driven	Process oriented
Tools	Traditional (ERD, data flow diagrams)	Dimensional modeling; a departure from relational modeling
End-user accessibility	Low	High
Philosophy		
Primary audience	IT professionals	End users
Place in the organization	Integral part of the corporate information factory	Transformer and retainer of operational data
Objective	Deliver a sound technical solution based on proven database methods and technologies	Deliver a solution that makes it easy for end users to directly query the data and still get reasonable response times

Sources: Based on M. Breslin, "Data Warehousing Battle of the Giants: Comparing the Basics of Kimball and Inmon Models," *Business Intelligence Journal*, Vol. 9, No. 1, Winter 2004, pp. 6–20; and T. Ariyachandra and H. Watson, "Which Data Warehouse Architecture Is Most Successful?" *Business Intelligence Journal*, Vol. 11, No. 1, First Quarter 2006.

provide many benefits along the way toward developing an EDW, especially if the organization is unable or unwilling to invest in a large-scale project. Data marts can also demonstrate feasibility and success in providing benefits. This could potentially lead to an investment in an EDW. Table 2.4 summarizes the most essential characteristic differences between the two models.

Additional Data Warehouse Development Considerations

Some organizations want to completely outsource their data warehousing efforts. They simply do not want to deal with software and hardware acquisitions, and they do not want to manage their information systems. One alternative is to use hosted data warehouses. In this scenario, another firm—ideally, one that has a lot of experience and expertise—develops and maintains the data warehouse. However, there are security and privacy concerns with this approach. See Technology Insight 2.1 for some details.

Representation of Data in Data Warehouse

A typical data warehouse structure is shown in Figure 2.1. Many variations of data warehouse architecture are possible (see Figure 2.5). No matter what the architecture was, the design of data representation in the data warehouse has always been based on the concept of dimensional modeling. **Dimensional modeling** is a retrieval-based system that supports high-volume query access. Representation and storage of data in a data warehouse should be designed in such a way that not only accommodates but also boosts the processing of complex multidimensional queries. Often, the star schema and the snowflakes schema are the means by which dimensional modeling is implemented in data warehouses.

The **star schema** (sometimes referenced as star join schema) is the most commonly used and the simplest style of dimensional modeling. A star schema contains a central fact table surrounded by and connected to several **dimension tables** (Adamson, 2009). The fact table contains a large number of rows that correspond to observed facts and external

---

TECHNOLOGY INSIGHT 2.1   Hosted Data Warehouses

A hosted data warehouse has nearly the same, if not more, functionality as an onsite data warehouse, but it does not consume computer resources on client premises. A hosted data warehouse offers the benefits of BI minus the cost of computer upgrades, network upgrades, software licenses, in-house development, and in-house support and maintenance.

A hosted data warehouse offers the following benefits:

- Requires minimal investment in infrastructure
- Frees up capacity on in-house systems
- Frees up cash flow
- Makes powerful solutions affordable
- Enables powerful solutions that provide for growth
- Offers better quality equipment and software
- Provides faster connections
- Enables users to access data from remote locations
- Allows a company to focus on core business
- Meets storage needs for large volumes of data

Despite its benefits, a hosted data warehouse is not necessarily a good fit for every organization. Large companies with revenue upward of $500 million could lose money if they already have underused internal infrastructure and IT staff. Furthermore, companies that see the paradigm shift of outsourcing applications as loss of control of their data are not prone to use a business intelligence service provider. Finally, the most significant and common argument against implementing a hosted data warehouse is that it may be unwise to outsource sensitive applications for reasons of security and privacy.

Sources: Based on M. Thornton and M. Lampa, "Hosted Data Warehouse," *Journal of Data Warehousing*, Vol. 7, No. 2, 2002, pp. 27–34; and M. Thornton, "What About Security? The Most Common, but Unwarranted, Objection to Hosted Data Warehouses," *DM Review*, Vol. 12, No. 3, March 18, 2002, pp. 30–43.

links (i.e., foreign keys). A fact table contains the descriptive attributes needed to perform decision analysis and query reporting, and foreign keys are used to link to dimension tables. The decision analysis attributes consist of performance measures, operational metrics, aggregated measures (e.g., sales volumes, customer retention rates, profit margins, production costs, crap rates)and all the other metrics needed to analyze the organization's performance. In other words, the fact table primarily addresses what the data warehouse supports for decision analysis.

Surrounding the central fact tables (and linked via foreign keys) are dimension tables. The dimension tables contain classification and aggregation information about the central fact rows. Dimension tables contain attributes that describe the data contained within the fact table; they address how data will be analyzed and summarized. Dimension tables have a one-to-many relationship with rows in the central fact table. In querying, the dimensions are used to slice and dice the numerical values in the fact table to address the requirements of an ad hoc information need. The star schema is designed to provide fast query-response time, simplicity, and ease of maintenance for read-only database structures. A simple star schema is shown in Figure 2.8a. The star schema is considered a special case of the snowflake schema.

The **snowflake schema** is a logical arrangement of tables in a multidimensional database in such a way that the entity relationship diagram resembles a snowflake in shape. Closely related to the star schema, the snowflake schema is represented by centralized fact tables (usually only one), which are connected to multiple dimensions. In the snowflake schema, however, dimensions are normalized into multiple related tables whereas the star schema's dimensions are denormalized with each dimension being represented by a single table. A simple snowflake schema is shown in Figure 2.8b.

Analysis of Data in Data Warehouse

Once the data are properly stored in a data warehouse, that data can be used in various ways to support organizational decision making. OLAP is arguably the most commonly used data analysis technique in data warehouses, and it has been growing in popularity due to the exponential increase in data volumes and the recognition of the business value of data-driven analytics. Simply, OLAP is an approach to quickly answer ad hoc questions by

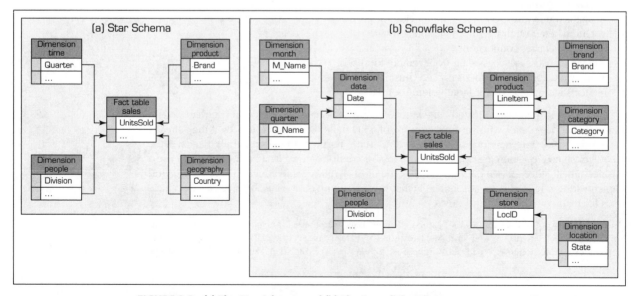

FIGURE 2.8 (a) The Star Schema, and (b) The Snowflake Schema.

executing multidimensional analytical queries against organizational data repositories (i.e., data warehouses, data marts).

OLAP versus OLTP

OLTP is a term used for transaction system that is primarily responsible for capturing and storing data related to day-to-day business functions such as ERP, CRM, SCM, POS, and so on. OLTP system addresses a critical business need, automating daily business transactions and running real-time reports and routine analysis. But these systems are not designed for ad hoc analysis and complex queries that deal with a number of data items. OLAP, on the other hand, is designed to address this need by providing ad hoc analysis of organizational data much more effectively and efficiently. OLAP and OLTP rely heavily on each other: OLAP uses the data captures by OLTP, and OLTP automates the business processes that are managed by decisions supported by OLAP. Table 2.5 provides a multi-criteria comparison between OLTP and OLAP.

OLAP Operations

The main operational structure in OLAP is based on a concept called cube. A **cube** in OLAP is a multidimensional data structure (actual or virtual) that allows fast analysis of data. It can also be defined as the capability of efficiently manipulating and analyzing data from multiple perspectives. The arrangement of data into cubes aims to overcome a limitation of relational databases: Relational databases are not well suited for near-instantaneous analysis of large amounts of data. Instead, they are better suited for manipulating records (adding, deleting, and updating data) that represent a series of transactions. Although many report-writing tools exist for relational databases, these tools are slow when a multidimensional query that encompasses many database tables needs to be executed.

Using OLAP, an analyst can navigate through the database and screen for a particular subset of the data (and its progression over time) by changing the data's orientations and defining analytical calculations. These types of user-initiated navigation of data through the specification of slices (via rotations) and drill down/up (via aggregation and disaggregation) are sometimes called "slice and dice." Commonly used OLAP operations include slice and dice, drill down, roll up, and pivot.

TABLE 2.5   A Comparison Between OLTP and OLAP

Criteria	OLTP	OLAP
Purpose	To carry out day-to-day business functions.	To support decision making and provide answers to business and management queries.
Data source	Transaction database (a normalized data repository primarily focused on efficiency and consistency).	Data warehouse or data mart (a non-normalized data repository primarily focused on accuracy and completeness).
Reporting	Routine, periodic, narrowly focused reports.	Ad hoc, multidimensional, broadly focused reports and queries.
Resource requirements	Ordinary relational databases.	Multiprocessor, large-capacity, specialized databases.
Execution speed	Fast (recording of business transactions and routine reports).	Slow (resource intensive, complex, large-scale queries).

- ***Slice:*** A slice is a subset of a multidimensional array (usually a two-dimensional representation) corresponding to a single value set for one (or more) of the dimensions not in the subset. A simple slicing operation on a three-dimensional cube is shown in Figure 2.9.
- ***Dice:*** The dice operation is a slice on more than two dimensions of a **data cube.**
- ***Drill Down/Up:*** Drilling down or up is a specific OLAP technique whereby the user navigates among levels of data ranging from the most summarized (up) to the most detailed (down).
- ***Roll up:*** A roll up involves computing all of the data relationships for one or more dimensions. To do this, a computational relationship or formula might be defined.
- ***Pivot:*** It is used to change the dimensional orientation of a report or an **ad hoc query**-page display.

VARIATIONS OF OLAP OLAP has a few variations; among them, ROLAP, MOLAP and HOLAP are the most common ones.

ROLAP stands for **Relational Online Analytical Processing**. ROLAP is an alternative to the **MOLAP (Multidimensional OLAP)** technology. While both ROLAP and MOLAP analytic tools are designed to allow analysis of data through the use of a multidimensional data model, ROLAP differs significantly in that it does not require the pre-computation and storage of information. Instead, ROLAP tools access the data in a relational database and generate SQL queries to calculate information at the appropriate level when an end user requests it. With ROLAP, it is possible to create additional database tables (summary tables or aggregations) that summarize the data at any desired combination of dimensions. While ROLAP uses a relational database source, generally the database must be carefully designed

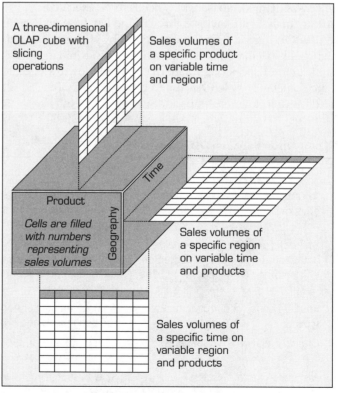

FIGURE 2.9 Slicing Operations on a Simple Three-Dimensional Data Cube.

for ROLAP use. A database that was designed for OLTP will not function well as a ROLAP database. Therefore, ROLAP still involves creating an additional copy of the data.

MOLAP is an alternative to the ROLAP technology. MOLAP differs from ROLAP significantly in that it requires the pre-computation and storage of information in the cube—the operation known as preprocessing. MOLAP stores this data in an optimized multidimensional array storage rather than in a relational database (which is often the case for ROLAP).

The undesirable trade-off between ROLAP and MOLAP with regard to the additional ETL cost and slow query performance has led to inquiries for better approaches where the pros and cons of these two approaches are optimized. These inquiries resulted in HOLAP (Hybrid Online Analytical Processing), which is a combination of ROLAP and MOLAP. HOLAP allows storing part of the data in a MOLAP store and another part of the data in a ROLAP store. The degree of control that the cube designer has over this partitioning varies from product to product. Technology Insight 2.2 provides opportunity for conducting a simple hands-on analysis on MicroStrategy BI tool.

TECHNOLOGY INSIGHT 2.2   Hands-On Data Warehousing with MicroStrategy

MicroStrategy is the leading independent provider of BI, data warehousing performance management, and business reporting solutions. The other big players in this market were recently acquired by large IT firms: Hyperion was acquired by Oracle, Cognos was acquired by IBM, and Business Objects was acquired by SAP. Despite these recent acquisitions, the BI and data warehousing market remains active, vibrant, and full of opportunities.

Following is a step-by-step approach to using MicroStrategy software to analyze a hypothetical business situation. A more comprehensive version of this hands-on exercise can be found at the TDUN Web site. According to this hypothetical scenario, you (the vice president of sales at a global telecommunications company) are planning a business visit to European region. Before meeting with the regional sales people on Monday, you want to know the sale representatives' activities for the last quarter (Quarter 4 of 2004). You are to create such an ad hoc report using MicroStrategy's Web access. In order to create this and many other OLAP reports, you will need the access code for the **TeradataStudentNetwork.com** Web site. It is free of charge for educational use, and only your professor will be able to get the necessary access code for you to utilize not only MicroStrategy software but also a large collection of other BI resources at this site.

Once you are in TeradataStudentNetwork, you need to go to "APPLY & DO" and select "MicroStrategy BI" from the "Software" section. On the "MicroStrategy/BI" Web page, follow these steps:

1. Click on the link for "MicroStrategy Application Modules." This will lead you to a page that shows a list of previously built MicroStrategy applications.
2. Select the "Sales Force Analysis Module." This module is designed to provide you with in-depth insight into the entire sales process. This insight in turn allows you to increase lead conversions, optimize product lines, take advantage of your organization's most successful sales practices, and improve your sales organization's effectiveness.
3. In the "Sales Force Analysis Module" site, you will see three sections: View, Create, and Tolls. In the View section, click on the link for "Shared Reports." This link will take you to a place where a number of previously created sales reports are listed for everybody's use.
4. In the "Shared Reports" page, click on the folder named "Pipeline Analysis." Pipeline Analysis reports provide insight into all open opportunities and deals in the sales pipeline. These reports measure the current status of the sales pipeline, detect changing trends and key events, and identify key open opportunities. Review what is in the pipeline for each sales rep, as well as whether or not the representatives hit their sales quota last quarter.

5. In the "Pipeline Analysis" page, click on the report named "Current Pipeline vs. Quota by Sales Region and District." This report presents the current pipeline status for each sales district within a sales region. It also projects whether target quotas can be achieved for the current quarter.

6. In the "Current Pipeline vs. Quota by Sales Region and District" page, select (with single click) "2004 Q4" as the report parameter, indicating that you want to see how the representatives performed against their quotas for the last quarter.

7. Run the report by clicking on the "Run Report" button at the bottom of the page. This will lead you to a sales report page where the values for each metric are calculated for all three European sales regions. In this interactive report, you can easily change the region from Europe to United States or Canada using the pull-down combo box, or you can drill in one of the three European regions by simply clicking on the appropriate regions heading to see more detailed analysis of the selected region.

SECTION 2.5 REVIEW QUESTIONS

1. List the benefits of data warehouses.
2. List several criteria for selecting a data warehouse vendor, and describe why they are important.
3. What is OLAP and how does it differ from OLTP?
4. What is a cube? What do drill down/roll up/slice and dice mean?
5. What are ROLAP, MOLAP, and HOLAP? How do they differ from OLAP?

2.6 DATA WAREHOUSING IMPLEMENTATION ISSUES

Implementing a data warehouse is generally a massive effort that must be planned and executed according to established methods. However, the project lifecycle has many facets, and no single person can be an expert in each area. Here we discuss specific ideas and issues as they relate to data warehousing. Inmon (2006) provided a set of actions that a data warehouse systems programmer may use to tune a data warehouse.

Reeves (2009) and Solomon (2005) provided some guidelines regarding the critical questions that must be asked, some **risks** that should be weighted, and some processes that can be followed to help ensure a successful data warehouse implementation. They compiled a list of 11 major tasks that could be performed in parallel:

1. Establishment of service-level agreements and data-refresh requirements
2. Identification of data sources and their governance policies
3. Data quality planning
4. Data model design
5. ETL tool selection
6. Relational database software and platform selection
7. Data transport
8. Data conversion
9. Reconciliation process
10. Purge and archive planning
11. End-user support

Following these guidelines should increase an organization's chances for success. Given the size and scope of an enterprise-level data warehouse initiative, failure to anticipate these issues greatly increases the risks of failure.

Hwang and Xu (2005) conducted a major survey of data warehousing success issues. The results established that data warehousing success is a multifaceted construct, and Hwang and Xu proposed that a data warehouse be constructed while keeping in mind the goal of improving user productivity. Extremely significant benefits of doing so include prompt information retrieval and enhanced quality information. The survey results also indicated that success hinges on factors of different dimensions.

People want to know how successful their BI and data warehousing initiatives are in comparison to those of other companies. Ariyachandra and Watson (2006a) proposed some benchmarks for BI and data warehousing success. Watson et al. (1999) researched data warehouse failures. Their results showed that people define a "failure" in different ways, and this was confirmed by Ariyachandra and Watson (2006a). The Data Warehousing Institute (**tdwi.org**) has developed a data warehousing maturity model that an enterprise can apply in order to benchmark its evolution. The model offers a fast means to gauge where the organization's data warehousing initiative is now and where it needs to go next. The maturity model consists of six stages: prenatal, infant, child, teenager, adult, and sage. Business value rises as the data warehouse progresses through each succeeding stage. The stages are identified by a number of characteristics, including scope, analytic structure, executive perceptions, types of analytics, stewardship, funding, technology platform, change management, and administration. See Eckerson et al. (2009) and Eckerson (2003) for more details.

Saunders (2009) provided an easy-to-understand cooking analogy to developing data warehouses. Weir (2002) specifically described some of the **best practices** for implementing a data warehouse. A list of the most pronounced implementation guidelines is as follows:

- The project must fit with corporate strategy and business objectives.
- There must be complete buy-in to the project by executives, managers, and users.
- It is important to manage user expectations about the completed project.
- The data warehouse must be built incrementally.
- Adaptability and scalability must be in consideration right from the start.
- The project must be managed by both IT and business professionals (a healthy business–supplier relationship must be developed).
- Only load data that are relevant to decision analysis, have been cleansed, and are from known/trusted source (both internal as well as external to the organization).
- Do not overlook training requirements (intended users may not be very computer literate).
- Choose proven tools and methodologies that fit nicely into the existing infrastructure.
- Be aware of the organizational forces, politics, and turf wars.

Data warehouse projects have many risks. Most of them are also found in other IT projects, but data warehousing risks are more serious because data warehouses are expensive, time-and-resource demanding, large-scale projects. Each risk should be assessed at the inception of the project. When developing a successful data warehouse, it is important to carefully consider various risks and avoid the following issues:

- ***Starting with the wrong sponsorship chain.***   You need an executive sponsor who has influence over the necessary resources to support and invest in the data warehouse. You also need an executive project driver, someone who has earned the respect of other executives, has a healthy skepticism about technology, and is decisive but flexible. You also need an IS/IT manager to head up the project.
- ***Setting expectations that you cannot meet.***   You do not want to frustrate executives at the moment of truth. Every data warehousing project has two phases: Phase 1 is the selling phase, in which you internally market the project by selling the benefits to those who have access to needed resources. Phase 2 is the struggle to meet the expectations described in Phase 1. For a mere $1 to $7 million, hopefully, you can deliver.

- ***Engaging in politically naive behavior.***   Do not simply state that a data warehouse will help managers make better decisions. This may imply that you feel they have been making bad decisions until now. Sell the idea that they will be able to get the information they need to help in decision making.
- ***Loading the data warehouse with information just because it is available.*** Do not let the data warehouse become a data landfill. This would unnecessarily slow down the use of the system. There is a trend toward real-time computing and analysis. Data warehouses must be shut down to load data in a timely way.
- ***Believing that data warehousing database design is the same as transactional database design.***   In general, it is not. The goal of data warehousing is to access aggregates rather than a single or a few records, as in transaction-processing systems. Content is also different, as is evident in how data are organized. DBMS tend to be nonredundant, normalized, and relational, whereas data warehouses are redundant, not normalized, and multidimensional.
- ***Choosing a data warehouse manager who is technology oriented rather than user oriented.***   One key to data warehouse success is to understand that the users must get what they need, not advanced technology for technology's sake.
- ***Focusing on traditional internal record-oriented data and ignoring the value of external data and of text, images, and, perhaps, sound and video.***   Data come in many formats and must be made accessible to the right people at the right time and in the right format. They must be cataloged properly.
- ***Delivering data with overlapping and confusing definitions.***   Data cleansing is a critical aspect of data warehousing. It includes reconciling conflicting data definitions and formats organization wide. Politically, this may be difficult because it involves change, typically at the executive level.
- ***Believing promises of performance, capacity, and scalability.***   Data warehouses generally require more capacity and speed than is originally budgeted for. Plan ahead to scale up.
- ***Believing that your problems are over when the data warehouse is up and running.***   DSS/BI projects tend to evolve continually. Each deployment is an iteration of the **prototyping** process. There will always be a need to add more and different data sets to the data warehouse, as well as additional analytic tools for existing and additional groups of decision makers. High energy and annual budgets must be planned for because success breeds success. Data warehousing is a continuous process.
- ***Focusing on ad hoc data mining and periodic reporting instead of alerts.*** The natural progression of information in a data warehouse is as follows: (1) Extract the data from legacy systems, cleanse them, and feed them to the warehouse; (2) Support ad hoc reporting until you learn what people want; and (3) Convert the ad hoc reports into regularly scheduled reports. This process of learning what people want in order to provide it seems natural, but it is not optimal or even practical. Managers are busy and need time to read reports. Alert systems are better than periodic reporting systems and can make a data warehouse mission critical. Alert systems monitor the data flowing into the warehouse and inform all key people who have a need to know as soon as a critical event occurs.

In many organizations, a data warehouse will be successful only if there is strong senior management support for its development and if there is a project champion who is high up in the organizational chart. Although this would likely be true for any large-scale IT project, it is especially important for a data warehouse realization. The successful implementation of a data warehouse results in the establishment of an architectural framework that may allow for decision analysis throughout an organization and in some cases also provides comprehensive SCM by granting access to information of an organization's customers and suppliers. The implementation of Web-based data warehouses (sometimes called *Webhousing*) has facilitated ease of access to vast amounts of data, but it is difficult to determine the hard benefits associated with a data warehouse. Hard benefits are defined as benefits to an organization that can be expressed in monetary terms. Many organizations have limited IT resources and must prioritize projects. Management support and a strong project champion can help ensure that a data warehouse project will receive the resources necessary for successful implementation. Data warehouse resources incur significant costs, in some cases requiring high-end processors and large increases in direct-access storage devices. Web-based data warehouses may also have special security requirements to ensure that only authorized users have access to the data.

User participation in the development of data and access modeling is a critical success factor in data warehouse development. During data modeling, expertise is required to determine what data are needed, define business rules associated with the data, and decide what aggregations and other calculations may be necessary. Access modeling is needed to determine how data are to be retrieved from a data warehouse, and it assists in the physical definition of the warehouse by helping to define which data require indexing. It may also indicate whether dependent data marts are needed to facilitate information retrieval. A set of team skills is needed to develop and implement a data warehouse; such skills may include in-depth knowledge of the database technology and development tools used. Source systems and development technology, as mentioned previously, reference the many inputs and the processes used to load and maintain a data warehouse.

Application Case 2.6 presents an excellent example for a large-scale implementation of an integrated data warehouse in the insurance industry.

Application Case 2.6

A Large Insurance Company Integrates Its Enterprise Data with AXIS

A large U.S. insurance company developed an integrated data management and reporting environment to provide a unified view of the enterprise performance and risk and to take a new strategic role in planning and management activities of the large number of business units.

XYZ Insurance Company (the actual name is not revealed) and its affiliated companies constitute one of the world's largest financial services organization. Incorporated a century ago, XYZ Insurance has grown and diversified to become a leading provider of domestic property and casualty insurance, life insurance, retirement savings, asset management, and strategic investment services. Today the firm is an industry powerhouse with over $150 billion in statutory assets, over $15 billion in annual revenue, 20,000+ employees, and more than 100 companies operating under XYZ Insurance umbrella.

Problem

For most of its years in business, the growing family of XYZ Insurance companies enjoyed considerable independence and autonomy. Over time, as the enterprise got bigger, such decentralized management style produced an equally diverse reporting and decision-making environment. With no common view of enterprise performance, corporate reporting was shortsighted, fragmented, slow, and often inaccurate. The burden of acquiring, consolidating, cleaning, and validating basic financial information crippled the organization's ability to support management with meaningful analysis and insight.

In order to address the pressing needs for integration, in January 2004, XYZ Insurance launched a needs-analysis initiative, which resulted in a shared vision for having a unified data management system. The integrated system, called AXIS, was envisioned to be capable of supporting enterprise-level planning, capital management, risk assessment, and managerial decision making with state-of-the-art reporting and analytical services that were timely, accurate, and efficient.

Solution

XYZ Insurance decided to develop AXIS using a best-of-breed approach. As opposed to buying all of the components from a single vendor, it chose the best fit for each module as determined by the needs analysis. The following tools/vendors were selected:

- The data warehouse: The AXIS environment has a hub-and-spoke architecture with a Teradata data warehouse at the center.
- Extraction, transportation, integration, and metadata management: All data movement from originating systems into the AXIS environment (and between systems within AXIS) is handled by Informatica PowerCenter.
- Reporting and analysis: Virtually all reporting and analytical functionality in the AXIS environment is provided through a suite of Hyperion tools that includes Essbase, Planning, Reporter, Analyzer, and Intelligence.
- Master data management: Reference data hierarchies and dimensions and business rules for interface translation and transformation are developed and maintained using master data management (MDM) software from Kalido.

Results

Implementing the AXIS environment was a monumental undertaking, even for an organization with XYZ Insurance's resources. More than 200 operational source system interfaces had to be created. At its peak, the development team employed 280 people (60% from internal IT and the business department and 40% external contractors) who dedicated 600,000 man-hours to the project. The system with full functionality was released in April 2006.

By standardizing the information assets along with the technology base and supporting processes, XYZ Insurance was able to consolidate much of the labor-intensive transactional and reporting activities. That freed up people and resources for more strategic, high-value contributions to the business. Another benefit is that business units across the organization now have consistent and accurate operating information to base their decisions on. Probably the most important benefit of AXIS environment is its ability to turn XYZ Insurance into an agile enterprise. Because they have access to corporate level data in timely manner, the business units can react to changing conditions (address problems and take advantage of opportunities) accurately and rapidly.

Source: Based on Teradata, "A Large US-based Insurance Company Masters Its Finance Data," Teradata Industry Solutions," **teradata.com/t/WorkArea/DownloadAsset.aspx?id=4858** (accessed July 2009).

Massive Data Warehouses and Scalability

In addition to flexibility, a data warehouse needs to support scalability. The main issues pertaining to scalability are the amount of data in the warehouse, how quickly the warehouse is expected to grow, the number of concurrent users, and the complexity of user queries. A data warehouse must scale both horizontally and vertically. The warehouse will grow as a function of data growth and the need to expand the warehouse to support new business functionality. Data growth may be a result of the addition of current cycle data (e.g., this month's results) and/or historical data.

Hicks (2001) described huge databases and data warehouses. Wal-Mart is continually increasing the size of its massive data warehouse. Wal-Mart is believed to use a warehouse with hundreds of terabytes of data to study sales trends and track inventory and other tasks. IBM recently publicized its 50-terabyte warehouse benchmark (IBM, 2009). The U.S. Department of Defense is using a 5-petabyte data warehouse and repository to hold medical records for 9 million military personnel. Because of the storage required to archive its news footage, CNN also has a petabyte-sized data warehouse.

Given that the size of data warehouses is expanding at an exponential rate, scalability is an important issue. Good scalability means that queries and other data-access functions will grow (ideally) linearly with the size of the warehouse. See Rosenberg (2006) for approaches to improve query performance. In practice, specialized methods have been developed to create scalable data warehouses. Scalability is difficult when managing hundreds of terabytes or more. Terabytes of data have considerable inertia, occupy a lot of physical space, and require powerful computers. Some firms use parallel processing, and others use clever indexing and search schemes to manage their data. Some spread their data across different physical data stores. As more data warehouses approach the petabyte size, better and better solutions to scalability continue to be developed.

Hall (2002) also addressed scalability issues. AT&T is an industry leader in deploying and using massive data warehouses. With its 26-terabyte data warehouse, AT&T can detect fraudulent use of calling cards and investigate calls related to kidnappings and other crimes. It can also compute millions of call-in votes from TV viewers selecting the next American Idol.

For a sample of successful data warehousing implementations, see Edwards (2003). Jukic and Lang (2004) examined the trends and specific issues related to the use of offshore resources in the development and support of data warehousing and BI applications. Davison (2003) indicated that IT-related offshore outsourcing had been growing at 20 to 25 percent per year. When considering offshoring data warehousing projects, careful consideration must be given to culture and security (for details, see Jukic and Lang, 2004).

SECTION 2.6 REVIEW QUESTIONS

1. What are the major DW implementation tasks that can be performed in parallel?
2. List and discuss the most pronounced DW implementation guidelines?
3. When developing a successful data warehouse, what are the most important risks and issues to consider and potentially avoid?
4. What is scalability? How does it apply to DW?

2.7 REAL-TIME DATA WAREHOUSING

Data warehousing and BI tools traditionally focus on assisting managers in making strategic and tactical decisions. Increased data volumes and accelerating update speeds are fundamentally changing the role of the data warehouse in modern business. For many businesses, making fast and consistent decisions across the enterprise requires more than a traditional data warehouse or data mart. Traditional data warehouses are not business critical. Data are commonly updated on a weekly basis, and this does not allow for responding to transactions in near real time.

More data, coming in faster and requiring immediate conversion into decisions, means that organizations are confronting the need for real-time data warehousing. This is because decision support has become operational, integrated BI requires closed-loop analytics, and yesterday's ODS will not support existing requirements.

In 2003, with the advent of real-time data warehousing, there was a shift toward using these technologies for operational decisions. **Real-time data warehousing (RDW)**, also known as **active data warehousing (ADW)**, is the process of loading and providing data via the data warehouse as they become available. It evolved from the EDW concept. The active traits of an RDW/ADW supplement and expand traditional data warehouse functions into the realm of tactical decision making. People throughout the organization who interact directly with customers and suppliers will be empowered with information-based decision making at their fingertips. Even further leverage results when an ADW provides information directly to customers and suppliers. The reach and impact of information access for decision making can positively affect almost all aspects of customer service, SCM, logistics, and beyond. E-business has become a major catalyst in

Application Case 2.7

Egg Plc Fries the Competition in Near Real Time

Egg plc (**egg.com**) is the world's largest online bank. It provides banking, insurance, investments, and mortgages to more than 3.6 million customers through its Internet site. In 1998, Egg selected Sun Microsystems to create a reliable, scalable, secure infrastructure to support its more than 2.5 million daily transactions. In 2001, the system was upgraded to eliminate latency problems. This new CDW used Sun, Oracle, and SAS software products. The initial data warehouse had about 10 terabytes of data and used a 16-CPU server. The system provides near-real-time data access. It provides data warehouse and data mining services to internal users, and it provides a requisite set of customer data to the customers themselves. Hundreds of sales and marketing campaigns are constructed using near-real-time data (within several minutes). And better, the system enables faster decision making about specific customers and customer classes.

Sources: Compiled from "Egg's Customer Data Warehouse Hits the Mark," *DM Review*, Vol. 15, No. 10, October 2005, pp. 24–28; Sun Microsystems, "Egg Banks on Sun to Hit the Mark with Customers," September 19, 2005, **sun.com/smi/Press/sunflash/2005-09/sunflash.20050919.1.xml** (accessed April 2006); and ZD Net UK, "Sun Case Study: Egg's Customer Data Warehouse," **whitepapers.zdnet.co.uk/0,39025945,60159401p-39000449q,00.htm** (accessed June 2009).

the demand for active data warehousing (Armstrong, 2000). For example, online retailer Overstock.com, Inc. (**overstock.com**) connected data users to a real-time data warehouse. At Egg plc, the world's largest purely online bank, a customer data warehouse (CDW) is refreshed in near real time (see Application Case 2.7).

As business needs evolve, so do the requirements of the data warehouse. At this basic level, a data warehouse simply reports what happened. At the next level, some analysis occurs. As the system evolves, it provides prediction capabilities, which lead to the next level of operationalization. At its highest evolution, the ADW is capable of making events happen (e.g., activities such as creating sales and marketing campaigns or identifying and exploiting opportunities). See Figure 2.10 for a graphic description of this evolutionary process. A recent survey on managing evolution of data warehouses can be found in Wrembel (2009).

Teradata Corp. provides the baseline requirements to support an EDW. It also provides the new traits of active data warehousing required to deliver data freshness, performance, and availability and to enable **enterprise decision management** (see Figure 2.11 for an example).

An ADW offers an integrated information repository to drive strategic and tactical decision support within an organization. With real-time data warehousing, instead of extracting operational data from an OLTP system in nightly batches into an ODS, data are assembled from OLTP systems as and when events happen and are moved at once into the data warehouse. This permits the instant updating of the data warehouse and the elimination of an ODS. At this point, tactical and strategic queries can be made against the RDW to use immediate as well as historical data.

According to Basu (2003), the most distinctive difference between a traditional data warehouse and an RDW is the shift in the data acquisition paradigm. Some of the business cases and enterprise requirements that led to the need for data in real time include the following:

- A business often cannot afford to wait a whole day for its operational data to load into the data warehouse for analysis.
- Until now, data warehouses have captured snapshots of an organization's fixed states instead of incremental real-time data showing every change and analogous patterns over time.

SAS
Enterprise Decisioning Management
ACTIVATING
MAKE it happen!
Real-Time Decisioning Applications
OPERATIONALIZING
WHAT IS
happening now?
Predictive Models
PREDICTING
WHAT WILL
happen?
Segmentation and Profiles
ANALYZING
WHY
did it happen?
REPORTING
WHAT
happened?
Primarily Batch and Some Ad Hoc Reports
Increase in Ad Hoc Analysis
Analytical Modeling Grows
Continuous Update and Time-sensitive Queries Become Important
Event-Based Triggering Takes Hold
Batch
Ad Hoc
Analytics
Continuous Update/Short Queries
Event-Based Triggering
Workload and Complexity
Data Sophistication

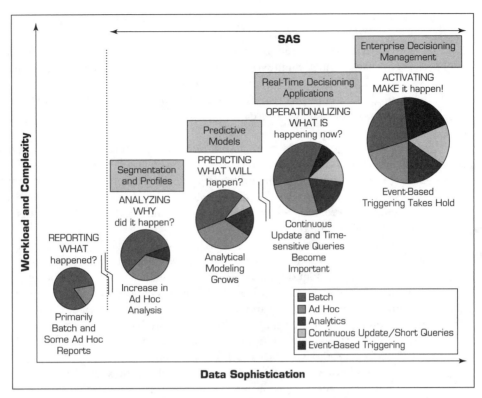

FIGURE 2.10 Enterprise Decision Evolution. *Source*: Courtesy of Teradata Corporation. Used with permission.

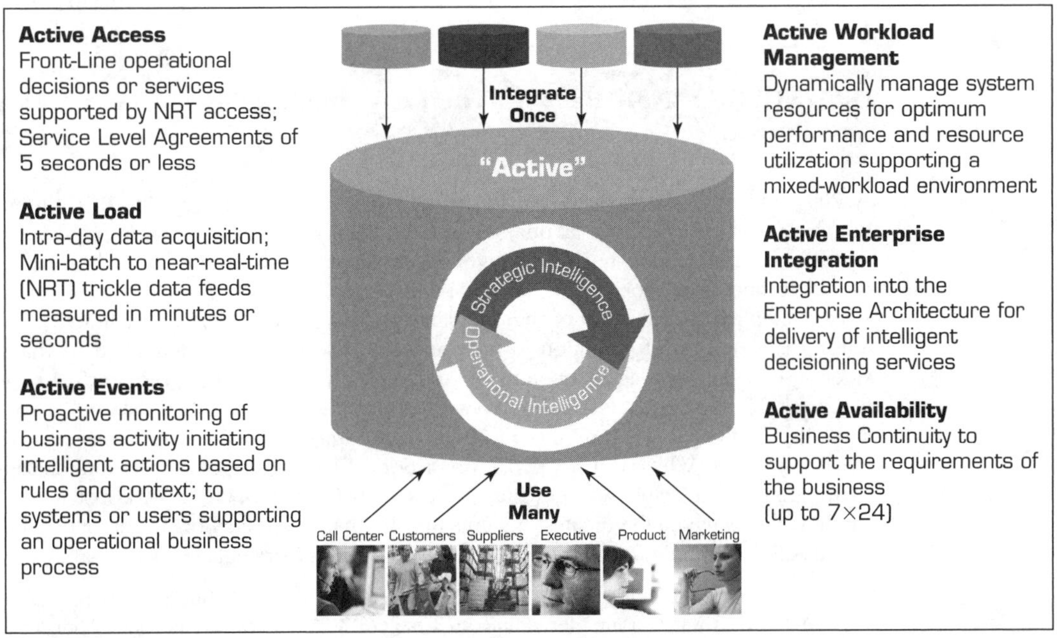

Active Access
Front-Line operational decisions or services supported by NRT access; Service Level Agreements of 5 seconds or less
Active Load
Intra-day data acquisition; Mini-batch to near-real-time (NRT) trickle data feeds measured in minutes or seconds
Active Events
Proactive monitoring of business activity initiating intelligent actions based on rules and context; to systems or users supporting an operational business process
Integrate Once
"Active"
Strategic Intelligence
Operational Intelligence
Use Many
Call Center
Customers
Suppliers
Executive
Product
Marketing
Active Workload Management
Dynamically manage system resources for optimum performance and resource utilization supporting a mixed-workload environment
Active Enterprise Integration
Integration into the Enterprise Architecture for delivery of intelligent decisioning services
Active Availability
Business Continuity to support the requirements of the business (up to 7×24)

FIGURE 2.11 The Teradata Active EDW. *Source*: Courtesy of Teradata Corporation.

- With a traditional hub-and-spoke architecture, keeping the metadata in sync is difficult. It is also costly to develop, maintain, and secure many systems as opposed to one huge data warehouse so that data are centralized for BI/BA tools.
- In cases of huge nightly batch loads, the necessary ETL setup and processing power for large nightly data warehouse loading might be very high, and the processes might take too long. An EAI with real-time data collection can reduce or eliminate the nightly batch processes.

Despite the benefits of an RDW, developing one can create its own set of issues. These problems relate to architecture, data modeling, physical database design, storage and scalability, and maintainability. In addition, depending on exactly when data are accessed, even down to the microsecond, different versions of the truth may be extracted and created, which can confuse team members. For details, refer to Basu (2003) and Terr (2004).

Real-time solutions present a remarkable set of challenges to BI activities. Although it is not ideal for all solutions, real-time data warehousing may be successful if the organization develops a sound methodology to handle project risks, incorporates proper planning, and focuses on quality assurance activities. Understanding the common challenges and applying best practices can reduce the extent of the problems that are often a part of implementing complex data warehousing systems that incorporate BI/BA methods. Details and real implementations are discussed by Burdett and Singh (2004) and Wilk (2003). Also see Akbay (2006) and Ericson (2006).

See Technology Insight 2.3 for some details on how the real-time concept evolved. The flight management dashboard application at Continental Airlines (see the End of Chapter Application Case) illustrates the power of real-time BI in accessing a data warehouse for use in face-to-face customer interaction situations. The operations staff uses the real-time system to identify issues in the Continental flight network. As another example, UPS invested $600 million so it could use real-time data and processes. The investment was expected to cut 100 million delivery miles and save 14 million gallons of fuel annually by managing its real-time package-flow technologies (Malykhina, 2003). Table 2.6 compares traditional data warehousing and active data warehousing environments.

TECHNOLOGY INSIGHT 2.3   The Real-Time Realities of Active Data Warehousing

By 2003, the role of data warehousing in practice was growing rapidly. Real-time systems, though a novelty, were the latest buzz, along with the major complications of providing data and information instantaneously to those who need them. Many experts, including Peter Coffee, *eWeek*'s technology editor, believe that real-time systems must feed a real-time decision-making process. Stephen Brobst, CTO of the Teradata division of NCR, indicated that active data warehousing is a process of evolution in how an enterprise uses data. *Active* means that the data warehouse is also used as an operational and tactical tool. Brobst provided a five-stage model that fits Coffee's experience (2003) of how organizations "grow" in their data utilization (Brobst et al., 2005). These stages (and the questions they purport to answer) are reporting (What happened?), analysis (Why did it happen?), prediction (What will happen?), operationalizing (What is happening?), and active warehousing (What do I want to happen?). The last stage, active data warehousing, is where the greatest benefits may be obtained. Many organizations are enhancing centralized data warehouses to serve both operational and strategic decision making.

Sources: Based on P. Coffee, "'Active' Warehousing," *eWeek*, Vol. 20, No. 25, June 23, 2003, p. 36; and Teradata Corp., "Active Data Warehousing," **teradata.com/t/page/87127/index.html** (accessed April 2006).

TABLE 2.6 Comparison Between Traditional and Active Data Warehousing Environments

Traditional Data Warehousing Environment	Active Data Warehousing Environment
Strategic decisions only	Strategic and tactical decisions
Results sometimes hard to measure	Results measured with operations
Daily, weekly, monthly data currency is acceptable; summaries are often appropriate	Only comprehensive detailed data available within minutes is acceptable
Moderate user concurrency	High number (1,000 or more) of users accessing and querying the system simultaneously
Highly restrictive reporting used to confirm or check existing processes and patterns; often uses predeveloped summary tables or data marts	Flexible ad hoc reporting as well as machine-assisted modeling (e.g., data mining) to discover new hypotheses and relationships
Power users, knowledge workers, internal users	Operational staffs, call centers, external users

Sources: Based on P. Coffee, "'Active' Warehousing," *eWeek*, Vol. 20, No. 25, June 23, 2003, p. 36; and Teradata Corp., "Active Data Warehousing," **teradata.com/t/page/87127/index.html** (accessed April 2006).

Real-time data warehousing, near-real-time data warehousing, zero-latency warehousing, and *active data warehousing* are different names used in practice to describe the same concept. Gonzales (2005) presented different definitions for ADW. According to Gonzales, ADW is only one option that provides blended tactical and strategic data on demand. The architecture to build an ADW is very similar to the corporate information factory architecture developed by Bill Inmon. The only difference between a corporate information factory and an ADW is the implementation of both data stores in a single environment. However, an SOA based on XML and Web services provide another option for blending tactical and strategic data on demand.

One critical issue in real-time data warehousing is that not all data should be updated continuously. This may certainly cause problems when reports are generated in real time, because one person's results may not match another person's. For example, a company using Business Objects Web Intelligence noticed a significant problem with real-time intelligence. Real-time reports produced at slightly different times differ (Peterson, 2003). Also, it may not be necessary to update certain data continuously (e.g., course grades that are 3 or more years old).

Real-time requirements change the way we view the design of databases, data warehouses, OLAP, and data mining tools, because they are literally updated concurrently while queries are active. But the substantial business value in doing so has been demonstrated, so it is crucial that organizations adopt these methods in their business processes. Careful planning is critical in such implementations.

SECTION 2.7 REVIEW QUESTIONS

1. What is an RDW?
2. List the benefits of an RDW.
3. What are the major differences between a traditional data warehouse and a real-time data warehouse?
4. List some of the drivers for RDW.

2.8 DATA WAREHOUSE ADMINISTRATION, SECURITY ISSUES, AND FUTURE TRENDS

Data warehouses provide a distinct competitive edge to enterprises that effectively create and use them. Due to its huge size and its intrinsic nature, a data warehouse requires especially strong monitoring in order to sustain satisfactory efficiency and productivity. The successful administration and management of a data warehouse entails skills and proficiency that go past what is required of a traditional database administrator (DBA). A **data warehouse administrator (DWA)** should be familiar with high-performance software, hardware, and networking technologies. He or she should also possess solid business insight. Because data warehouses feed BI systems and DSS that help managers with their decision-making activities, the DWA should be familiar with the decision-making processes so as to suitably design and maintain the data warehouse structure. It is particularly significant for a DWA to keep the existing requirements and capabilities of the data warehouse stable while simultaneously providing flexibility for rapid improvements. Finally, a DWA must possess excellent communications skills. See Benander et al. (2000) for a description of the key differences between a DBA and a DWA.

Security and privacy of information is a main and significant concern for a data warehouse professional. The U.S. government has passed regulations (e.g., the Gramm-Leach Bliley privacy and safeguards rules, the Health Insurance Portability and Accountability Act of 1996 [HIPAA]), instituting obligatory requirements in the management of customer information. Hence, companies must create security procedures that are effective yet flexible to conform to numerous privacy regulations. According to Elson and LeClerc (2005), effective security in a data warehouse should focus on four main areas:

1. Establishing effective corporate and security policies and procedures. An effective security policy should start at the top, with executive management, and should be communicated to all individuals within the organization.
2. Implementing logical security procedures and techniques to restrict access. This includes user authentication, access controls, and encryption technology.
3. Limiting physical access to the data center environment.
4. Establishing an effective internal control review process with an emphasis on security and privacy.

See Technology Insight 2.4 for a description of Ambeo's important software tool that monitors security and privacy of data warehouses. Finally, keep in mind that accessing a

---

TECHNOLOGY INSIGHT 2.4   Ambeo Delivers Proven Data Access Auditing Solution

Since 1997, Ambeo (**ambeo.com**; now Embarcadero Technologies, Inc.) has deployed technology that provides performance management, data usage tracking, data privacy auditing, and monitoring to Fortune 1000 companies. These firms have some of the largest database environments in existence. Ambeo data access auditing solutions play a major role in an enterprise information security infrastructure.

The Ambeo technology is a relatively easy solution that records everything that happens in the databases, with low or zero overhead. In addition, it provides data access auditing that identifies exactly who is looking at data, when they are looking, and what they are doing with the data. This real-time monitoring helps quickly and effectively identify security breaches.

Sources: Based on "Ambeo Delivers Proven Data Access Auditing Solution," *Database Trends and Applications*, Vol. 19, No. 7, July 2005; and Ambeo, "Keeping Data Private (and Knowing It): Moving Beyond Conventional Safeguards to Ensure Data Privacy," **am-beo.com/why_ambeo_white_papers.html** (accessed May 2009).

data warehouse via a mobile device should always be performed cautiously. In this instance, data should only be accessed as read only.

In the near term, data warehousing developments will be determined by noticeable factors (e.g., data volumes, increased intolerance for latency, the diversity and complexity of data types) and less noticeable factors (e.g., unmet end-user requirements for dashboards, balanced scorecards, master data management, information quality). Given these drivers, Moseley (2009) and Agosta (2006) suggested that data warehousing trends will lean toward simplicity, value, and performance.

The Future of Data Warehousing

The field of data warehousing is/has been a vibrant area in information technology in the last couple of decades, and the evidence in the BI world shows that the importance of the field will only get better. Following are some of the recently popularized concepts and technologies that will play a significant role in defining the future of data warehousing.

- ***Sourcing***   (acquisition of data from diverse and dispersed sources)
  - ***Open source software.***   Use of open source software tools is increasing at an unprecedented level in warehousing, business intelligence, and data integration. There are good reasons for the upswing of open source software used in data warehousing (Russom, 2009): (1) The recession has driven up interest in low-cost open source software; (2) Open source tools are coming into a new level of maturity, and (3) Open source software augments traditional enterprise software without replacing it.
  - ***SaaS (software as a service), "The Extended ASP Model."***   SaaS is a creative way of deploying information systems application where the provider licenses its applications to customers for use as a service on demand (usually over the Internet). SaaS software vendors may host the application on their own servers or upload the application to the consumer site. In essence, SaaS is the new and improved version of the ASP model. For data warehouse customers, finding SaaS-based software applications and resources that meet specific needs and requirements can be challenging. As these software offerings become more agile, the appeal and the actual use of SaaS as the choice of data warehousing platform will also increase.
  - ***Cloud computing.***   **Cloud computing** is perhaps the newest and the most innovative platform choice to come along in years, where numerous hardware and software resources are pooled and virtualized, so that they can be freely allocated to applications and software platforms as resources are needed. This enables information systems applications to dynamically scale up as workloads increase. Although cloud computing and similar virtualization techniques are fairly established for operational applications today, they are just now starting to be used as data warehouse platforms of choice. The dynamic allocation of a cloud is particularly useful when the data volume of the warehouse varies unpredictably, making capacity planning difficult.
  - ***Data warehouse appliances.***   One of the most widely discussed data warehouse option of the recent years has to be the data warehouse appliances. Its original definition referred to a holistic solution by simply providing a whole-technology stack (software, hardware, etc.) for data warehousing. Since then, the definition has been modified to include options to mix and match parts and pieces in a way so that it fits the specific needs of the customers. Future is expected to move in the direction of this best-of-breed philosophy.
- ***Infrastructure***   (architectural—hardware and software—enhancements)
  - ***Real-time data warehousing.***   RDW implies that the refresh cycle of an existing data warehouse to update the data is more frequent (almost at the same time as the data become available at operational databases). These real-time data warehouse systems can achieve near-real-time update of data, where the data latency

typically is in the range from minutes to hours. As the latency gets smaller, the cost of data update seems to be increasing exponentially. Future advancements in many technological fronts (ranging from automatic data acquisition to intelligent **software agents**) are needed to make the real-time data warehousing a reality with affordable price tag.

- ***Data management technologies and practices.*** Some of the most pressing needs for a next generation data warehouse platform involve technologies and practices that we generally don't think of as part of the platform. In particular, many users need to update the data management tools that process data for use through the data warehousing. Future holds strong growth for master data management (MDM). This relatively new but extremely important concept is gaining popularity for many reasons including: (1) Tighter integration with operational systems demands MDM, (2) Most data warehouses still lack MDM and data quality functions, and (3) Regulatory and financial reports must be perfectly clean and accurate.

- ***In-memory processing (64-bit computing) or "super computing."*** Sixty-four-bit systems typically offer faster CPUs and more power-efficient hardware than older systems. But, for data warehousing, the most compelling benefit of 64-bit systems is the large space of addressable memory, allowing to deploy an in-memory database for reporting or analytic applications that need very fast query response. In-memory databases provide such speed because they don't have disk input/output to slow them down. The in-memory database is usually a function of a DBMS, but some BI platforms for reporting and analysis also support in-memory data stores and related processing.

  Tools for ETL commonly support in-memory processing in a 64-bit environment so that complex joins and transformations are executed in a large memory space without the need to land data to disk in temporary tables. This makes an ETL data flow a true "pipe," which means the ETL tool can scale up to large data volumes that are processed in relatively short time periods.

- ***New DBMS*** A data warehouse platform consists of several basic components, of which the most critical one is the **database management system (DBMS)**. It is only natural; given the fact that DBMS is the component of the platform where most work must be done to implement a data model and optimize it for query performance. Therefore, the DBMS is where many next-generation innovations are expected to happen.

- ***Advanced analytics.*** There are different analytic methods users can choose as they move beyond basic OLAP-based methods and into advanced analytics. Some users choose advanced analytic methods based on data mining, predictive analytics, statistics, artificial intelligence, and so on. Still, the majority of users seem to be choosing SQL-based methods. SQL-based or not, advanced analytic methods seem to be among the most important promises of the next generation data warehousing.

The future of data warehousing seems to be full of promises and significant challenges. As the world of business becomes more global and complex, the need for business intelligence and data warehousing tools also becomes more prominent. The fast improving information technology tools and techniques seem to be moving in the right direction to address the needs of the future business intelligence systems.

SECTION 2.8 REVIEW QUESTIONS

1. What steps can an organization take to ensure the security and confidentiality of customer data in its data warehouse?
2. What skills should a DWA possess? Why?
3. What are the recent technologies that may shape the future of data warehousing? Why?

2.9 RESOURCES, LINKS, AND THE TERADATA UNIVERSITY NETWORK CONNECTION

The use of this chapter and most other chapters in this book can be enhanced by the tools described in the following sections.

Resources and Links

We recommend looking at the following resources and links for further reading and explanations:

- The Data Warehouse Institute (**tdwi.com**)
- *DM Review* (**dmreview.com**)
- DSS Resources (**dssresources.com**)

Cases

All major MSS vendors (e.g., MicroStrategy, Microsoft, Oracle, IBM, Hyperion, Cognos, Exsys, Fair Isaac, SAP, Information Builders) provide interesting customer success stories. Academic-oriented cases are available at the Harvard Business School Case Collection (**harvardbusinessonline.hbsp.harvard.edu**), Business Performance Improvement Resource (**bpir.com**), Idea Group Publishing (**idea-group.com**), Ivy League Publishing (**ivylp.com**), ICFAI Center for Management Research (**icmr.icfai.org/casestudies/icmr_case_studies.htm**), KnowledgeStorm (**knowledgestorm.com**), and other sites. For additional case resources, see Teradata University Network (**teradatauniversitynetwork.com**). For data warehousing cases, we specifically recommend the following from the Teradata University Network (**teradatauniversitynetwork.com**): "Continental Airlines Flies High with Real-Time Business Intelligence," "Data Warehouse Governance at Blue Cross and Blue Shield of North Carolina," "3M Moves to a Customer Focus Using a Global Data Warehouse," "Data Warehousing Supports Corporate Strategy at First American Corporation," "Harrah's High Payoff from Customer Information," and "Whirlpool." We also recommend the Data Warehousing Failures Assignment, which consists of eight short cases on data warehousing failures.

Vendors, Products, and Demos

A comprehensive list of vendors, products, and demos is available at *DM Review* (**dmreview.com**). Vendors are listed in Table 2.2. Also see **technologyevaluation.com**.

Periodicals

We recommend the following periodicals:

- *Baseline* (**baselinemag.com**)
- *Business Intelligence Journal* (**tdwi.org**)
- *CIO* (**cio.com**)
- *CIO Insight* (**cioinsight.com**)
- *Computerworld* (**computerworld.com**)
- *Decision Support Systems* (**elsevier.com**)
- *DM Review* (**dmreview.com**)
- *eWeek* (**eweek.com**)
- *InfoWeek* (**infoweek.com**)
- *InfoWorld* (**infoworld.com**)
- *InternetWeek* (**internetweek.com**)

- *Management Information Systems Quarterly* (*MIS Quarterly*, **misq.org**)
- *Technology Evaluation* (**technologyevaluation.com**)
- *Teradata Magazine* (**teradata.com**)

Additional References

For additional information on data warehousing, see the following.

- C. Imhoff, N. Galemmo, and J. G. Geiger. (2003). *Mastering Data Warehouse Design: Relational and Dimensional Techniques.* New York: Wiley.
- D. Marco and M. Jennings. (2004). *Universal Meta Data Models.* New York: Wiley.
- J. Wang. (2005). *Encyclopedia of Data Warehousing and Mining.* Hershey, PA: Idea Group Publishing.

For more on databases, the structure on which data warehouses are developed, see the following:

- R. T. Watson. (2006). *Data Management*, 5th ed., New York: Wiley.

The Teradata University Network (TUN) Connection

TUN (**teradatauniversitynetwork.com**) provides a wealth of information and cases on data warehousing. One of the best is the Continental Airlines case, which we require you to solve in a later exercise. Other recommended cases are mentioned earlier in this chapter. At TUN, if you click the Courses tab and select Data Warehousing, you will see links to many relevant articles, assignments, book chapters, course Web sites, PowerPoint presentations, projects, research reports, syllabi, and Web seminars. You will also find links to active data warehousing software demonstrations. Finally, you will see links to Teradata (**teradata.com**), where you can find additional information, including excellent data warehousing success stories, white papers, Web-based courses, and the online version of *Teradata Magazine.*

Chapter Highlights

- A data warehouse is a specially constructed data repository where data are organized so that they can be easily accessed by end users for several applications.
- Data marts contain data on one topic (e.g., marketing). A data mart can be a replication of a subset of data in the data warehouse. Data marts are a less expensive solution that can be replaced by or can supplement a data warehouse. Data marts can be independent of or dependent on a data warehouse.
- An ODS is a type of customer-information-file database that is often used as a staging area for a data warehouse.
- Data integration comprises three major processes: data access, data federation, and change capture.

When these three processes are correctly implemented, data can be accessed and made accessible to an array of ETL and analysis tools and data warehousing environments.

- ETL technologies pull data from many sources, cleanse them, and load them into a data warehouse. ETL is an integral process in any data-centric project.
- Real-time or active data warehousing supplements and expands traditional data warehousing, moving into the realm of operational and tactical decision making by loading data in real time and providing data to users for active decision making.
- The security and privacy of data and information is a critical issue for a data warehouse professional.

Key Terms

active data warehousing (ADW)	decision support systems (DSS)	extraction, transformation, and load (ETL)	parallel processing
ad hoc query	dependent data mart	grain	prototyping
best practices	dimensional modeling	graphical user interface (GUI)	real-time data warehousing (RDW)
cloud computing	dimension tables	independent data mart	relational database
cube	drill down	metadata	Relational Online Analytical Processing (ROLAP)
data cube	enterprise application integration (EAI)	multidimensional analysis	
data integration		multidimensional database	risk
data mart	enterprise data warehouse (EDW)	multidimensional OLAP (MOLAP)	scenario
data quality			software agent
data warehouse (DW)	enterprise decision management	oper marts	speech recognition
data warehouse administrator (DWA)	enterprise information integration (EII)	operational data store (ODS)	SQL
database management system (DBMS)	expert		snowflake schema
	extraction		star schema

Questions for Discussion

1. Compare data integration and ETL. How are they related?
2. What is a data warehouse, and what are its benefits? Why is Web accessibility important to a data warehouse?
3. A data mart can replace a data warehouse or complement it. Compare and discuss these options.
4. Discuss the major drivers and benefits of data warehousing to end users.
5. List the differences and/or similarities between the roles of a database administrator and a data warehouse administrator.
6. Describe how data integration can lead to higher levels of data quality.
7. Compare the Kimball and Inmon approaches toward data warehouse development. Identify when each one is most effective.
8. Discuss security concerns involved in building a data warehouse.
9. Investigate current data warehouse development implementation through offshoring. Write a report about it. In class, debate the issue in terms of the benefits and costs, as well as social factors.

Exercises

Teradata University and Other Hands-on Exercises

1. Consider the case describing the development and application of a data warehouse for Coca-Cola Japan (a summary appears in Application Case 2.4), available at the DSS Resources Web site, **dssresources.com/cases/ cocacolajapan/index.html**. Read the case and answer the nine questions for further analysis and discussion.
2. Read the Ball (2005) article and rank-order the criteria (ideally for a real organization). In a report, explain how important each criterion is and why.
3. Explain when you should implement a two- or three-tiered architecture when considering developing a data warehouse.
4. Read the full Continental Airlines case (summarized in the End of Chapter Application Case) at **teradata studentnetwork.com** and answer the questions.

5. At **teradatastudentnetwork.com**, read and answer the questions to the case "Harrah's High Payoff from Customer Information." Relate Harrah's results to how airlines and other casinos use their customer data.
6. At **teradatastudentnetwork.com**, read and answer the questions of the assignment "Data Warehousing Failures." Because eight cases are described in that assignment, the class may be divided into eight groups, with one case assigned per group. In addition, read Ariyachandra and Watson (2006a), and for each case identify how the failure occurred as related to not focusing on one or more of the reference's success factor(s).
7. At **teradatastudentnetwork.com**, read and answer the questions with the assignment "Ad-Vent Technology: Using the MicroStrategy Sales Analytic Model." The MicroStrategy software is accessible from the TUN site.

Also, you might want to use Barbara Wixom's PowerPoint presentation about the MicroStrategy software ("Demo Slides for MicroStrategy Tutorial Script"), which is also available at the TUN site.

8. At **teradatastudentnetwork.com**, watch the Web seminars titled "Real-Time Data Warehousing: The Next Generation of Decision Support Data Management" and "Building the Real-Time Enterprise." Read the article "Teradata's Real-Time Enterprise Reference Architecture: A Blueprint for the Future of IT," also available at this site. Describe how real-time concepts and technologies work and how they can be used to extend existing data warehousing and BI architectures to support day-to-day decision making. Write a report indicating how real-time data warehousing is specifically providing competitive advantage for organizations. Describe in detail the difficulties in such implementations and operations, and describe how they are being addressed in practice.

9. At **teradatastudentnetwork.com**, watch the Web seminars "Data Integration Renaissance: New Drivers and Emerging Approaches," "In Search of a Single Version of the Truth: Strategies for Consolidating Analytic Silos," and "Data Integration: Using ETL, EAI, and EII Tools to Create an Integrated Enterprise." Also read the "Data Integration" research report. Compare and contrast the presentations. What is the most important issue described in these seminars? What is the best way to handle the strategies and challenges of consolidating data marts and spreadsheets into a unified data warehousing architecture? Perform a Web search to identify the latest developments in the field. Compare the presentation to the material in the text and the new material that you found.

10. Consider the future of data warehousing. Perform a Web search on this topic. Also, read these two articles: L. Agosta, "Data Warehousing in a Flat World: Trends for 2006," *DM Direct Newsletter*, March 31, 2006; and J. G. Geiger, "CIFe: Evolving with the Times," *DM Review*, November 2005, pp. 38–41. Compare and contrast your findings.

11. Access **teradatastudentnetwork.com**. Identify the latest articles, research reports, and cases on data warehousing. Describe recent developments in the field. Include in your report how data warehousing is used in BI and DSS.

Team Assignments and Role-Playing Projects

1. Kathryn Avery has been a DBA with a nationwide retail chain (Big Chain) for the past 6 years. She has recently been asked to lead the development of Big Chain's first data warehouse. The project has the sponsorship of senior management and the chief information officer. The rationale for developing the data warehouse is to advance the reporting systems, particularly in sales and marketing, and, in the longer term, to improve Big Chain's CRM. Kathryn has been to a Data Warehousing Institute conference and has been doing some reading, but she is still mystified about development methodologies. She knows there are two groups—EDW (Inmon) and architected data marts (Kimball)—that have equally robust features.

Initially, she believed that the two methodologies were extremely dissimilar, but as she has examined them more carefully, she isn't so certain. Kathryn has a number of questions that she would like answered:

a. What are the real differences between the methodologies?
b. What factors are important in selecting a particular methodology?
c. What should be her next steps in thinking about a methodology?

Help Kathryn answer these questions. (This exercise was based on K. Duncan, L. Reeves, and J. Griffin, "BI Experts' Perspective," *Business Intelligence Journal*, Vol. 8, No. 4, Fall 2003, pp. 14–19.)

2. Jeet Kumar is the administrator of data warehousing at a big regional bank. He was appointed 5 years ago to implement a data warehouse to support the bank's CRM business strategy. Using the data warehouse, the bank has been successful in integrating customer information, understanding customer profitability, attracting customers, enhancing customer relationships, and retaining customers.

Over the years, the bank's data warehouse has moved closer to real time by moving to more frequent refreshes of the data warehouse. Now, the bank wants to implement customer self-service and call-center applications that require even fresher data than is currently available in the warehouse.

Jeet wants some support in considering the possibilities for presenting fresher data. One alternative is to entirely commit to implementing real-time data warehousing. His ETL vendor is prepared to assist him make this change. Nevertheless, Jeet has been informed about EAI and EII technologies and wonders how they might fit into his plans.

In particular, he has the following questions:

a. What exactly are EAI and EII technologies?
b. How are EAI and EII related to ETL?
c. How are EAI and EII related to real-time data warehousing?
d. Are EAI and EII required, complementary, or alternatives to real-time data warehousing?

Help Jeet answer these questions. (This exercise is based on S. Brobst, E. Levy, and C. Muzilla, "Enterprise Application Integration and Enterprise Information Integration," *Business Intelligence Journal*, Vol. 10, No. 2, Spring 2005, pp. 27–32.)

3. Interview administrators in your college or executives in your organization to determine how data warehousing could assist them in their work. Write up a proposal describing your findings. Include cost estimates and benefits in your report.

4. Go through the list of data warehousing risks described in this chapter and find two examples of each in practice.

5. Access **teradata.com** and read the white papers "Measuring Data Warehouse ROI" and "Realizing ROI: Projecting and Harvesting the Business Value of an Enterprise Data

Warehouse." Also, watch the Web-based course "The ROI Factor: How Leading Practitioners Deal with the Tough Issue of Measuring DW ROI." Describe the most important issues described in them. Compare these issues to the success factors described in Ariyachandra and Watson (2006a).

6. Read the article K. Liddell Avery and Hugh J. Watson, "Training Data Warehouse End-users," *Business Intelligence Journal*, Vol. 9, No. 4, Fall 2004, pp. 40–51 (which is available at **teradatastudentnetwork.com**). Consider the different classes of end users, describe their difficulties, and discuss the benefits of appropriate training for each group. Have each member of the group take on one of the roles and have a discussion about how an appropriate type of data warehousing training would be good for each of you.

Internet Exercises

1. Search the Internet to find information about data warehousing. Identify some newsgroups that have an interest in this concept. Explore ABI/INFORM in your library, e-library, and Google for recent articles on the topic. Begin with **tdwi.com**, **technologyevaluation.com**, and the major vendors: **teradata.com**, **sas.com**, **oracle**

.com, and **ncr.com**. Also check **cio.com**, **dmreview .com**, **dssresources.com**, and **db2mag.com**.

2. Survey some ETL tools and vendors. Start with **fairisaac .com** and **egain.com**. Also consult **dmreview.com**.

3. Contact some data warehouse vendors and obtain information about their products. Give special attention to vendors that provide tools for multiple purposes, such as Cognos, Software A&G, SAS Institute, and Oracle. Free online demos are available from some of these vendors. Download a demo or two and try them. Write a report describing your experience.

4. Explore **teradata.com** for developments and success stories about data warehousing. Write a report about what you have discovered.

5. Explore **teradata.com** for white papers and Web-based courses on data warehousing. Read the former and watch the latter. (Divide up the class so that all the sources are covered.) Write up what you have discovered in a report.

6. Find recent cases of successful data warehousing applications. Go to data warehouse vendors' sites and look for cases or success stories. Select one and write a brief summary to present to your class.

End of Chapter Application Case

Continental Airlines Flies High With Its Real-Time Data Warehouse

As business intelligence (BI) becomes a critical component of daily operations, real-time data warehouses that provide end users with rapid updates and alerts generated from transactional systems are increasingly being deployed. Real-time data warehousing and BI, supporting its aggressive Go Forward business plan, have helped Continental Airlines alter its industry status from "worst to first" and then from "first to favorite." Continental Airlines is a leader in real-time BI. In 2004, Continental won the Data Warehousing Institute's Best Practices and Leadership Award.

Problem(s)

Continental Airlines was founded in 1934, with a single-engine Lockheed aircraft in the southwestern United States. As of 2006, Continental was the fifth largest airline in the United States and the seventh largest in the world. Continental has the broadest global route network of any U.S. airline, with more than 2,300 daily departures to more than 227 destinations.

Back in 1994, Continental was in deep financial trouble. It had filed for Chapter 11 bankruptcy protection twice and was heading for its third, and probably final, bankruptcy. Ticket sales were hurting because performance on factors that are important to customers was dismal, including a low percentage of on-time departures, frequent baggage arrival problems, and too many customers turned away due to overbooking.

Solution

The revival of Continental began in 1994 when Gordon Bethune became CEO and initiated the Go Forward plan, which consisted of four interrelated parts to be implemented simultaneously. Bethune targeted the need to improve customer-valued performance measures by better understanding customer needs as well as customer perceptions of the value of services that were and could be offered. Financial management practices were also targeted for a significant overhaul. As early as 1998, the airline had separate databases for marketing and operations, all hosted and managed by outside vendors. Processing queries and instigating marketing programs to its high-value customers were time consuming and ineffective. In addition, information that the workforce needed to make quick decisions was simply not available. In 1999, Continental chose to integrate its marketing, IT, revenue, and operational data sources into a single, in-house, EDW. The data warehouse provided a variety of early, major benefits.

As soon as Continental returned to profitability and ranked first in the airline industry in many performance metrics, Bethune and his management team raised the bar by escalating the vision. Instead of just performing best, they wanted Continental to be their customers' favorite airline. The Go Forward plan established more actionable ways to move from first to favorite among customers. Technology became increasingly critical for supporting these new initiatives. In the early days, having access to historical, integrated information was sufficient. This produced substantial strategic value. But it became increasingly imperative for the data warehouse to provide real-time, actionable information to support enterprise-wide tactical decision making and business processes.

Luckily, the warehouse team had expected and arranged for the real-time shift. From the very beginning, the team had created an architecture to handle real-time data feeds into the warehouse, extracts of data from legacy systems into the warehouse, and tactical queries to the warehouse that required almost immediate response times. In 2001, real-time data became available from the warehouse, and the amount stored grew rapidly. Continental moves real-time data (ranging from to-the-minute to hourly) about customers, reservations, check-ins, operations, and flights from its main operational systems to the warehouse. Continental's real-time applications include the following:

- Revenue management and accounting
- Customer relationship management (CRM)
- Crew operations and payroll
- Security and fraud
- Flight operations

Results

In the first year alone, after the data warehouse project was deployed, Continental identified and eliminated over $7 million in fraud and reduced costs by $41 million. With a $30 million investment in hardware and software over 6 years, Continental has reached over $500 million in increased revenues and cost savings in marketing, fraud detection, demand forecasting and tracking, and improved data center management. The single, integrated, trusted view of the business (i.e., the single version of the truth) has led to better, faster decision making.

Continental is now identified as a leader in real-time BI, based on its scalable and extensible architecture, practical decisions on what data are captured in real time, strong relationships with end users, a small and highly competent data warehouse staff, sensible weighing of strategic and tactical decision support requirements, understanding of the synergies between decision support and operations, and changed business processes that

use real-time data. (For a sample output screen from the Continental system, see **teradata.com/t/page/139245/**.)

Sources: Adapted from H. Wixom, J. Hoffer, R. Anderson-Lehman, and A. Reynolds, "Real-Time Business Intelligence: Best Practices at Continental Airlines," *Information Systems Management Journal*, Winter 2006, pp. 7–18; R. Anderson-Lehman, H. Watson, B. Wixom, and J. Hoffer, "Continental Airlines Flies High with Real-Time Business Intelligence," *MIS Quarterly Executive*, Vol. 3, No. 4, December 2004, pp. 163–176 (available at **teradatauniversitynetwork.com**); H. Watson, "Real Time: The Next Generation of Decision-Support Data Management," *Business Intelligence Journal*, Vol. 10, No. 3, 2005, pp. 4–6; M. Edwards, "2003 Best Practices Awards Winners: Innovators in Business Intelligence and Data Warehousing," *Business Intelligence Journal*, Fall 2003, pp. 57–64; R. Westervelt, "Continental Airlines Builds Real-Time Data Warehouse," August 20, 2003, **searchoracle.techtarget.com**; R. Clayton, "Enterprise Business Performance Management: Business Intelligence + Data Warehouse = Optimal Business Performance," *Teradata Magazine*, September 2005, **teradata.com/t/page/139245/**; and The Data Warehousing Institute, "2003 Best Practices Summaries: Enterprise Data Warehouse," 2003, **tdwi.org/display.aspx?ID=6749**.

QUESTIONS FOR END OF CHAPTER APPLICATION CASE

1. Describe the benefits of implementing the Continental Go Forward strategy.
2. Explain why it is important for an airline to use a real-time data warehouse.
3. Examine the sample system output screen at **teradata.com/t/page/139245/**. Describe how it can assist the user in identifying problems and opportunities.
4. Identify the major differences between the traditional data warehouse and a real-time data warehouse, as was implemented at Continental.
5. What strategic advantage can Continental derive from the real-time system as opposed to a traditional information system?

References

Adamson, C. (2009). *The Star Schema Handbook: The Complete Reference to Dimensional Data Warehouse Design*, Hoboken, NJ: Wiley.

Agosta, L. (2006, January). "The Data Strategy Adviser: The Year Ahead—Data Warehousing Trends 2006." *DM Review*, Vol. 16, No. 1.

Akbay, S. (2006, Quarter 1). "Data Warehousing in Real Time." *Business Intelligence Journal*, Vol. 11, No. 1.

Ambeo. "Keeping Data Private (and Knowing It): Moving Beyond Conventional Safeguards to Ensure Data Privacy." **am-beo.com/why_ambeo_white_papers.html** (accessed May 2009).

Ambeo. (2005, July). "Ambeo Delivers Proven Data Access Auditing Solution." *Database Trends and Applications*, Vol. 19, No. 7.

Anthes, G. H. (2003, June 30). "Hilton Checks into New Suite." *Computerworld*, Vol. 37, No. 26.

Ariyachandra, T., and H. Watson. (2006a, January). "Benchmarks for BI and Data Warehousing Success." *DM Review*, Vol. 16, No. 1.

Ariyachandra, T., and H. Watson. (2006b). "Which Data Warehouse Architecture Is Most Successful?" *Business Intelligence Journal*, Vol. 11, No. 1.

Ariyachandra, T., and H. Watson. (2005). "Key Factors in Selecting a Data Warehouse Architecture." *Business Intelligence Journal*, Vol. 10, No. 2.

Armstrong, R. (2000, Quarter 3). "E-nalysis for the E-business." *Teradata Magazine Online*, **teradata.com**.

Ball, S. K. (2005, November 14). "Do You Need a Data Warehouse Layer in Your Business Intelligence Architecture?"

datawarehouse.ittoolbox.com/documents/industry-articles/do-you-need-a-data-warehouse-layer-in-your-business-intelligencearchitecture-2729 (accessed June 2009).

Basu, R. (2003, November). "Challenges of Real-Time Data Warehousing." *DM Review*.

Bell, L. D. (2001, Spring). "MetaBusiness Meta Data for the Masses: Administering Knowledge Sharing for Your Data Warehouse." *Journal of Data Warehousing*, Vol. 6, No. 2.

Benander, A., B. Benander, A. Fadlalla, and G. James. (2000, Winter). "Data Warehouse Administration and Management." *Information Systems Management*, Vol. 17, No. 1.

Bonde, A., and M. Kuckuk. (2004, April). "Real World Business Intelligence: The Implementation Perspective." *DM Review*, Vol. 14, No. 4.

Breslin, M. (2004, Winter). "Data Warehousing Battle of the Giants: Comparing the Basics of Kimball and Inmon Models." *Business Intelligence Journal*, Vol. 9, No. 1.

Briggs, L. L. "DirecTV Connects with Data Integration Solution," *Business Intelligence Journal*, Vol. 14, No. 1, 2009, pp. 14–16.

Brobst, S., E. Levy, and C. Muzilla. (2005, Spring). "Enterprise Application Integration and Enterprise Information Integration." *Business Intelligence Journal*, Vol. 10, No. 2.

Brody, R. (2003, Summer). "Information Ethics in the Design and Use of Metadata." *IEEE Technology and Society Magazine*, Vol. 22, No. 2.

Brown, M. (2004, May 9–12). "8 Characteristics of a Successful Data Warehouse." *Proceedings of the Twenty-Ninth Annual SAS Users Group International Conference* (SUGI 29). Montreal, Canada.

Burdett, J., and S. Singh. (2004). "Challenges and Lessons Learned from Real-Time Data Warehousing." *Business Intelligence Journal*, Vol. 9, No. 4.

Coffee, P. (2003, June 23). "'Active' Warehousing." *eWeek*, Vol. 20, No. 25.

Cooper, B. L., H. J. Watson, B. H. Wixom, and D. L. Goodhue. (2000). "Data Warehousing Supports Corporate Strategy at First American Corporation." *MIS Quarterly*, Vol. 24, No. 4, pp. 547–567.

Cooper, B. L., H. J. Watson, B. H. Wixom, and D. L. Goodhue. (1999, August 15–19). "Data Warehousing Supports Corporate Strategy at First American Corporation." SIM International Conference, Atlanta.

Davison, D. (2003, November 14). "Top 10 Risks of Offshore Outsourcing." META Group (now Gartner, Inc.) Research Report, Stamford, CT.

Dragoon, A. (2003, July 1). "All for One View." *CIO*.

Eckerson, W. (2005, April 1). "Data Warehouse Builders Advocate for Different Architectures." *Application Development Trends*.

Eckerson, W. (2003, Fall). "The Evolution of ETL." *Business Intelligence Journal*, Vol. 8, No. 4.

Eckerson, W., R. Hackathorn, M. McGivern, C. Twogood, and G. Watson. (2009). "Data Warehousing Appliances." *Business Intelligence Journal*, Vol. 14, No. 1, pp. 40–48.

Edwards, M. (2003, Fall). "2003 Best Practices Awards Winners: Innovators in Business Intelligence and Data Warehousing." *Business Intelligence Journal*, Vol. 8, No.4.

"Egg's Customer Data Warehouse Hits the Mark." (2005, October). *DM Review*, Vol. 15, No. 10, pp. 24–28.

Elson, R., and R. LeClerc. (2005). "Security and Privacy Concerns in the Data Warehouse Environment." *Business Intelligence Journal*, Vol. 10, No. 3.

Ericson, J. (2006, March). "Real-Time Realities." *BI Review*.

Furtado, P. (2009). "A Survey of Parallel and Distributed Data Warehouses." *International Journal of Data Warehousing and Mining*, Vol. 5, No. 2, pp. 57–78.

Golfarelli, M., and Rizzi, S. (2009). *Data Warehouse Design: Modern Principles and Methodologies*. San Francisco, CA: McGraw-Hill Osborne Media.

Gonzales, M. (2005, Quarter 1). "Active Data Warehouses Are Just One Approach for Combining Strategic and Technical Data." *DB2 Magazine*.

Hall, M. (2002, April 15). "Seeding for Data Growth." *Computerworld*, Vol. 36, No. 16.

Hicks, M. (2001, November 26). "Getting Pricing Just Right." *eWeek*, Vol. 18, No. 46.

Hoffer, J. A., M. B. Prescott, and F. R. McFadden. (2007). *Modern Database Management*, 8th ed. Upper Saddle River, NJ: Prentice Hall.

Hwang, M., and H. Xu. (2005, Fall). "A Survey of Data Warehousing Success Issues." *Business Intelligence Journal*, Vol. 10, No. 4.

IBM. (2009). *50 TB Data Warehouse Benchmark on IBM System Z*. Armonk, NY: IBM Redbooks.

Imhoff, C. (2001, May). "Power Up Your Enterprise Portal." *E-Business Advise*.

Inmon, W. H. (2006, January). "Information Management: How Do You Tune a Data Warehouse?" *DM Review*, Vol. 16, No. 1.

Inmon, W. H. (2005). *Building the Data Warehouse*, 4th ed. New York: Wiley.

Jukic, N., and C. Lang. (2004, Summer). "Using Offshore Resources to Develop and Support Data Warehousing Applications." *Business Intelligence Journal*, Vol. 9, No. 3.

Kalido. "BP Lubricants Achieves BIGS Success." **kalido.com/collateral/Documents/English-US/CS-BP%20BIGS.pdf** (accessed August 2009).

Kalido. "BP Lubricants Achieves BIGS, Key IT Solutions." **keyitsolutions.com/asp/rptdetails/report/95/cat/1175/** (accessed August 2009).

Karacsony, K. (2006, January). "ETL Is a Symptom of the Problem, not the Solution." *DM Review*, Vol. 16, No. 1.

Kassam, S. (2002, April 16). "Freedom of Information." *Intelligent Enterprise*, Vol. 5, No. 7.

Kay, R. (2005, September 19). "EII." *Computerworld*, Vol. 39, No. 38.

Kelly, C. (2001, June 14). "Calculating Data Warehousing ROI." *SearchSQLServer.com Tips*.

Malykhina, E. (2003, January 3). "The Real-Time Imperative." *InformationWeek*, Issue 1020.

Manglik, A., and V. Mehra. (2005, Winter). "Extending Enterprise BI Capabilities: New Patterns for Data Integration." *Business Intelligence Journal*, Vol. 10, No. 1.

Martins, C. (2005, December 13). "HP to Consolidate Data Marts into Single Warehouse." *Computerworld*.

Matney, D. (2003, Spring). "End-User Support Strategy." *Business Intelligence Journal*, Vol. 8, No. 2.

McCloskey, D. W. (2002). *Choosing Vendors and Products to Maximize Data Warehousing Success*. New York: Auerbach Publications.

Mehra, V. (2005, Summer). "Building a Metadata-Driven Enterprise: A Holistic Approach." *Business Intelligence Journal*, Vol. 10, No. 3.

Moseley, M. (2009). "Eliminating Data Warehouse Pressures with Master Data Services and SOA." *Business Intelligence Journal*, Vol. 14, No. 2, pp. 33–43.

Murtaza, A. (1998, Fall). "A Framework for Developing Enterprise Data Warehouses." *Information Systems Management*, Vol. 15, No. 4.

Nash, K. S. (2002, July). "Chemical Reaction." *Baseline*.

Orovic, V. (2003, June). "To Do & Not to Do." *eAI Journal*.

Parzinger, M. J., and M. N. Frolick. (2001, July). "Creating Competitive Advantage Through Data Warehousing." *Information Strategy*, Vol. 17, No. 4.

Peterson, T. (2003, April 21). "Getting Real About Real Time." *Computerworld*, Vol. 37, No. 16.

Reeves, L. (2009). *Manager's Guide to Data Warehousing*. Hoboken, NJ: Wiley.

Romero, O., and A. Abelló. (2009). "A Survey of Multidimensional Modeling Methodologies." *International Journal of Data Warehousing and Mining*, Vol. 5, No. 2, pp. 1–24.

Rosenberg, A. (2006, Quarter 1). "Improving Query Performance in Data Warehouses." *Business Intelligence Journal*, Vol. 11, No. 1.

Russom, P. (2009). "Next Generation Data Warehouse Platforms." TDWI Best Practices Report, available at tdwi.org/research/reportseries/reports.aspx?pid=842 tdwi.org (accessed January 2010).

Saunders, T. (2009). "Cooking up a Data Warehouse." *Business Intelligence Journal*, Vol. 14, No. 2, pp. 16–22.

Schwartz, K. D. "Decisions at the Touch of a Button." *Teradata Magazine*, **teradata.com/t/page/117774/index.html** (accessed June 2009).

Schwartz, K. D. (2004, March). "Decisions at the Touch of a Button." *DSS Resources*, pp. 28–31. dssresources.com/cases/coca-colajapan/index.html (accessed April 2006).

Sen, A. (2004, April). "Metadata Management: Past, Present, and Future." *Decision Support Systems*, Vol. 37, No. 1.

Sen, A., and P. Sinha (2005). "A Comparison of Data Warehousing Methodologies." *Communications of the ACM*, Vol. 48, No. 3.

Solomon, M. (2005, Winter)."Ensuring a Successful Data Warehouse Initiative." *Information Systems Management*, Vol. 22, No. 1 26-36.

Songini, M. L. (2004, February 2). "ETL Quickstudy." *Computerworld*, Vol. 38, No. 5.

Sun Microsystems. (2005, September 19). "Egg Banks on Sun to Hit the Mark with Customers." **sun.com/smi/Press/sunflash/2005-09/sunflash.20050919.1.xml** (accessed April 2006; no longer available online).

Tannenbaum, A. (2002, Spring). "Identifying Meta Data Requirements." *Journal of Data Warehousing*, Vol. 7, No. 2.

Teradata Corp. "A Large US-based Insurance Company Masters Its Finance Data." **teradata.com/t/WorkArea/DownloadAsset.aspx?id=4858** (accessed July 2009).

Teradata Corp. "Active Data Warehousing." **teradata.com/t/page/87127/index.html** (accessed April 2006).

Teradata Corp. "Coca-Cola Japan Puts the Fizz Back in Vending Machine Sales." **teradata.com/t/page/118866/index.html** (accessed June 2009).

Teradata Corp. "Enterprise Data Warehouse Delivers Cost Savings and Process Efficiencies." **teradata.com/t/resources/case-studies/NCR-Corporation-eb4455/** (accessed June 2009).

Terr, S. (2004, February). "Real-Time Data Warehousing: Hardware and Software." *DM Review*, Vol. 14, No. 2.

Thornton, M. (2002, March 18). "What About Security? The Most Common, but Unwarranted, Objection to Hosted Data Warehouses." *DM Review*, Vol. 12, No. 3, pp. 30–43.

Thornton, M., and M. Lampa. (2002). "Hosted Data Warehouse." *Journal of Data Warehousing*, Vol. 7, No. 2, pp. 27–34.

Vaduva, A., and T. Vetterli. (2001, September). "Metadata Management for Data Warehousing: An Overview." *International Journal of Cooperative Information Systems*, Vol. 10, No. 3.

Van den Hoven, J. (1998). "Data Marts: Plan Big, Build Small." *Information Systems Management*, Vol. 15, No. 1.

Watson, H. J. (2002). "Recent Developments in Data Warehousing." *Communications of the ACM*, Vol. 8, No. 1.

Watson, H. J., D. L. Goodhue, and B. H. Wixom. (2002). "The Benefits of Data Warehousing: Why Some Organizations Realize Exceptional Payoffs." *Information & Management*, Vol. 39.

Watson, H., J. Gerard, L. Gonzalez, M. Haywood, and D. Fenton. (1999), "Data Warehouse Failures: Case Studies and Findings." *Journal of Data Warehousing*, Vol. 4, No. 1.

Weir, R. (2002, Winter). "Best Practices for Implementing a Data Warehouse." *Journal of Data Warehousing*, Vol. 7, No. 1.

Wilk, L. (2003, Spring). "Data Warehousing and Real-Time Computing." *Business Intelligence Journal*, Vol. 8, No. 2.

Wrembel, R. (2009). "A Survey of Managing the Evolution of Data Warehouses." *International Journal of Data Warehousing and Mining*, Vol. 5, No. 2, pp. 24–56.

ZD Net UK. "Sun Case Study: Egg's Customer Data Warehouse." **whitepapers.zdnet.co.uk/0,39025945,60159401p-39000449q,00.htm** (accessed June 2009).

Zhao, X. (2005, October 7). "Meta Data Management Maturity Model," *DM Direct Newsletter*.

CHAPTER

3

Business Performance Management

LEARNING OBJECTIVES

- Understand the all-encompassing nature of business performance management (BPM)
- Understand the closed-loop processes linking strategy to execution
- Describe some of the best practices in planning and management reporting
- Describe the difference between performance management and measurement

- Understand the role of methodologies in BPM
- Describe the basic elements of the balanced scorecard (BSC) and Six Sigma methodologies
- Describe the differences between scorecards and dashboards
- Understand some of the basics of dashboard design

Business performance management (BPM) is an outgrowth of decision support systems (DSS), enterprise information systems (EIS), and business intelligence (BI). From a market standpoint, it was over 25 years in the making. As with decision support, BPM is more than just a technology. It is an integrated set of processes, methodologies, metrics, and applications designed to drive the overall financial and operational performance of an enterprise. It helps enterprises translate their strategies and objectives into plans, monitor performance against those plans, analyze variations between actual results and planned results, and adjust their objectives and actions in response to this analysis.

This chapter examines the processes, methodologies, metrics, and systems underlying BPM. Because BPM is distinguished from DSS and BI by its focus on strategy and objectives, this chapter begins with an exploration of the notions of enterprise strategy and execution and the gap that often exists between them. The specific sections are:

OPENING VIGNETTE: Double Down at Harrah's

Harrah's Entertainment, Inc. is the largest gaming company in the world and has been in operation since 1937. For most of its history, it has enjoyed financial success and unprecedented growth. In 2000, it had 21 hotel-casinos in 17 markets across the United States, employed over 40,000 people, and served over 19 million customers. By 2008, those numbers had risen to 51 hotel-casinos on 6 continents, 85,000 employees, and over 40 million customers. Much of Harrah's growth is attributable to savvy marketing operations and customer service, as well as its acquisition strategy.

PROBLEM

Besides being a leader in the gaming industry, Harrah's has been a long-time leader in the business intelligence and performance management arena. Unlike its competitors, Harrah's has generally avoided investing vast sums of money in lavish hotels, shopping malls, and attractions. Instead, it has operated on the basis of a business strategy that focuses on "knowing their customers well, giving them great service, and rewarding their loyalty so that they seek out a Harrah's casino whenever and wherever they play" (Watson and Volonino, 2001). The execution of this strategy has involved creative marketing, innovative uses of information technology, and operational excellence.

The strategy actually started back in the late 1990s when Harrah's hired Gary Loveman as its chief operating officer. Today, Loveman is Harrah Entertainment's chairman, president, and chief executive officer (CEO). Prior to joining Harrah's, Loveman had been an associate professor at the Harvard University Graduate School of Business Administration, with extensive experience in retail marketing and service management. When he arrived at Harrah's, he was given the task of turning Harrah's into a "market-driven company that would build customer loyalty" (Swabey, 2007). At the time, Harrah's actually had little choice. Harrah's didn't have the capital to build new luxury casinos and entertainment centers, a strategy being pursued by its rivals like the Bellagio. Instead, it decided to maximize its return on investment (ROI) by understanding its customers' behavior and preferences. It reasoned that in the highly competitive gaming market, the need to attract and retain customers is critical to business success, because customer loyalty and satisfaction can make or break a company. Attraction and retention require more than opulent accommodations and surroundings. Instead, the goal should be to persuade gamblers to spend a greater share at Harrah's properties.

Because it had a couple of years' worth of loyalty card data, Harrah's already knew a lot about its customers (Swabey, 2007). But focus groups revealed what management suspected—they might have cards, but they weren't loyal. Nearly 65 percent of their gambling expenditures went elsewhere. The first step was to find out who its customers were. The analysis revealed two facts: (1) Over 80 percent of revenues came from over 25 percent of customers and (2) Most of the customers were "average folks" (middle aged or seniors) and not the high rollers attracted by the luxury hotels (Shill and

Thomas, 2005). How could Harrah's collect, utilize, and leverage data, analysis, and findings of this type to maximize the lifetime value of a customer?

SOLUTION

Harrah's answer was Total Gold, a patented customer loyalty program that is now known as the Total Rewards program. Not only did the program serve to reward customers with cash and comps for their gaming and other activities at any of Harrah's properties, but, more important, it provided Harrah's with a vast collection of high volume, real-time transaction data regarding its customers and their behaviors. The data are collected via the Total Rewards card, which is used to record guest activities of all sorts (e.g., purchases at restaurants and wins and losses from any type of gaming activity).

The data are fed to a centralized data warehouse. Staff at any of Harrah's properties can access the data. The data warehouse forms the base of a "closed-loop" marketing system that enables Harrah's to clearly define the objectives of its marketing campaigns, to execute and monitor those campaigns, and to learn what types of campaigns provide the highest return for particular types of customers. The overall result is that Harrah's has established a "differentiated loyalty and service framework to continuously improve customer service interactions and business outcomes" (Stanley, 2006). The system also acts as a real-time feed to Harrah's operational systems, which can impact the experience of customers while they gamble and participate in other activities at Harrah's properties.

RESULTS AND A NEW PROBLEM

Harrah's Total Rewards loyalty card program and closed-loop marketing system has produced substantial returns over the past decade, including (Watson and Volonino, 2001):

- A brand identity for Harrah's casinos
- An increase in customer retention worth several million dollars
- An increase in the number of customers who play at more than one Harrah's property, increasing profitability by millions of dollars
- A high internal rate of return on its information technology investments

The bottom line is that customers' discretionary spending versus their competitors has increased substantially from year to year, resulting in hundreds of millions of dollars in additional revenue.

The system has won a number of awards (e.g., TDWI Best Practices Award) and has been the subject of many case studies. It has been recognized as the "most spectacularly successful example of analytics in action today" (Swabey, 2007). Of course, awards and accolades are no guarantee of future success, especially in the face of a global economic downturn.

For the 10 years leading up to the end of 2007, the U.S. gaming industry had the highest performing equity index of any industry in America (Knowledge@W.P. Carey, 2009). The past 2 years have been a different **story**. Once thought to be immune to economic downturns, the gaming industry has suffered substantially from the collapse of the capital markets and the world economy. In cities like Las Vegas, not only have hotel occupancy rates declined, but the average spend per visitor has also dwindled. The plight of many casinos remains precarious, because they relied on huge amounts of debt to build newer and bigger hotel-casino projects and lacked the reserves to handle declining revenues.

Unlike its competitors, Harrah's has never had an "edifice" complex (Shill and Thomas, 2005). Yet, like its competitors, Harrah's still faces substantial economic problems. In the first 3 months of 2009, it posted operating losses of $127 million, although this was an improvement over 2008. In the first 3 months of 2008, it had operating losses of $270 million. In 2008, Harrah's also doubled its debt load (to the tune of $24 billion) when it was taken private in January 2008 by the equity firms Apollo Management and TPG Capital. Today, its debt load has left it facing potential bankruptcy.

So, even though Harrah's has had an award-winning performance management system in place for years and is a recognized leader in the use of data and predictive analytics, it still confronts the same strategic problems and economic issues that its "lesser equipped" competitors face.

Harrah's has continued to rely on its marketing campaigns to boost demand. Additionally, it has instituted a number of initiatives designed to reduce its debt and to cut costs. In December 2008, Harrah's completed a debt-exchange deal that reduced its overall debt by $1.16 billion, and it is in the midst of another debt-reduction and maturity-extension program involving $2.8 million in notes. Like most other gaming companies, it laid off 1,600 workers in Las Vegas, cut managers' pay, and suspended 401K contributions during the downturn. It delayed the completion of 660 more rooms at Caesar's Palace, although it is still working on a new convention center at Caesar's, which has had strong bookings.

Management has also been encouraged by the results of an "efficiency-management" process, pioneered by Toyota, called Lean Operations Management. Lean Operations Management is a performance management framework focused primarily on efficiency rather than effectiveness. Harrah's has launched pilot programs at several properties and planned to roll it out company-wide in 2009.

QUESTIONS FOR THE OPENING VIGNETTE

1. Describe Harrah's marketing strategy. How does Harrah's strategy differ from its competitors?
2. What is Harrah's Total Rewards program?
3. What are the basic elements of Harrah's closed-loop marketing system?
4. What were the results of Harrah's marketing strategy?
5. What economic issues does Harrah's face today? Could the Total Rewards system be modified in any way to handle these issues?

WHAT WE CAN LEARN FROM THIS VIGNETTE

For a number of years, Harrah's closed-loop marketing system enabled it to execute a strategy that clearly differentiated it from its competitors. The system also provided the means to monitor key indicators of operational and tactical importance. One of the problems with the system is that it is predicated on the assumption of growing, or at least stable, demand. What it could not do, at least in the short run, was predict drastically reduced or nonexistent demand or fundamental changes in the economy. As Loveman, Harrah's CEO, has said, "We are not experiencing a recession, but a fundamental restructuring of financial interaction that we have grown accustomed to over a very long period of time. And it's not at all clear yet where that's going."

Sources: Compiled from Knowledge@W.P. Carey, "High-Rolling Casinos Hit a Losing Streak," March 2, 2009, **knowledge.wpcarey.asu.edu/article.cfm?articleid=1752#** (accessed January 2010); S. Green, "Harrah's Reports Loss, Says LV Properties Hit Hard," *Las Vegas Sun*, March 13, 2009, **lasvegassun.com/news/2009/mar/13/harrahs-reports-loss-says-lv-properties-hit-hard** (accessed January 2010); W. Shill and R. Thomas, "Exploring the Mindset of the High Performer," *Outlook Journal*, October 2005, **accenture.com/Global/Research_and_Insights/Outlook/By_Issue/Y2005/ExploringPerformer.htm** (accessed January 2010); T. Stanley, "High-Stakes Analytics," *InformationWeek*, February 1, 2006, **informationweek.com/shared/printableArticle.jhtml?articleID=177103414** (accessed January 2010); P. Swabey, "Nothing Left to Chance," *Information Age*, January 18, 2007, **information-age.com/channels/information-management/features/272256/nothing-left-to-chance.thtml** (accessed January 2010); and H. Watson and L. Volonino, "Harrah's High Payoff from Customer Information," *The Data Warehousing Institute Industry Study 2000—Harnessing Customer Information for Strategic Advantage: Technical Challenges and Business Solutions*, January 2001, **terry.uga.edu/~hwatson/Harrahs.doc** (accessed January 2010).

3.1 BUSINESS PERFORMANCE MANAGEMENT (BPM) OVERVIEW

As this chapter will show, Harrah's closed-loop marketing system has all the hallmarks of a performance management system. Essentially, the system allowed Harrah's to align its strategies, plans, analytical systems, and actions in such a way that it substantially improved its performance. Harrah's recent experience also shows that successful performance also requires a broad focus, as opposed to a narrow one (e.g., just on marketing or customer loyalty), as well as the ability to question and explore assumptions, especially during times of uncertainty. Organizations need to adapt constantly if they are to achieve sustained success. An organization's performance management processes are the principal mechanism for assessing the impact of change and tuning the business in order to survive and prosper (Axson, 2007).

BPM Defined

In the business and trade literature, performance management has a number of names, including corporate performance management (CPM), enterprise performance management (EPM), strategic enterprise management (SEM), and business performance management (BPM). CPM was coined by the market analyst firm Gartner (**gartner.com**). EPM is a term associated with Oracle's PeopleSoft offering by the same name. SEM is the term that SAP (**sap.com**) uses. In this chapter, BPM is used rather than the other terms, because the term was originally coined by the BPM Standards Group and is still used by the BPM Forum. The term **business performance management (BPM)** refers to the business processes, methodologies, metrics, and technologies used by enterprises to measure, monitor, and manage business performance. It encompasses three key components (Colbert, 2009):

1. A set of integrated, closed-loop management and analytic processes, supported by technology, that addresses financial as well as operational activities
2. Tools for businesses to define strategic goals and then measure and manage performance against those goals
3. A core set of processes, including financial and operational planning, consolidation and reporting, modeling, analysis, and monitoring of key performance indicators (KPIs), linked to organizational strategy

BPM and BI Compared

BPM is an outgrowth of BI and incorporates many of its technologies, applications, and techniques. When BPM was first introduced as a separate concept, there was confusion about the differences between BPM and BI. Was it simply a new term for the same concept? Was BPM the next generation of BI, or were there substantial differences between the two? The confusion persists even today for the following reasons:

- BPM is promoted and sold by the same companies that market and sell the BI tools and suites.
- BI has evolved so that many of the original differences between the two no longer exist (e.g., BI used to be focused on departmental rather than on enterprise-wide projects).
- BI is a crucial element of BPM.

The term *BI* now describes the technology used to access, analyze, and report on data relevant to an enterprise. It encompasses a wide spectrum of software, including ad hoc querying, reporting, online analytical processing (OLAP), dashboards, scorecards, search, visualization, and more. These software products started as stand-alone tools, but BI software vendors have incorporated them into their BI suites.

BPM has been characterized as "BI + Planning," meaning that BPM is the convergence of BI and planning on a unified platform—the cycle of plan, monitor, and analyze (Calumo Group, 2009). The processes that BPM encompasses are not new. Virtually every medium and large organization has processes in place (e.g., budgets, detailed plans, execution, and measurement) that feed back to the overall strategic plan, as well as the operational plans. What BPM adds is a framework for integrating these processes, methodologies, metrics, and systems into a unified solution.

BI practices and software are almost always part of an overall BPM solution. BPM, however, is not just about software. BPM is an enterprise-wide strategy that seeks to prevent organizations from optimizing local business at the expense of overall corporate performance. BPM is not a "one-off" project or departmentally focused. Instead, BPM is an ongoing set of processes that, if done correctly, impacts an organization from top to bottom. Critical to the success of BPM is alignment throughout an organization. It "helps users take action in pursuit of their 'common cause': achieving performance targets, executing company strategy, and delivering value to stakeholders" (Tucker and Dimon, 2009).

This is not to say that a BI project cannot be strategically oriented, centrally controlled, or impact a substantial part of an organization. For example, the Transportation Security Administration (TSA) uses a BI system called the Performance Information System (PIMS) to track passenger volumes, screen performance (attrition, absenteeism, overtime, and injuries), dangerous items, and total passenger throughput (Henschen, 2008). The system is built on BI software from MicroStrategy (**microstrategy.com**) and is used by over 2,500 "power users" on a daily basis and 9,500 casual users on a weekly basis. The information in PIMS is critical to the operation of the TSA and in some cases is mandated by Congress. It is used by TSA employees from the top of the agency to the bottom, and it reduced agency costs by approximately $100 million for fiscal year 2007–2008. Clearly, the system has strategic and operational importance. However, it is not a BPM system.

The primary distinction is that a BPM system is strategy driven. It encompasses a closed-loop set of processes that link strategy to execution in order to optimize business performance (see Figure 3.1). The loop implies that optimum performance is achieved by

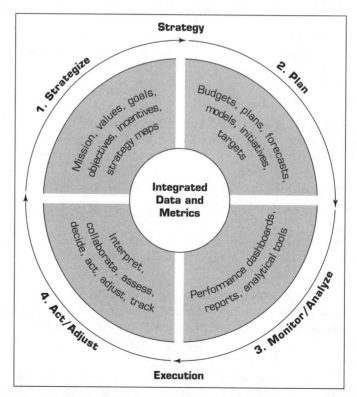

FIGURE 3.1 BPM Cycle. *Source*: W. Eckerson, "Performance Management Strategies: How to Create and Deploy Performance Management Strategies." *TDWI Best Practices Report*, 2009.

setting goals and objectives (i.e., strategize), establishing initiatives and plans to achieve those goals (i.e., plan), monitoring actual performance against the goals and objectives (i.e., monitor), and taking corrective action (i.e., act and adjust). In Sections 3.3 through 3.6, each of these major processes is examined in detail.

SECTION 3.1 REVIEW QUESTIONS

1. Define BPM.
2. How does BPM differ from BI? How are they the same?
3. Briefly describe TSA's PIMS.
4. List the major BPM processes.

3.2 STRATEGIZE: WHERE DO WE WANT TO GO?

For the moment, imagine that you are a distance runner and are in the process of training for an upcoming event. In preparation, suppose your coach said to you, "I haven't thought much about the race. I'm not even sure what the distance is, but I think you should just go out and run for 8 hours a day until race day. Things will work out in the end." If a coach said this, you would think your coach was nuts. Obviously, for your training plan to make sense, you would need to know what race you were running (e.g., is it a marathon, a half marathon, or 10 miler) and what sort of time you were shooting for (e.g., a top-5 finish with a time of 2 hours, 10 minutes). You would also need to know what your strengths and weaknesses were in order to determine whether the goal was realistic and what sorts of things you would need to work on to achieve your goal (e.g., trouble with finishing speed over the last few miles of a race).

You would be surprised at the number of companies that operate much like the coach, especially during uncertain and challenging times. The general refrain is something like, "Setting a strategy and developing a formal plan is too slow and inflexible. You need actions that are far bolder and more attuned to the unique nature of our time. If you take the time to define your goals, set your priorities, develop your strategies, and manage your outcomes, someone will beat you to the finish line." However, without specific goals or objectives, it is difficult to evaluate alternative courses of action. Without specific priorities, there is no way to determine how to allocate resources among the alternatives selected. Without plans, there is no way to guide the actions among those working on the alternatives. Without analysis and evaluation, there is no way to determine which of the opportunities are succeeding or failing. Goals, objectives, priorities, plans, and critical thinking are all part of a well-defined strategy.

Strategic Planning

The term *strategy* has many definitions. To add to the confusion, it is also often used in combination with a variety of other terms such as *strategic vision* and *strategic focus*. Regardless of the differences in meaning, they all address the question "Where do we want to go in the future?" For most companies, the answer to this question is provided in a strategic plan. You can think of a strategic plan as a map, detailing a course of action for moving an organization from its current state to its future vision.

Typically, strategic plans start at the top and begin with an enterprise-wide view. From there, strategic plans are created for the company's business units or functional units. The following tasks are quite common to the strategic planning process, regardless of the level at which the planning is done—enterprise-wide, business unit, or functional unit:

1. ***Conduct a current situation analysis.*** This analysis reviews the company's current situation ("Where are we?") and establishes a baseline, as well as key trends, for financial performance and operational performance.

2. ***Determine the planning horizon.*** Traditionally, organizations produce plans on a yearly basis, with the planning horizon running 3 to 5 years. In large part, the time horizon is determined by the volatility and predictability of the market, product life cycles, the size of the organization, the rate of technological innovation, and the capital intensity of the industry. The more volatile, the less predictable; the shorter the life cycles, the smaller the organization; the faster the rate of innovation, and the less the capital intensity, the shorter the planning horizon.

3. ***Conduct an environment scan.*** An environment scan is a standard strengths, weaknesses, opportunities, and threats assessment of the company. It identifies and prioritizes the key customer, market, competitor, government, demographic, stake-holder, and industry factors potentially or actually affecting the company.

4. ***Identify critical success factors.*** **Critical success factors (CSFs)** delineate those things that an organization must excel at to be successful in its market space. For a product-focused company, product quality and product innovation are examples of CSF. For a low-cost provider such as Wal-Mart, distribution capabilities are the CSF.

5. ***Complete a gap analysis.*** Like the environment scan, a gap analysis is used to identify and prioritize the internal strengths and weaknesses in an organization's processes, structures, and technologies and applications. The gaps reflect what the strategy actually requires and what the organization actually provides.

6. ***Create a strategic vision.*** An organization's **strategic vision** provides a picture or mental image of what the organization should look like in the future—the shift in its products and markets. Generally, the vision is couched in terms of its strategy focus and identifies the as-is state and the desired state.

7. ***Develop a business strategy.*** The challenge in this step is to produce a strategy that is based on the data and information from the previous steps and is consistent with the strategic vision. Common sense tells us that the strategy needs to exploit the organization's strengths, take advantage of its opportunities, address weaknesses, and respond to threats. The company needs to ensure that the strategy is internally consistent, that the organizational culture is aligned with the strategy, and that sufficient resources and capital are available to implement the strategy.

8. ***Identify strategic objectives and goals.*** A strategic plan that fails to provide clear directions for the operational and financial planning process is incomplete. Before an operational or financial plan can be established, strategic objectives must be established and refined into well-defined goals or targets. A **strategic objective** is a broad statement or general course of action that prescribes targeted directions for an organization. Before a strategic objective can be linked to an operational plan or a financial plan, it should be converted into a well-defined goal or target. A **strategic goal** is a quantification of an objective for a designated period of time. For example, if an organization has an objective of improving return on assets (ROA) or increasing overall profitability, these objectives need to be turned into quantified targets (e.g., an increase of ROA from 10 to 15 percent or an increase in profit margin from 5 to 7 percent) before the organization can begin to detail the operational plans needed to achieve these targets. Strategic goals and targets guide operational execution and allow progress to be tracked against overall objectives.

The Strategy Gap

It's one thing to create a long-term strategy and another to execute it. Over the past couple of decades, a number of surveys have highlighted the gap that routinely exists in many organizations between their strategic plans and the execution of those plans. Recent surveys of senior executives by the Monitor Group (Kaplan and Norton, 2008) and the

Conference Board (2008) pinpointed "strategy execution" as the executive's number one priority. Similarly, statistics from the Palladium Group (Norton, 2007) suggest that 90 percent of organizations fail to execute their strategies successfully. The reasons for the "strategy gap" are varied, although many studies pinpoint one of the following four reasons:

1. ***Communication.***   In many organizations, a very small percentage of the employees understand the organization's strategy. The Palladium Group (Norton, 2007) put the figure at less than 10 percent. On the one hand, it is difficult, if not impossible, for employees to make decisions and act in accordance with the strategic plan if they have never seen nor heard the plan. On the other hand, even when the plan is communicated, the strategy often lacks clarity so that no one is quite sure whether their actions are in line or at variance with the plan.

2. ***Alignment of rewards and incentives.***   Linking pay to performance is important for successful execution. However, incentive plans are often linked to short-term financial results, not to the strategic plan or even to the strategic initiatives articulated in the operational plan. Maximizing short-term gains leads to less than rational decision making. Again, the Palladium Group (Norton, 2007) indicated that 70 percent of organizations failed to link middle management incentives to their strategy.

3. ***Focus.***   Management often spends time on the periphery of issues rather than concentrating on the core elements. Hours can be spent debating line items on a budget, with little attention given to the strategy, the linkage of the financial plan to the strategy, or the assumptions underlying the linkage. The Palladium Group (Norton, 2007) suggested that in many organizations 85 percent of managers spend less than 1 hour per month discussing strategy.

4. ***Resources.***   Unless strategic initiatives are properly funded and resourced, their failure is virtually assured. The Palladium Group (Norton, 2007) found that less than 40 percent of organizations tied their budgets to their strategic plans.

SECTION 3.2 REVIEW QUESTIONS

1. Why does a company need a well-formulated strategy?
2. What are the basic tasks in the strategic planning process?
3. What are some of the sources of the gap between formulating a strategy and actually executing the strategy?

3.3 PLAN: HOW DO WE GET THERE?

When operational managers know and understand the *what* (i.e., the organizational objectives and goals), they will be able to come up with the *how* (i.e., detailed operational and financial plans). Operational and financial plans answer two questions: What tactics and initiatives will be pursued to meet the performance targets established by the strategic plan? What are the expected financial results of executing the tactics?

Operational Planning

An operational plan translates an organization's strategic objectives and goals into a set of well-defined tactics and initiatives, resource requirements, and expected results for some future time period, usually, but not always, a year. In essence, an operational plan is like a project plan that is designed to ensure that an organization's strategy is realized. Most operational plans encompass a portfolio of tactics and initiatives. The key to successful operational planning is integration. Strategy drives tactics, and tactics drive results. Basically, the tactics and initiatives defined in an operational plan need to be directly linked to key objectives and targets in the strategic plan. If there is no linkage between an individual tactic and one or more strategic objectives or targets, management should question whether the tactic and its associated initiatives are really needed at all. The BPM methodologies discussed in Section 3.8 are designed to ensure that these linkages exist.

Operational planning can be either tactic centric or budget centric (Axson, 2007). In a *tactic-centric* plan, tactics are established to meet the objectives and targets established in the strategic plan. Conversely, in a *budget-centric* plan, a financial plan or budget is established that sums to the targeted financial values. Best practice organizations use tactic-centric operational planning. This means that they begin the operational planning process by defining the alternative tactics and initiatives that can be used to reach a particular target. For example, if a business is targeting a 10 percent growth in profit margin (i.e., the ratio of the difference between revenue and expenses divided by revenue), the business will first determine whether it plans to increase the margin by increasing revenues, by reducing expenses, or by using some combination of both. If it focuses on revenues, then the question will become whether it plans to enter new markets or increase sales in existing markets, enhance existing products or introduce new products, or apply some combination of these. The alternate scenarios and associated initiatives have to be weighed in terms of their overall risk, resource requirements, and financial viability.

Financial Planning and Budgeting

In most organizations, resources tend to be scarce. If they were not, organizations could simply throw people and money at their opportunities and problems and overwhelm the competition. Given the scarcity of resources, an organization needs to put its money and people where its strategies and linked tactics are. An organization's strategic objectives and key metrics should serve as top-down drivers for the allocation of an organization's tangible and intangible assets. While continuing operations clearly need support, key resources should be assigned to the most important strategic programs and priorities. Most organizations use their budgets and compensation programs to allocate resources. By implication, both of these need to be carefully aligned with the organization's strategic objectives and tactics in order to achieve strategic success.

The best way for an organization to achieve this alignment is to base its financial plan on its operational plan or, more directly, to allocate and budget its resources against specific tactics and initiatives. For example, if one of the tactics is to develop a new sales channel, budgeted revenues and costs need to be assigned to the channel rather than simply having costs assigned to particular functional units such as marketing and research and development. Without this type of tactical resource planning, there is no way to measure the success of those tactics and hence the strategy. This type of linkage helps organizations avoid the problem of "random" budget cuts that inadvertently affect associated strategies. Tactic-based budgeting ensures that the link between particular budget-line items and particular tactics or initiatives is well established and well known.

The financial planning and budgeting process has a logical structure that typically starts with those tactics that generate some form of revenue or income. In organizations that sell goods or services, the ability to generate revenue is based on either the ability to directly produce goods and services or acquire the right amount of goods and services to sell. After a revenue figure has been established, the associated costs of delivering that level of revenue can be generated. Quite often, this entails input from several departments or tactics. This means the process has to be collaborative and that dependencies between functions need to be clearly communicated and understood. In addition to the collaborative input, the organization also needs to add various overhead costs, as well as the costs of the capital required. This information, once consolidated, shows the cost by tactic as well as the cash and funding requirements to put the plan into operation.

SECTION 3.3 REVIEW QUESTIONS

1. What is the goal of operational planning?
2. What is tactic-centric planning? What is budget-centric planning?
3. What is the primary goal of a financial plan?

3.4 MONITOR: HOW ARE WE DOING?

When the operational and financial plans are under way, it is imperative that the performance of the organization be monitored. A comprehensive framework for monitoring performance should address two key issues: what to monitor and how to monitor. Because it is impossible to look at everything, an organization needs to focus on monitoring specific issues. After the organization has identified the indicators or measures to look at, it needs to develop a strategy for monitoring those factors and responding effectively.

In Sections 3.7 and 3.8, we examine in detail how to determine what should be measured by a BPM system. For the moment, we simply note that the "what" is usually defined by the CSF and the goals or targets established in the strategic planning process. For example, if an instrument manufacturer has a specified strategic objective of increasing the overall profit margin of its current product lines by 5 percent annually over the next 3 years, then the organization needs to monitor the profit margin throughout the year to see whether it is trending toward the targeted annual rate of 5 percent. In the same vein, if this company plans to introduce a new product every quarter for the next two years, the organization needs to track new product introduction over the designated time period.

Diagnostic Control Systems

Most companies use what is known as a *diagnostic control system* to monitor organizational performance and correct deviations from present performance standards. This is true even for those organizations that do not have formal BPM processes or systems. A **diagnostic control system** is a cybernetic system, meaning that it has inputs, a process for transforming the inputs into outputs, a standard or benchmark against which to compare the outputs, and a feedback channel to allow information on variances between the outputs and the standard to be communicated and acted upon. Virtually any information system can be used as a diagnostic control system if it is possible to (1) set a goal in advance, (2) measure outputs, (3) compute or calculate absolute or relative performance variances, and (4) use the variance information as feedback to alter inputs and/or processes to bring performance back in line with present goals and standards. The key elements of a diagnostic control system are depicted in Figure 3.2. Balanced scorecards, performance dashboards, project monitoring systems, human resources systems, and financial reporting systems are all examples of systems that can be used diagnostically.

An effective diagnostic control system encourages *management by exception.* Instead of constantly monitoring a variety of internal processes and target values and comparing actual results with planned results, managers regularly receive schedule exception reports. Measures that are aligned with expectations receive little attention. If, however, a significant variation is identified, then—and only then—managers need to invest time and attention to investigate the cause of the deviation and initiate appropriate remedial action.

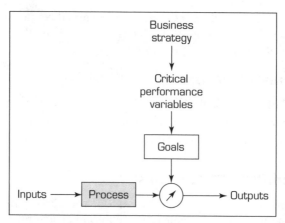

FIGURE 3.2 **Diagnostic Control System.** *Source*: R. Simons, *Performance Measurement and Control Systems for Implementing Strategy*, Prentice Hall, Upper Saddle River, NJ, 2002, p. 207.

Pitfalls of Variance Analysis

In many organizations, the vast majority of the exception analysis focuses on negative variances when functional groups or departments fail to meet their targets. Rarely are positive variances reviewed for potential opportunities, and rarely does the analysis focus on assumptions underlying the variance patterns. Consider, for a moment, the two paths depicted in Figure 3.3. In this figure, the dashed line from A to B represents planned or targeted results over a specified period of time. Recognizing that there will be minor deviations from the plan, we might expect the actual results to deviate slightly from the targeted results. When the deviation is larger than expected, this is typically viewed as an operational error that needs to be corrected. At this point, managers usually direct their employees to do whatever it takes to get the plan back on track. If revenues are below plan, they are chided to sell harder. If costs are above plan, they are told to stop spending.

However, what happens if our strategic assumptions—not the operations—are wrong? What if the organization needs to change strategic directions toward point C rather than continuing with the original plan? As Application Case 3.1 exemplifies, the results of proceeding on the basis of fallacious assumptions can be disastrous. The only way to make this sort of determination is to monitor more than actual versus targeted performance. Whatever diagnostic control system is being used needs to track underlying assumptions, cause-and-effect relationships, and the overall validity of the intended strategy. Consider, for instance, a growth strategy that is focused on the introduction of a new product. This sort of strategy is usually based on certain assumptions about market demand or the availability of parts from particular suppliers. As the strategy unfolds, management needs to monitor not only the revenues and costs associated with the new product but also the variations in the market demand or availability of parts or any other key assumptions.

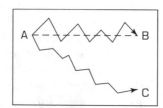

FIGURE 3.3 **Operational Variance or Strategic Issue?**

Application Case 3.1

Discovery-Driven Planning: The Coffee Wars

For the last couple of years, Starbucks, Dunkin' Donuts (**dunkindonuts.com**), and McDonald's have been locked in a battle to capture the specialty coffee market. For Starbucks and Dunkin' Donuts, a major part of the battle revolves around the growth in the number of stores. This is not an issue for McDonald's, because it already has a worldwide presence.

Since 2000, Starbucks has been opening stores at a "remarkable pace." Its store count went from just over 3,000 stores in 2000 to approximately 15,000 stores in 2007. The underlying assumption was that there was pent-up demand for specialty coffee and unless it opened new stores to service this demand, its competitors would. One of these competitors was Dunkin' Donuts. In 2007, Dunkin' Donuts decided to expand its franchises both in numbers and geographical reach. Prior to 2007, most of Dunkin' Donuts' 5,000 franchises were in the Northeast (Weier, 2007). Its new goal was to increase to 15,000 franchises worldwide. Unlike Starbucks, Dunkin' Donuts does not own its stores. Instead, it relies on individuals to apply for franchises, to pay a franchise fee after the approval process, and pay royalties from ongoing operations.

To help keep track of its progress toward its franchise goal, Dunkin' Donuts instituted a new dashboard (see Section 3.10) application that would tell it where deals were stalling, whether there were any deals in close proximity to one another, what the average cycle time was for closing a franchise deal, and the average size of the deals (Weier, 2007). Suppose that Dunkin' Donuts found that the average cycle time was longer than expected or that the deals were stalling, what would its response be?

Given Dunkin' Donuts' sunk costs in its strategy, the first responses would certainly revolve around increasing the cycle time or determining why the deals were stalling. Its last response would probably be to question the whole strategy of opening new franchises and the underlying assumption about pent-up demand. This is certainly what happened to Starbucks.

Starbucks continued to open stores at a rapid rate even in the face of substantial decline in comparative-store sales, which measures how fast sales are growing at stores open at least a year (Wailgum, 2008).

Starbucks' first response to the issue was to focus on the decline in sales. In 2007, it announced a set of strategic initiatives aimed at addressing the problem. It was going to move to new blends of coffees, replace existing espresso machines with new equipment, institute a customer rewards program, and open a new Web site. It was not until January 2008 that Starbucks realized that it needed to modify its growth strategy. Essentially, the new stores were cannibalizing sales at existing outlets. In response, Starbucks scaled back its growth plans, lowered its yearly targets for new store openings, retracted its long-term goal of opening 40,000 stores, and began closing unprofitable locations in the United States.

Discovery-Driven Planning

When a major company like Starbucks or Dunkin' Donuts embarks on an enterprise-wide growth strategy, considerable effort is made to ensure that everyone is on board. When things go astray, a variety of biases often come into play, directly and indirectly putting pressure on employees to stick to the plan at all costs. Especially, in very competitive, well-publicized circumstances of this sort, there is a tendency for companies to have:

- ***Confirmation bias.*** Embracing new information that confirms existing assumptions and rejecting information that challenges them.
- ***Recency bias.*** Forgetting that key assumptions were made in the first place, making it difficult to interpret or learn from unfolding experiences.
- ***Winner's bias.*** Overvaluing winning in competitive situations, even when the price exceeds the prize.
- ***Social or political bias.*** Sticking to a "public" plan, rather than admitting either ignorance or a mistake.

Part of the problem is that conventional planning processes of the sort used by Starbucks and Dunkin' Donuts provide little in the way of probing or analyzing the underlying assumptions on which the plan is based. As an alternative to conventional

(Continued)

Application Case 3.1   (Continued)

planning, McGrath and MacMillan (2009) suggested that companies use discovery-driven planning (DDP). With most growth strategies, the outcomes are initially uncertain and unpredictable. They also rest on a variety of critical assumptions that will certainly change as the plan unfolds. As the strategic plan unfolds, the key is to reduce the "assumption-to-knowledge" ratio (turning assumptions into facts). This is the focus of discovery-driven planning. Discovery-driven planning (DDP) offers a systematic way to uncover problematic assumptions that otherwise remain unnoticed and unchallenged. It is called *discovery-driven* because as plans evolve new data are uncovered and new potentials are discovered.

DDP consists of a series of steps. Some are similar to conventional planning (e.g., establishing a growth strategy), whereas others are not. In the context of this discussion, three steps distinguish DDP from conventional planning:

1. *Reverse financials.*   The first step is to use a set of financial documents to model how all the various assumptions in a plan affect one another and to determine, as information is gained, whether the plan is gaining traction or is at risk.
2. *Deliverables specification.*   The second step is to lay out all the activities required to produce, sell, service, and deliver the product or service to the customer. Together, these activities represent the allowable costs.
3. *Assumption checklist.*   All of the activities required to build a business rest on key assumptions. In this step, a written checklist of each of the assumptions associated with the project deliverables laid out in step 2 is created.

Suppose you plan to open an upscale French restaurant and your goal is to break even the first

year of operation (based on $2 million in sales). One question to ask is, "Is this a realistic sales number?" More specifically, "What activities would it take to generate $2 million in sales, and do these activities make sense?"

One way to answer these questions is to consider the number of customers your restaurant will need to serve on a yearly basis and how much they will have to spend on average when they dine at your restaurant. In terms of the average spend per person, you could make a guess about the types of courses in an average meal (an appetizer, entrée, etc.) and the average cost of those courses, or you could look at the average bill at comparable restaurants. So, for instance if the average meal at other high-end French restaurants in your region of the country is $120 to $150 per person. Given these figures, you would need to serve to somewhere between 13,333 and 16,667 customers a year, or between 44 and 56 customers a night. The question is: Do these figures make sense? Are they too optimistic? If so, you might need to adjust your goals. No matter what the answers are, you would still need to lay out all the other activities and associated costs needed to meet your specific goals.

Once a new growth plan is under way, DDP helps identify key checkpoints and assumption checklists that enable a company to assess not only its current performance but also the ongoing validity of the assumptions on which the plan was and is based. If Starbucks had employed DDP, it might have discovered the flaws in its growth strategy earlier.

Sources: Compiled from R. McGrath and I. MacMillan, *Discovery-Driven Growth*, Cambridge, MA, Harvard University Press, 2009; T. Wailgum, "How IT Systems Can Help Starbucks Fix Itself," *CIO*, January 25, 2008, **cio.com/article/176003/How_IT_Systems_Can_Help_Starbucks_Fix_Itself** (accessed January 2010); M. Weier, "Dunkin' Donuts Uses Business Intelligence in War Against Starbucks," *InformationWeek*, April 16, 2007.

SECTION 3.4 REVIEW QUESTIONS

1. What are the critical questions that a monitoring framework answers?
2. What are the key elements of a diagnostic control system?
3. What is management by exception?
4. What is one of the major pitfalls of variance analysis, from a managerial perspective?

3.5 ACT AND ADJUST: WHAT DO WE NEED TO DO DIFFERENTLY?

Whether a company is interested in growing its business or simply improving its operations, virtually all strategies depend on new projects—creating new products, entering new markets, acquiring new customers or businesses, or streamlining some processes. Most companies approach these new projects with a spirit of optimism rather than objectivity, ignoring the fact that most new projects and ventures fail. What is the chance of failure? Obviously, it depends on the type of project (Slywotzky and Weber, 2007). Hollywood movies have around a 60 percent chance of failure. The same is true for mergers and acquisitions. IT projects fail at the rate of 70 percent. For new food products, the failure rate is 80 percent. For new pharmaceutical products, it is even higher, around 90 percent. Overall, the rate of failure for most new projects or ventures runs between 60 and 80 percent.

A project can fail in a number of different ways, ranging from considering too few options or scenarios, failing to anticipate a competitor's moves, ignoring changes in the economic or social environment, inaccurately forecasting demand, or underestimating the investment required to succeed, just to name a few of the possibilities. This is why it is critical for a company to continually monitor its results, analyze what has happened, determine why it has happened, and adjust its actions accordingly.

Reconsider Harrah's closed-loop marketing system discussed in the Opening Vignette. The system is depicted in Figure 3.4. As the figure indicates, the process has five basic steps:

1. The loop begins by *defining* quantifiable objectives of a marketing campaign or test procedure in the form of expected values or outcomes for customers who are in the experimental test group versus those in the control groups.

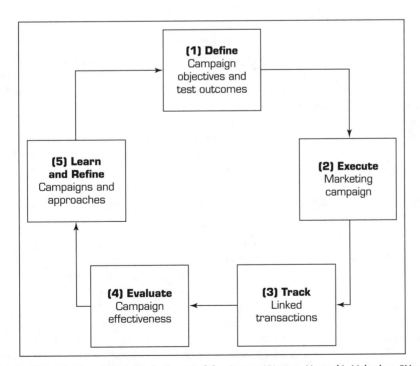

FIGURE 3.4 **Harrah's Closed-Loop Marketing Model.** *Source:* Watson, H., and L. Volonino. "Harrah's High Payoff from Customer Information," *The Data Warehousing Institute Industry Study 2000— Harnessing Customer Information for Strategic Advantage: Technical Challenges and Business Solutions,* Jan 2001. **terry.uga.edu/~hwatson/Harrahs.doc** (accessed January 2010).

2. Next, the campaign or test is *executed*. The campaign is designed to provide the right offer and message at the right time. The selection of particular customers and the treatments they receive are based on their prior experiences with Harrah's.
3. Each customer's response to the campaign is *tracked*. Not only are response rates measured, but other metrics are as well, such as revenues generated by the incentive and whether the incentive induced a positive change in behavior (e.g., increased frequency of visit, profitability of the visit, or cross-play among the various casinos).
4. The effectiveness of a campaign is *evaluated* by determining the net value of the campaign and its profitability relative to other campaigns.
5. Harrah's *learns* which incentives have the most effective influence on customer behavior or provide the best profitability improvement. This knowledge is used to continuously refine its marketing approaches.

Over the years, Harrah's has run literally thousands of these tests. Although all five steps are critical, it is the fact that Harrah's is continually analyzing and adjusting its strategy to produce optimal results that sets it apart from its competitors.

Like Harrah's, most organizations spend an enormous amount of money and time developing plans, collecting data, and generating management reports. However, most of these organizations pale in comparison when it comes to performance management practices. As research from the Saxon Group has suggested (Axson, 2007),

> Most organizations are trying to manage increasingly volatile and complex processes with management practices that are more than half a century old. Detailed five year strategic plans, static annual budgets, calendar-driven reporting, and mind numbing detailed financial forecasts are largely ineffective tools for managing change, uncertainty, and complexity, yet for many organizations they remain the foundation for the management process.

The Saxon Group consulting firm is headed by David Axson, who was formerly with the Hackett Group, a global strategic advisory firm who is a leader in best practice advisory, benchmarking, and transformation consulting services. Axson has personally participated in well over 300 benchmarking studies. Between mid-2005 and mid-2006, the Saxon Group conducted surveys or working sessions with over 1,000 financial executives from North America, Europe, and Asia in an effort to determine the current state of the art with respect to business management. Companies from all major industry groups were represented. Approximately 25 percent of the companies had annual revenues of less than $500 million, 55 percent between $500 million and $5 billion, and 20 percent in excess of $5 billion.

The following is a summary of the Saxon Group's findings (Axson, 2007):

- Only 20 percent of the organizations utilized an integrated performance management system, although this was up from less than 10 percent just 5 years prior.
- Fewer than 3 out of 10 companies developed plans that clearly identified the expected results of major projects or initiatives. Instead, they focused on the wrong things. Financial plans did not show the expected costs and benefits of each initiative nor did they identify the total investment involved. Tactical plans failed to describe major initiatives to be undertaken.
- More than 75 percent of the information reported to management was historic and internally focused; less than 25 percent was predictive of the future or focused on the marketplace.
- The average knowledge worker spent less than 20 percent of his or her time focused on the so-called higher-value analytical and decision support tasks. Basic tasks such

as assembling and validating data needed for higher-valued tasks consumed most of the average knowledge workers time.

The overall impact of the planning and reporting practices of the average company was that management had little time to review results from a strategic perspective, decide what should be done differently, and act on the revised plans. The fact that there was little tie between a company's strategy, tactics, and expected outcomes (Axson, 2007)

> . . . leaves many organizations dangerously exposed when things do not turn out exactly as projected—which is most of the time. Without a clear understanding of the cause-and-effect relationships between tactics and objectives, you can have little confidence that today's actions will produce tomorrow's desired results. Best practice organizations do not necessarily develop better predictions or plans; however, they are far better equipped to quickly identify changes or problems, diagnose the root causes, and take corrective action.

SECTION 3.5 REVIEW QUESTIONS

1. Why do 60 to 80 percent of all new projects or ventures fail?
2. Describe the basic steps in Harrah's closed-loop model.
3. According to the Saxon Group's research results, what are some of the performance management practices of the average company?
4. Why do few companies have time to analyze their strategic and tactical results and take corrective action based on this analysis?

3.6 PERFORMANCE MEASUREMENT

Underlying BPM is a performance measurement system. According to Simons (2002), **performance measurement systems**:

> Assist managers in tracking the implementations of business strategy by comparing actual results against strategic goals and objectives. A performance measurement system typically comprises systematic methods of setting business goals together with periodic feedback reports that indicate progress against goals.

All measurement is about comparisons. Raw numbers are rarely of little value. If you were told that a salesperson completed 50 percent of the deals he or she was working on within a month, that would have little meaning. Now, suppose you were told that the same salesperson had a monthly close rate of 30 percent last year. Obviously, the trend is good. What if you were also told that the average close rate for all salespeople at the company was 80 percent? Obviously, that particular salesperson needs to pick up the pace. As Simons' definition suggests, in performance measurement, the key comparisons revolve around strategies, goals, and objectives.

KPIs and Operational Metrics

There is a difference between a "run of the mill" metric and a "strategically aligned" metric. The term **key performance indicator (KPI)** is often used to denote the latter. A KPI represents a strategic objective and measures performance against a goal. According to

Eckerson (2009), KPIs are multidimensional. Loosely translated, this means that KPIs have a variety of distinguishing features, including:

- **Strategy.** KPIs embody a strategic objective.
- **Targets.** KPIs measure performance against specific targets. Targets are defined in strategy, planning, or budget sessions and can take different forms (e.g., achievement targets, reduction targets, absolute targets).
- **Ranges.** Targets have performance ranges (e.g., above, on, or below target).
- **Encodings.** Ranges are encoded in software, enabling the visual display of performance (e.g., green, yellow, red). Encodings can be based on percentages or more complex rules.
- **Time frames.** Targets are assigned time frames by which they must be accomplished. A time frame is often divided into smaller intervals to provide performance mileposts.
- **Benchmarks.** Targets are measured against a baseline or benchmark. The previous year's results often serve as a benchmark, but arbitrary numbers or external benchmarks may also be used.

A distinction is sometimes made between KPIs that are "outcomes" and those that are "drivers." Outcome KPIs—sometimes known as *lagging indicators*—measure the output of past activity (e.g., revenues). They are often financial in nature, but not always. Driver KPIs—sometimes known as *leading indicators* or *value drivers*—measure activities that have a significant impact on outcome KPIs (e.g., sales leads).

In some circles, driver KPIs are sometimes called *operational KPIs*, which is a bit of an oxymoron (Hatch, 2008). Most organizations collect a wide range of operational metrics. As the name implies, these metrics deal with the operational activities and performance of a company. The following list of examples illustrates the variety of operational areas covered by these metrics:

- **Customer performance.** Metrics for customer satisfaction, speed and accuracy of issue resolution, and customer retention.
- **Service performance.** Metrics for service-call resolution rates, service renewal rates, service level agreements, delivery performance, and return rates.
- **Sales operations.** New pipeline accounts, sales meetings secured, conversion of inquiries to leads, and average call closure time.
- **Sales plan/forecast.** Metrics for price-to-purchase accuracy, purchase order-to-fulfillment ratio, quantity earned, forecast-to-plan ratio, and total closed contracts.

Whether an operational metric is strategic or not depends on the company and its use of the measure. In many instances, these metrics represent critical drivers of strategic outcomes. For instance, Hatch (2008) recalls the case of a mid-tier wine distributor that was being squeezed upstream by the consolidation of suppliers and downstream by the consolidation of retailers. In response, it decided to focus on four operational measures: on-hand/on-time inventory availability, outstanding "open" order value, net-new accounts, and promotion costs and return on marketing investment. The net result of its efforts was a 12 percent increase in revenues in 1 year. Obviously, these operational metrics were key drivers. However, as described in the following section, in many cases, companies simply measure what is convenient with minimal consideration as to why the data are being collected. The result is a significant waste of time, effort, and money.

Problems with Existing Performance Measurement Systems

If you were to survey most companies today, you would have a hard time finding a company that would not claim that it had a performance measurement system (as opposed to a performance management system). The most popular system in use is some variant of Kaplan and Norton's balanced scorecard (BSC). Various surveys and benchmarking studies indicate that anywhere from 50 to over 90 percent of all companies have implemented some form of a BSC at one time or another. For example, every year since 1993, Bain & Company (Rigby and Bilodeau, 2009) has surveyed a broad spectrum of international executives to determine which management tools are in widespread use. The 2008 survey results were based on responses from over 1,400 executives. According to the survey, 53 percent of the companies indicated they were currently using a BSC. In most of these sorts of surveys, when the same executives are asked to describe their BSC, there seems to be some confusion about what constitutes "balance." There is no confusion for the originators of the BSC, Kaplan and Norton (1996):

> Central to the BSC methodology is a holistic vision of a measurement system tied to the strategic direction of the organization. It is based on a four-perspective view of the world, with financial measures supported by customer, internal, and learning and growth metrics.

Yet, as the Saxon Group found, the overwhelming majority of performance measures are financial in nature (65%), are focused on lagging indicators (80%), and are internal rather than external in nature (75%). What these companies really have is a "scorecard"— a set of reports, charts, and specialized displays that enable them to compare actual results with planned results for a miscellaneous collection of measures.

Calendar-driven financial reports are a major component of most performance measurement systems. This is no surprise. First, most of these systems are under the purview of the finance department. Second, most organizations (Saxon puts it at 67%) view the planning process as a financial exercise that is completed annually. Third, most executives place little faith in anything except financial or operational numbers. Research indicates that executives value a variety of different types of information (e.g., financial, operational, market, customer), but they think that outside the financial or operational arenas, most of the data are suspect, and they are unwilling to bet their jobs on the quality of that information.

The drawbacks of using financial data as the core of a performance measurement system are well known. Among the limitations most frequently cited are:

- Financial measures are usually reported by organizational structures (e.g., research and development expenses) and not by the processes that produced them.
- Financial measures are lagging indicators, telling what happened, not why it happened or what is likely to happen in the future.
- Financial measures (e.g., administrative overhead) are often the product of allocations that are not related to the underlying processes that generated them.
- Financial measures are focused on the short term and provide little information about the long term.

Financial myopia is not the only problem plaguing many of the performance measurement systems in operation today. Measurement overload and measurement obliquity are also major problems confronting the current crop of systems.

It is not uncommon to find companies proudly announcing that they are tracking 200 or more measures at the corporate level. It is hard to imagine trying to drive a car with 200 dials on the dashboard. Yet, we seem to have little trouble driving companies with 200 dials on the corporate dashboard, even though we know that humans have major difficulty keeping track of more than a handful of issues and that anything else is simply shoved to the side. This sort of overload is exacerbated by the fact that companies rarely retire the measures they collect. If some new data or request for data comes along, it is simply added to the list. If the number of measures is 200 today, it will be 201 tomorrow, and 202 the day after that. Even though plans change and opportunities and problems come and go with increasing frequency, little effort is made to determine whether the list of measures being tracked is still applicable to the current situation.

For many of the measures being tracked, management lacks direct control. Michael Hammer (2003) called this the *principle of obliquity*. On the one hand, measures such as earnings per share, return on equity, profitability, market share, and customer satisfaction need to be monitored. On the other hand, these measures can only be pursued in an oblique fashion. What can be controlled are the actions of individual workers or employees. Unfortunately, the impact of any individual action on a corporate strategy or business unit strategy is negligible. What is required to tie the critical with the controllable is a strategic business model or methodology that starts at the top and links corporate goals and objectives all the way down to the bottom-level initiatives being carried out by individual performers.

Effective Performance Measurement

A number of books provide recipes for determining whether a collection of performance measures is good or bad. Among the basic ingredients of a good collection are the following:

- Measures should focus on key factors.
- Measures should be a mix of past, present, and future.
- Measures should balance the needs of shareholders, employees, partners, suppliers, and other stakeholders.
- Measures should start at the top and flow down to the bottom.
- Measures need to have targets that are based on research and reality rather than be arbitrary.

As the section on KPIs notes, although all of these characteristics are important, the real key to an effective performance measurement system is to have a good strategy. Measures need to be derived from the corporate and business unit strategies and from an analysis of the key business processes required to achieve those strategies. Of course, this is easier said than done. If it were simple, most organizations would already have effective performance measurement systems in place, but they do not.

Application Case 3.2, which describes the Web-based KPI scorecard system at **Expedia.com**, offers insights into the difficulties of defining both outcome and driver KPIs and the importance of aligning departmental KPIs to overall company objectives.

Application Case 3.2

Expedia.com's Customer Satisfaction Scorecard

Expedia, Inc., is the parent company to some of the world's leading travel companies, providing travel products and services to leisure and corporate travelers in the United States and around the world. It owns and operates a diversified portfolio of well-recognized brands, including **Expedia.com**, **Hotels.com**, **Hotwire.com**, TripAdvisor, Egencia, Classic Vacations, and a range of other domestic and international businesses. The company's travel offerings consist of airline flights, hotel stays, car rentals, destination services, cruises, and package travel provided by various airlines, lodging properties, car rental companies, destination service providers, cruise lines, and other travel product and service companies on a stand-alone and package basis. It also facilitates the booking of hotel rooms, airline seats, car rentals, and destination services from its travel suppliers. It acts as an agent in the transaction, passing reservations booked by its travelers to the relevant airline, hotel, car rental company, or cruise line. Together, these popular brands and innovative businesses make Expedia the largest online travel agency in the world, the third largest travel company in the United States, and the fourth largest travel company in the world. Its mission is to become the largest and most profitable seller of travel in the world, by helping everyone everywhere plan and purchase everything in travel.

Problem

Customer satisfaction is key to Expedia's overall mission, strategy, and success. Because **Expedia.com** is an online business, the customer's shopping experience is critical to Expedia's revenues. The online shopping experience can make or break an online business. It is also important that the customer's shopping experience is mirrored by a good trip experience. Because the customer experience is critical, all customer issues need to be tracked, monitored, and resolved as quickly as possible. Unfortunately, a few years back, Expedia lacked visibility into the "voice of the customer." It had no uniform way of measuring satisfaction, of analyzing the drivers of satisfaction, or of determining the impact of satisfaction on the company's profitability or overall business objectives.

Solution

Expedia's problem was not lack of data. The customer satisfaction group at Expedia knew that it had lots of data. In all, there were 20 disparate databases with 20 different owners. Originally, the group charged one of its business analysts with the task of pulling together and aggregating the data from these various sources into a number of key measures for satisfaction. The business analyst spent 2 to 3 weeks every month pulling and aggregating the data, leaving virtually no time for analysis. Eventually, the group realized that it wasn't enough to aggregate the data. The data needed to be viewed in the context of strategic goals, and individuals had to take ownership of the results.

To tackle the problem, the group decided it needed a refined vision. It began with a detailed analysis of the fundamental drivers of the department's performance and the link between this performance and Expedia's overall goals. Next, the group converted these drivers and links into a scorecard. This process involved three steps:

1. *Deciding how to measure satisfaction.* This required the group to determine which measures in the 20 databases would be useful for demonstrating a customer's level of satisfaction. This became the basis for the scorecards and KPIs.
2. *Setting the right performance targets.* This required the group to determine whether KPI targets had short-term or long-term payoffs. Just because a customer was satisfied with his or her online experience does not mean that the customer was satisfied with the vendor providing the travel service.
3. *Putting data into context.* The group had to tie the data to ongoing customer satisfaction projects.

Figure 3.5 provides a technical overview of the system. The various real-time data sources are fed into a main database (called the Decision Support Factory). In the case of the customer satisfaction group, these include customer surveys, CRM systems, interactive voice response systems, and other customer-service systems. The data in the DSS Factory are loaded on a daily basis into several data marts and multidimensional cubes. Users can access the data in a variety of ways that are relevant to their particular business needs.

Benefits

Ultimately, the customer satisfaction group came up with 10 to 12 objectives that linked directly to Expedia's corporate initiatives. These objectives were, in turn, linked to more than 200 KPIs within the customer satisfaction group. KPI owners can build, manage, and consume their own scorecards, and managers and executives have a transparent view of how well actions are aligning with the strategy. The scorecard also provides the customer satisfaction group with the ability to drill down into the data underlying any of the trends or patterns observed. In the past, all of this would have taken

(Continued)

Application Case 3.2 (Continued)

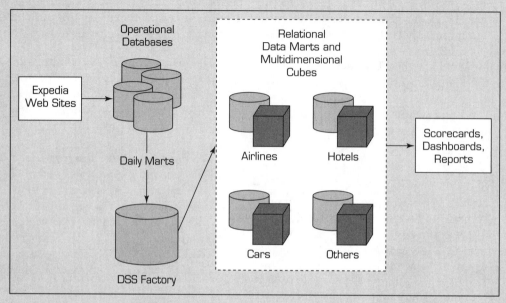

FIGURE 3.5 Expedia Scorecarding System.

weeks or months to do, if it was done at all. With the scorecard, the Customer Service group can immediately see how well it is doing with respect to the KPIs, which, in turn, are reflected in the group's objectives and the company's objectives.

As an added benefit, the data in the system not only support the customer satisfaction group, but also other business units in the company. For example, a frontline manager can analyze airline expenditures on a market-by-market basis to evaluate negotiated contract performance or determine the savings potential for consolidating spend with a single carrier. A travel manager can leverage the business intelligence to discover areas with high volumes of unused tickets or offline bookings and devise strategies to adjust behavior and increase overall savings.

Sources: Based on Microsoft, "Expedia: Scorecard Solution Helps Online Travel Company Measure the Road to Greatness," April 12, 2006, **microsoft.com/casestudies/Case_Study_Detail.aspx? CaseStudyID=49076** (accessed January 2010); R. Smith, "Expedia-5 Team Blog: Technology," April 5, 2007, **expedia-team5.blogspot .com** (accessed January 2010).

SECTION 3.6 REVIEW QUESTIONS

1. What is a performance measurement system?
2. What is a KPI, and what are its distinguishing characteristics?
3. How does a KPI differ from an operational metric?
4. What are some of the drawbacks of relying solely on financial metrics for measuring performance?
5. What is the principle of obliquity?
6. What are some of the characteristics of a "good" collection of performance measures?

3.7 BPM METHODOLOGIES

There is more to performance measurement than simply keeping score. An effective performance measurement system should help do the following:

- Align top-level strategic objectives and bottom-level initiatives.
- Identify opportunities and problems in a timely fashion.
- Determine priorities and allocate resources based on those priorities.
- Change measurements when the underlying processes and strategies change.
- Delineate responsibilities, understand actual performance relative to responsibilities, and reward and recognize accomplishments.
- Take action to improve processes and procedures when the data warrant it.
- Plan and forecast in a more reliable and timely fashion.

A holistic or systematic performance measurement framework is required to accomplish these aims, as well as others. Over the past 40 or more years, various systems have been proposed. Some of them, such as activity-based costing (ABC) or activity-based management, are financially focused. Others, such as total quality management, are process oriented. In the discussion that follows, we examine two widely used approaches that support the basic processes underlying BPM: the balanced scorecard (see **thepalladiumgroup .com**) and Six Sigma (see **motorola.com/motorolauniversity.jsp**).

Balanced Scorecard (BSC)

Probably the best-known and most widely used performance management system is the balanced scorecard (BSC). Kaplan and Norton first articulated this methodology in their *Harvard Business Review* article "The Balanced Scorecard: Measures That Drive Performance," which appeared in 1992. A few years later, in 1996, these same authors produced a groundbreaking book—*The Balanced Scorecard: Translating Strategy into Action*—that documented how companies were using the BSC to not only supplement their financial measures with nonfinancial measures, but also to communicate and implement their strategies. Over the past few years, BSC has become a generic term (much like Coke or Xerox) that is used to represent virtually every type of scorecard application and implementation, regardless of whether it is balanced or strategic. In response to this bastardization of the term, Kaplan and Norton released a new book in 2000, *The Strategy-Focused Organization: How Balanced Scorecard Companies Thrive in the New Business Environment*. This book was designed to reemphasize the strategic nature of the BSC methodology. This was followed a few years later, in 2004, by *Strategy Maps: Converting Intangible Assets into Tangible Outcomes*, which describes a detailed process for linking strategic objectives to operational tactics and initiatives. Finally, their latest book, *The Execution Premium*, published in 2008, focuses on the strategy gap—linking strategy formulation and planning with operational execution.

THE MEANING OF BALANCE   From a high-level viewpoint, the **balanced scorecard (BSC)** is both a performance measurement and a management methodology that helps translate an organization's financial, customer, internal process and **learning** and growth objectives and targets into a set of actionable initiatives. As a measurement methodology, BSC is designed to overcome the limitations of systems that are financially focused. It does this by translating an organization's vision and strategy into a set of interrelated financial and nonfinancial objectives, measures, targets, and initiatives. The nonfinancial objectives fall into one of three perspectives:

- *Customer.*   This objective defines how the organization should appear to its customers if it is to accomplish its vision.

	Strategy Map: Linked Objectives	Balanced Scorecard: Measures and Targets		Strategic Initiatives: Action Plans
Financial	*Increase Net Income*	Net income growth	Increase 25%	
Customer	*Increase Customer Retention*	Maintenance retention rate	Increase 15%	Change licensing and maintenance contracts
Process	*Improve Call Center Performance*	Issue turnaround time	Improve 30%	Standardized call center processes
Learning and Growth	*Reduce Employee Turnover*	Voluntary turnover rate	Reduce 25%	Salary and bonus upgrade

FIGURE 3.6 Strategy Map and Balanced Scorecard.

- *Internal business process.* This objective specifies the processes the organization must excel at in order to satisfy its shareholders and customers.
- *Learning and growth.* This objective indicates how an organization can improve its ability to change and improve in order to achieve its vision.

Basically, nonfinancial objectives form a simple causal chain with "learning and growth" driving "internal business process" change, which produces "customer" outcomes that are responsible for reaching a company's "financial" objectives. A simple chain of this sort is exemplified in Figure 3.6.

In BSC, the term *balance* arises because the combined set of measures is supposed to encompass indicators that are:

- Financial and nonfinancial
- Leading and lagging
- Internal and external
- Quantitative and qualitative
- Short term and long term

ALIGNING STRATEGIES AND ACTIONS As a strategic management methodology, BSC enables an organization to align its actions with its overall strategies. BSC accomplishes this task through a series of interrelated steps. The specific steps that are involved vary from one book to the next. In their latest rendition, Kaplan and Norton (2008) lay out a six-stage process:

1. *Developing and formulating a strategy.* Develop and clarify the organization's mission, values, and vision; identify through strategic analysis the internal and external forces impacting the strategy; and define the organization's strategic direction, specifying where and how the organization will compete.
2. *Planning the strategy.* Convert statements of strategic direction into specific objectives, measures, targets, initiatives, and budgets that guide actions and align the organization for effective strategy execution.

3. ***Aligning the organization.*** Ensure that business-unit and support-unit strategies are in line with the corporate strategy and that employees are motivated to execute the corporate strategy.

4. ***Planning the operations.*** Ensure that the changes required by strategy are translated into changes in operational processes and that resource capacity, operational plans, and budgets reflect the directions and needs of the strategy.

5. ***Monitoring and learning.*** Determine through formal operational review meetings whether short-term financial and operational performances are in line with specified targets and through strategy review meetings whether the overall strategy is being executed successfully.

6. ***Testing and adapting the strategy.*** Determine through strategy testing and adapting meetings whether the strategy is working, whether fundamental assumptions are still valid, and whether the strategy needs to be modified or adapted over time.

On the surface, these steps are very similar to the closed-loop BPM cycle depicted in Figure 3.1. This should not be a surprise, because the BSC methodology is a BPM methodology. However, one thing that distinguishes the BSC methodology from other methodologies is its use of two innovative tools that are unique to the methodology—strategy maps and balanced scorecards.

Strategy maps and balanced scorecards work hand in hand. A **strategy map** delineates the process of value creation through a series of cause-and-effect relationships among the key organizational objectives for all four BSC perspectives—financial, customer, process, and learning and growth. A balanced scorecard tracks the actionable measures and targets associated with the various objectives. Together, strategy maps and BSCs help companies translate, communicate, and measure their strategies.

Figure 3.6 displays a strategy map and balanced scorecard for a fictitious company. It also includes the portfolio of initiatives designed to help the organization achieve its targets. From the map, we can see that the organization has seven objectives across the four BSC perspectives. Like other strategy maps, this one begins at the top with a financial objective (i.e., increase net income). This objective is driven by a customer objective (i.e., increase customer retention). In turn, the customer objective is the result of an internal process objective (i.e., improve call center performance). The map continues down to the bottom of the hierarchy, where the learning objective is found (e.g., reduce employee turnover).

Each objective that appears in a strategy map has an associated measure, target, and initiative. For example, the objective "increase customer retention" might be measured by "maintenance retention rate." For this measure, we might be targeting a 15 percent increase over last year's figures. One of the ways of accomplishing this improvement is by changing (simplifying) licensing and maintenance contracts.

Overall, strategy maps like the one in Figure 3.6 represent a hypothetical model of a segment of the business. When specific names (of people or teams) are assigned to the various initiatives, the model serves to align the bottom-level actions of the organization with the top-level strategic objectives. When actual results are compared with targeted results, a determination can be made about whether the strategy that the hypothesis represents should be called into question or whether the actions of those responsible for various parts of the hypothesis need to be adjusted.

The strategy map shown in Figure 3.6 is relatively simple and straightforward and only represents a segment of the business. Most strategy maps are more complex and cover a broader range of objectives. Because of these complexities, Kaplan and Norton have recently introduced the concept of "strategic themes." "Strategic themes split a strategy into several distinct value-creating processes." Each **strategic theme** represents a collection of related strategic objectives. For example, in Figure 3.6, this collection of objectives might be labeled "customer management." If the fictitious company represented by Figure 3.6 was also trying to increase net income by acquiring a competitor, then it might have a theme of "mergers and acquisitions." The idea behind strategic themes is to simplify the processes of formulating, executing, tracking, and adjusting a strategy.

Six Sigma

Since its inception in the mid-1980s, Six Sigma has enjoyed widespread adoption by companies throughout the world. For the most part, it has not been used as a performance management methodology. Instead, most companies use it as a process improvement methodology that enables them to scrutinize their processes, pinpoint problems, and apply remedies. In recent years, some companies, such as Motorola, have recognized the value of using Six Sigma for strategic purposes. In these instances, Six Sigma provides the means to measure and monitor key processes related to a company's profitability and to accelerate improvement in overall business performance. Because of its focus on business processes, Six Sigma also provides a straightforward way to address performance problems after they are identified or detected.

SIX SIGMA DEFINED   The history of Six Sigma dates to the late 1970s, although many of its ideas can be traced to earlier quality initiatives (see **en.wikipedia.org/wiki/ Six_Sigma**). The term *Six Sigma* was coined by Bill Smith, an engineer at Motorola. In fact, Six Sigma is a federally registered trademark of Motorola. In the late 1970s and early to mid-1980s, Motorola was driven to Six Sigma by internal and external pressures. Externally, it was being beaten in the marketplace by competitors who were able to produce higher-quality products at a lower price. Internally, when a Japanese firm took over a U.S. Motorola factory that manufactured Quasar television and was able to produce TV sets with 5 percent the number of defects produced under regular operating procedures, Motorola executives had to admit that their quality was not good. In response to these pressures, Motorola's CEO, Bob Galvin, led the company down a quality path called Six Sigma. Since that time, hundreds of companies around the world, including General Electric, Allied Signal, DuPont, Ford, Merrill Lynch, Caterpillar, and Toshiba, have used Six Sigma to generate billions of dollars of top-line growth and bottom-line earnings improvement.

In Six Sigma, a business is viewed as a collection of processes. A *business process* is a set of activities that transforms a set of inputs, including suppliers, assets, resources (e.g., capital, material, people), and information into a set of outputs (i.e., goods or services) for another person or process. Table 3.1 lists some categories of business processes that can affect overall corporate performance.

Sigma, σ, is a letter in the Greek alphabet that statisticians use to measure the variability in a process. In the quality arena, *variability* is synonymous with the number of defects. Generally, companies have accepted a great deal of variability in their business processes. In numeric terms, the norm has been 6,200 to 67,000 defects per million opportunities (DPMO). For instance, if an insurance company handles 1 million claims, then under normal operating procedures 6,200 to 67,000 of those claims would be defective (e.g., mishandled, have errors in the forms). This level of variability represents a three- to four-sigma level of performance. To achieve a Six Sigma level of performance, the company would have to reduce the number of defects to no more than 3.4 DPMO. Therefore, **Six Sigma** is a performance management methodology aimed at reducing the number of defects in a business process to as close to zero DPMO as possible.

TABLE 3.1   Categories of Business Processes

Accounting and measurements
Administrative and facility management
Audits and improvements
Business planning and execution
Business policies and procedures
Global marketing and sales
Information management and analysis
Leadership and profitability
Learning and innovation
Maintenance and collaboration
Partnerships and alliances
Production and service
Purchasing and supply chain management
Recruitment and development
Research and development

THE DMAIC PERFORMANCE MODEL   Six Sigma rests on a simple performance improvement model known as DMAIC. Like BPM, **DMAIC** is a closed-loop business improvement model, and it encompasses the steps of defining, measuring, analyzing, improving, and controlling a process. The steps can be described as follows:

1. *Define.*   Define the goals, objectives, and boundaries of the improvement activity. At the top level, the goals are the strategic objectives of the company. At lower levels—department or project levels—the goals are focused on specific operational processes.
2. *Measure.*   Measure the existing system. Establish quantitative measures that will yield statistically valid data. The data can be used to monitor progress toward the goals defined in the previous step.
3. *Analyze.*   Analyze the system to identify ways to eliminate the gap between the current performance of the system or process and the desired goal.
4. *Improve.*   Initiate actions to eliminate the gap by finding ways to do things better, cheaper, or faster. Use project management and other planning tools to implement the new approach.
5. *Control.*   Institutionalize the improved system by modifying compensation and incentive systems, policies, procedures, manufacturing resource planning, budgets, operation instructions, or other management systems.

For new processes, the model that is used is called *DMADV* (define, measure, analyze, design, and verify). Traditionally, DMAIC and DMADV have been used primarily with operational issues. However, nothing precludes the application of these methodologies to strategic issues such as company profitability.

LEAN SIX SIGMA   In recent years, there has been a focus on combining the Six Sigma methodology with the methodology known as **Lean Manufacturing,** *Lean Production,* or simply as *Lean* (see **en.wikipedia.org/wiki/Lean_manufacturing** for a summary of the methodology). The early concepts of lean date back to Henry Ford's use of mass

TABLE 3.2 Comparison of Lean Production with Six Sigma

Feature	Lean	Six Sigma
Purpose	Remove waste	Reduce variation
Focus	Flow focused	Problem focused
Approach	Many small improvements	Removing root causes
Performance measure	Reduced flow time	Uniform output
Results	Less waste with increased efficiency	Less variation with consistent output

Source: Compiled from P. Gupta, *Six Sigma Business Scorecard,* 2nd ed., McGraw-Hill Professional, New York, 2006.

production based on work flow. More recently, the concept has been associated with the production processes used by Toyota (which are known as the Toyota Production System). The term *Lean Production* was coined in 1988 by John Krafcik in an article entitled the "Triumph of the Lean Production System" published in the *Sloan Management Review* (Krafcik, 1988) and based on his master's thesis at the Sloan School of Management at MIT. Before his stint at MIT, Krafcik was a quality engineer at a joint project between Toyota and General Motors.

Six Sigma and Lean Production both deal with quality. The two methodologies are compared in Table 3.2.

As Table 3.2 indicates, Lean focuses on the elimination of waste or non-value-added activities, whereas Six Sigma focuses on reducing the variation or improving the consistency of a process. From a Lean perspective, waste (or "muda") comes in a variety of forms (Six Sigma Institute, 2009):

- Overproduction ahead of demand
- Waiting for the next process step of information
- Transporting materials unnecessarily
- Over- and non-value-added processing
- Inventory that is more than bare minimum
- Unnecessary motion by employees
- Producing nonconforming parts

Lean can be applied to any sort of production or workflow, not just manufacturing. The goal is to examine the flow in order to eliminate waste. The following are some examples of waste that can arise in handling customer requests or complaints at a call center:

- Overproduction—sending all information to everyone
- Waiting—people waiting for information
- Transportation—call transfers to many operators
- Processing—excessive approvals for information release
- Inventory—caller awaiting to be answered
- Motion—retrieving printed instruction manual
- Defect—errors in information provided to callers

What Lean adds to Six Sigma is speed (Poppendieck, 2009). It does this by eliminating non-value-added steps. Once the process flow consists only of value-added steps, Six Sigma can be used to ensure that those steps are performed as consistently as possible. For instance, in the call center example, once the appropriate steps for retrieving printed instructions (motion) are identified, the next step would be to determine how the steps could be carried out in a consistent manner.

THE PAYOFF FROM SIX SIGMA   Six Sigma experts and pundits are quick to praise the methodology and point to companies such as General Electric (GE) and Honeywell as proof of its value. Jack Welch, the former CEO of GE who instituted the program back in the 1995, publically stated that "Six Sigma helped drive operating margins to 18.9 percent in 2000 from 14.8 percent four years earlier." More recently, an earnings announcement from Caterpillar Inc. (2009) indicated that it will realize $3 billion in savings from its Six Sigma program. Others have pointed to companies like Home Depot as evidence that Six Sigma can also fail (Richardson, 2007). Home Depot's well-publicized adoption of Six Sigma was driven by its former CEO Robert Nardelli, who came from GE. When Home Depot's fortunes started to wane and it lost ground to its archrival Lowes, Nardelli departed the company and claims were made that Six Sigma hadn't panned out as promised. In the same vein, opponents of Six Sigma have noted that the framework works well if a company is solely interested in manufacturing efficiency. It does not work well if a company is interested in driving growth through innovation (Hindo, 2007). A statement by a Honeywell spokesman provides a more balanced view of the overall debate when he noted that "Six Sigma is not the end all be all. It is simply a set of process tools. We would never suggest that a company's performance is solely linked to the adoption of these tools" (Richardson, 2007).

Six Sigma is no different than any other business initiative. You make plans and develop metrics to evaluate the progress. When the deployment is not going as expected, you make adjustments. The following can dramatically increase the success of Six Sigma (Wurtzel, 2008):

- *Six Sigma is integrated with business strategy.*   Six Sigma techniques are powerful in reducing process variation. Today, an increasing number of companies are implementing a Six Sigma approach to business excellence as part of the business strategy.
- *Six Sigma supports business objectives.*   Successful deployments are based on some major business challenge or risk that the company can overcome only through Six Sigma. Identifying the challenge means all the company's business leaders are clear about why the company is adopting strategies based on Six Sigma principles.
- *Key executives are engaged in the process.*   A company must involve all key business leaders in helping to design its Six Sigma deployment. Managers will never fully support Six Sigma if they view it as taking away from their resources rather than adding capability and helping them become more successful in achieving their goals; nor will they actively support it if they think it is eating up vital budgetary allotments rather than setting the stage for significant financial payback.
- *Project selection process is based on value potential.*   The most effective Six Sigma companies have rigorous project selection processes driven by an evaluation of how much shareholder value a project can generate. It can be characterized as a trade-off decision comparing value delivered to effort expended.
- *There is a critical mass of projects and resources.*   Some companies start their deployments by training a handful of people and launching a few "demonstration" projects. Others ramp up for immediate corporate-wide deployment, training hundreds of Black Belts and launching dozens of projects within the first 6 months. In this context, a Black Belt refers to an employee who is trained or certified in Six Sigma and who devotes 100 percent of his or her time to the execution of a Six

Sigma project. Either approach is workable, but for every company, there is a critical level of Six Sigma effort.

- ***Projects in process are actively managed.*** Given that most companies want to generate measurable, significant results within 6 months or a year, the tendency is to push as many projects into the Lean Six Sigma deployment as possible. It is better to focus on getting a few high-potential projects done right than to just flood the workplace with dozens of less-important projects. With the right resources working on the right projects, learning and results are maximized by short cycle times.
- ***Team leadership skills are emphasized.*** Use of Six Sigma does involve some technical skills—the ability to process and analyze data, for example. But good leadership skills are even more important. This emphasis on leadership also relates to how a company chooses people to fill Black Belt roles. Placing the most promising people in the Black Belt role is painful at first, yet it yields fast results and a rapid transformation of the organization.
- ***Results are rigorously tracked.*** Six Sigma results should "pay as you go" and be confirmed by objective parties. Too many companies discount the necessity of having a reliable means to judge project results and impact, or they underestimate the difficulty in creating such a system. As a deployment is planned, a company must think in terms of leading measurements or key performance indicators of the potential financial results. At a minimum, project cycle times and project values must be measured on a regular basis and to gain an understanding of the level of variation in these numbers.

In an effort to increase the probability of success of their Six Sigma initiatives, some companies, such as Motorola and Duke University Hospital, have combined these initiatives with the BSC initiatives. In this way, their quality initiatives are directly tied to their strategic objectives and targets. In the same vein, Gupta (2006) developed a hybrid methodology called Six Sigma Business Scorecard that directly ties the process improvement aspects of Six Sigma to the financial perspective of the BSC. The benefits and structure of this combination are discussed in Technology Insight 3.1.

TECHNOLOGY INSIGHT 3.1   BSC Meets Six Sigma

A recent book by Praveen Gupta (2006) entitled *Six Sigma Business Scorecard* provides a summary of the differences between the balanced scorecard and Six Sigma methodologies. This summary is shown in Table 3.3. In a nutshell, BSC is focused on improving strategy, whereas Six Sigma is focused on improving process.

Because of these differences, most companies have treated their BSC and Six Sigma implementations as separate initiatives. However, according to Stan Elbaum, senior vice president of research at Aberdeen Group in Boston, these are complementary programs. The true benefits of each cannot be achieved unless the two are integrated (Leahy, 2005). The BSC approach enables companies to quickly and accurately identify critical performance weaknesses and uncover opportunities for improvement and growth. What BSC has a hard time doing is showing how to fix the performance problems. In contrast, Six Sigma projects often flounder because project teams "bounce all over the organization looking for performance weaknesses or focusing attention on areas where improvements will yield only marginal returns" (Leahy, 2005). The methodologies are complementary because BSC provides the strategic context for targeted improvement initiatives, and Six Sigma can dig down to the underlying causes of a performance shortfall and provide solutions for closing the gap between targets and results.

TABLE 3.3 Comparison of Balanced Scorecard and Six Sigma

Balanced Scorecard	Six Sigma
Strategic management system	Performance measurement system
Relates to the longer-term view of the business	Provides snapshot of business' performance and identifies measures that drive performance toward profitability
Designed to develop balanced set of measures	Designed to identify a set of measurements that impact profitability
Identifies measurements around vision and values	Establishes accountability for leadership for wellness and profitability
Critical management processes are to clarify vision/strategy, communicate, plan, set targets, align strategic initiatives, and enhance feedback	Includes all business processes—management and operational
Balances customer and internal operations without a clearly defined leadership role	Balances management and employees' roles; balances costs and revenue of heavy processes
Emphasizes targets for each measurement	Emphasizes aggressive rate of improvement for each measurement, irrespective of target
Emphasizes learning of executives based on the feedback	Emphasizes learning and innovation at all levels based on the process feedback. Enlists all employees' participation
Focuses on growth	Focuses on maximizing profitability
Heavy on strategic content	Heavy on execution for profitability
Management system consisting of measures	Measurement system based on process management

Source: P. Gupta, *Six Sigma Business Scorecard*, 2nd ed., McGraw-Hill Professional, New York, 2006.

A while back, a survey (Docherty, 2005) of companies that had adopted BSC or Six Sigma programs revealed that nearly half the programs had failed to break even in the first 3 years of adoption, but those companies that made them work had achieved substantial financial benefits. The companies with the biggest net returns were those that had found a way to integrate the two methods. Integration was achieved by doing the following:

- ***Translating their strategy into quantifiable objectives.*** This was done by mapping the strategy and using a scorecard to monitor the associated metrics.
- ***Cascading objectives through the organization.*** They broke enterprise-wide goals into lower-level operational objectives by applying the causal reasoning underlying Six Sigma.
- ***Setting targets based on the voice of the customer.*** They used BSC and Six Sigma together to ensure that operational targets would directly impact customer expectations.
- ***Implementing strategic projects using Six Sigma.*** They used Six Sigma to drive improvements in product and process quality.
- ***Executing processes in a consistent fashion to deliver business results.*** They viewed the organization from a process perspective. Six Sigma was used to control process variation, and process measures were included in their BSC.

Companies that have successfully combined the two methodologies say that they can't understand why an organization would want to do one without the other. However, they also

(Continued)

advise that it takes about a year to provide the necessary workforce training and to overcome existing cultural and organizational barriers.

Sources: Compiled from P. Gupta, *Six Sigma Business Scorecard,* 2nd ed., McGraw-Hill Professional, New York, 2006; P. Docherty, "From Six Sigma to Strategy Execution," 2005, **i-solutionsglobal.com/secure/ FromSixSigmaToStrateg_AAC8C.pdf** (accessed January 2010); and T. Leahy, "The One-Two Performance Punch." *Business Finance,* February 2005, **businessfinancemag.com/magazine/archives/article. html?articleID=14364** (accessed January 2010).

SECTION 3.7 REVIEW QUESTIONS

1. What are the characteristics of an effective performance measurement system?
2. What are the four perspectives in BSC?
3. What does the term *balanced* refer to in BSC?
4. How does a BSC align strategies and actions?
5. What is a strategy map?
6. What is a strategic theme?
7. What does Six Sigma refer to?
8. What are the basic processes in the DMAIC model?
9. Compare Lean Production with Six Sigma.
10. What are some of the ways that the success of Six Sigma implementations is improved?
11. Compare BSC with Six Sigma.
12. How can BSC and Six Sigma be integrated?

3.8 BPM TECHNOLOGIES AND APPLICATIONS

At the beginning of this chapter, we defined *BPM* as an umbrella term covering the processes, methodologies, metrics, and technologies used by enterprises to measure, monitor, and manage business performance. Sections 3.3 through 3.8 examined the process, metrics, and methodologies. This section briefly describes the remaining element—the supporting technologies and applications.

BPM Architecture

The term **system architecture** refers to both the logical and physical design of a system. The *logical design* entails the functional elements of a system and their interactions. The *physical design* specifies how the logical design is actually implemented and deployed across a specific set of technologies such as Web browsers, application servers, communication protocols, databases, and the like. From a physical standpoint, any particular BPM solution or implementation is likely to be quite complex. From a logical standpoint, they are usually quite simple. Logically speaking, a BPM system consists of three basic parts or layers (see Figure 3.7). Included are:

- *BPM applications.* This layer supports the BPM processes used to transform user interactions and source data into budgets, plans, forecasts, reports, analysis, and the like. The particular applications used from one BPM implementation to the next will vary from organization to organization, depending on their specific needs and strategic focus. Any BPM solution should be flexible and extensible enough to allow an organization to find its own path, including decisions about which applications to include and when to roll them out. Practically speaking, however, there are some BPM applications that are used quite frequently. These applications are discussed momentarily.

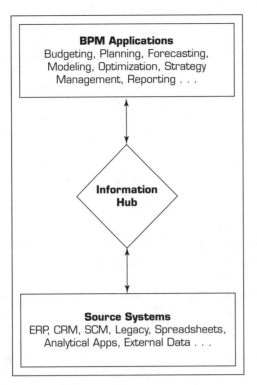

FIGURE 3.7 BPM Logical System Architecture.

- *Information Hub.* Most BPM systems require data and information from a variety of source systems (e.g., ERP or CRM systems). The data and information can be accessed in a number of ways. However, in a well-designed BPM system, the data from these systems are usually mapped to and stored at a central location, typically a data warehouse or data mart.

- *Source systems.* This layer represents all of the data sources containing information fed into the BPM information hub. For most large enterprises, this will include financial and other operational data from a variety of enterprise systems. Complete solutions will also access key external information, such as industry trends and competitor intelligence, to provide deeper context and insight into company performance. Rarely are source data accessed directly by the BPM applications. Typically, an extraction, transformation, and load (ETL) application, an enterprise application integration system, or Web Services are used to move or connect the data to the information hub.

BPM APPLICATIONS In BPM, a wide variety of applications are needed to cover the closed-loop processes running from strategic planning to operational planning and budgeting to monitoring to adjustment and action. Despite the breadth of the processes, the industry analyst group Gartner contends that the majority of the processes can be handled by the following applications (Chandler et al., 2009):

1. *Strategy management.* Strategy management applications provide a packaged approach to support strategic planning, modeling, and monitoring to improve corporate performance, accelerate management decision making, and facilitate collaboration. These solutions are usually tied to strategy maps or methodologies

such as the balanced scorecard. Strategy management can encompass capabilities for the following:

- Creation and and evaluation of high-level business plans using a "base case plus" or "initiative-based" approach, along with scenario modeling.
- Initiative/goal management using project-management-like tools to enable responsible managers to execute specific tasks related to a strategy.
- Scorecards and strategy maps to record strategies, objectives, and tasks; measure performance; and provide a collaborative environment for effective, enterprise-wide communication.
- Dashboards (or cockpits) to aggregate and display metrics and KPIs so they can be examined at a glance before further exploration via additional BI tools.

BPM suites should, at the very least, provide dashboard capabilities to help display performance information in a way that is easily understood by users. However, more-sophisticated organizations are implementing strategy maps (linked frameworks of KPIs) using scorecard software to link BPM to other aspects of performance management. Strategy management is, therefore, becoming an increasingly important aspect of BPM suites.

2. **Budgeting, planning, and forecasting.**   These applications support the development of all aspects of budgets, plans, and forecasts. They encompass short-term financially focused budgets, longer-term plans, and high-level strategic plans. These applications should deliver workflow capabilities to manage budget/plan creation, submission, and approval, and they provide the facility to dynamically create forecasts and scenarios. They should also support the development of an enterprise-wide planning model that links operational plans to financial budgets. In addition, they must be capable of sharing data with domain-specific applications such as supply chain planning.

3. **Financial consolidation.**   This type of application enables organizations to reconcile, consolidate, summarize, and aggregate financial data based on different accounting standards and federal regulations. These applications are a fundamental part of BPM because they create the audited, enterprise-level view of financial information that must be shared with other BPM applications to analyze variance from targets.

4. **Profitability modeling and optimization.**   These applications include activity-based costing (ABC) applications that determine and allocate costs at a highly granular level and activity-based management applications that provide capabilities to enable users to model the impact on profitability of different cost and resource allocation strategies. Some applications have moved beyond the traditional ABC focus to enable revenue to be allocated in addition to costs for model packaging, bundling, pricing, and channel strategies.

5. **Financial, statutory, and management reporting.**   BPM applications require specialized reporting tools that can format output as structured financial statements. They may also need to support specific generally accepted accounting principles (GAAP) presentation rules, such as U.S. GAAP or international financial reporting standards. They also include visualization techniques that are specifically designed to support the analysis of variance from budgets or targets, such as hyperbolic trees.

Commercial BPM Suites

The BPM market consists of those software companies offering suites with at least three of the core BPM applications (i.e., budgeting, planning, and forecasting; profitability modeling and **optimization**; scorecarding; financial consolidation; and statutory and financial reporting). According to estimates by Gartner (Chandler et al., 2009), the commercial software market for BPM suites in 2007 was approximately $1.8 billion in license fees and maintenance revenue. This represented a 19 percent increase from 2006. In contrast, the research firm International Data Corporation (IDC) estimated that the BPM application market was approximately $2 billion in 2007 and was expected to grow to $3.2 billion in 2012 (Vessette and McDonough, 2008). This is a growth rate of over 10 percent per annum.

The primary driver for this growth is that users continue to replace spreadsheet-based applications with more-robust analytics. BPM is relevant to every organization, regardless of industry sector, because all organizations need analytics (e.g., profitability analysis and performance to financial planning), as well as the management information (e.g., financial management reports, budgets, and statutory reports) to support the CFO and finance team and to deliver management information to the leadership team, which is one of the main areas of focus for BPM.

Over the past 3 to 4 years, the biggest change in the BPM market has been the consolidation of the BPM vendors. A few years back, the BPM market was dominated by the pure-play vendors Hyperion, Cognos, and SAS. This was before Oracle acquired Hyperion, IBM acquired Cognos, and SAP acquired Business Objects. Today, the market is dominated by the mega-vendors, including Oracle Hyperion, IBM Cognos, and SAP Business Objects. These mega-vendors, along with Infor and SAS, account for 70 percent of the BPM market.

As it does with a number of the software markets that it follows, Gartner has established a *magic quadrant* for vendors of CPM suites (Chandler et al., 2009). The quadrant positions companies in terms of their ability to execute (as a company) and the completeness of their visions. The combination of the two dimensions results in four categories of companies (see Table 3.4). According to Gartner, Oracle Hyperion, SAP Business Objects, and IBM Cognos are all in the Leaders quadrant. This simply validates the fact that the mega-vendors lead the BPM market.

The fact that a suite is required to have at least three of the basic BPM applications in order to be considered for Gartner's magic quadrant means that the various suites provide similar sorts of capabilities. Table 3.5 provides a summary of the various applications associated with the three BPM suites in the Leaders quadrant.

BPM Market versus the BI Platform Market

In addition to the BPM market, Gartner also follows the BI platform market. In Gartner's terms, a BI platform differs from simple niche BI offerings in terms of its overall breadth of capabilities. According to Gartner, the key functions include (McKay, 2009):

- BI infrastructure
- Metadata management
- BI application development
- Workflow and collaboration

TABLE 3.4   Gartner's Magic Quadrant

Execution	Vision	
	Limited	Strong
Strong	Challengers	Leaders
Limited	Niche	Visionaries

TABLE 3.5	**BPM Applications Provided by SAP, Oracle, and IBM**		
BPM Application	SAP Business Objects Enterprise Performance Management	Oracle Hyperion Performance Management	IBM Cognos BI and Financial Performance Management
BPM Application	SAP Business Objects Enterprise Performance Management	Oracle Hyperion Performance Management	IBM Cognos BI and Financial Performance Management
Strategy Management	Strategy Management	Strategic Finance, Performance Scorecard	BI Scorecarding, BI Analysis
Budgeting, Planning, and Forecasting	Business Planning and Consolidation	Planning	Planning
Financial Consolidation	Financial Consolidation, Intercompany Reconciliation	Financial Management	Controller
Profitability Modeling and Optimization	Profitability and Cost Management	Profitability and Cost Management	
Financial, Statutory, and Management Reporting	Business Objects BI, XBRL Publishing	Performance Scorecard	BI Reporting, BI Scorecarding, BI Dashboards
Other BPM Applications	Spend Performance Management, Supply Chain Performance Management	Capital Asset Planning, Workforce Planning, Integrated Operational Planning	
Data Management Applications	Financial Information Management	Financial Data Quality Management, Data Relationship Management	DecisionStream

Source: Compiled from **sap.com/solutions/sapbusinessobjects/large/enterprise-performance-management/index.epx** (accessed January 2010); **oracle.com/appserver/business-intelligence/hyperion-financial-performance-management/hyperion-financial-performance-management.html** (accessed January 2010); **ibm.com/software/data/cognos** (accessed January 2010).

- Reporting
- Dashboards
- Ad hoc querying
- Microsoft Office integration
- OLAP
- Advanced visualization
- Predictive modeling and data mining
- Scorecards

In comparison to the BPM market, the size of the BI platform market is much larger. Various estimates placed the overall size of the BPM market in 2009 at anywhere between $2 billion to $3.5 billion, growing at a rate of at least 25 percent per annum. In contrast, the market for BI (platform) software was estimated at more than $5 billion for 2007, with a growth rate exceeding 10 percent per annum.

While all of the BPM market leaders also offer BI platforms, the BI platform market is much more diverse than the BPM market. In 2009, Gartner's "Leaders" category in its BI platform magic quadrant included not only the BPM market leaders—IBM, Oracle, and SAP—but also Information Builders, Microsoft, SAS, and MicroStrategy. All of the vendors in this quadrant have strong offerings, differing slightly in ease of use and analytical capabilities. Among these leaders, MicroStrategy is somewhat distinguished by its connection with Teradata University (**teradatastudentnetwork.com**), which enables university students to utilize their offering for education and research purposes.

SECTION 3.8 REVIEW QUESTIONS

1. What is a logical system architecture?
2. What are the three key elements of a BPM architecture?
3. Describe the major categories of BPM applications.
4. What major change has occurred in the BPM market in the last 3 to 4 years?
5. What are the basic categories in Gartner's magic quadrant? Who are some of the vendors in the BPM Leaders quadrant?
6. What is a BI platform? Who are the major vendors in Gartner's BI platform magic quadrant?

3.9 PERFORMANCE DASHBOARDS AND SCORECARDS

Scorecards and dashboards are common components of most, if not all, performance management systems, performance measurement systems, BPM suites, and BI platforms. **Dashboards** and **scorecards** both provide visual displays of important information that is consolidated and arranged on a single screen so that information can be digested at a single glance and easily explored. A typical dashboard is shown in Figure 3.8. This particular dashboard displays a variety of KPIs for a hypothetical software company that produces specialized charting and visual display components for software developers. The company sells its products over the Web and uses banner ads placed at a handful of sites to drive traffic to the main Web page. From the dashboard, it is easy to see that the banner ad placed on "The Code House" site is driving the most traffic to its site and that "The Code House" has the highest percentage of click-throughs per impression (which in this case shows that every 100 times the software company's banner ad is displayed on "The Code House" site, a little over two of the visitors will click the banner ad). Overall, the banner pipeline indicates that there have been over 205 million impressions. These have resulted in 2.2 million visits to the main page followed by 1.2 visits to the product pages and eventually 1 million downloads. Finally, the gauges indicate that the percentage increase year-to-date in "visits through banner(s)" and "visitors who download(ed)" has exceeded their targets (i.e., they are above shaded zones), and the cost per click is about 80 cents. This particular dashboard enables end users to see the differences in the banner statistics and the metrics on the gauges by time period or product (the dropdowns on the upper right).

Dashboards versus Scorecards

In the trade journals, the terms *dashboard* and *scorecard* are used almost interchangeably, even though, as we saw in Table 3.4, the various BPM vendors usually offer separate dashboard and scorecard applications. Although dashboards and scorecards have much in common, there are differences between the two. On the one hand, executives, managers, and staff use scorecards to monitor strategic alignment and success with strategic objectives and targets. As noted, the best-known example is the BSC. On the other hand, dashboards are used at the operational and tactical levels. Managers, supervisors,

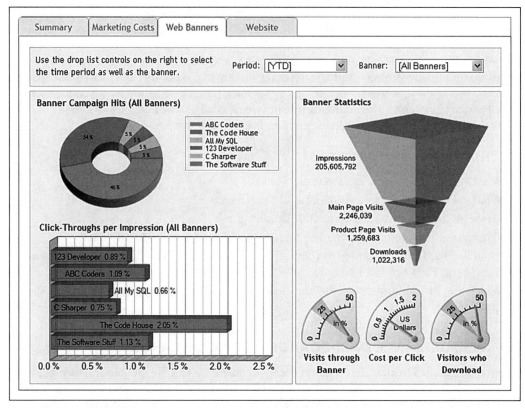

FIGURE 3.8   Sample Dashboard.   *Source:* Dundas Data Visualization, Inc., **dundas.com/Gallery/Flash/Dashboards/index.aspx** (accessed January 2009).

and operators use operational dashboards to monitor detailed operational performance on a weekly, daily, or even hourly basis. For example, operational dashboards might be used to monitor production quality. In the same vein, managers and staff use tactical dashboards to monitor tactical initiatives. For example, tactical dashboards might be used to monitor a marketing campaign or sales performance.

Dashboard Design

Dashboards are not a new concept. Their roots can be traced at least to the EIS of the 1980s. Today, dashboards are ubiquitous. For example, a few years back, Forrester Research estimated that over 40 percent of the largest 2,000 companies in the world use the technology (Ante and McGregor, 2006). The Dashboard Spy Web site (**dashboardspy.com/about**) provides further evidence of their ubiquity. The site contains descriptions and screenshots of thousands of BI dashboards, scorecards, and BI interfaces used by businesses of all sizes and industries, nonprofits, and government agencies. One of the more recent dashboards covered by the site—New York City's Citywide Performance Reporting System—is described in detail in the case at the end of the chapter.

According to Eckerson (2006), a well-known expert on BI in general and dashboards in particular, the most distinctive feature of a dashboard is its three layers of information:

1. *Monitoring.*   Graphical, abstracted data to monitor key performance metrics.
2. *Analysis.*   Summarized dimensional data to analyze the root cause of problems.
3. *Management.*   Detailed operational data that identify what actions to take to resolve a problem.

Because of these layers, dashboards pack of lot of information into a single screen. According to Few (2005), "The fundamental challenge of dashboard design is to display all the required information on a single screen, clearly and without distraction, in a manner that can be assimilated quickly." To speed assimilation of the numbers, the numbers need to be placed in context. This can be done by comparing the numbers of interest to other baseline or target numbers, by indicating whether the numbers are good or bad, by denoting whether a trend is better or worse, and by using specialized display widgets or components to set the comparative and evaluative context.

Some of the common comparisons that are typically made in a BPM system include comparisons against past values, forecasted values, targeted values, benchmark or average values, multiple instances of the same measure, and the values of other measures (e.g., revenues vs. costs). In Figure 3.8, the various KPIs are set in context by comparing them with targeted values, the revenue figure is set in context by comparing it with marketing costs, and the figures for the various stages of the sales pipeline are set in context by comparing one stage with another.

Even with comparative measures, it is important to specifically point out whether a particular number is good or bad and whether it is trending in the right direction. Without these sorts of evaluative designations, it can be time consuming to determine the status of a particular number or result. Typically, either specialized visual objects (e.g., traffic lights) or visual attributes (e.g., color coding) are used to set the evaluative context. Again, for the dashboard in Figure 3.8, color coding is used with the gauges to designate whether the KPI is good or bad, and green up arrows are used with the various stages of the sales pipeline to indicate whether the results for those stages are trending up or down and whether up or down is good or bad. Although not used in this particular example, additional colors—red and orange, for instance—could be used to represent other states on the various gauges.

What to Look for in a Dashboard

Although performance dashboards and standard performance scorecards differ, they do share some of the same characteristics. First, they both fit within the larger BPM or performance measurement system. This means that their underlying architecture is the BI or performance management architecture of the larger system. Second, all well-designed dashboards and scorecards possess the following characteristics (Novell, 2009):

- They use visual components (e.g., charts, performance bars, sparklines, gauges, meters, stoplights) to highlight, at a glance, the data and exceptions that require action.
- They are transparent to the user, meaning that they require minimal training and are extremely easy to use.
- They combine data from a variety of systems into a single, summarized, unified view of the business.
- They enable drill-down or drill-through to underlying data sources or reports, providing more detail about the underlying comparative and evaluative context.
- They present a dynamic, real-world view with timely data refreshes, enabling the end user to stay up to date with any recent changes in the business.
- They require little, if any, customized coding to implement, deploy, and maintain.

Data Visualization

Data visualization has been defined as, "the use of visual representations to explore, make sense of, and communicate data" (Few, 2008). It is closely related to the fields of information graphics, information visualization, scientific visualization, and statistical graphics. Until recently, the major forms of data visualization available in both BPM and BI applications have included charts and graphs, as well as the other types of visual elements used in scorecards and dashboards (e.g., stoplights and gauges). As Seth Grimes (2009) has noted, there is a "growing palate" of data visualization techniques and tools that enable the users of BPM and BI systems to better "communicate relationships, add historical context, uncover hidden correlations and tell persuasive stories that clarify and call to action."

In BPM and BI applications, the key challenges for visualization have revolved around the intuitive representation of large, complex data sets with multiple dimensions and measures. For the most part, the typical charts, graphs, and other visual elements used in these applications usually involve two dimensions, sometimes three, and fairly small subsets of data sets. In contrast, the data in these systems reside in a data warehouse. At a minimum, these warehouses involve a range of dimensions (e.g., product, location, organizational structure, time), a range of measures, and millions of cells of data. In an effort to address these challenges, a number of researchers have developed a variety of new visualization techniques.

Some of these new techniques involve extensions to standard charts and graphs. For instance, the interactive bubble charts available at the Gapminder Web site (**gapminder.org**) provide an intriguing way of exploring world health and population data from a multidimensional perspective. Figure 3.9 depicts the sorts of displays available at the site (this is a facsimile, not an actual chart from the site). On the surface, this particular figure shows the relationship between life expectancy and fertility rate for nations of the world. Each bubble represents a single nation. Within the chart, the size of a bubble represents the population size of the nation, while the color represents the

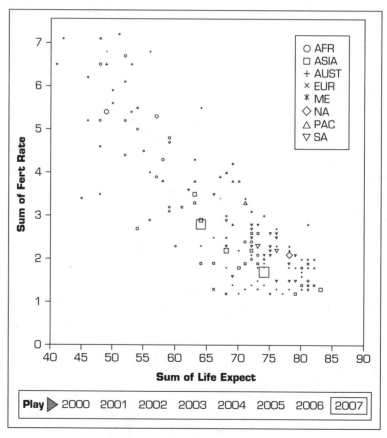

FIGURE 3.9 Interactive Bubble Chart of Population Data.

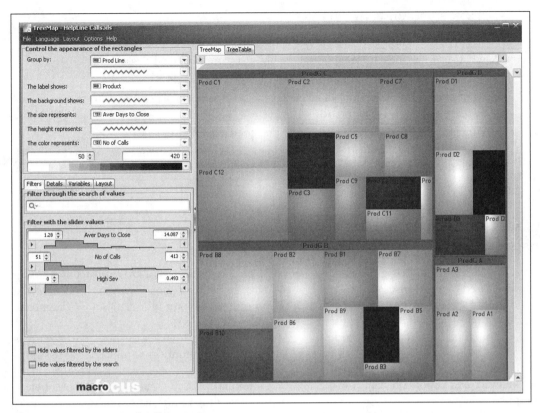

FIGURE 3.10 **Treemap of Call Center Data.**

continent where the nation is located. At the bottom of the display is a menu that enables the user to select a particular year for analysis along with a button for running an animation showing the changes in values overtime.

Other techniques involve relatively new forms of visualizations. One example is the treemap display devised by Ben Shneiderman at the University of Maryland. A treemap displays hierarchical data as a set of nested rectangles (see Figure 3.10). For this reason, it is well suited to display data associated with the dimensions in a data warehouse. Each branch of a hierarchical dimension can be represented by a rectangle, which is then tiled with smaller rectangles representing the children (or sub-branches) of the parent (branch). The area of each rectangle is proportional to a specified measure (usually some aggregate total). For example, a treemap could be used by a software company to analyze total defects associated with particular releases of their product offerings. At the top level, the rectangles could be used to display the number of issues associated with particular product categories. Within each of the rectangles, the smaller tiled rectangles could be used to represent the total issues associated with the individual products within those categories. Additionally, the color of the rectangles could be used to represent the length of time the current release has been on the market. In general, a treemap enables the user to spot patterns that would be difficult to spot in other ways. Also, because treemaps make efficient use of space, they can be used to display thousands of items at one time.

Other examples of new data visualization techniques can be found at **webdesignerdepot.com/2009/06/50-great-examples-of-data-visualization** and **smashingmagazine.com/2007/08/02/data-visualization-modern-approaches**. Also, Grimes (2009) provides a listing and description of major data visualization vendors and products (e.g., **tableausoftware.com**) that specialize in BPM and BI applications.

SECTION 3.9 REVIEW QUESTIONS

1. What are the major differences between a scorecard and a dashboard?
2. What distinguishes an operational dashboard from a tactical dashboard?
3. What layers of information are provided by a dashboard?
4. What criteria are important in selecting the particular display widgets to use with particular metrics on a dashboard?
5. What are the characteristics of a well-designed dashboard?
6. What is data visualization? What are some of the major challenges associated with displaying BPM and BI application data.

Chapter Highlights

- BPM refers to the processes, methodologies, metrics, and technologies used by enterprises to measure, monitor, and manage business performance.
- BPM is an outgrowth of BI, and it incorporates many of its technologies, applications, and techniques.
- BI has become the term describing the technology used to access, analyze, and report on data relevant to an enterprise.
- BI practices and software are almost always part of an overall BPM solution.
- The primary difference between BI and BPM is that BPM is always strategy driven.
- BPM encompasses a closed-loop set of processes that link strategy to execution in order to optimize business performance.
- The key processes in BPM are strategize, plan, monitor, act, and adjust.
- Strategy answers the question "Where do we want to go in the future?"
- Decades of research highlight the gap between strategy and execution.
- The gap between strategy and execution is found in the broad areas of communication, alignment, focus, and resources.
- Operational and tactical plans address the question "How do we get to the future?"
- The tactics and initiatives defined in an operational plan need to be directly linked to key objectives and targets in the strategic plan.
- An organization's strategic objectives and key metrics should serve as top-down drivers for the allocation of the organization's tangible and intangible assets.
- Monitoring addresses the question of "How are we doing?"

- BSCs, performance dashboards, project monitoring systems, human resources systems, and financial reporting systems are all examples of diagnostic control systems.
- Most monitoring focuses on negative variances and pays little attention to underlying assumptions or strategies.
- Conventional planning suffers from a number of biases, including confirmation, recency, winner's, and social or political bias.
- Discovery-driven planning provides a way to systematically uncover problematic assumptions that otherwise remain unnoticed or unchallenged in the planning and monitoring process.
- The failure rate for new projects and ventures runs between 60 and 80 percent.
- The overall impact of the planning and reporting practices of the average company is that management has little time to review results from a strategic perspective, decide what should be done differently, and act on the revised plans.
- Performance measurement systems assist managers in tracking the implementation of business strategy by comparing actual results against strategic goals and objectives.
- The drawbacks of using financial data as the core of a performance measurement system are well known.
- There is a difference between a "run of the mill" metric and a "strategically aligned" metric.
- Performance measures need to be derived from the corporate and business unit strategies and from an analysis of the key business processes required to achieve those strategies.
- Probably the best-known and most widely used performance management system is the BSC.

- Central to the BSC methodology is a holistic vision of a measurement system tied to the strategic direction of the organization.
- As a measurement methodology, BSC is designed to overcome the limitations of systems that are financially focused.
- Calendar-driven financial reports are a major component of most performance measurement systems.
- As a strategic management methodology, BSC enables an organization to align its actions with its overall strategies.
- In BSC, strategy maps provide a way to formally represent an organization's strategic objectives and the causal connections among them.
- Most companies use Six Sigma as a process improvement methodology that enables them to scrutinize their processes, pinpoint problems, and apply remedies.
- Six Sigma is a performance management methodology aimed at reducing the number of defects in a business process to as close to zero DPMO as possible.
- Six Sigma uses DMAIC, a closed-loop business improvement model that involves the steps of defining, measuring, analyzing, improving, and controlling a process.
- In recent years, there has been a focus on combining the Six Sigma methodology with the Lean strategy.
- Lean focuses on the elimination of waste or non-value-added activities, whereas Six Sigma focuses

on reducing the variation or improving the consistency of a process.
- Substantial performance benefits can be gained by integrating BSC and Six Sigma.
- The standard BPM architecture is multilayered and consists of BPM applications, an information hub, and data from a variety of source systems.
- The major BPM applications include strategy management; budgeting, planning, and forecasting; financial consolidation; profitability analysis and optimization; and financial, statutory, and management reporting.
- Over the past 3 to 4 years, the biggest change in the BPM market has been the consolidation of the BPM vendors.
- Scorecards and dashboards are common components of most, if not all, performance management systems, performance measurement systems, and BPM suites.
- Although scorecards and dashboards both provide visual displays of performance, there are significant differences between them.
- The most distinctive feature of a dashboard is its three layers: monitoring, analysis, and management.
- The fundamental challenge of dashboard design is to display all the required information on a single screen, clearly and without distraction, in a manner that can be assimilated quickly.
- Newer data visualization techniques have been developed to assist with the analysis of the types of large, complex multidimensional data sets found in BPM and BI applications.

Key Terms

balanced scorecard (BSC)
business performance management (BPM)
critical success factors (CSFs)
dashboards
data visualization
diagnostic control system
DMAIC
key performance indicator (KPI)
Lean Manufacturing
learning
optimization
performance measurement systems
scorecards
Six Sigma
strategic goal
strategic objective
strategic vision
strategy map
strategic theme
system architecture

Questions for Discussion

1. SAP uses the term *strategic enterprise management* (SEM), Cognos uses the term *corporate performance management* (CPM), and Hyperion uses the term *business performance management* (BPM). Are they referring to the same basic ideas? Provide evidence to support your answer.

2. BPM encompasses five basic processes: strategize, plan, monitor, act, and adjust. Select one of these processes and discuss the types of software tools and applications that are available to support it. Figure 3.1 provides some hints. Also, refer to Bain & Company's list of management tools for assistance (**bain.com/management_tools/home.asp**).

3. Select a public company of interest. Using the company's 2008 annual report, create three strategic financial objectives for 2009. For each objective, specify a strategic goal or target. The goals should be consistent with the company's 2008 financial performance.

4. Netflix's strategy of moving to online video downloads has been widely discussed in a number of articles that can be found online. What are the basic objectives of Netflix's strategy? What are some of the major assumptions underlying the strategy? Given what you know about discovery-driven planning, do these assumptions seem reasonable?

5. In recent years, the Beyond Budgeting Round Table (BBRT; **bbrt.org**) has called into question traditional budgeting practices. A number of articles on the Web discuss the BBRT's position. In the BBRT's view, what is wrong with today's budgeting practices? What does the BBRT recommend as a substitute?

6. Describe how a BSC fits the description of a diagnostic control system.

7. Distinguish performance management and performance measurement.

8. The EFQM "excellence model" provides an alternative performance measurement and management framework. First, what does EFQM stand for? Second, using materials from the Web, discuss the major tenets of the framework. Compare the framework to BSC and Six Sigma.

9. Create a measure for some strategic objective of interest (you can use one of the objectives formulated in discussion question 3). For the selected measure, complete the measurement template found in Table W3.2.1 in the online file for this chapter.

10. Create a strategy for a hypothetical company, using the four perspectives of the BSC. Express the strategy as a series of strategic objectives. Produce a strategy map depicting the linkages among the objectives.

11. Compare and contrast the DMAIC model with the closed-loop processes of BPM.

12. Select two of the companies (other than SAP, Oracle, or IBM) appearing on Gartner's magic quadrant (Table 3.4). What terms do they use to describe their BPM suites. Compare and contrast their offerings in terms of BPM applications and functionality.

Exercises

Teradata University and Other Hands-on Exercises

1. Go to **teradatastudentnetwork.com**. Select the "Articles" content type. Browse down the list of articles and locate one entitled "Business/Corporate Performance Management: Changing Vendor Landscape and New Market Targets." Based on the article, answer the following questions:
  a. What is the basic focus of the article?
  b. What are the major "take aways" from the article?
  c. In the article, which organizational function or role is most intimately involved in CPM?
  d. Which applications are covered by CPM?
  e. How are these applications similar to or different from the applications covered by Gartner's CPM?
  f. What is GRC, and what is its link to corporate performance?
  g. What are some of the major acquisitions that occurred in the CPM marketplace over the last couple of years?
  h. Select two of the companies discussed by the article (not SAP, Oracle, or IBM). What are the CPM strategies of each of the companies? What do the authors think about these strategies?

2. Go to **teradatastudentnetwork.com**. Select the "Case Studies" content type. Browse down the list of cases and locate one entitled "Real-Time Dashboards at Western Digital." Based on the article, answer the following questions:
  a. What is VIS?
  b. In what ways is the architecture of VIS similar to or different from the architecture of BPM?

  c. What are the similarities and differences between the closed-loop processes of BPM and the processes in the OODA decision cycle?
  d. What types of dashboards are in the system? Are they operational or tactical, or are they actually scorecards? Explain.
  e. What are the basic benefits provided by Western Digital's VIS and dashboards?
  f. What sorts of advice can you provide to a company that is getting ready to create its own VIS and dashboards?

3. Go to Stephen Few's blog "the Perceptual Edge" (**perceptualedge.com**). Go to the section of "Examples." In this section, he provides critiques of various dashboard examples. Read a handful of these examples. Now go to **dundas.com.** Select the "Gallery" section of the site. Once there, click the "Digital Dashboard" selection. You will be shown a variety of different dashboard demos. Run a couple of the demos.
  a. What sorts of information and metrics are shown on the demos? What sorts of actions can you take?
  b. Using some of the basic concepts from Few's critiques, describe some of the good design points and bad design points of the demos.

4. Develop a prototype dashboard to display the financial results of a public company. The prototype can be on paper or use Excel. Use data from the 2008 annual plans of two public companies to illustrate the features of your dashboard.

Team Assignments and Role-Playing Projects

1. Virtually every BPM/CPM vendor provides case studies on their Web sites. As a team, select two of these vendors (you can get their names from the Gartner or AMR lists). Select two case studies from each of these sites. For each, summarize the problem the customer was trying to address, the applications or solutions implemented, and the benefits the customer received from the system.

2. Go to the Dashboard Spy Web sitemap for executive dashboards (**enterprise-dashboard.com/sitemap**). This site provides a number of examples of executive dashboards. As a team, select a particular industry (e.g., health care, banking, airlines). Locate a handful of example dashboards for that industry. Describe the types of metrics found on the dashboards. What types of displays are used to provide the information? Using what you know about dashboard design, provide a paper prototype of a dashboard for this information.

Internet Exercises

1. A survey conducted by Economist Intelligence Unit and reported in S. Taub, "Closing the Strategy-to-Performance Gap," *CFO Magazine*, February 22, 2005 (**cfo.com/article.cfm/3686974?f=related**), explores the relationship between strategy development and execution. Based on the survey, which is more important for performance management—strategy development or execution? What reasons do respondents give for poor execution? In what ways do respondents think they can improve performance?

2. Go to the NYC Citywide Performance Report site (**nyc.gov/html/ops/cpr/html/home/home**). The performance reports are organized by "Themes" (see End of Chapter Application Case). Use the site to answer the following questions:

   a. How many performance indicators are there for the whole city? For community service? For education?

   b. Overall, how many of the indicators are improving or are stable? Declining?

   c. How many of the education performance indicators are improving or stable? Declining?

   d. Select "Citywide Themes" (on the upper left). One of the themes is "Social Services." Select this theme. Now select "View the performance report for Social Services." How many social service indicators are there? How many are declining by more than 10 percent?

What are some of these indicators that are declining? How can NYC use this specific information to address the problem tracked by the performance indicator?

3. One of the more famous BSCs is the one created by Southwest Airlines to manage its business. An earlier article by Anthes provides a strategy map of the system (see **computerworld.com/action/article.do?command=viewArticleBasic&articleId=78512**). Retrieve the article. Using the strategy map, describe this segment of Southwest's strategy. What major measures and targets is Southwest using to track its performance against its strategic objectives? Based on what you know about today's economy in general and the airline industry specifically, do you think this strategy will work in today's world?

4. Annually, TDWI (The Data Warehouse Institute) identifies and honors companies that have demonstrated excellence (i.e., best practices) in developing, deploying, and maintaining business intelligence and data warehousing applications. Go to the Web page with the 2008 winners (**tdwi.org/research/display.aspx?id=9000**). What categories does TDWI honor? Who were some of the winners? What were some of the reasons that they won their particular award?

5. A number of Web sites provide examples and directions for creating executive dashboards and executive balanced scorecards. Using some of the capabilities described by these sites, create an Excel prototype of each.

6. A recent white paper titled "Business Intelligence and Enterprise Performance Management: Trends for Midsize Companies" by Oracle (see **oracle.com/appserver/business-intelligence/hyperion-financial-performance-management/docs/bi-epm-trends-for-emerging-businesses.pdf**) compares the BI and performance management practices of middle-sized and large-sized companies. First, in the survey, what is a middle-sized company? Second, what sorts of practices are these companies surveying? Based on the survey results, what are some of the similarities and differences between the practices of the two types of companies? What conclusions and advice do they give to vendors?

7. Go to **webdesignerdepot.com/2009/06/50-great-examples-of-data-visualization.** Select two of the data visualization techniques and describe how the techniques could be used to discover and explore the data in a BI or BPM application. In your description be sure to highlight both the benefits and limitations of each of the techniques.

End of Chapter Application Case

Tracking Citywide Performance

Massive systems produce massive amounts of metrics. The challenge is to determine how to slice the data in ways that benefit users rather than confuse them, especially when the users have a wide variety of experiences with information

technologies. This was one of the major issues facing New York City when it decided to develop its Citywide Performance Reporting (CPR) Online System, an interactive dashboard providing agencies and citizens with "user-friendly access to the most critical performance indicators for every city agency, with monthly updates and automatic evaluation of trends within specified program areas."

Development of CPR

CPR is part of NYCStat (**nyc.gov/html/ops/nycstat/html/home/home.shtml**). NYCStat is New York City's one-stop-shop for all essential data, reports, and statistics related to city services. NYCStat provides access to a wide variety of performance-related information, including citywide and agency-specific information, 311-related data, and interactive mapping features for selected performance data and quality-of-life indicators.

CPR was launched in February 2008. Initial plans for CPR were developed by the Mayor's Office of Operations in concert with the Department of Information Technology and Communications (DoITT) in mid-2005 (NYCStat, 2009). The project had three components:

- *Performance management application.* A back-end computer system providing a single point of access for agencies to input data.
- *Analytics tool/dashboard.* The front-end system to provide standardized reporting format with drill-down capabilities, performance summaries, and trend graphics.
- *Data definition.* Review and identification of the topics measures and critical indicators to be included in the CPR system for 44 mayorial agencies.

Development of these components continued through July 2007. At this time, the system was opened to the 44 agencies and the mayor's office for review. At the end of the summer, Mayor Bloomberg directed that the system be made available to the public through the city's NYC.gov Web site as soon as possible. Subsequent work on the system focused on making the dashboard as easy and flexible as possible for public use. The system was finally opened on February 14, 2008, as part of the release of the Preliminary Fiscal 2008 Mayor's Management Report.

Refining Metrics

CPR is an offshoot of the Mayor's Management Report (MMR), an annual evaluation of the city's agencies that measures 1,000 performance indicators, including everything from grade school test scores to the time it takes to fix a pot-hole. Rather than simply providing an online version of the MMR, the CPR required the agencies to take a fresh look at the services they were delivering and how best to measure the outcomes of those services. Initially, this resulted in thousands of measures, many of which did not exist at the time. Eventually, the list of initial measures was reduced to 525 critical measures. The majority of these measures represent final outcomes of services that directly impact the city's residents. This is why the decision was made to open up the system to the public.

In addition to refining the measures, other key decisions had to be made. Because data was available by month,

year-to-date, and full year, choices had to be made about how to best slice and dice the data and make comparisons across the various periods. Decisions also had to be made on how to measure and present trends and performance against preset targets—designating the desired direction of each measure and thresholds for good and bad performance. Finally, because the total number of measures and agencies was so large and none of the public was likely to be familiar with each of the individual agencies, the presentation and navigation needed to be simplified. The developers decided to categorize the measures into eight citywide "themes" that captured the way the city government serves the people who work and live in New York City. The themes included: citywide administration, community services, economic development and business affairs, infrastructure, education, legal affairs, public safety, and social services.

Impact of CPR

From the viewpoint of the mayor's office, CPR improves performance management in three ways—accountability, transparency, and accessibility. It does this by providing the following capabilities (NYCStat, 2009):

- Tracks performance for the most important "outcome" measures that directly reflect how the lives of the public are affected by city government.
- Measures performance by comparing current data to prior data for the year before, thereby holding agencies accountable for year-over-year improvements.
- Highlights agency performance through graphs and color coding, making positive or negative performance trends immediately obvious.
- Drill-down capability, allowing users to review comparative trends over a 5-year period.
- Aggregates important measures into citywide themes, which cut across agency silos and disciplines to reveal the overall picture about city government performance.
- Updates each measure monthly, quarterly, or annually so that the most recent data is always available.
- Offers the ability to download data in a variety of formats for more detailed review and analysis.
- Provides detailed information about each measure, including an explanation of what the measure means, its reporting frequency, and other useful details.

In March 2009, the CPR system was recognized by the Ash Institute for Democratic Governance and Innovation at the JFK School of Government at Harvard University as one of the top 50 government innovations for the year (*New York Nonprofit Press,* 2009).

Lessons Learned

According to Sarlin, "It is interesting to see how government agencies at all levels are implementing best practices to be more run like a business." In the case of New York City's Mayoral Operations Office, you might expect this, because Mayor Bloomberg comes from the world of business, more specifically, the world of real-time financial information (see **bloomberg.com**). However, other government agencies have announced online dashboards even though they have virtually no connection with business. For instance, the new U.S. Chief Information Officer Vivek Kundra recently announced the U.S. Federal IT Dashboard, which provides public access to data reported to the Office of Management and Budget (OMB), including general information on over 7,000 federal IT investments and detailed data for nearly 800 of these investments classified as "major." Mr. Kundra has spent his entire career in government positions. These efforts suggest that business may be able to learn quite a bit from these initiatives.

These government dashboard initiatives demonstrate the following (Buytendijk, 2008):

- ***Transparency makes a difference.*** These initiatives provide widespread, public access to large collections of performance data. Many businesses could learn from the depth and breadth of the information these agencies are sharing.
- ***Importance of collaboration.*** Many BI projects suffer from a silo approach, with different departments doing their own dashboards or scorecards. Each department may realize a short-term ROI. However, the combination will be suboptimal and is not likely to lead to an overall ROI. Both the CPR dashboard and the federal IT dashboard show that it is possible to create an organization-wide initiative spanning multiple domains.
- ***Continuous Improvement.*** CPR is based on trends, not targets. This means that the performance indicators

are aimed at continuous improvement instead of static goals. It sets a good example for how an operational or tactical dashboard should look.

QUESTIONS FOR END OF CHAPTER APPLICATION CASE

1. What are the major components of the CPR dashboard?
2. How many agencies were involved in the definition and implementation of the CPR dashboard?
3. What were the major steps used in defining and implementing the CPR?
4. What role did "themes" play in the CPR dashboard?
5. What are the major capabilities of the CPR dashboard?
6. What can businesses learn from a government initiative like the CPR?

Sources: Compiled from NYCStat, "CPR Fact Sheet," Mayor's Office of Operations, February 2009, **nyc.gov/html/ops/cpr/downloads/pdf/cpr_fact_sheet.pdf** (accessed January 2010); B. Sarlin, "Mayor Unveils Web Database Tracking Performance," *New York Sun*, February 15, 2008, **nysun.com/new-york/mayor-unveils-web-database-tracking-performance/71347/?print=5119866421** (accessed January 2010); F. Buytendijk, "The Mother of All Accountability Tools," February 20, 2008, **blogs.oracle.com/frankbuytendijk/2008/02/the_mother_of_all_accountabili.htm** (accessed January 2010); *New York Nonprofit Press*, "Eight NYC Programs Among 50 Selected for National Honors," March 31, 2009, **nynp.biz/index.php/breaking-news/620-eight-nyc-programs-among-50-selected-for-national-honors-** (accessed January 2010); J. Hiner, "U.S. Federal IT Dashboard is a Great Example of How to Promote IT," July 1, 2009, **blogs.zdnet.com/BTL/?p=20157** (accessed January 2010).

References

Ante, S., and J. McGregor. (2006, February 13). "Giving the Boss the Big Picture." *BusinessWeek.* **businessweek.com/magazine/content/06_07/b3971083.htm** (accessed January 2010).

Axson, D. (2007). *Best Practices in Planning and Performance Management: From Data to Decisions.* New York: Wiley.

Buytendijk, F. (2008, February 20). "The Mother of All Accountability Tools." **blogs.oracle.com/frankbuytendijk/2008/02/the_mother_of_all_accountabili.html** (accessed January 2010).

Calumo Group. (2009, January 30). "Planning on Microsoft BI Platform." **calumo.com/newsblog** (accessed January 2010).

Caterpillar Inc. (2009, September). "Caterpillar Inc. Announces 2Q 2009 Results." *Caterpillar Press Release.* **cat.com/cda/components/fullArticleNoNav?m=37523&x=7&id=1654623** (accessed January 2010).

Chandler, N., N. Rayner, J. Van Decker, and J. Holincheck. (2009, April 30). "Magic Quadrant for Corporate Performance Management Suites." *Gartner RAS Core Research Note G00165786.* **mediaproducts.gartner.com/reprints/oracle/article51/article51.html** (accessed January 2010).

Colbert, J. (2009, June). "Captain Jack and the BPM Market: Performance Management in Turbulent Times." *BPM Magazine.* **bmpmag.net/mag/captain_jack_bpm** (accessed January 2010).

Conference Board. (2008, December 2). "Weakening Global Economy and Growing Financial Pressures are Increasing CEO Concerns." Press Release. **conference-board.org/utilities/pressDetail.cfm?press_id=3529** (accessed January 2010).

Docherty, P. (2005). "From Six Sigma to Strategy Execution." **i-solutionsglobal.com/secure/FromSixSigmaToStrateg_AAC8C.pdf** (accessed January 2010).

Eckerson, W. (2009, January). "Performance Management Strategies: How to Create and Deploy Effective Metrics." *TDWI Best Practices Report.* **tdwi.org/research/display.aspx?ID=9390** (accessed January 2010).

Eckerson, W. (2006). *Performance Dashboards.* Hoboken, NJ: Wiley.

Few, S. (2005, Winter). "Dashboard Design: Beyond Meters, Gauges, and Traffic Lights." *Business Intelligence Journal*, Vol. 10, No. 1.

Few, S. (2008). "Data Visualization and Analysis—BI Blind Spots." *Visual Perceptual Edge.* **perceptualedge.com/ blog/?p=367** (accessed January 2010).

Green, S. (2009, March 13). "Harrah's Reports Loss, Says LV Properties Hit Hard." *Las Vegas Sun.* **lasvegassun.com/ news/2009/mar/13/harrahs-reports-loss-says-lv-prop erties-hit-hard** (accessed January 2010).

Grimes, S. (2009, May 2) "Seeing Connections: Visualizations Makes Sense of Data." *Intelligent Enterprise.* **i.cmpnet. com/intelligententerprise/next-era-business-intelli gence/Intelligent_Enterprise_Next_Era_BI_Visualiza tion.pdf** (accessed January 2010).

Gupta, P. (2006). *Six Sigma Business Scorecard,* 2nd ed. New York: McGraw-Hill Professional.

Hammer, M. (2003). *Agenda: What Every Business Must Do to Dominate the Decade.* Pittsburgh, PA: Three Rivers Press.

Hatch, D. (2008, January). "Operational BI: Getting 'Real Time' about Performance." *Intelligent Enterprise.* **intelligententerprise.com/showArticle.jhtml?articleI D=205920233** (accessed January 2010).

Henschen, D. (2008, September). "Special Report: Business Intelligence Gets Smart." **intelligententerprise.com/ showArticle.jhtml?articleID=210500374** (accessed January 2010).

Hindo, B. (2007, June 11). "At 3M: A Struggle between Efficiency and Creativity." *BusinessWeek.* **businessweek. com/magazine/content/07_24/b4038406.htm?chan= top+news_top+news+index_best+of+bw** (accessed January 2010).

Hiner, J. (2009, July 1). "U.S. Federal IT Dashboard is a Great Example of How to Promote IT." **blogs.zdnet.com/ BTL/?p=20157** (accessed January 2010).

Kaplan, R., and D. Norton. (2008). *The Execution Premium.* Boston, MA: Harvard Business School Press.

Kaplan, R., and D. Norton. (2004). *Strategy Maps: Converting Intangible Assets into Tangible Outcomes.* Boston, MA: Harvard Business School Press.

Kaplan, R., and D. Norton. (2000). *The Strategy-Focused Organization: How Balanced Scorecard Companies Thrive in the New Business Environment.* Boston, MA: Harvard Business School Press.

Kaplan, R., and D. Norton. (1996). *The Balanced Scorecard: Translating Strategy into Action.* Boston, MA: Harvard University Press.

Kaplan, R., and D. Norton. (1992, January–February). "The Balanced Scorecard—Measures That Drive Performance." *Harvard Business Review*, pp. 71–79.

Knowledge@W.P. Carey. (2009, March 2). "High-Rolling Casinos Hit a Losing Streak." **knowledge.wpcarey.asu. edu/article.cfm?articleid=1752#** (accessed January 2010).

Krafcik, J. (1988, Fall). "Triumph of the lean production system." *Sloan Management Review*, Vol. 30, No. 1.

Leahy, T. (2005, February). "The One-Two Performance Punch." *Business Finance.* **businessfinancemag.com/ magazine/archives/article.html?articleID=1436** (accessed January 2010).

McGrath, R., and I. MacMillan. (2009). *Discovery-Driven Growth.* Boston, MA: Harvard Business School Press.

McKay, L. (2009, February). "Megavendors Look Smart in Gartner Magic Quadrant for Business Intelligence." **destinationcrm.com/Articles/CRM-News/Daily-News/ Megavendors-Look-Smart-in-Gartner-Magic-Quadrant- for-Business-Intelligence-52600.aspx** (accessed January 2010).

Microsoft. (2006, April 12). "Expedia: Scorecard Solution Helps Online Travel Company Measure the Road to Greatness." **microsoft.com/casestudies/Case_Study_Detail.aspx? CaseStudyID=49076** (accessed January 2010).

New York Nonprofit Press. (2009, March 31). "Eight NYC Programs Among 50 Selected for National Honors." **nynp.biz/index.php/breaking-news/620-eight-nyc- programs-among-50-selected-for-national-honors-** (accessed January 2010).

Norton, D. (2007). "Strategy Execution—A Competency that Creates Competitive Advantage." The Palladium Group. **thepalladiumgroup.com/KnowledgeObjectRepository/ Norton_StrategyExec creates competitive adv WP.pdf** (accessed January 2010).

Novell. (2009, April). "Executive Dashboards Elements of Success." Novell White Paper. **novell.com/rc/docreposi tory/public/37/basedocument.2009-03-23.4871823014/ Executive Dashboards_Elements_of_Success_White_ Paper_en.pdf** (accessed January 2010).

NYCStat. (2009, February). "CPR Fact Sheet." Mayor's Office of Operations. **nyc.gov/html/ops/cpr/downloads/ pdf/cpr_fact_sheet.pdf** (accessed January 2010).

Poppendieck, LLC. (2009). "Why the Lean in Six Sigma." **poppendieck.com/lean-six-sigma.htm** (accessed January 2010).

Richardson, K. (2007, January 4). "The Six Sigma Factor for Home Depot." *Wall Street Journal Online.* **sukimcintosh. com/articles/WSJJan4.pdf** (accessed January 2010).

Rigby, D., and B. Bilodeau. (2009). "Management Tools and Trends 2009." Bain & Co. **bain.com/management_tools/ Management_Tools_and_Trends_2009_Global_Results. pdf** (accessed January 2010).

Sarlin, B. (2008, February 15). "Mayor Unveils Web Database Tracking Performance." *New York Sun.* **nysun.com/new york/mayor-unveils-web-database-tracking-perform ance/71347/?print=5119866421** (accessed January 2010).

Shill, W., and R. Thomas. (2005, October). "Exploring the Mindset of the High Performer." *Outlook Journal.* **accenture.com/Global/Research_and_Insights/Out look/By_Issue/Y2005/ExploringPerformer.htm** (accessed January 2010).

Simons, R. (2002). *Performance Measurement and Control Systems for Implementing Strategy.* Upper Saddle River, NJ: Prentice Hall.

Six Sigma Institute. (2009). "Lean Enterprise." **sixsigmainstitute. com/lean/index_lean.shtml** (accessed August 2009).

Slywotzky, A., and K. Weber. (2007). *The Upside: The 7 Strategies for Turning Big Threats into Growth Breakthroughs.* New York: Crown Publishing.

Smith, R. (2007, April 5). "Expedia-5 Team Blog: Technology." **expedia-team5.blogspot.com** (accessed January 2010).

Stanley, T. (2006, February 1). "High-Stakes Analytics." *Information Week.* **informationweek.com/shared/ printableArticle.jhtml?articleID=177103414** (accessed January 2010).

Swabey, P. (2007, January 18). "Nothing Left to Chance." *Information Age.* **information-age.com/channels/ information-management/features/272256/nothing-left-to-chance.thtml** (accessed January 2010).

Tucker, S., and R. Dimon. (2009, April 17). "Design to Align: The Key Component in BPM Success." *BPM Magazine.* **bpmmag.net/mag/design-to-align-key-component-in-bpm-success-0417** (accessed January 2010).

Vessette, D., and B. McDonough. (2008, November). "Worldwide Business Analytics Software 2008–2012 Forecast and 2007 Vendor Shares." **DC Doc # 214904. sas.com/ offices/europe/denmark/pdf/idc_ba_1108.pdf** (accessed January 2010).

Wailgum, T. (2008, January 25). "How IT Systems Can Help Starbucks Fix Itself." *CIO.* **cio.com/article/176003/ How_IT_Systems_Can_Help_Starbucks_Fix_Itself** (accessed January 2010).

Watson, H., and L. Volonino. (2001, January). "Harrah's High Payoff from Customer Information." *The Data Warehousing Institute Industry Study 2000—Harnessing Customer Information for Strategic Advantage: Technical Challenges and Business Solutions.* **terry.uga.edu/~hwatson/ Harrahs.doc** (accessed January 2010).

Weier, M. (2007, April 16). "Dunkin' Donuts Uses Business Intelligence In War Against Starbucks." *Information Week.*

Wurtzel, M. (2008, June 13). "Reasons for Six Sigma Deployment Failures." *BPM Institute.* **bpminstitute.org/articles/ article/article/reasons-for-six-sigma-deployment-failures.html** (accessed January 2010).

4

Data Mining for Business Intelligence

LEARNING OBJECTIVES

- Define data mining as an enabling technology for business intelligence (BI)
- Understand the objectives and benefits of business analytics and data mining
- Recognize the wide range of applications of data mining
- Learn the standardized data mining processes

- Understand the steps involved in data preprocessing for data mining
- Learn different methods and algorithms of data mining
- Build awareness of the existing data mining software tools
- Understand the pitfalls and myths of data mining

Generally speaking, data mining is a way to develop business intelligence (BI) from data that an organization collects, organizes, and stores. A wide range of data mining techniques are being used by organizations to gain a better understanding of their customers and their own operations and to solve complex organizational problems. In this chapter, we study data mining as an enabling technology for business intelligence, learn about the standard processes of conducting data mining projects, understand and build expertise in the use of major data mining techniques, develop awareness of the existing software tools, and explore common myths and pitfalls of data mining.

OPENING VIGNETTE: Data Mining Goes to Hollywood!

Predicting box-office receipts (i.e., financial success) of a particular motion picture is an interesting and challenging problem. According to some domain experts, the movie industry is the "land of hunches and wild guesses" due to the difficulty associated with forecasting product demand, making the movie business in Hollywood a risky endeavor. In support of such observations, Jack Valenti (the longtime president and CEO of the Motion Picture Association of America) once mentioned that "no one can tell you how a movie is going to do in the marketplace. . . not until the film opens in darkened theatre and sparks fly up between the screen and the audience." Entertainment industry trade journals and magazines have been full of examples, statements, and experiences that support such a claim.

Like many other researchers who have attempted to shed light on this challenging real-world problem, Ramesh Sharda and Dursun Delen have been exploring the use of data mining to predict the financial performance of a motion picture at the box office before it even enters production (while the movie is nothing more than a conceptual idea). In their highly publicized prediction models, they convert the forecasting (or regression) problem into a classification problem; that is, rather than forecasting the point estimate of box-office receipts, they classify a movie based on its box-office receipts in one of nine categories, ranging from "flop" to "blockbuster," making the problem a multinomial classification problem. Table 4.1 illustrates the definition of the nine classes in terms of the range of box-office receipts.

DATA

Data was collected from variety of movie-related databases (e.g., ShowBiz, IMDb, IMSDb, AllMovie) and consolidated into a single dataset. The dataset for the most recently developed models contained 2,632 movies released between 1998 and 2006. A summary of the independent variables along with their specifications is provided in Table 4.2. For more descriptive details and justification for inclusion of these independent variables, the reader is referred to Sharda and Delen (2007).

METHODOLOGY

Using a variety of data mining methods, including **neural networks**, **decision trees**, **support vector machines (SVM)**, and three types of ensembles, Sharda and Delen developed the prediction models. The data from 1998 to 2005 were used as training data to build the prediction models, and the data from 2006 were used as the test data to assess and compare the models' prediction accuracy. Figure 4.1 shows a screenshot of SPSS's PASW Modeler (formerly, Clementine data mining tool) depicting the process map employed for the prediction problem. The upper-left side of the process map shows the model development process, and the lower-right corner of the process map shows the model assessment (i.e., testing or scoring) process (more details on PASW Modeler tool and its usage can be found on the book's Web site).

TABLE 4.1 Movie Classification Based on Receipts

Class No.	1	2	3	4	5	6	7	8	9
Range (in millions of dollars)	< 1	> 1	> 10	> 20	> 40	> 65	> 100	> 150	> 200
	(Flop)	< 10	> 20	< 40	< 65	< 100	< 150	< 200	(Blockbuster)

TABLE 4.2 Summary of Independent Variables

Independent Variable	Number of Values	Possible Values
MPAA rating	5	G, PG, PG-13, R, NR
Competition	3	High, medium, low
Star value	3	High, medium, low
Genre	10	Sci-fi, historic epic drama, modern drama, politically related, thriller, horror, comedy, cartoon, action, documentary
Special effects	3	High, medium, low
Sequel	1	Yes, no
Number of screens	1	Positive integer

RESULTS

Table 4.3 provides the prediction results of all three data mining methods as well as the results of the three different ensembles. The first performance measure is the percent correct classification rate, which is called *bingo*. Also reported in the table is the *1-Away* correct classification rate (i.e., within one category). The results indicate that SVM performed the best among the individual prediction models, followed by ANN; the worst of the three was the CART decision tree algorithm. In general, the ensemble models performed better than the individual predictions models, of which the fusion algorithm performed the best.

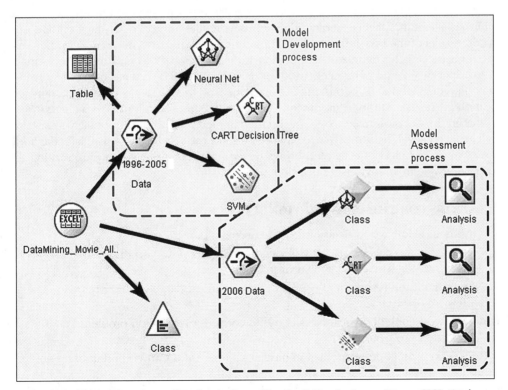

FIGURE 4.1 Process Flow Screenshot for the Box-office Prediction System. *Source:* SPSS. Used with permission.

TABLE 4.3 Tabulated Prediction Results for Individual and Ensemble Models

	Prediction Models					
	Individual Models			**Ensemble Models**		
Performance Measure	**SVM**	**ANN**	**C&RT**	**Random Forest**	**Boosted Tree**	**Fusion (Average)**
Count (*Bingo*)	192	182	140	189	187	194
Count (*1-Away*)	104	120	126	121	104	120
Accuracy (*% Bingo*)	55.49%	52.60%	40.46%	54.62%	54.05%	56.07%
Accuracy (*% 1-Away*)	85.55%	87.28%	76.88%	89.60%	84.10%	90.75%
Standard deviation	0.93	0.87	1.05	0.76	0.84	0.63

What is probably more important to decision makers, and standing out in the results table, is the significantly low standard deviation obtained from the ensembles compared to the individual models.

CONCLUSION

The researchers claim that these prediction results are better than any reported in the published literature for this problem domain. Beyond the attractive accuracy of their prediction results of the box-office receipts, these models could also be used to further analyze (and potentially optimize) the decision variables in order to maximize the financial return. Specifically, the parameters used for modeling could be altered using the already-trained prediction models in order to better understand the impact of different parameters on the end results. During this process, which is commonly referred to as *sensitivity analysis*, the decision maker of a given entertainment firm could find out, with a fairly high accuracy level, how much value a specific actor (or a specific release date, the addition of more technical effects, etc.) brings to the financial success of a film, making the underlying system an invaluable decision aid.

QUESTIONS FOR THE OPENING VIGNETTE

1. Why should Hollywood decision makers use data mining?
2. What are the top challenges for Hollywood managers? Can you think of other industry segments that face similar problems?
3. Do you think the researchers used all of the relevant data to build prediction models?
4. Why do you think the researchers chose to convert a regression problem into a classification problem?
5. How do you think these prediction models can be used? Can you think of a good production system for such models?
6. Do you think the decision makers would easily adapt to such an information system?
7. What can be done to further improve the prediction models explained in this case?

WHAT WE CAN LEARN FROM THIS VIGNETTE

The entertainment industry is full of interesting and challenging problems for decision makers. Making the right decisions to manage large amounts of money is critical to success (or mere survival) of many companies in this marketplace. Data mining is a prime candidate for better management of this data-rich, knowledge-poor business environment. The study described in the opening vignette clearly illustrates the power of data mining in predicting and explaining the financial outlook of a motion picture, which most still think is a form of art and hence cannot be forecasted. In this chapter, you will see a wide variety of data mining applications solving complex problems in a variety of industries where the data can be used to leverage competitive business advantage.

Sources: R. Sharda and D. Delen, "Predicting Box-Office Success of Motion Pictures with Neural Networks," *Expert Systems with Applications,* Vol. 30, 2006, pp. 243–254; D. Delen, R. Sharda, and P. Kumar, "Movie Forecast Guru: A Web-based DSS for Hollywood Managers," *Decision Support Systems,* Vol. 43, No. 4, 2007, pp. 1151–1170.

4.1 DATA MINING CONCEPTS AND DEFINITIONS

In an interview with *Computerworld* magazine in January 1999, Dr. Arno Penzias (Nobel laureate and former chief scientist of Bell Labs) identified data mining from organizational databases as a key application for corporations of the near future. In response to *Computerworld*'s age-old question of "What will be the killer applications in the corporation?" Dr. Penzias replied: "Data mining." He then added, "Data mining will become much more important and companies will throw away nothing about their customers because it will be so valuable. If you're not doing this, you're out of business." Similarly, in an article in *Harvard Business Review*, Thomas Davenport (2006) argued that the latest strategic weapon for companies is analytical decision making, providing examples of companies such as Amazon.com, Capital One, Marriott International, and others that have used analytics to better understand their customers and optimize their extended supply chains to maximize their returns on investment while providing the best customer service. This level of success is highly dependent on a company understanding its customers, vendors, business processes, and the extended supply chain very well.

A large component of this understanding comes from analyzing the vast amount of data that a company collects. The cost of storing and processing data has decreased dramatically in the recent past, and as a result, the amount of data stored in electronic form has grown at an explosive rate. With the creation of large databases, the possibility of analyzing the data stored in them has emerged. The term *data mining* was originally used to describe the process through which previously unknown patterns in data were discovered. This definition has since been stretched beyond those limits by some software vendors to include most forms of data analysis in order to increase sales with the popularity of data mining label. In this chapter, we accept the original definition of data mining.

Although the term *data mining* is relatively new, the ideas behind it are not. Many of the techniques used in data mining have their roots in traditional statistical analysis and artificial intelligence work done since the early part of 1980s. Why, then, has it suddenly gained the attention of the business world? Following are some of most pronounced reasons:

- More intense competition at the global scale driven by customers' ever-changing needs and wants in an increasingly saturated marketplace.
- General recognition of the untapped value hidden in large data sources.

- Consolidation and integration of database records, which enables a single view of customers, vendors, transactions, and so on.
- Consolidation of databases and other data repositories into a single location in the form of a data warehouse.
- The exponential increase in data processing and storage technologies.
- Significant reduction in the cost of hardware and software for data storage and processing.
- Movement toward the de-massification (conversion of information resources into nonphysical form) of business practices.

Data generated by the Internet are increasing rapidly in both volume and complexity. Large amounts of genomic data are being generated and accumulated all over the world. Disciplines such as astronomy and nuclear physics create huge quantities of data on a regular basis. Medical and pharmaceutical researchers constantly generate and store data that can then be used in data mining applications to identify better ways to accurately diagnose and treat illnesses and to discover new and improved drugs.

On the commercial side, perhaps the most common use of data mining has been in the finance, retail, and health care sectors. Data mining is used to detect and reduce fraudulent activities, especially in insurance claims and credit card use (Chan et al., 1999); to identify customer buying patterns; to reclaim profitable customers; to identify trading rules from historical data; and to aid in increased profitability using market-basket analysis. Data mining is already widely used to better target clients, and with the widespread development of e-commerce, this can only become more imperative with time. See Application Case 4.1 for information on how 1-800-Flowers has used business analytics and data mining to excel in business.

Application Case 4.1

Business Analytics and Data Mining Help 1-800-Flowers Excel in Business

1-800-Flowers is one of the best-known and most successful brands in the gift-retailing business. For more than 30 years, the New York-based company has been providing customers around the world with the freshest flowers and finest selection of plants, gift baskets, gourmet foods, confections, and plush stuffed animals for every occasion. Founded by Jim McCann in 1976, 1-800-Flowers has quickly become the leader in direct-order e-commerce after opening its own Web site more than 14 years ago.

Problem

As successful as it has been, like many other companies involved in e-commerce, 1-800-Flowers needed to make decisions in real time to increase retention, reduce costs, and keep its best customers coming back for more again and again. As the business has grown from one flower shop to an online gift retailer serving more than 30 million customers, it has needed

to stay ahead of the competition by being the best that it can be.

Solution

Strongly believing in the value of close customer relationships, 1-800-Flowers wanted to better understand its customers' needs and wants by analyzing every piece of data that it had about them. 1-800-Flowers decided to use SAS data mining tools to dig deep into its data assets to discover novel patterns about its customers and turn that knowledge into business transactions.

Results

According to McCann, business analytics and data mining tools from SAS have enabled 1-800-Flowers to grow its business regardless of the conditions of the larger economy. At a time when other retailers are struggling to survive, 1-800-Flowers has seen revenues grow, nearly doubling in the last 5 years. Specific benefits of the analysis were as follows:

- **More efficient marketing campaigns.** 1-800-Flowers has drastically reduced the time it takes to segment customers for direct mailing. "It used to take 2 or 3 weeks—now it takes 2 or 3 days," says Aaron Cano, vice president of customer knowledge management. "That leaves us time to do more analysis and make sure we're sending relevant offers."
- **Reduced mailings, increased response rates.** The company has been able to significantly reduce marketing mailings while increasing response rates and be much more selective about TV and radio advertisements.
- **Better customer experience.** When a repeat customer logs on to 1-800-Flowers.com, the Web site immediately shows selections that are related to that customer's interests. "If a customer usually buys tulips for his wife, we

show him our newest and best tulip selections," Cano says.

- **Increased repeat sales.** The company's best customers are returning more often because 1-800-Flowers knows who the customer is and what he or she likes. The company makes the shopping experience easy and relevant and markets to customers at the point of contact.

As a result of using business analytics and data mining, 1-800-Flowers reduced its operating expenses, increased the retention rate of its best customer segment to more than 80 percent, attracted 20 million new customers, and grew the overall repeat business from less than 40 percent to greater than 50 percent (a 10-basis-point increase in repeat sales across all brands translates into a $40 million additional revenue for the business).

Sources: Based on "SAS Helps 1-800-Flowers.com Grow Deep Roots with Customers," **sas.com/success/1800flowers.html** (accessed on May 23, 2009); "Data Mining at 1-800-Flowers," **kdnuggets.com/news/2009/n10/3i.html** (accessed on May 26, 2009).

Definitions, Characteristics, and Benefits

Simply defined, **data mining** is a term used to describe discovering or "mining" knowledge from large amounts of data. When considered by analogy, one can easily realize that the term *data mining* is a misnomer; that is, mining of gold from within rocks or dirt is referred to as "gold" mining rather than "rock" or "dirt" mining. Therefore, data mining perhaps should have been named "knowledge mining" or "knowledge discovery." Despite the mismatch between the term and its meaning, *data mining* has become the choice of the community. Many other names that are associated with data mining include *knowledge extraction, pattern analysis, data archeology, information harvesting, pattern searching,* and *data dredging.*

Technically speaking, data mining is a process that uses statistical, mathematical, and artificial intelligence techniques to extract and identify useful information and subsequent knowledge (or patterns) from large sets of data. These patterns can be in the form of business rules, affinities, correlations, trends, or prediction models (Nemati and Barko, 2001). Most literature defines data mining as "the nontrivial process of identifying valid, novel, potentially useful, and ultimately understandable patterns in data stored in structured databases," where the data are organized in records structured by categorical, ordinal and continuous variables (Fayyad et al., 1996). In this definition, the meanings of the key term are as follows:

- *Process* implies that data mining comprises many iterative steps.
- *Nontrivial* means that some experimentation-type search or inference is involved; that is, it is as straightforward as a computation of predefined quantities.
- *Valid* means that the discovered patterns should hold true on new data with sufficient degree of certainty.

- *Novel* means that the patterns are not previously known to the user within the context of the system being analyzed.
- *Potentially useful* means that the discovered patterns should lead to some benefit to the user or task.
- *Ultimately understandable* means that the pattern should make business sense that leads to user saying "mmm! It makes sense; why didn't I think of that" if not immediately, at least after some postprocessing.

Data mining is not a new discipline but rather a new definition for the use of many disciplines. Data mining is tightly positioned at the intersection of many disciplines, including statistics, **artificial intelligence**, **machine learning**, management science, information systems, and databases (see Figure 4.2). Using advances in all of these disciplines, data mining strives to make progress in extracting useful information and knowledge from large databases. It is an emerging field that has attracted much attention in a very short time.

The following are the major characteristics and objectives of data mining:

- Data are often buried deep within very large databases, which sometimes contain data from several years. In many cases, the data are cleansed and consolidated into a data warehouse.
- The data mining environment is usually a client/server architecture or a Web-based information systems architecture.
- Sophisticated new tools, including advanced visualization tools, help to remove the information ore buried in corporate files or archival public records. Finding it involves massaging and synchronizing the data to get the right results. Cutting-edge data miners are also exploring the usefulness of soft data (i.e., unstructured text stored in such places as Lotus Notes databases, text files on the Internet, or enterprise-wide intranets).
- The miner is often an end user, empowered by data drills and other power query tools to ask ad hoc questions and obtain answers quickly, with little or no programming skill.

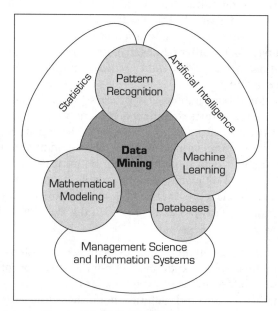

FIGURE 4.2 **Data Mining as a Blend of Multiple Disciplines.**

- Striking it rich often involves finding an unexpected result and requires end users to think creatively throughout the process, including the interpretation of the findings.
- Data mining tools are readily combined with spreadsheets and other software development tools. Thus, the mined data can be analyzed and deployed quickly and easily.
- Because of the large amounts of data and massive search efforts, it is sometimes necessary to use parallel processing for data mining.

A company that effectively leverages data mining tools and technologies can acquire and maintain a strategic competitive advantage. Data mining offers organizations an indispensable decision-enhancing environment to exploit new opportunities by transforming data into a strategic weapon. See Nemati and Barko (2001) for a more detailed discussion on the strategic benefits of data mining.

TECHNOLOGY INSIGHT 4.1 Data in Data Mining

Data refers to a collection of facts usually obtained as the result of experiences, observations, or experiments. Data may consist of numbers, words, images, and so on as measurements of a set of variables. Data are often viewed as the lowest level of abstraction from which information and knowledge are derived.

At the highest level of abstraction, one can classify data as categorical or numeric. The categorical data can be subdivided into nominal or ordinal data, whereas numeric data can be subdivided into interval or ratio. Figure 4.3 shows a simple taxonomy of data in data mining.

- *Categorical data* represent the labels of multiple classes used to divide a variable into specific groups. Examples of categorical variables include race, sex, age group, and educational level. Although the latter two variables may also be considered in a numerical manner by using exact values for age and highest grade completed, it is often more informative to categorize such variables into a relatively small number of ordered classes. The categorical data may also be called discrete data implying that it represents a finite number of values with no continuum between them. Even if the values used for the categorical (or discrete) variables are numeric, these numbers are nothing more than symbols and do not imply the possibility of calculating fractional values.
- *Nominal data* contain measurements of simple codes assigned to objects as labels, which are not measurements. For example, the variable *marital status* can be generally categorized as (1) single, (2) married, and (3) divorced. Nominal data can be represented with binomial values having two possible values (e.g., yes/no, true/false, good/bad), or multinomial values having three or more possible values (e.g., brown/green/blue, white/black/Latino/Asian, single/married/divorced).

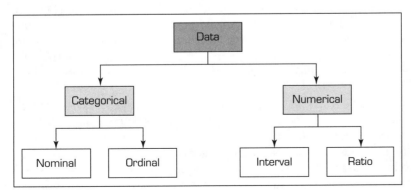

FIGURE 4.3 A Simple Taxonomy of Data in Data Mining.

- ***Ordinal data*** contain codes assigned to objects or events as labels that also represent the rank order among them. For example, the variable *credit score* can be generally categorized as (1) low, (2) medium, and (3) high. Similar ordered relationships can be seen in variables such as age group (i.e., child, young, middle aged, elderly) and educational level (i.e., high school, college, graduate school). Some data mining algorithms, such as *ordinal multiple logistic regression,* take into account this additional rank-order information to build a better classification model.
- ***Numeric data*** represent the numeric values of specific variables. Examples of numerically valued variables include age, number of children, total household income (in U.S. dollars), travel distance (in miles), and temperature (in Fahrenheit degrees). Numeric values representing a variable can be integer (taking only whole numbers) or real (taking also the fractional number). The numeric data may also be called continuous data, implying that the variable contains continuous measures on a specific scale that allows insertion of interim values. Unlike a discrete variable, which represents finite, countable data, a continuous variable represents scalable measurements, and it is possible for the data to contain an infinite number of fractional values.
- ***Interval data*** are variables that can be measured on interval scales. A common example of interval scale measurement is temperature on the Celsius scale. In this particular scale, the unit of measurement is 1/100 of the difference between the melting temperature and the boiling temperature of water in atmospheric pressure; that is, there is not an absolute zero value.
- ***Ratio data*** include measurement variables commonly found in the physical sciences and engineering. Mass, length, time, plane angle, energy, and electric charge are examples of physical measures that are ratio scales. The scale type takes its name from the fact that measurement is the estimation of the ratio between a magnitude of a continuous quantity and a unit magnitude of the same kind. Informally, the distinguishing feature of a ratio scale is the possession of a nonarbitrary zero value. For example, the Kelvin temperature scale has a nonarbitrary zero point of absolute zero, which is equal to –273.15 degrees Celsius. This zero point is nonarbitrary, because the particles that comprise matter at this temperature have zero kinetic energy.
- Other data types include date/time, unstructured text, image, and audio. These data types need to be converted into some form of categorical or numeric representation before they can be processed by data mining algorithms. Data can also be classified as static or dynamic (i.e., temporal or time series).

Some data mining methods are particular about the data types they can handle. Providing them with incompatible data types may lead to incorrect models or (more often) halt of the model development process. For example, some data mining methods need all of the variables (both input as well as output) represented as numerically valued variables (e.g., neural networks, support vector machines, logistic regression). The nominal or ordinal variables are converted into numeric representations using some type of *1-of-N* pseudo variables (e.g., a categorical variable with three unique values can be transformed into three pseudo variables with binary values—1 or 0). Because this process may increase the number of variables, one should be cautious about the effect of such representations, especially for the categorical variables that have large number of unique values.

Similarly, some data mining methods, such as ID3 (a classic decision tree algorithm) and rough sets (a relatively new rule induction algorithm), need all of the variables represented as categorically valued variables. Early versions of these methods required the user to discretize numeric variables into categorical representations before they could be processed by the **algorithm**. The good news is that most implementations of these algorithms in widely available software tools accept a mix of numeric and nominal variables and internally make the necessary conversions before processing the data.

Application Case 4.2

Police Department Fights Crime with Data Mining

Shrinking resources, few leads, and aging cases complicate the fight against crime. At a police department in the United Kingdom, investigators find that these challenges limit the cases they can tackle. High-volume cases without definite leads, such as house burglaries and vehicle thefts that lack clear evidence, are often filed away until new evidence is found. Therefore, the challenge for the police department was to determine a way to quickly and easily find patterns and trends in unsolved criminal cases.

Each electronic case file at the police department contains physical descriptions of the thieves as well as their modus operandi (MO). Whereas many cases lacking evidence were previously filed away, the department is now reexamining them, and doing it more quickly than ever before. In PASW Modeler, the data modeler uses two Kohonen networks to cluster similar physical descriptions and MOs and then combines clusters to see whether groups of similar physical descriptions coincide with groups of similar MOs. If a good match is found and the perpetrators are known for one or more of the offenses, it is possible that the unsolved cases were committed by the same individuals.

The analytical team further investigates the clusters, using statistical methods to verify the similarities' importance. If clusters indicate that the same criminal might be at work, the department is likely to reopen and investigate the other crimes. Or, if the criminal is unknown but a large cluster indicates the same offender, the leads from these cases can be combined and the case reprioritized. The department is also investigating the behavior of prolific repeat offenders, with the goal of identifying crimes that seem to fit their behavioral pattern. The department hopes that the PASW Modeler will enable it to reopen old cases and make connections with known perpetrators.

Police departments around the globe are enhancing their crime-fighting techniques with innovative twenty-first-century approaches of applying data mining technology to prevent criminal activity. Success stories can be found on Web sites of major data mining tool and solution providers (e.g., SPSS, SAS, StatSoft, Salford Systems) as well as the major consultancy companies.

Source: "Police Department Fights Crime with SPSS Inc. Technology," **spss.com/success/pdf/WMPCS-1208.pdf** (accessed on May 25, 2009).

How Data Mining Works

Using existing and relevant data, data mining builds models to identify patterns among the attributes presented in the dataset. Models are the mathematical representations (simple linear relationships and/or complex highly nonlinear relationships) that identify the patterns among the attributes of the objects (e.g., customers) described in the dataset. Some of these patterns are explanatory (explaining the interrelationships and affinities among the attributes), whereas others are predictive (foretelling future values of certain attributes). In general, data mining seeks to identify four major types of patterns:

1. *Associations* find the commonly co-occurring groupings of things, such as beer and diapers going together in market-basket analysis.
2. *Predictions* tell the nature of future occurrences of certain events based on what has happened in the past, such as predicting the winner of the Super Bowl or forecasting the absolute temperature of a particular day.
3. *Clusters* identify natural groupings of things based on their known characteristics, such as assigning customers in different segments based on their demographics and past purchase behaviors.
4. *Sequential relationships* discover time-ordered events, such as predicting that an existing banking customer who already has a checking account will open a savings account followed by an investment account within a year.

These types of patterns have been *manually* extracted from data by humans for centuries, but the increasing volume of data in modern times has created a need for more automatic approaches. As datasets have grown in size and complexity, direct manual data analysis has increasingly been augmented with indirect, automatic data processing tools that use sophisticated methodologies, methods, and algorithms. The manifestation of such evolution of automated and semiautomated means of processing large datasets is now commonly referred to as *data mining*.

Generally speaking, data mining tasks can be classified into three main categories: prediction, association, and clustering. Based on the way in which the patterns are extracted from the historical data, the **learning algorithms** of data mining methods can be classified as either supervised or unsupervised. With supervised learning algorithms, the training data include both the descriptive attributes (i.e., independent variables or decision variables) as well as the class attribute (i.e., output variable or **result variable**). In contrast, with **unsupervised learning**, the training data include only the descriptive attributes. Figure 4.4 shows a simple taxonomy for data mining tasks, along with the learning methods, and popular algorithms for each of the data mining tasks.

PREDICTION **Prediction** is commonly referred to as the act of telling about the future. It differs from simple guessing by taking into account the experiences, opinions, and other relevant information in conducting the task of foretelling. A term that is commonly associated with prediction is *forecasting*. Even though many believe that these two terms are synonymous, there is a subtle but critical difference between the two. Whereas prediction

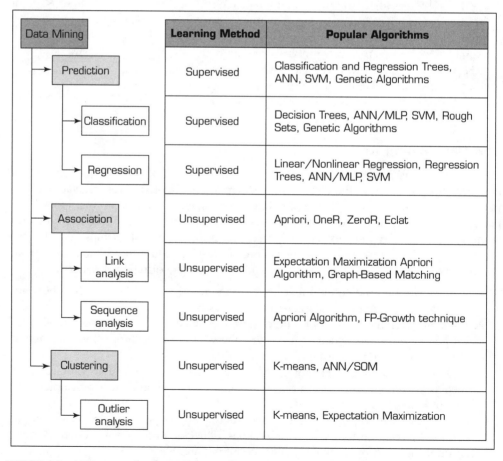

FIGURE 4.4 A Taxonomy for Data Mining Tasks.

is largely experience and opinion based, forecasting is data and model based. That is, in order of increasing reliability, one might list the relevant terms as *guessing, predicting,* and *forecasting,* respectively. In data mining terminology, *prediction* and *forecasting* are used synonymously, and the term *prediction* is used as the common representation of the act. Depending on the nature of what is being predicted, prediction can be named more specifically as classification (where the predicted thing, such as tomorrow's forecast, is a class label such as "rainy" or "sunny") or regression (where the predicted thing, such tomorrow's temperature, is a real number such as "65°F").

CLASSIFICATION **Classification**, or supervised induction, is perhaps the most common of all data mining tasks. The objective of classification is to analyze the historical data stored in a database and automatically generate a model that can predict future behavior. This induced model consists of generalizations over the records of a training dataset, which help distinguish predefined classes. The hope is that the model can then be used to predict the classes of other unclassified records and, more important, to accurately predict actual future events.

Common classification tools include neural networks and decision trees (from machine learning), logistic regression and discriminant analysis (from traditional statistics), and emerging tools such as rough sets, support vector machines, and **genetic algorithms**. Statistics-based classification techniques (e.g., logistic regression and discriminant analysis) have received their share of criticism—that they make unrealistic assumptions about the data, such as independence and normality—which limits their use in classification-type data mining projects.

Neural networks (see Section 4.5 for a detailed coverage of this popular machine-learning algorithm) involve the development of mathematical structures (somewhat resembling the biological neural networks in human brain) that have the capability to learn from past experiences presented in the form of well-structured datasets. They tend to be more effective when the number of variables involved is rather large and the relationships among them are complex and imprecise. Neural networks have disadvantages as well as advantages. For example, it is usually very difficult to provide a good rationale for the predictions made by a neural network. Also, neural networks tend to need considerable training. Unfortunately, the time needed for training tends to increase exponentially as the volume of data increases, and in general, neural networks cannot be trained on very large databases. These and other factors have limited the applicability of neural networks in data-rich domains.

Decision trees classify data into a finite number of classes based on the values of the input variables. Decision trees are essentially a hierarchy of if-then statements and are thus significantly faster than neural networks. They are most appropriate for categorical and interval data. Therefore, incorporating continuous variables into a decision tree framework requires *discretization*; that is, converting continuous valued numerical variables to ranges and categories.

A related category of classification tools is rule induction. Unlike with a decision tree, with rule induction the if-then statements are induced from the training data directly, and they need not be hierarchical in nature. Other, more recent techniques such as SVM, rough sets, and genetic algorithms are gradually finding their way into the arsenal of classification algorithms as representatives of advanced intelligent systems.

CLUSTERING **Clustering** partitions a collection of things (e.g., objects and events presented in a structured dataset) into segments (or natural groupings) whose members share similar characteristics. Unlike in classification, in clustering, the class labels are unknown. As the selected algorithms go through the dataset, identifying the commonalities of things based on their characteristics, the clusters are established. Because the clusters are determined using a heuristic-type algorithm, and because different algorithms may end up with different sets of clusters for the same dataset, it may be necessary for an expert to interpret, and potentially modify, the suggested clusters before the results of clustering techniques are put to actual use. After reasonable clusters have been identified, they can be used to classify and interpret new data.

Not surprisingly, clustering techniques include optimization. The goal of clustering is to create groups so that the members within each group have maximum similarity and the members across groups have minimum similarity. The most commonly used clustering techniques include *k*-means (from statistics) and self-organizing maps (from machine learning), which is a unique neural network architecture developed by Kohonen (1982).

Firms often effectively use their data mining systems to perform market segmentation with cluster analysis. Cluster analysis is a means of identifying classes of items so that items in a cluster have more in common with each other than with items in other clusters. It can be used in segmenting customers and directing appropriate marketing products to the segments at the right time in the right format at the right price. Cluster analysis is also used to identify natural groupings of events or objects so that a common set of characteristics of these groups can be identified to describe them. Application Case 4.3 describes how cluster analysis was combined with other data mining techniques to identify the causes of accidents.

ASSOCIATIONS Associations, or *association rule learning in data mining,* is a popular and well-researched technique for discovering interesting relationships among variables in large databases. Thanks to automated data-gathering technologies such as bar code

Application Case 4.3
Motor Vehicle Accidents and Driver Distractions

Driver distraction is at center stage in highway safety. A study published in 1996 by the National Highway Traffic Safety Administration concluded that roughly 25 to 30 percent of the injuries caused by car crashes were due to driver distraction. In 1999, according to the Fatality Analysis Reporting System (FARS) developed by the National Centre for Statistics and Analysis, 11 percent of fatal crashes (i.e., 4,462 fatalities) were due to driver inattention.

A study was conducted to extract the patterns of distraction factors at traffic accidents. Data mining was used to draw the correlations and associations of factors from the crash datasets provided by FARS. Three data mining techniques (Kohonen type neural networks, decision trees, and multilayer perceptron-type neural networks) were used to find different combinations of distraction factors that correlated with and potentially explained the high accident rates. The Kohonen type neural network identified natural clusters and revealed patterns of input variables in the collection of data. Decision trees explored and classified the effect of each incident on

successive events and also suggested the relationship between inattentive drivers and physical/mental conditions. Finally, a multilayer perceptron type neural network model was trained and tested to discover the relationships between inattention and other driver-related factors in these traffic crashes. Clementine from SPSS was used to mine the data obtained from the FARS database for all three model types.

The prediction and exploration model identified 1,255 drivers who were involved in accidents in which inattention was one of the leading driver factors that led to a crash. Rear, head-on, and angled collisions, among other various output variables, were among the factors that had significant impact on the occurrence of crashes and their severity.

Sources: Based on W. S. Tseng, H. Nguyen, J. Liebowitz, and W. Agresti, "Distractions and Motor Vehicle Accidents: Data Mining Application on Fatality Analysis Reporting System (FARS) Data Files," *Industrial Management & Data Systems,* Vol. 105, No. 9, January 2005, pp. 1188–1205; and J. Liebowitz, "New Trends in Intelligent Systems," Presentation made at University of Granada, **docto-si.ugr. es/seminario2006/presentaciones/jay.ppt** (accessed May 2009).

scanners, the use of association rules for discovering regularities among products in large-scale transactions recorded by point-of-sale (POS) systems in supermarkets has become a common knowledge-discovery task in the retail industry. In the context of the retail industry, association rule mining is often called *market-basket analysis.*

Two commonly used derivatives of association rule mining are **link analysis** and **sequence mining**. With link analysis, the linkage among many objects of interest is discovered automatically, such as the link between Web pages and referential relationships among groups of academic publication authors. With sequence mining, relationships are examined in terms of their order of occurrence to identify associations over time. Algorithms used in association rule mining include the popular Apriori (where frequent itemsets are identified) and FP-Growth, OneR, ZeroR, and Eclat.

VISUALIZATION AND TIME-SERIES FORECASTING Two techniques often associated with data mining are *visualization* and *time-series forecasting.* Visualization can be used in conjunction with other data mining techniques to gain a clearer understanding of underlying relationships. With time-series forecasting, the data are a series of values of the same variable that is captured and stored over time. These data are then used to develop models to extrapolate the future values of the same phenomenon.

HYPOTHESIS- OR DISCOVERY-DRIVEN DATA MINING Data mining can be hypothesis driven or discovery driven. **Hypothesis-driven data mining** begins with a proposition by the user, who then seeks to validate the truthfulness of the proposition. For example, a marketing manager may begin with the following proposition: "Are DVD player sales related to sales of television sets?"

Discovery-driven data mining finds patterns, associations, and other relationships hidden within datasets. It can uncover facts that an organization had not previously known or even contemplated.

SECTION 4.1 REVIEW QUESTIONS

1. Define data mining. Why are there many different names and definitions for data mining?
2. What recent factors have increased the popularity of data mining?
3. Is data mining a new discipline? Explain.
4. What are some major data mining methods and algorithms?
5. What are the key differences between the major data mining methods?

4.2 DATA MINING APPLICATIONS

Data mining has become a popular tool in addressing many complex businesses issues. It has been proven to be very successful and helpful in many areas, some of which are shown by the following representative examples. The goal of many of these business data mining applications is to solve a pressing problem or to explore an emerging business opportunity in order to create a sustainable competitive advantage.

- *Customer relationship management.* Customer relationship management (CRM) is the new and emerging extension of traditional marketing. The goal of CRM is to create one-on-one relationships with customers by developing an intimate understanding of their needs and wants. As businesses build relationships with their customers over time through a variety of transactions (e.g., product inquiries, sales, service requests, warranty calls), they accumulate tremendous amount of data. When combined with demographic and socioeconomic attributes, this information-rich data can be used to (1) identify most likely responders/buyers of new products/services (i.e., customer profiling); (2) understand the root causes of customer attrition in order to improve customer retention (i.e., churn analysis); (3) discover time-variant associations between products and services to maximize sales and customer value; and (4) identify the most profitable customers and their preferential needs to strengthen relationships and to maximize sales.

- *Banking.* Data mining can help banks with the following: (1) automating the loan application process by accurately predicting the most probable defaulters; (2) detecting fraudulent credit card and online-banking transactions; (3) identifying ways to maximize customer value by selling them products and services that they are most likely to buy; and (4) optimizing the cash return by accurately forecasting the cash flow on banking entities (e.g., ATM machines, banking branches).
- *Retailing and logistics.* In the retailing industry, data mining can be used to (1) predict accurate sales volumes at specific retail locations in order to determine correct inventory levels; (2) identify sales relationships between different products (with market-basket analysis) to improve the store layout and optimize sales promotions; (3) forecast consumption levels of different product types (based on seasonal and environmental conditions) to optimize logistics and hence maximize sales; and (4) discover interesting patterns in the movement of products (especially for the products that have a limited shelf life because they are prone to expiration, perishability, and contamination) in a supply chain by analyzing sensory and RFID data.
- *Manufacturing and production.* Manufacturers can use data mining to (1) predict machinery failures before they occur through the use of sensory data (enabling what is called *condition-based maintenance*); (2) identify anomalies and commonalities in production systems to optimize manufacturing capacity; and (3) discover novel patterns to identify and improve product quality.
- *Brokerage and securities trading.* Brokers and traders use data mining to (1) predict when and how much certain bond prices will change; (2) forecast the range and direction of stock fluctuations; (3) assess the effect of particular issues and events on overall market movements; and (4) identify and prevent fraudulent activities in securities trading.
- *Insurance.* The insurance industry uses data mining techniques to (1) forecast claim amounts for property and medical coverage costs for better business planning; (2) determine optimal rate plans based on the analysis of claims and customer data; (3) predict which customers are more likely to buy new policies with special features; and (4) identify and prevent incorrect claim payments and fraudulent activities.
- *Computer hardware and software.* Data mining can be used to (1) predict disk drive failures well before they actually occur; (2) identify and filter unwanted Web content and e-mail messages; (3) detect and prevent computer network security bridges; and (4) identify potentially unsecure software products.
- *Government and defense.* Data mining also has a number of military applications. It can be used to (1) forecast the cost of moving military personnel and equipment; (2) predict an adversary's moves to develop more successful strategies for military engagements; (3) predict resource consumption for better planning and budgeting; and (4) identify classes of unique experiences, strategies, and lessons

learned from military operations for better knowledge sharing throughout the organization.

- **Travel industry (airlines, hotels/resorts, rental car companies).** Data mining has a variety of uses in the travel industry. It is successfully used to (1) predict sales of different services (seat types in airplanes, room types in hotels/resorts, car types in rental car companies) in order to optimally price services to maximize revenues as a function of time-varying transactions (commonly referred to as *yield management*); (2) forecast demand at different locations to better allocate limited organizational resources; (3) identify the most profitable customers and provide them with personalized services to maintain their repeat business; and (4) retain valuable employees by identifying and acting on the root causes for attrition.

- **Health care.** Data mining has a number of health care applications. It can be used to (1) identify people without health insurance and the factors underlying this undesired phenomenon; (2) identify novel cost-benefit relationships between different treatments to develop more effective strategies; (3) forecast the level and the time of demand at different service locations to optimally allocate organizational resources; and (4) understand the underlying reasons for customer and employee attrition.

- **Medicine.** Use of data mining in medicine should be viewed as an invaluable complement to traditional medical research, which is mainly clinical and biological in nature. Data mining analyses can (1) identify novel patterns to improve survivability of patients with cancer; (2) predict success rates of organ transplantation patients to develop better donor-organ matching policies; (3) identify the functions of different genes in the human **chromosome** (known as genomics); and (4) discover the relationships between symptoms and illnesses (as well as illnesses and successful treatments) to help medical professionals make informed and correct decisions in a timely manner.

- **Entertainment industry.** Data mining is successfully used by the entertainment industry to (1) analyze viewer data to decide what programs to show during prime time and how to maximize returns by knowing where to insert advertisements; (2) predict the financial success of movies before they are produced to make investment decisions and to optimize the returns; (3) forecast the demand at different locations and different times to better schedule entertainment events and to optimally allocate resources; and (4) develop optimal pricing policies to maximize revenues.

- **Homeland security and law enforcement.** Data mining has a number of homeland security and law enforcement applications. Data mining is often used to (1) identify patterns of terrorist behaviors (see Application Case 4.4 for a recent example of use of data mining to track funding of terrorists' activities); (2) discover crime patterns (e.g., locations, timings, criminal behaviors, and other related attributes) to help solve criminal cases in a timely manner; (3) predict and eliminate potential biological and chemical attacks to a nation's critical infrastructure by analyzing special-purpose sensory data; and (4) identify and stop malicious attacks on critical information infrastructures (often called *information warfare*).

- **Sports.** Data mining was used to improve the performance of National Basketball Association (NBA) teams in the United States. The NBA developed Advanced Scout, a PC-based data mining application that coaching staff use to discover interesting patterns in basketball game data. The pattern interpretation is facilitated by allowing the user to relate patterns to videotape. See Bhandari et al. (1997) for details.

Application Case 4.4

A Mine on Terrorist Funding

The terrorist attack on the World Trade Center on September 11, 2001, underlined the importance of open source intelligence. The USA PATRIOT Act and the creation of the U.S. Department of Homeland Security heralded the potential application of information technology and data mining techniques to detect money laundering and other forms of terrorist financing. Law enforcement agencies have been focusing on money laundering activities via normal transactions through banks and other financial service organizations.

Law enforcement agencies are now focusing on international trade pricing as a terrorism funding tool. International trade has been used by money launderers to move money silently out of a country without attracting government attention. This transfer is achieved by overvaluing imports and undervaluing exports. For example, a domestic importer and foreign exporter could form a partnership and overvalue imports, thereby transferring money from the home country, resulting in crimes related to customs fraud, income tax evasion, and money laundering. The foreign exporter could be a member of a terrorist organization.

Data mining techniques focus on analysis of data on import and export transactions from the U.S. Department of Commerce and commerce-related entities. Import prices that exceed the upper quartile import prices and export prices that are lower than the lower quartile export prices are tracked. The focus is on abnormal transfer prices between corporations that may result in shifting taxable income and taxes out of the United States. An observed price deviation may be related to income tax avoidance/evasion, money laundering, or terrorist financing. The observed price deviation may also be due to an error in the U.S. trade database.

Data mining will result in efficient evaluation of data, which, in turn, will aid in the fight against terrorism. The application of information technology and data mining techniques to financial transactions can contribute to better intelligence information.

Sources: Based on J. S. Zdanowic, "Detecting Money Laundering and Terrorist Financing via Data Mining," *Communications of the ACM,* Vol. 47, No. 5, May 2004, p. 53; and R. J. Bolton, "Statistical Fraud Detection: A Review," *Statistical Science,* Vol. 17, No. 3, January 2002, p. 235.

SECTION 4.2 REVIEW QUESTIONS

1. What are the major application areas for data mining?
2. Identify at least five specific applications of data mining and list five common characteristics of these applications.
3. What do you think is the most prominent application area for data mining? Why?
4. Can you think of other application areas for data mining not discussed in this section? Explain.

4.3 DATA MINING PROCESS

In order to systematically carry out data mining projects, a general process is usually followed. Based on best practices, data mining researchers and practitioners have proposed several processes (workflows or simple step-by-step approaches) to maximize the chances of success in conducting data mining projects. These efforts have led to several standardized processes, some of which (a few of the most popular ones) are described in this section.

One such standardized process, arguably the most popular one, Cross-Industry Standard Process for Data Mining—**CRISP-DM**—was proposed in the mid-1990s by a European consortium of companies to serve as a nonproprietary standard methodology

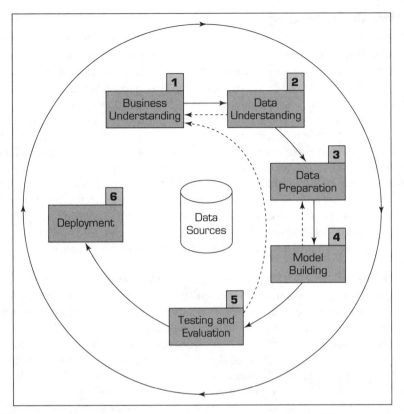

FIGURE 4.5   **The Six-Step CRISP-DM Data Mining Process.**   *Source:* Adapted from **CRISP-DM.org**.

for data mining (CRISP-DM, 2009). Figure 4.5 illustrates this proposed process, which is a sequence of six steps that starts with a good understanding of the business and the need for the data mining project (i.e., the application domain) and ends with the deployment of the solution that satisfied the specific business need. Even though these steps are sequential in nature, there is usually a great deal of backtracking. Because the data mining is driven by experience and experimentation, depending on the problem situation and the knowledge/experience of the analyst, the whole process can be very iterative (i.e., one should expect to go back and forth through the steps quite a few times) and time consuming. Because latter steps are built on the outcome of the former ones, one should pay extra attention to the earlier steps in order not to put the whole study on an incorrect path from the onset.

Step 1: Business Understanding

The key element of any data mining study is to know what the study is for. Answering such a question begins with a thorough understanding of the managerial need for new knowledge and an explicit specification of the business objective regarding the study to be conducted. Specific questions such as "What are the common characteristics of the customers we have lost to our competitors recently?" or "What are typical profiles of our customers, and how much value does each of them provide to us?" need to be addressed. Then a project plan for finding such knowledge is developed that specifies the people responsible for collecting the data, analyzing the data, and reporting the findings. At this early stage, a budget to support the study should also be established, at least at a high level with rough numbers.

Step 2: Data Understanding

A data mining study is specific to addressing a well-defined business task, and different business tasks require different sets of data. Following the business understanding, the main activity of the data mining process is to identify the relevant data from many available databases. Some key points must be considered in the data identification and selection phase. First and foremost, the analyst should be clear and concise about the description of the data mining task so that the most relevant data can be identified. For example, a retail data mining project may seek to identify spending behaviors of female shoppers, who purchase seasonal clothes, based on their demographics, credit card transactions, and socioeconomic attributes. Furthermore, the analyst should build an intimate understanding of the data sources (e.g., where the relevant data are stored and in what form; what the process of collecting the data is—automated versus manual; who the collectors of it are; and how often it is updated) and the variables (e.g., What are the most relevant variables? Is there any synonymous and/or homonymous variables? Are the variables independent of each other—do they stand as a complete information source without overlapping or conflicting information?).

In order to better understand the data, the analyst often uses a variety of statistical and graphical techniques, such as simple statistical summaries of each variable (e.g., for numeric variables, the average, minimum/maximum, median, standard deviation are among the calculated measures, whereas for categorical variables, the mode and frequency tables are calculated), correlation analysis, scatter plots, histograms, and box plots. A careful identification and selection of data sources and the most relevant variables can make it easier for data mining algorithms to quickly discover useful knowledge patterns.

Data sources for data selection can vary. Normally, data sources for business applications include demographic data (such as income, education, number of households, and age), sociographic data (such as hobby, club membership, and entertainment), transactional data (sales record, credit card spending, and issued checks), and so on.

Data can be categorized as quantitative and qualitative. Quantitative data are measured using numeric values. This data can be discrete (such as integers) or continuous (such as real numbers). Qualitative data, also known as categorical data, contain both nominal and ordinal data. Nominal data have finite nonordered values (e.g., gender data, which have two values: male and female). Ordinal data have finite ordered values. For example, customer credit ratings are considered ordinal data because the ratings can be excellent, fair, and bad.

Quantitative data can be readily represented by some sort of probability distribution. A probability distribution describes how the data are dispersed and shaped. For instance, normally distributed data are symmetric and are commonly referred to as being a bell-shaped curve. Qualitative data may be coded to numbers and then described by frequency distributions. Once the relevant data are selected according to the data mining business objective, data preprocessing should be pursued.

Step 3: Data Preparation

The purpose of data preparation (or more commonly called as *data preprocessing*) is to take the data identified in the previous step and prepare them for analysis by data mining methods. Compared to the other steps in CRISP-DM, data preprocessing consumes the most time and effort; most believe that this step accounts for roughly 80 percent of the total time spent on a data mining project. The reason for such an enormous effort spent on this step is the fact that real-world data are generally incomplete (lacking attribute values, lacking certain attributes of interest, or containing only aggregate data), noisy (containing errors or outliers), and inconsistent (containing discrepancies in codes or names). Figure 4.6 shows the four main steps needed to convert the raw, real-world data into minable datasets.

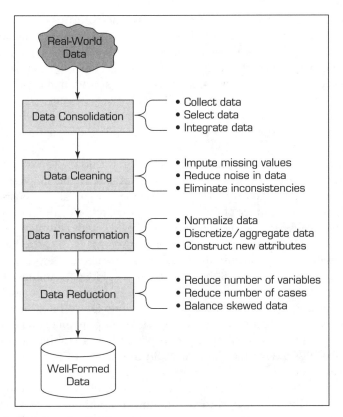

FIGURE 4.6 **Data Preprocessing Steps.**

In the first phase of data preprocessing, the relevant data are collected from the identified sources (accomplished in the previous step—Data Understanding—of CRISP-DM process), the necessary records and variables are selected (based on an intimate understanding of the data, the unnecessary sections are filtered out), and the records coming from multiple data sources are integrated (again, using the intimate understanding of the data, the synonyms and homonyms are to be handled properly).

In the second phase of data preprocessing, the data are cleaned (this step is also known as data scrubbing). In this step, the values in the dataset are identified and dealt with. In some cases, missing values are an anomaly in the dataset, in which case, they need to be imputed (filled with a most probable value) or ignored; in other cases, the missing values are a natural part of the dataset (e.g., the *household income* field is often left unanswered by people who are in the top-income tier). In this step, the analyst should also identify noisy values in the data (i.e., the outliers) and smooth them out. Additionally, inconsistencies (unusual values within a variable) in the data should be handled using domain knowledge and/or expert opinion.

In the third phase of data preprocessing, the data are transformed for better processing. For instance, in many cases, the data are normalized between a certain minimum and maximum for all variables in order to mitigate the potential bias of one variable (having large numeric values, such as for household income) dominating other variables (such as *number of dependents* or *years in service,* which may potentially be more important) having smaller values. Another transformation that takes place is discretization and/or aggregation. In some cases, the numeric variables are converted to categorical values (e.g., low, medium, and high); in other cases, a nominal variable's unique value range is reduced to a smaller set using concept hierarchies (e.g., as opposed to using the individual states with 50 different values, one may choose to use several regions for a variable that shows location) in order to have a dataset that is more amenable to computer processing. Still, in other cases, one might choose to create new variables based on the existing ones in order to magnify the information found in a collection of variables in the dataset. For instance, in an organ transplantation dataset, one might choose to use a single variable showing the blood-type match (1: match; 0: no-match) as opposed to separate multinominal values for the blood type of both the donor and the recipient. Such simplification may increase the information content while reducing the complexity of the relationships in the data.

The final phase of data preprocessing is data reduction. Even though data miners like to have large datasets, too much data is also a problem. In the simplest sense, one can visualize the data commonly used in data mining projects as a flat file consisting of two dimensions: variables (the number of columns) and cases/records (the number of rows). In some cases (e.g., image processing and genome projects with complex microarray data), the number of variables can be rather large, and the analyst must reduce the number down to a manageable size. Because the variables are treated as different dimensions that describe the phenomenon from different perspectives, in data mining, this process is commonly called *dimensional reduction*. Even though there is not a single best way to accomplish this task, one can use the findings from previously published literature; consult domain experts; run appropriate statistical tests (e.g., principle component analysis or independent component analysis); and, more preferably, a combination of these techniques to successfully reduce the dimensions in the data into a more manageable and most relevant subset.

With respect to the other dimension (i.e., the number of cases), some datasets may include millions or billions of records. Even though computing power is increasing exponentially, processing such a large number of records may not be practical or feasible. In such cases, one may need to sample a subset of the data for analysis. The underlying assumption of sampling is that the subset of the data will contain all relevant patterns of the complete dataset. In a homogenous dataset, such an assumption may hold well, but real-world data are hardly ever homogenous. The analyst should be extremely careful in selecting a subset of the data that reflects the essence of the complete dataset and is not specific to a subgroup or subcategory. The data are usually sorted on some variable, and taking a section of the data from the top or bottom may lead to a biased dataset on specific values of the indexed variable; therefore, one should always try to randomly select the records on the sample set. For skewed data, straightforward random sampling may not be sufficient, and stratified sampling (a proportional representation of different subgroups in the data is represented in the sample dataset) may be required. Speaking of skewed data, it is a good practice to balance the highly skewed data by either oversampling the less represented or undersampling the more represented classes. Research has shown that balanced datasets tend to produce better prediction models than unbalanced ones (Wilson and Sharda, 1994).

The essence of data preprocessing is summarized in Table 4.4, which maps the main phases (along with their problem descriptions) to a representative list of tasks and algorithms.

Step 4: Modeling Building

In this step, various modeling techniques are selected and applied to an already prepared dataset in order to address the specific business need. The model-building step also encompasses the assessment and comparative analysis of the various models built. Because there is not a universally known *best* method or algorithm for a data mining task, one should use a variety of viable model types along with a well-defined experimentation

TABLE 4.4 A Summary of Data Preprocessing Tasks and Potential Methods

Main Task	Subtasks	Popular Methods
Data consolidation	Access and collect the data	SQL queries, software agents, Web services.
	Select and filter the data	Domain expertise, SQL queries, statistical tests.
	Integrate and unify the data	SQL queries, domain expertise, ontology-driven data mapping.
Data cleaning	Handle missing values in the data	Fill in missing values (imputations) with most appropriate values (mean, median, min/max, mode, etc.); recode the missing values with a constant such as "ML"; remove the record of the missing value; do nothing.
	Identify and reduce noise in the data	Identify the outliers in data with simple statistical techniques (such as averages and standard deviations) or with cluster analysis; once identified, either remove the outliers or smooth them by using binning, regression, or simple averages.
	Find and eliminate erroneous data	Identify the erroneous values in data (other than outliers), such as odd values, inconsistent class labels, and odd distributions; once identified, use domain expertise to correct the values or remove the records holding the erroneous values.
Data transformation	Normalize the data	Reduce the range of values in each numerically valued variable to a standard range (e.g., 0 to 1 or −1 to +1) by using a variety of normalization or scaling techniques.
	Discretize or aggregate the data	If needed, convert the numeric variables into discrete representations using range or frequency-based binning techniques; for categorical variables, reduce the number of values by applying proper concept hierarchies.
	Construct new attributes	Derive new and more informative variables from the existing ones using a wide range of mathematical functions (as simple as addition and multiplication or as complex as a hybrid combination of log transformations).
Data reduction	Reduce number of attributes	Principle component analysis, independent component analysis, Chi-square testing, correlation analysis, and decision tree induction.
	Reduce number of records	Random sampling, stratified sampling, expert–knowledge-driven purposeful sampling.
	Balance skewed data	Oversample the less represented or undersample the more represented classes.

and assessment strategy to identify the "best" method for a given purpose. Even for a single method or algorithm, a number of parameters need to be calibrated to obtain optimal results. Some methods may have specific requirements on the way that the data are to be formatted; thus, stepping back to the data preparation step is often necessary.

Depending on the business need, the data mining task can be of a prediction (either classification or regression), an association, or a clustering type. Each of these data mining tasks can use a variety of data mining methods and algorithms. Some of these data mining methods were explained earlier in this chapter, and some of the most popular algorithms, including decision trees for classification, *k*-means for clustering, and the **Apriori algorithm** for association rule mining, are described later in this chapter.

Step 5: Testing and Evaluation

In step 5, the developed models are assessed and evaluated for their accuracy and generality. This step assesses the degree to which the selected model (or models) meets the business objectives and, if so, to what extent (i.e., do more models need to be developed and assessed). Another option is to test the developed model(s) in a real-world scenario if time and budget constraints permit. Even though the outcome of the developed models are expected to relate to the original business objectives, other findings that are not necessarily related to the original business objectives but that might also unveil additional information or hints for future directions are often discovered.

The testing and evaluation step is a critical and challenging task. No value is added by the data mining task until the business value obtained from discovered knowledge patterns is identified and recognized. Determining the business value from discovered knowledge patterns is somewhat similar to playing with puzzles. The extracted knowledge patterns are pieces of the puzzle that need to be put together in the context of the specific business purpose. The success of this identification operation depends on the interaction among data analysts, **business analysts**, and decision makers (such as business managers). Because data analysts may not have the full understanding of the data mining objectives and what they mean to the business and the business analysts and decision makers may not have the technical knowledge to interpret the results of sophisticated mathematical solutions, interaction among them is necessary. In order to properly interpret knowledge patterns, it is often necessary to use a variety of tabulation and visualization techniques (e.g., pivot tables, cross-tabulation of findings, pie charts, histograms, box plots, scatter plots).

Step 6: Deployment

Development and assessment of the models is not the end of the data mining project. Even if the purpose of the model is to have a simple exploration of the data, the knowledge gained from such exploration will need to be organized and presented in a way that the end user can understand and benefit from it. Depending on the requirements, the deployment phase can be as simple as generating a report or as complex as implementing a repeatable data mining process across the enterprise. In many cases, it is the customer, not the data analyst, who carries out the deployment steps. However, even if the analyst will not carry out the deployment effort, it is important for the customer to understand up front what actions need to be carried out in order to actually make use of the created models.

The deployment step may also include maintenance activities for the deployed models. Because everything about the business is constantly changing, the data that reflect the business activities also are changing. Over time, the models (and the patterns embedded within them) built on the old data may become obsolete, irrelevant, or misleading. Therefore, monitoring and maintenance of the models is important if the data mining results are to become a part of the day-to-day business and its environment. A careful preparation of a maintenance strategy helps to avoid unnecessarily long periods of incorrect usage of data mining results. In order to monitor the deployment of the data mining result(s), the project needs a detailed plan on the monitoring process, which may not be a trivial task for complex data mining models.

Application Case 4.5

Data Mining in Cancer Research

According to the American Cancer Society, approximately 1.5 million new cancer cases will be diagnosed in 2009. Cancer is the second-most common cause of death in the United States and in the world, exceeded only by cardiovascular disease. In the year 2010, 562,340 Americans are expected to die of cancer—more than 1,500 people a day—accounting for nearly one of every four deaths.

Cancer is a group of diseases generally characterized by uncontrolled growth and spread of abnormal cells. If the growth and/or spread is not controlled, it can result in death. Even though the exact reasons are not known, cancer is believed to be caused by both external factors (e.g., tobacco, infectious organisms, chemicals, and radiation) and internal factors (e.g., inherited mutations, hormones, immune conditions, and mutations that occur from metabolism). These causal factors may act together or in sequence to initiate or promote carcinogenesis. Cancer is treated with surgery, radiation, chemotherapy, hormone therapy, biological therapy, and targeted therapy. Survival statistics vary greatly by cancer type and stage at diagnosis.

The 5-year relative survival rate for all cancers diagnosed in 1996–2004 is 66 percent, up from 50 percent in 1975–1977. The improvement in survival reflects progress in diagnosing certain cancers at an earlier stage and improvements in treatment. Further improvements are needed to prevent and treat cancer.

Even though cancer research has traditionally been clinical and biological in nature, in recent years, data-driven analytic studies have become a common complement. In medical domains where data- and analytics-driven research have been applied successfully, novel research directions have been identified to further advance the clinical and biological studies. Using various types of data, including molecular, clinical, literature-based, and clinical-trial data, along with suitable data mining tools and techniques, researchers have been able to identify novel patterns, paving the road toward a cancer-free society.

In one study, Delen (2009) used three popular data mining techniques (decision trees, artificial neural networks (ANN), and support vector machines) in conjunction with logistic regression to develop prediction models for prostate cancer survivability. The dataset contained around 120,000 records and 77 variables. A k-fold cross-validation methodology was used in model building, evaluation, and comparison. The results showed that support vector models are the most accurate predictor (with a test set accuracy of 92.85%) for this domain, followed by artificial neural networks and decision trees. Furthermore, using a sensitivity-analysis-based evaluation method, the study also revealed novel patterns related to prognostic factors of prostate cancer.

In a related study, Delen et al. (2006) used two data mining algorithms (artificial neural networks and decision trees) and logistic regression to develop prediction models for breast cancer survival using a large dataset (more than 200,000 cases). Using a 10-fold cross-validation method to measure the unbiased estimate of the prediction models for performance comparison purposes, the results indicated that the decision tree (C5 algorithm) was the best predictor, with 93.6 percent accuracy on the holdout sample (which was the best prediction accuracy reported in the literature); followed by artificial neural networks, with 91.2 percent accuracy; and logistic regression, with 89.2 percent accuracy. Further analysis of prediction models revealed prioritized importance of the prognostic factors, which can then be used as basis for further clinical and biological research studies.

These examples (among many others in the medical literature) show that advanced data mining techniques can be used to develop models that possess a high degree of predictive as well as explanatory power. Although data mining methods are capable of extracting patterns and relationships hidden deep in large and complex medical databases, without the cooperation and feedback from the medical experts, their results are not be of much use. The patterns found via data mining methods

(Continued)

Application Case 4.5   (Continued)

should be evaluated by medical professionals who have years of experience in the problem domain to decide whether they are logical, actionable, and novel to warrant new research directions. In short, data mining is not to replace medical professionals and researchers, but to complement their invaluable efforts to provide data-driven new research directions and to ultimately save more human lives.

Sources: D. Delen, "Analysis of Cancer Data: A Data Mining Approach," *Expert Systems,* Vol. 26, No. 1, 2009, pp. 100–112; J. Thongkam, G. Xu, Y. Zhang, and F. Huang, "Toward Breast Cancer Survivability Prediction Models Through Improving Training Space," *Expert Systems with Applications,* 2009, in press; D. Delen, G. Walker, and A. Kadam, "Predicting Breast Cancer Survivability: A Comparison of Three Data Mining Methods," *Artificial Intelligence in Medicine,* Vol. 34, No. 2, 2005, pp. 113–127.

Other Data Mining Standardized Processes and Methodologies

In order to be applied successfully, a data mining study must be viewed as a process that follows a standardized methodology rather than as a set of automated software tools and techniques. In addition to CRISP-DM, there is another well-known methodology developed by the SAS Institute, called SEMMA (2009). The acronym **SEMMA** stands for "sample, explore, modify, model, and assess."

Beginning with a statistically representative sample of the data, SEMMA makes it easy to apply exploratory statistical and visualization techniques, select and transform the most significant predictive variables, model the variables to predict outcomes, and confirm a model's accuracy. A pictorial representation of SEMMA is given in Figure 4.7.

By assessing the outcome of each stage in the SEMMA process, the model developer can determine how to model new questions raised by the previous results and thus proceed back to the exploration phase for additional refinement of the data; that is, as with CRISP-DM, SEMMA is driven by a highly iterative experimentation cycle. The main difference between CRISP-DM and SEMMA is that CRISP-DM takes a more comprehensive approach—including understanding of the business and the relevant data—to data mining projects, whereas SEMMA implicitly assumes that the data mining project's goals and objectives along with the appropriate data sources have been identified and understood.

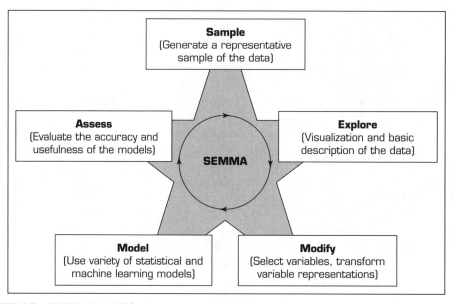

FIGURE 4.7   SEMMA Data Mining Process.

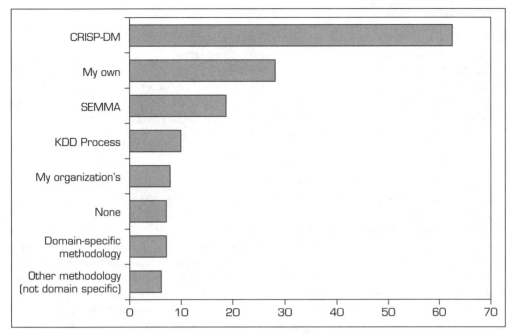

FIGURE 4.8   **Ranking of Data Mining Methodologies/Processes.**   *Source:* **kdnuggets.com**. Used with permission.

Some practitioners commonly use the term **knowledge discovery in databases (KDD)** as a synonym for data mining. Fayyad et al. (1996) defined *knowledge discovery in databases* as a process of using data mining methods to find useful information and patterns in the data, as opposed to data mining, which involves using algorithms to identify patterns in data derived through the KDD process. KDD is a comprehensive process that encompasses data mining. The input to the KDD process consists of organizational data. The enterprise data warehouse enables KDD to be implemented efficiently because it provides a single source for data to be mined. Dunham (2003) summarized the KDD process as consisting of the following steps: data selection, data preprocessing, data transformation, data mining, and interpretation/evaluation. Figure 4.8 shows the polling results for the question, "What main methodology are you using for data mining?" (conducted by **kdnuggets.com** in August 2007).

SECTION 4.3 REVIEW QUESTIONS

1. What are the major data mining processes?
2. Why do you think the early phases (understanding of the business and understanding of the data) take the longest in data mining projects?
3. List and briefly define the phases in the CRISP-DM process.
4. What are the main data preprocessing steps? Briefly describe each step and provide relevant examples.
5. How does CRISP-DM differ from SEMMA?

4.4   DATA MINING METHODS

A variety of methods are available for performing data mining studies, including classification, regression, clustering, and association. Most data mining software tools employ more than one technique (or algorithm) for each of these methods. This section describes the most popular data mining methods and explains their representative techniques.

Classification

Classification is perhaps the most frequently used data mining method for real-world problems. As a popular member of the machine-learning family of techniques, classification learns patterns from past data (a set of information—traits, variables, features—on characteristics of the previously labeled items, objects, or events) in order to place new instances (with unknown labels) into their respective groups or classes. For example, one could use classification to predict whether the weather on a particular day will be "sunny," "rainy," or "cloudy." Popular classification tasks include credit approval (i.e., good or bad credit risk), store location (e.g., good, moderate, bad), target marketing (e.g., likely customer, no hope), fraud detection (i.e., yes, no), and telecommunication (e.g., likely to turn to another phone company, yes/no). If what is being predicted is a class label (e.g., "sunny," "rainy," or "cloudy"), the prediction problem is called a classification, whereas if it is a numeric value (e.g., temperature such as 68°F), the prediction problem is called a **regression**.

Even though clustering (another popular data mining method) can also be used to determine groups (or class memberships) of things, there is a significant difference between the two. Classification learns the function between the characteristics of things (i.e., independent variables) and their membership (i.e., output variable) through a **supervised learning** process, where both types (input and output) of variables are presented to the algorithm; in clustering, the membership of the objects is learned through an unsupervised learning process where only the input variables are presented to the algorithm. Unlike classification, clustering does not have a supervising (or controlling) mechanism that enforces the learning process; instead, clustering algorithms use one or more **heuristics** (e.g., multidimensional distance measure) to discover natural groupings of objects.

The most common two-step methodology of classification-type prediction involves model development/training and model testing/deployment. In the model development phase, a collection of input data, including the actual class labels, is used. After a model has been trained, the model is tested against the holdout sample for accuracy assessment and eventually deployed for actual use where it is to predict classes of new data instances (where the class label is unknown). Several factors are considered in assessing the model, including the following:

- *Predictive accuracy.* The model's ability to correctly predict the class label of new or previously unseen data. Prediction accuracy is the most commonly used assessment factor for classification models. To compute this measure, actual class labels of a test dataset are matched against the class labels predicted by the model. The accuracy can then be computed as the *accuracy rate,* which is the percentage of test dataset samples correctly classified by the model (more on this topic is provided later in this chapter).
- *Speed.* The computational costs involved in generating and using the model, where faster is deemed to be better.
- *Robustness.* The model's ability to make reasonably accurate predictions, given noisy data or data with missing and erroneous values.
- *Scalability.* The ability to construct a prediction model efficiently given a rather large amount of data.
- *Interpretability.* The level of understanding and insight provided by the model (e.g., how and/or what the model concludes on certain predictions).

Estimating the True Accuracy of Classification Models

In classification problems, the primary source for accuracy estimation is the *confusion matrix* (also called a *classification matrix* or a *contingency table*). Figure 4.9 shows a confusion matrix for two-class classification problem. The numbers along the diagonal

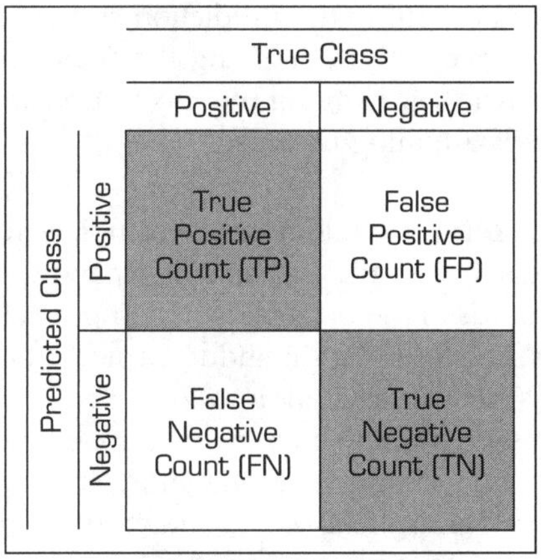

FIGURE 4.9 **A Sample Confusion Matrix for Tabulation of Two-Class Classification Results.**

from the upper left to the lower right represent correct decisions, and the numbers outside this diagonal represent the errors.

Table 4.5 provides equations for common accuracy metrics for classification models.

When the classification problem is not binary, the confusion matrix gets bigger (a square matrix with the size of the unique number of class labels), and accuracy metrics becomes limited to *per class accuracy rates* and the *overall classifier accuracy*.

$$(True\ Classification\ Rate)_i = \frac{(True\ Classification)_i}{\sum_{i=1}^{n}(False\ Classification)_i}$$

$$(Overall\ Classifier\ Accuracy)_i = \frac{\sum_{i=1}^{n}(False\ Classification)_i}{Total\ Number\ of\ Cases}$$

Estimating the accuracy of a classification model (or classifier) induced by a supervised learning algorithms is important for the following two reasons: First, it can be used to estimate its future prediction accuracy, which could imply the level of confidence one

TABLE 4.5 **Common Accuracy Metrics for Classification Models**

Metric	Description
$True\ Positive\ Rate = \dfrac{TP}{TP + FN}$	The ratio of correctly classified positives divided by the total positive count (i.e., hit rate or recall)
$True\ Negative\ Rate = \dfrac{TN}{TN + FP}$	The ratio of correctly classified negatives divided by the total negative count (i.e., false alarm rate)
$Accuracy = \dfrac{TP + TN}{TP + TN + FP + FN}$	The ratio of correctly classified instances (positives and negatives) divided by the total number of instances
$Precision = \dfrac{TP}{TP + FP}$	The ratio of correctly classified positives divided by the sum of correctly classified positives and incorrectly classified positives
$Recall = \dfrac{TP}{TP + FN}$	Ratio of correctly classified positives divided by the sum of correctly classified positives and incorrectly classified negatives

should have in the classifier's output in the prediction system. Second, it can be used for choosing a classifier from a given set (identifying the "best" classification model among the many trained). The following are among the most popular estimation methodologies used for classification-type data mining models.

SIMPLE SPLIT The **simple split** (or holdout or test sample estimation) partitions the data into two mutually exclusive subsets called a *training set* and a *test set* (or *holdout set*). It is common to designate two-thirds of the data as the training set and the remaining one-third as the test set. The training set is used by the inducer (model builder), and the built classifier is then tested on the test set. An exception to this rule occurs when the classifier is an artificial neural network. In this case, the data are partitioned into three mutually exclusive subsets: training, validation, and testing. The validation set is used during model building to prevent overfitting (more on artificial neural networks can be found in Chapter 6). Figure 4.10 shows the simple split methodology.

The main criticism of this method is that it makes the assumption that the data in the two subsets are of the same kind (i.e., have the exact same properties). Because this is a simple random partitioning, in most realistic datasets where the data are skewed on the classification variable, such an assumption may not hold true. In order to improve this situation, stratified sampling is suggested, where the strata become the output variable. Even though this is an improvement over the simple split, it still has a bias associated from the single random partitioning.

K-FOLD CROSS-VALIDATION In order to minimize the bias associated with the random sampling of the training and holdout data samples in comparing the predictive accuracy of two or more methods, one can use a methodology called **k-fold cross-validation**. In k-fold cross-validation, also called *rotation estimation,* the complete dataset is randomly split into k mutually exclusive subsets of approximately equal size. The classification model is trained and tested k times. Each time, it is trained on all but one fold and then tested on the remaining single fold. The cross-validation estimate of the overall accuracy of a model is calculated by simply averaging the k individual accuracy measures, as shown in the following equation:

$$CVA = \frac{1}{k}\sum_{i=1}^{k}A_i$$

where *CVA* stands for cross-validation accuracy, k is the number of folds used, and *A* is the accuracy measure (e.g., hit-rate, sensitivity, specificity) of each fold.

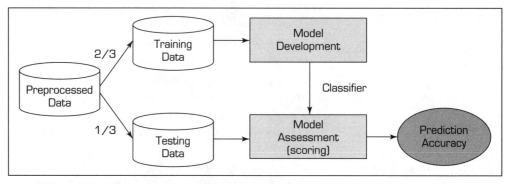

FIGURE 4.10 Simple Random Data Splitting.

ADDITIONAL CLASSIFICATION ASSESSMENT METHODOLOGIES Other popular assessment methodologies include the following:

- *Leave-one-out.*   The leave-one-out method is similar to the *k*-fold cross-validation where the *k* takes the value of 1; that is, every data point is used for testing once on as many models developed as there are number of data points. This is a time-consuming methodology, but for small datasets, sometimes it is a viable option.
- *Bootstrapping.*   With **bootstrapping**, a fixed number of instances from the original data are sampled (with replacement) for training and the rest of the dataset is used for testing. This process is repeated as many times as desired.
- *Jackknifing.*   Similar to the leave-one-out methodology; with jackknifing, the accuracy is calculated by leaving one sample out at each iteration of the estimation process.
- *Area under the ROC curve.*   The **area under the ROC curve** is a graphical assessment technique where the true positive rate is plotted on the *Y*-axis and false positive rate is plotted on the *X*-axis. The area under the ROC curve determines the accuracy measure of a classifier: A value of 1 indicates a perfect classifier whereas 0.5 indicates no better than random chance; in reality, the values would range between the two extreme cases. For example, in Figure 4.11, *A* has a better classification performance than *B*, while *C* is not any better than random chance of flipping a coin.

CLASSIFICATION TECHNIQUES A number of techniques (or algorithms) are used for classification modeling, including the following:

- *Decision tree analysis.*   Decision tree analysis (a machine-learning technique) is arguably the most popular classification technique in the data mining arena. A detailed description of this technique is given in the following section.

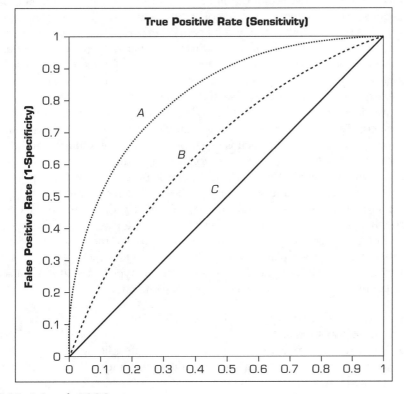

FIGURE 4.11 A Sample ROC Curve.

- *Statistical analysis.* Statistical techniques were the primary classification algorithm for many years until the emergence of machine-learning techniques. Statistical classification techniques include logistic regression and discriminant analysis, both of which make the assumptions that the relationships between the input and output variables are linear in nature, the data are normally distributed, and the variables are not correlated and are independent of each other. The questionable nature of these assumptions has led to the shift toward machine-learning techniques.
- *Neural networks.* These are among the most popular machine-learning techniques that can be used for classification-type problems. A detailed description of this technique is presented later in this chapter.
- *Case-based reasoning.* This approach uses historical cases to recognize commonalities in order to assign a new case into most probable category.
- *Bayesian classifiers.* This approach uses probability theory to build classification models based on the past occurrences that are capable of placing a new instance into a most probable class (or category).
- *Genetic algorithms.* The use of the analogy of natural evolution to build directed-search-based mechanisms to classify data samples.
- *Rough sets.* This method takes into account the partial membership of class labels to predefined categories in building models (collection of rules) for classification problems.

A complete description of all of these classification techniques is beyond the scope of this book; so, only a few of the most popular ones are presented here.

DECISION TREES Before describing the details of decision trees, we need to discuss some simple terminology. First, decision trees include many input variables that may have an impact on the classification of different patterns. These input variables are usually called *attributes.* For example, if we were to build a model to classify loan risks on the basis of just two characteristics—income and a credit rating—these two characteristics would be the attributes and the resulting output would be the *class label* (e.g., low, medium, or high risk). Second, a tree consists of branches and nodes. A *branch* represents the outcome of a test to classify a pattern (on the basis of a test) using one of the attributes. A *leaf node* at the end represents the final class choice for a pattern (a chain of branches from the root node to the leaf node that can be represented as a complex if-then statement).

The basic idea behind a decision tree is that it recursively divides a training set until each division consists entirely or primarily of examples from one class. Each nonleaf node of the tree contains a *split point,* which is a test on one or more attributes and determines how the data are to be divided further. Decision tree algorithms, in general, build an initial tree from the training data such that each leaf node is pure, and they then prune the tree to increase its generalization, and hence the prediction accuracy on test data.

In the growth phase, the tree is built by recursively dividing the data until each division is either pure (i.e., contains members of the same class) or relatively small. The basic idea is to ask questions whose answers would provide the most information, similar to what we may do when playing the game "Twenty Questions."

The split used to partition the data depends on the type of the attribute used in the split. For a continuous attribute A, splits are of the form value(A)

1. Create a root node and assign all of the training data to it.
2. Select the *best* splitting attribute.
3. Add a branch to the root node for each value of the split. Split the data into mutually exclusive (nonoverlapping) subsets along the lines of the specific split and mode to the branches.
4. Repeat the steps 2 and 3 for each and every leaf node until the stopping criteria is reached (e.g., the node is dominated by a single class label).

Many different algorithms have been proposed for creating decision trees. These algorithms differ primarily in terms of the way in which they determine the splitting attribute (and its split values), the order of splitting the attributes (splitting the same attribute only once or many times), the number of splits at each node (binary versus ternary), the stopping criteria, and the pruning of the tree (pre- versus postpruning). Some of the most well-known algorithms are ID3 (followed by C4.5 and C5 as the improved versions of ID3) from machine learning, classification and regression trees (CART) from statistics, and the chi-squared automatic interaction detector (CHAID) from pattern recognition.

When building a decision tree, the goal at each node is to determine the attribute and the split point of that attribute that best divides the training records in order to purify the class representation at that node. To evaluate the goodness of the split, some splitting indices have been proposed. Two of the most common ones are the Gini index and information gain. The Gini index is used in CART and SPRINT (Scalable PaRalleizable Induction of Decision Trees) algorithms. Versions of information gain are used in ID3 (and its newer versions, C4.5 and C5).

The **Gini index** has been used in economics to measure the diversity of a population. The same concept can be used to determine the purity of a specific class as a result of a decision to branch along a particular attribute or variable. The best split is the one that increases the purity of the sets resulting from a proposed split. A more detailed description on Gini index and its mathematical formulation can be found in Hastie et al (2009).

Information gain is the splitting mechanism used in ID3, which is perhaps the most widely known decision tree algorithm. It was developed by Ross Quinlan in 1986, and since then, he has evolved this algorithm into the C4.5 and C5 algorithms. The basic idea behind ID3 (and its variants) is to use a concept called *entropy* in place of the Gini index. **Entropy** measures the extent of uncertainty or randomness in a dataset. If all the data in a subset belong to just one class, there is no uncertainty or randomness in that dataset; so the entropy is zero. The objective of this approach is to build subtrees so that the entropy of each final subset is zero (or close to zero). A more detailed description on Information gain and its mathematical formulation can be found in Quinlan (1986).

Application Case 4.6

Highmark, Inc., Employs Data Mining to Manage Insurance Costs

Highmark, Inc., based in Pittsburgh, Pennsylvania, has a long tradition of providing access to affordable, quality health care to its members and communities. Highmark was formed in 1996 by the merger of two Pennsylvania licensees of the Blue Cross and Blue Shield Association: Pennsylvania Blue Shield (now Highmark Blue Shield) and a Blue Cross plan in western Pennsylvania (now Highmark Blue Cross Blue Shield). Highmark is currently one of the largest health insurers in the United States.

Data in Managed Care Organizations

The amount of data floating around in managed care organizations such as Highmark is vast. These data, often considered to be occupying storage space and viewed as a menace to be dealt with, have recently been recognized as a source of new knowledge. Data mining tools and techniques provide practical means for analyzing patient data and unraveling mysteries that can lead to better managed care at lower costs—a mission that most managed care companies are trying to achieve.

Each day, managed care companies receive millions of data items about their customers, and each piece of information updates the case history of each member. Companies have become aware of the usefulness of the data at their disposal and use analytic software tools to extract patient clusters that are more costly than average to treat. Earlier efforts

(Continued)

Application Case 4.6 (Continued)

at using computer technology in order to extract patient-related actionable information were limited in establishing a connection between two different diseases. For example, the software tool could scan through the data and report that diabetics or people suffering from coronary heart diseases were the most expensive to treat. However, these reporting-based software tools were inefficient in finding why these patients were getting sick or why some patients were more adversely affected by certain diseases than others. Data mining tools can solve some of these problems by analyzing multidimensional information and generating succinct relationships and correlations among different diseases and patient profiles.

Managed care organizations are inundated with data, and some of the companies do not want to add to the complexity by adding data mining applications. They may want to scan data for various reasons but are unable to decide why or how to analyze their data. Things are becoming brighter for patients as well as companies, however, because health insurance regulations are clearing the way for efficient data and structuring analysis.

The Need for Data Mining

Market pressures are driving managed care organizations to become more efficient, and hence to take data mining seriously. Customers are demanding more and better service, and competitors are becoming relentless, all of which are leading to the design and delivery of more customized products in a timely manner.

This customization brings us to the originating point of why and where the major portions of medical costs are occurring. Many organizations have started to use data mining software to

predict who is more likely to fall sick and who is more likely to be the most expensive to treat. A look into the future has enabled organizations to filter out their costly patients and lower their Medicare costs by using preventive measures. Another important application of predictive studies is the management of premiums. An employer group that has a large number of employees falling in a higher cost bracket would see its rates increase.

Based on the historical data, predictive modeling might be able to foretell which patients are more likely to become a financial burden for the company. For example, a predictive modeling application might rate a diabetic patient as a high risk of increased medical costs, which by itself might not be actionable information. However, data mining implementation at Highmark draws a relationship between a diabetic patient and other patient- and environment-related parameters; that is, a patient with a specific cardiac condition might be at high risk of contracting diabetes. This relationship is drawn because the cardiac medication could lead the patient to developing diabetes later in life. Highmark officials testify to this fact by saying that they would not have monitored the patients for the cardiac medication and might not have drawn a relationship between the cardiac medication and diabetes. Medical research has been successful in codifying many of the complexities associated with patient conditions. Data mining has laid the foundation for better detection and proper intervention programs.

Sources: Based on G. Gillespie, "Data Mining: Solving Care, Cost Capers," *Health Data Management,* November 2004, **findarticles.com/p/articles/mi_km2925/is_200411/ai_n8622737** (accessed May 2009); and "Highmark Enhances Patient Care, Keeps Medical Costs Down with SAS," **sas.com/success/highmark.html** (accessed April 2006).

Cluster Analysis for Data Mining

Cluster analysis is an essential data mining method for classifying items, events, or concepts into common groupings called *clusters*. The method is commonly used in biology, medicine, genetics, social network analysis, anthropology, archaeology, astronomy, character recognition, and even in management information system development. As data mining has increased in popularity, the underlying techniques have been applied to business, especially to marketing. Cluster analysis has been used extensively for fraud detection (both credit card and e-commerce fraud) and market segmentation of customers in contemporary CRM systems. More applications in business continue to be developed as the strength of cluster analysis is recognized and used.

Cluster analysis is an exploratory data analysis tool for solving classification problems. The objective is to sort cases (e.g., people, things, events) into groups, or clusters, so that the degree of association is strong among members of the same cluster and weak among members of different clusters. Each cluster describes the class to which its members belong. An obvious one-dimensional example of cluster analysis is to establish score ranges into which to assign class grades for a college class. This is similar to the cluster analysis problem that the U.S. Treasury faced when establishing new tax brackets in the 1980s. A fictional example of clustering occurs in J. K. Rowling's *Harry Potter* books. The Sorting Hat determines to which House (e.g., dormitory) to assign first-year students at the Hogwarts School. Another example involves determining how to seat guests at a wedding. As far as data mining goes, the importance of cluster analysis is that it may reveal associations and structures in data that were not previously apparent but are sensible and useful once found.

Cluster analysis results may be used to:

- Identify a classification scheme (e.g., types of customers)
- Suggest statistical models to describe populations
- Indicate rules for assigning new cases to classes for identification, targeting, and diagnostic purposes
- Provide measures of definition, size, and change in what were previously broad concepts
- Find typical cases to label and represent classes
- Decrease the size and complexity of the problem space for other data mining methods
- Identify outliers in a specific domain (e.g., rare-event detection)

DETERMINING THE OPTIMAL NUMBER OF CLUSTERS Clustering algorithms usually require one to specify the number of clusters to find. If this number is not known from prior knowledge, it should be chosen in some way. Unfortunately, there is not an optimal way of calculating what this number is supposed to be. Therefore, several different heuristic methods have been proposed. The following are among the most commonly referenced ones:

- Look at the percentage of variance explained as a function of the number of clusters; that is, choose a number of clusters so that adding another cluster would not give much better modeling of the data. Specifically, if one graphs the percentage of variance explained by the clusters, there is a point at which the marginal gain will drop (giving an angle in the graph), indicating the number of clusters to be chosen.
- Set the number of clusters to $(n/2)^{1/2}$, where n is the number of data points.
- Use the Akaike Information Criterion, which is a measure of the goodness of fit (based on the concept of entropy) to determine the number of clusters.
- Use Bayesian Information Criterion, which is a model-selection criterion (based on maximum likelihood estimation) to determine the number of clusters.

ANALYSIS METHODS Cluster analysis may be based on one or more of the following general methods:

- Statistical methods (including both hierarchical and nonhierarchical), such as *k*-means, *k*-modes, and so on.
- Neural networks (with the architecture called self-organizing map or SOM)

- **Fuzzy logic** (e.g., fuzzy *c*-means algorithm)
- Genetic algorithms

Each of these methods generally works with one of two general method classes:

- *Divisive.* With divisive classes, all items start in one cluster and are broken apart.
- *Agglomerative.* With agglomerative classes, all items start in individual clusters, and the clusters are joined together.

Most cluster analysis methods involve the use of a **distance measure** to calculate the closeness between pairs of items. Popular distance measures include Euclidian distance (the ordinary distance between two points that one would measure with a ruler) and Manhattan distance (also called the rectilinear distance, or taxicab distance, between two points). Often, they are based on true distances that are measured, but this need not be so, as is typically the case in IS development. Weighted averages may be used to establish these distances. For example, in an IS development project, individual modules of the system may be related by the similarity between their inputs, outputs, processes, and the specific data used. These factors are then aggregated, pairwise by item, into a single distance measure.

K-MEANS CLUSTERING ALGORITHM The *k*-means clustering algorithm (where *k* stands for the predetermined number of clusters) is arguably the most referenced clustering algorithm. It has its roots in traditional statistical analysis. As the name implies, the algorithm assigns each data point (customer, event, object, etc.) to the cluster whose center (also called *centroid*) is the nearest. The center is calculated as the average of all the points in the cluster; that is, its coordinates are the arithmetic mean for each dimension separately over all the points in the cluster. The algorithm steps are listed below and shown graphically in Figure 4.12:

Initialization step: Choose the number of clusters (i.e., the value of *k*).
   Step 1: Randomly generate *k* random points as initial cluster centers.
   Step 2: Assign each point to the nearest cluster center.
   Step 3: Recompute the new cluster centers.

Repetition step: Repeat steps 2 and 3 until some convergence criterion is met (usually that the assignment of points to clusters becomes stable).

Association Rule Mining

Association rule mining is a popular data mining method that is commonly used as an example to explain what data mining is and what it can do to a technologically less-savvy audience. Most of you might have heard the famous (or infamous, depending on how to

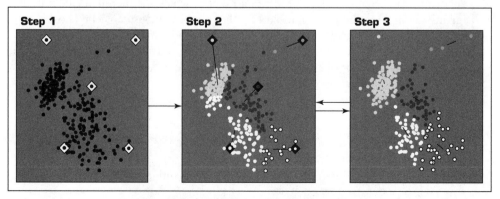

FIGURE 4.12 A Graphical Illustration of the Steps in *k*-Means Algorithm.

look at it) relationship discovered between the sales of beer and diapers at grocery stores. As the story goes, a large supermarket chain (maybe Wal-Mart, maybe not; there is no consensus on which supermarket chain it was) did an analysis of customers' buying habits and found a statistically significant correlation between purchases of beer and purchases of diapers. It was theorized that the reason for this was that fathers (presumably young men) were stopping off at the supermarket to buy diapers for their babies (especially on Thursdays) and, since they could no longer go down to the sports bar as often, would buy beer as well. As a result of this finding, the supermarket chain is alleged to have placed the diapers next to the beer, resulting in increased sales of both.

In essence, association rule mining aims to find interesting relationships (affinities) between variables (items) in large databases. Because of its successful application to business problems, it is commonly called a *market-basket analysis*. The main idea in market-basket analysis is to identify strong relationships among different products (or services) that are usually purchased together (shows up in the same basket together, either a physical basket at a grocery store or a virtual basket at an e-commerce Web site). For instance, market-basket analysis may find a pattern like, "If a customer buys laptop computer and virus protection software, he/she also buys extended service plan 70 percent of the time." The input to market-basket analysis is the simple point-of-sale transaction data, where a number of products and/or services purchased together (just like the content of a purchase receipt) are tabulated under a single transaction instance. The outcome of the analysis is invaluable information that can be used to better understand customer-purchase behavior in order to maximize the profit from business transactions. A business can take advantage of such knowledge by (1) putting the items next to each other to make it more convenient for the customers to pick them up together and not forget to buy one when buying the others (increasing sales volume); (2) promoting the items as a package (do not put one on sale if the other(s) is on sale); and (3) placing them apart from each other so that the customer has to walk the aisles to search for it, and by doing so potentially seeing and buying other items.

Applications of market-basket analysis include cross-marketing, cross-selling, store design, catalog design, e-commerce site design, optimization of online advertising, product pricing, and sales/promotion configuration. In essence, market-basket analysis helps businesses infer customer needs and preferences from their purchase patterns. Outside the business realm, association rules are successfully used to discover relationships between symptoms and illnesses, diagnosis and patient characteristics and treatments (to be used in medical decision support systems [DSS]), and genes and their functions (to be used in genomics projects), among others.

A good question to ask with respect to the patterns/relationships that association rule mining can discover is, "Are all association rules interesting and useful?" In order to answer such a question, association rule mining uses two common metrics: **support** and **confidence**. Before defining these terms, let's get a little technical by showing what an association rule looks like:

$$X \Rightarrow Y[S\%, C\%]$$

{Laptop Computer, Antivirus Software} $\Rightarrow$ {Extended Service Plan}[30%, 70%]

Here, X (products and/or service; called the *left-hand side, LHS,* or the antecedent) is associated with Y (products and/or service; called the *right-hand side, RHS,* or *consequent*). S is the support, and C is the confidence for this particular rule. The support (S) of a rule is the measure of how often these products and/or services (i.e., LHS + RHS = Laptop Computer, Antivirus Software, and Extended Service Plan) appear together in the same transaction; that is, the proportion of transactions in the dataset that contain all of the products and/or services mentioned in a specific rule. In this example, 30 percent of all transactions in the hypothetical store database had all three products present in a single sales ticket. The confidence of a rule is the measure of how often the products and/or services on the RHS (consequent) go together with the products and/or services on the LHS (antecedent); that is, the proportion of transactions that include LHS while also including the RHS. In other words, it is the conditional probability of finding the RHS of the rule present in transactions where the LHS of the rule already exists.

Several algorithms are available for generating association rules. Some well-known algorithms include Apriori, Eclat, and FP-Growth. These algorithms only do half the job, which is to identify the frequent itemsets in the database. A frequent itemset is an arbitrary number of items that frequently go together in a transaction (e.g., shopping basket). Once the frequent itemsets are identified, they need to be converted into rules with antecedent and consequent parts. Determination of the rules from frequent itemsets is a straightforward matching process, but the process may be time consuming with large transaction databases. Even though there can be many items on each section of the rule, in practice, the consequent part usually contains a single item. In the following section, one of the most popular algorithms for identification of frequent itemsets is explained.

APRIORI ALGORITHM The **Apriori algorithm** is the most commonly used algorithm to discover association rules. Given a set of itemsets (e.g., sets of retail transactions, each listing individual items purchased), the algorithm attempts to find subsets that are common to at least a minimum number of the itemsets (i.e., complies with a minimum support). Apriori uses a bottom-up approach, where frequent subsets are extended one item at a time (a method known as *candidate generation,* whereby the size of frequent subsets increases from one-item subsets to two-item subsets, then three-item subsets, etc.), and groups of candidates at each level are tested against the data for minimum support. The algorithm terminates when no further successful extensions are found.

As an illustrative example, consider the following. A grocery store tracks sales transactions by SKU (stock-keeping unit) and thus knows which items are typically purchased together. The database of transactions, along with the subsequent steps in identifying the frequent itemsets, is shown in Figure 4.13. Each SKU in the transaction database corresponds to a product, such as "1 = butter," "2 = bread," "3 = water," and so on. The first step in Apriori is to count up the frequencies (i.e., the supports) of each item (one-item itemsets). For this overly simplified example, let us set the minimum support to 3 (or 50%; meaning an itemset is considered to be a frequent itemset if it shows up in at least three out of six transactions in the database). Because all of the one-item itemsets have at least 3 in the support column, they are all considered frequent itemsets. However, had any of the one-item itemsets not been frequent, they would not have been included as a possible member of possible two-item pairs. In this way, Apriori *prunes* the tree of all possible itemsets. As Figure 4.13 shows, using one-item itemsets, all possible two-item itemsets are generated and the transaction database is used to calculate their support values. Because the two-item itemset {1, 3} has a support less than 3, it should not be included in the frequent itemsets that will be used to generate the next-level itemsets (three-item itemsets). The algorithms seem deceivingly simple, but only for small dataset. In much larger datasets, especially those with huge amounts of items present in low quantities and small amounts of items present in big quantities, the search and calculation becomes a computationally intensive process.

SECTION 4.4 REVIEW QUESTIONS

1. Identify at least three of the main data mining methods.
2. Give examples of situations in which classification would be an appropriate data mining technique. Give examples of situations in which regression would be an appropriate data mining technique.

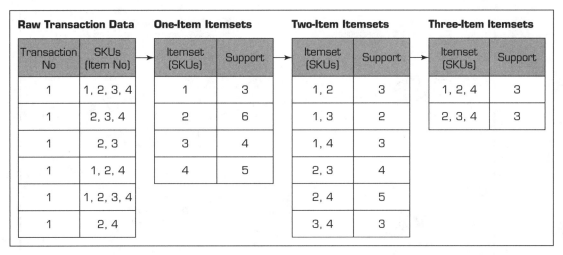

Raw Transaction Data		One-Item Itemsets		Two-Item Itemsets		Three-Item Itemsets	
Transaction No	SKUs (Item No)	Itemset (SKUs)	Support	Itemset (SKUs)	Support	Itemset (SKUs)	Support
1	1, 2, 3, 4	1	3	1, 2	3	1, 2, 4	3
1	2, 3, 4	2	6	1, 3	2	2, 3, 4	3
1	2, 3	3	4	1, 4	3		
1	1, 2, 4	4	5	2, 3	4		
1	1, 2, 3, 4			2, 4	5		
1	2, 4			3, 4	3		

FIGURE 4.13   **Identification of Frequent Itemsets in Apriori Algorithm.**

3. List and briefly define at least two classification techniques.

4. What are some of the criteria for comparing and selecting the best classification technique?

5. Briefly describe the general algorithm used in decision trees.

6. Define Gini index. What does it measure?

7. Give examples of situations in which cluster analysis would be an appropriate data mining technique.

8. What is the major difference between cluster analysis and classification?

9. What are some of the methods for cluster analysis?

10. Give examples of situations in which association would be an appropriate data mining technique.

4.5   ARTIFICIAL NEURAL NETWORKS FOR DATA MINING

Neural networks have emerged as advanced data mining tools in cases where other techniques may not produce satisfactory solutions. As the term implies, neural networks have a biologically inspired modeling capability (representing a brain metaphor) for information processing. Neural networks have been shown to be very promising computational systems in many forecasting and business classification applications due to their ability to "learn" from the data, their nonparametric nature (i.e., no rigid assumptions), and their ability to generalize (Haykin, 2009). **Neural computing** refers to a pattern-recognition methodology for machine learning. The resulting model from neural computing is often called an **artificial neural network (ANN)** or a **neural network**. Neural network computing is a key component of any data mining tool kit. Applications of neural networks abound in finance, marketing, manufacturing, operations management, information systems, social behavior analysis, and so on.

Biological neural networks are composed of many massively interconnected **neurons**. Each neuron possesses **axons** and **dendrites,** fingerlike projections that enable the neuron to communicate with its neighboring neurons by transmitting and receiving electrical and chemical signals. More or less resembling the structure of their biological counterparts, ANNs are composed of interconnected, simple processing elements (PE) called artificial neurons. When processing information, the processing elements in an ANN operate concurrently and collectively, similar to biological neurons. ANNs possess

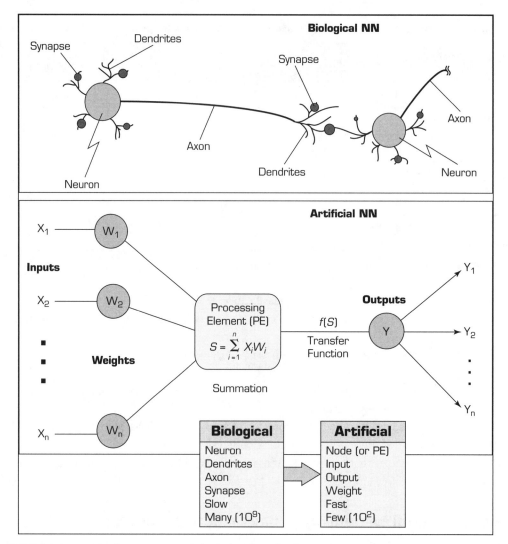

FIGURE 4.14   An Analogy Between Biological and Artificial Neural Networks.

some desirable traits similar to those of biological neural networks, such as the abilities to learn, to self-organize, and to support fault tolerance. Figure 4.14 shows the resemblance between biological and artificial neural networks.

Elements of ANN

PROCESSING ELEMENTS (PE)   The PE of an ANN are essentially artificial neurons. Similar to biological neurons, each PE receives inputs, processes them, and delivers an output, as shown in the bottom part of Figure 4.14. The input can be raw input data or the output of other PE. The output can be the final result or it can be an input to other neurons.

INFORMATION PROCESSING   The inputs received by a neuron go through a two-step process to turn into outputs: **summation function** and **transformation function** (see the bottom half of Figure 4.14). The summation function generates the sum product of the inputs and their respective **connection weights**. The transformation function takes the value produced by the summation function and pushes it through a nonlinear (often a **sigmoid**) function to generate the output of the neuron.

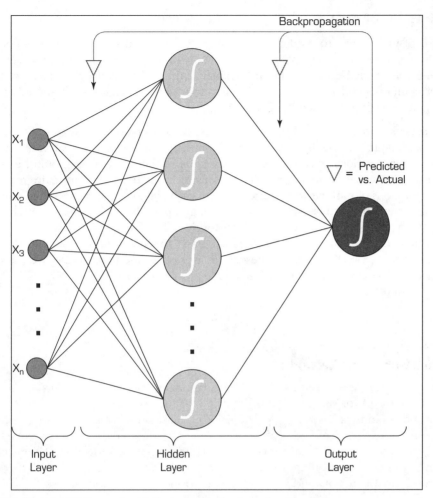

FIGURE 4.15   An MLP Network with Backpropagation Learning Algorithm.

NETWORK STRUCTURE   Each ANN is composed of a collection of neurons (or PE) that are grouped into layers. A typical layered structure of a neural network is shown in Figure 4.15. Note the three layers: input, intermediate (called the hidden layer), and output. A **hidden layer** is a layer of neurons that takes input from the previous layer and converts those inputs into outputs for further processing. Several hidden layers can be placed between the input and output layers, although it is common to use only one hidden layer. This layered structure of ANN is commonly called as **multi-layered percep-tron (MLP).** MLP architecture is known to produce highly accurate prediction models for both classification as well as regression type prediction problems. In addition to MLP, ANN also has other architectures such as **Kohonen's self-organizing feature maps** (commonly used for clustering type problems), Hopfield network (used to solve complex computational problems), recurrent networks (as opposed to feedforward, this architecture allows for backward connections as well), and probabilistic networks (where the weights are adjusted based on the statistical measures obtained from the training data).

BACKPROPAGATION   **Backpropagation** is the learning mechanism for feedforward MLP networks. It follows an iterative process where the difference between the network output and the desired output is fed back to the network so that the network weights would gradually be adjusted to produce outputs closer to the actual values.

Applications of ANN

Because of their ability to model highly complex real-world problems, researchers and practitioners have found many uses for ANN. Many of these uses have led to solutions for problems previously believed to be unsolvable. At the highest conceptual level, common uses of neural networks can be classified into four general classes (corresponding to all of the general tasks addressed by data mining):

1. ***Classification.*** A neural network can be trained to predict a categorical (i.e., class-label) output variable. In a mathematical sense, this involves dividing an n-dimensional space into various regions, and given a point in the space, one should be able to determine to which region it belongs. This idea has been used in many real-world applications of **pattern recognition**, where each pattern is transformed into a multidimensional point and classified into a certain group, each of which represents a known pattern. Types of ANN used for this task include feedforward networks (such as MLP with backpropagation learning), radial basis functions, and probabilistic neural networks. Application Case 4.7 presents an interesting case where predictive features of neural networks are used to analyze and improve beer flavors.

Application Case 4.7

Coors Improves Beer Flavors with Neural Networks

Coors Brewers Ltd., based in Burton-upon-Trent, Britain's brewing capital, is proud of having the United Kingdom's top beer brands, a 20-percent share of the market, years of experience, and some of the best people in the business. Popular brands include Carling (the country's bestselling lager), Grolsch, Coors Fine Light Beer, Sol, and Korenwolf.

Problem

Today's customer has a wide variety of options regarding what he or she drinks. A drinker's choice depends on various factors, including mood, venue, and occasion. Coors' goal is to ensure that the customer chooses a Coors brand no matter what the circumstances are.

According to Coors, creativity is the key to long-term success. To be the customer's choice brand, Coors needs to be creative and anticipate the customer's ever so rapidly changing moods. An important issue with beers is the flavor; each beer has a distinctive flavor. These flavors are mostly determined through panel tests. However, such tests take time. If Coors could understand the beer flavor based solely on its chemical composition, it would open up new avenues to create beer that would suit customer expectations.

The relationship between chemical analysis and beer flavor is not clearly understood yet. Substantial data exist on the chemical composition of a beer and sensory analysis. Coors needed a mechanism to link those two together. Neural networks were applied to create the link between chemical composition and sensory analysis.

Solution

Over the years, Coors has accumulated a significant amount of data related to the final product analysis, which has been supplemented by sensory data provided by the trained in-house testing panel. Some of the analytical inputs and sensory outputs are shown in the following table:

Analytical Data: Inputs	Sensory Data: Outputs
Alcohol	Alcohol
Color	Estery
Calculated bitterness	Malty
Ethyl acetate	Grainy
Isobutyl acetate	Burnt
Ethyl butyrate	Hoppy
Isoamyl acetate	Toffee
Ethyl hexanoate	Sweet

A single neural network, restricted to a single quality and flavor, was first used to model the relationship between the analytical and sensory data. The neural network was based on a package solution supplied by NeuroDimension, Inc. (**nd.com**). The neural network consisted of an MLP architecture with two hidden layers. Data were normalized within the network, thereby enabling comparison between the results for the various sensory outputs. The neural network was trained (to learn the relationship between the inputs and outputs) through the presentation of many combinations of relevant input/output combinations. When there was no observed improvement in the network error in the last 100 epochs, training was automatically terminated. Training was carried out 50 times to ensure that a considerable mean network error could be calculated for comparison purposes. Prior to each training run, a different training and cross-validation dataset was presented by randomizing the source data records, thereby removing any bias.

This technique produced poor results, due to two major factors. First, concentrating on a single product's quality meant that the variation in the data was pretty low. The neural network could not extract useful relationships from the data. Second, it was probable that only one subset of the provided inputs would have an impact on the selected beer flavor. Performance of the neural network was affected by "noise" created by inputs that had no impact on flavor.

A more diverse product range was included in the training range to address the first factor. It was more challenging to identify the most important analytical inputs. This challenge was addressed by using a software switch that enabled the neural network to be trained on all possible combinations of inputs. The switch was not used to disable a significant input; if the significant input were disabled, we could expect the network error to increase. If the disabled input was insignificant, then the network error would either remain unchanged or be reduced due to the removal of noise. This approach is called an *exhaustive search* because all possible combinations are evaluated. The technique, although conceptually simple, was computationally impractical with the numerous inputs; the number of possible combinations was 16.7 million per flavor.

A more efficient method of searching for the relevant inputs was required. A genetic algorithm was the solution to the problem. A genetic algorithm was able to manipulate the different input switches in response to the error term from the neural network. The objective of the genetic algorithm was to minimize the network error term. When this minimum was reached, the switch settings would identify the analytical inputs that were most likely to predict the flavor.

Results

After determining what inputs were relevant, it was possible to identify which flavors could be predicted more skillfully. The network was trained using the relevant inputs previously identified multiple times. Before each training run, the network data were randomized to ensure that a different training and cross-validation dataset was used. Network error was recorded after each training run. The testing set used for assessing the performance of the trained network contained approximately 80 records out of the sample data. The neural network accurately predicted a few flavors by using the chemical inputs. For example, "burnt" flavor was predicted with a correlation coefficient of 0.87.

Today, a limited number of flavors are being predicted by using the analytical data. Sensory response is extremely complex, with many potential interactions and hugely variable sensitivity thresholds. Standard instrumental analysis tends to be of gross parameters, and for practical and economical reasons, many flavor-active compounds are simply not measured. The relationship of flavor and analysis can be effectively modeled only if a large number of flavor-contributory analytes are considered. What is more, in addition to the obvious flavor-active materials, mouth-feel and physical contributors should also be considered in the overall sensory profile. With further development of the input parameters, the accuracy of the neural network models will improve.

Sources: Based on C. I. Wilson and L. Threapleton, "Application of Artificial Intelligence for Predicting Beer Flavours from Chemical Analysis," *Proceedings of the 29th European Brewery Congress,* Dublin, Ireland, May 17–22, 2003, **neurosolutions.com/resources/apps/beer.html** (accessed January 2010); R. Nischwitz, M. Goldsmith, M. Lees, P. Rogers, and L. MacLeod, "Developing Functional Malt Specifications for Improved Brewing Performance," The Regional Institute Ltd., **regional.org.au/au/abts/1999/nischwitz.htm** (accessed December 2009).

2. *Regression.* A neural network can be trained to predict an output variable whose values are of numeric (i.e., real or integer numbers) type. If a network fits well in modeling a known sequence of values, it can be used to predict future results. An obvious example of the regression task is stock market index predictions. Types of ANN used for this task include feedforward networks (such as MLP with backpropagation learning) and radial basis functions.

3. *Clustering.* Sometimes a dataset is so complicated that there is no obvious way to classify the data into different categories. ANN can be used to identify special features of these data and classify them into different categories without prior knowledge of the data. This technique is useful in identifying natural grouping of things for commercial as well as scientific problems. Types of ANN used for this task include **Adaptive Resonance Theory** networks and SOM.

4. *Association.* A neural network can be trained to "remember" a number of unique patterns so that when a distorted version of a particular pattern is presented, the network associates it with the closest one in its memory and returns the original version of that particular pattern. This can be useful for restoring noisy data and identifying objects and events where the data are noisy or incomplete. Types of ANN used for this task include Hopfield networks.

SECTION 4.5 REVIEW QUESTIONS

1. What are neural networks?
2. What are the commonalities and differences between biological and artificial neural networks?
3. What is a neural network architecture? What are the most common neural network architectures?
4. How does an MLP type neural network learn?

4.6 DATA MINING SOFTWARE TOOLS

Many software vendors provide powerful data mining tools. Examples of these vendors include SPSS (PASW Modeler), SAS (Enterprise Miner), StatSoft (Statistica Data Miner), Salford (CART, MARS, TreeNet, RandomForest), Angoss (KnowledgeSTUDIO, KnowledgeSeeker), and Megaputer (PolyAnalyst). As can be seen, most of the more popular tools are developed by the largest statistical software companies (SPSS, SAS, and StatSoft). Most of the business intelligence tool vendors (e.g., IBM Cognos, Oracle Hyperion, SAP Business Objects, MicroStrategy, Teradata, and Microsoft) also have some level of data mining capabilities integrated into their software offerings. These BI tools are still primarily focused on multidimensional modeling and data visualization and are not considered to be direct competitors of the data mining tool vendors.

In addition to these commercial tools, several open source and/or free data mining software tools are available online. Probably the most popular free (and open source) data mining tool is **Weka**, which is developed by a number of researchers from the University Waikato in New Zealand (the tool can be downloaded from **cs.waikato.ac.nz/ml/weka/**). Weka includes a large number of algorithms for different data mining tasks and has an intuitive user interface. Another recently released free (for noncommercial use) data mining tool is **RapidMiner** (developed by Rapid-I;

it can be downloaded from **rapid-i.com**). Its graphically enhanced user interface, employment of a rather large number of algorithms, and incorporation of a variety of data visualization features set it apart from the rest of the free tools. The main difference between commercial tools, such as Enterprise Miner, PASW, and Statistica, and free tools, such as Weka and RapidMiner, is computational efficiency. The same data mining task involving a rather large dataset may take a whole lot longer to complete with the free software, and in some cases, it may not even be feasible (i.e., crashing due to the inefficient use of computer memory). Table 4.6 lists a few of the major products and their Web sites.

A suite of business intelligence capabilities that has become increasingly more popular for data mining studies is Microsoft's SQL Server, where data and the models are stored in the same relational database environment, making model management a considerably easier task. The **Microsoft Enterprise Consortium** serves as the worldwide source for access to Microsoft's SQL Server 2008 software suite for academic purposes—teaching and research. The consortium has been established to enable universities around the world to access enterprise technology without having to maintain the necessary hardware and software on their own campus. The consortium provides a wide range of business intelligence development tools (e.g., data mining, cube building, business reporting) as well as a number of large, realistic datasets from Sam' Club, Dillard's, and Tyson Foods. A screenshot that shows development of a decision tree for churn analysis in SQL Server 2008 Business Intelligence Development

TABLE 4.6 Selected Data Mining Software

Product Name	Web Site (URL)
Clementine	spss.com/Clementine
Enterprise Miner	sas.com/technologies/bi/analytics/index.html
Statistica	statsoft.com/products/dataminer.htm
Intelligent Miner	ibm.com/software/data/iminer
PolyAnalyst	megaputer.com/polyanalyst.php
CART, MARS, TreeNet, RandomForest	salford-systems.com
Insightful Miner	insightful.com
XLMiner	xlminer.net
KXEN (Knowledge eXtraction ENgines)	kxen.com
GhostMiner	fqs.pl/ghostminer
Microsoft SQL Server Data Mining	microsoft.com/sqlserver/2008/data-mining.aspx
Knowledge Miner	knowledgeminer.net
Teradata Warehouse Miner	ncr.com/products/software/teradata_mining.htm
Oracle Data Mining (ODM)	otn.oracle.com/products/bi/9idmining.html
Fair Isaac Business Science	fairisaac.com/edm
DeltaMaster	bissantz.de
iData Analyzer	infoacumen.com
Orange Data Mining Tool	ailab.si/orange/
Zementis Predictive Analytics	zementis.com

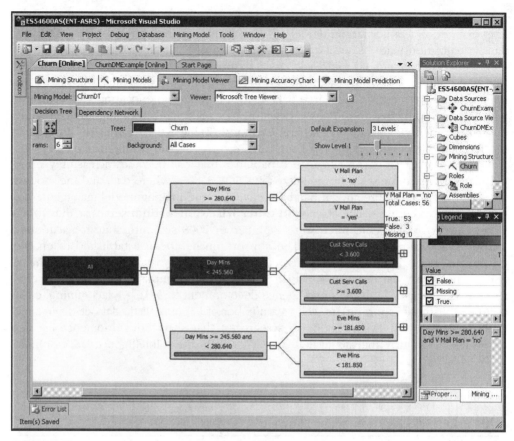

FIGURE 4.16 A Screenshot of a Decision Tree Development in SQL Server 2008. *Source:* Microsoft Enterprise Consortium and Microsoft SQL Server 2008; Used with permission from Microsoft.

Suite is shown in Figure 4.16. The Microsoft Enterprise Consortium is free of charge and can only be used for academic purposes. The Sam M. Walton College of Business at the University of Arkansas hosts the enterprise system and allows consortium members and their students to access these resources using a simple remote desktop connection. The details about becoming a part of the consortium along with easy-to-follow tutorials and examples can be found at **enterprise.waltoncollege. uark.edu/mec/**.

A May 2009 survey by **kdnuggets.com** polled the data mining community on the following question: "What data mining tools have you used for a real project (not just for evaluation) in the past 6 months?" In order to make the results more representative, votes from tool vendors were removed. In previous years, there was a very strong correlation between the use of SPSS Clementine and SPSS Statistics as well as **SAS Enterprise Miner** and SAS Statistics; thus the votes for these two tool families were grouped together. In total, 364 unique votes were counted toward the rankings. The most popular tools were **SPSS PASW Modeler**, RapidMiner, SAS Enterprise Miner, and Microsoft Excel. Compared to poll results in previous years (see 2008 data at **kdnuggets.com/polls/**

2008/data-mining-software-tools-used.htm), among commercial tools, SPSS PASW Modeler, StatSoft Statistica, and SAS Enterprise Miner showed the most growth; among the free tools, RapidMiner and Orange showed the most growth. The results are shown in Figure 4.17.

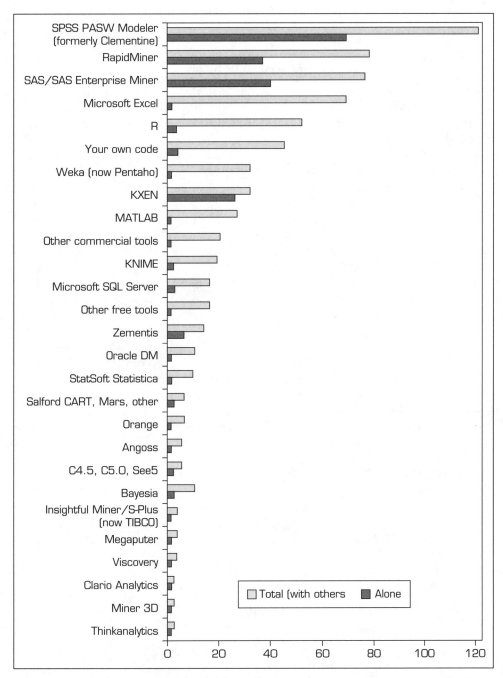

FIGURE 4.17 **Popular Commercial Data Mining Software Tools.** *Source:* kdnuggets.com. Used with permission.

Application Case 4.8

Predicting Customer Churn—A Competition of Different Tools

In 2003, the Duke University/NCR Teradata Center sought to identify the best predictive modeling techniques to help manage a vexing problem for wireless telecommunications providers: customer churn. Although other industries are also faced with customers who defect to competitors, at the retail level, wireless customers switch service providers at a rate of about 25 percent per year or 25 per month. In the early 1990s, when new subscriber growth rates were in the 50 percent range, telecommunications companies were tempted to focus on new customer acquisition rather than on customer retention. However, in a new era of slower growth rates—as low as 10 percent—it is becoming clear that customer retention is vital to overall profitability.

The key to customer retention is predicting which customers are most at risk of defecting to a competitor and offering the most valuable of them incentives to stay. To execute such a strategy effectively, one must be able to develop highly accurate predictions—churn scorecards—so that the retention effort is focused on the relevant customers.

The Data

The data were provided by a major wireless telecommunications company using its own customer records for the second half of 2001. Account summary data were provided for 100,000 customers who had been with the company for at least 6 months. To assist in the modeling process, churners (those who left the company by the end of the following 60 days) were oversampled so that one-half of the sample consisted of churners, and the other half were customers remaining with the company at least another 60 days. A broad range of 171 potential predictors was made available, spanning all the types of data a typical service provider would routinely have. Predictor data included:

- **Demographics:** Age, location, number, ages of children, and so on.
- **Financials:** Credit score and credit card ownership

- **Product details:** Handset price, handset capabilities, and so on.
- **Phone usage:** Number and duration of various categories of calls.

Evaluation Criteria

The data were provided to support predictive modeling development. Participants (a mix of data mining software companies, university research centers, other nonprofits and consultancy companies) were asked to use their best models to predict the probability of churn for two different groups of customers: a "current" sample of 51,306 drawn from the latter half of 2001 and a "future" sample of 100,462 customers drawn from the first quarter of 2002. Predicting "future" data is generally considered more difficult because external factors and behavioral patterns may change over time. In the real world, predictive models are always applied to future data, and the tournament organizers wanted to reproduce a similar context.

Each contestant in the tournament was asked to rank the current and future score samples in descending order by probability of churn. Using the actual churn status available to the tournament organizers, two performance measures were calculated for each predictive model: the overall Gini index and the lift in the top decile. The two measures were calculated for the two samples, current and future, so that there were four performance scores available for every contestant. Evaluation criteria are described in detail in a number of locations, including the tournament Web site. The top-decile lift is the easiest to explain: It measures the number of actual churners captured among the customers ranked most likely to churn by a model.

The Results

Contestants were free to develop a separate model for each measure if they wished to try to optimize their models to the time period, the evaluation criterion, or both. Salford Systems was declared the winner in all categories. Salford Systems used its TreeNet software to create the model. TreeNet is an innovative form of boosted decision tree analysis that is well known for building accurate classification models. Across all the entries, the judges found that decision trees and logistic regression methods were generally the best at predicting churn, though they acknowledged that not all methodologies were adequately represented in the competition.

Salford's TreeNet models captured the most churners across the board and discovered which of the 171 possible variables were most important for predicting churn. In the top 10 percent of customers, TreeNet found 35 to 45 percent more churners than the competition average, and three times more than would be found in a random sample. For companies with large subscriber bases, this could translate to the identification of thousands more potential churners each month. Targeting these customers with an appropriate retention campaign could save a company millions of dollars each year.

Source: Salford Systems, "The Duke/NCR Teradata Churn Modeling Tournament," **salford-systems.com/churn.php** (accessed April 20, 2009); and W. Yu, D. N. Jutla, and S. C. Sivakumar, "A Churn-Strategy Alignment Model for Managers in Mobile Telecom," *Proceedings of the Communication Networks and Services Research Conference*, IEEE Publications, 2005, pp. 48–53.

SECTION 4.6 REVIEW QUESTIONS

1. What are the most popular commercial data mining tools?
2. Why do you think the most popular tools are developed by statistics companies?
3. What are the most popular free data mining tools?
4. What are the main differences between commercial and free data mining software tools?
5. What would be your top five selection criteria for a data mining tool? Explain.

4.7 DATA MINING MYTHS AND BLUNDERS

Data mining is a powerful analytical tool that enables business executives to advance from describing the nature of the past to predicting the future. It helps marketers find patterns that unlock the mysteries of customer behavior. The results of data mining can be used to increase revenue, reduce expenses, identify fraud, and locate business opportunities, offering a whole new realm of competitive advantage. As an evolving and maturing field, data mining is often associated with a number of myths, including the following (Zaima, 2003):

Myth	Reality
Data mining provides instant, crystal-ball-like predictions.	Data mining is a multistep process that requires deliberate, proactive design and use.
Data mining is not yet viable for business applications.	The current state of the art is ready to go for almost any business.
Data mining requires a separate, dedicated database.	Because of advances in database technology, a dedicated database is not required, even though it may be desirable.
Only those with advanced degrees can do data mining.	Newer Web-based tools enable managers at all educational levels to do data mining.
Data mining is only for large firms that have lots of customer data.	If the data accurately reflect the business or its customers, a company can use data mining.

Data mining visionaries have gained enormous competitive advantage by understanding that these myths are just that: myths.

The following 10 data mining mistakes are often made in practice (Skalak, 2001; and Shultz, 2004), and you should try to avoid them:

1. Selecting the wrong problem for data mining.
2. Ignoring what your sponsor thinks data mining is and what it really can and cannot do.
3. Leaving insufficient time for data preparation. It takes more effort than is generally understood.
4. Looking only at aggregated results and not at individual records. IBM's DB2 IMS can highlight individual records of interest.
5. Being sloppy about keeping track of the data mining procedure and results.
6. Ignoring suspicious findings and quickly moving on.
7. Running mining algorithms repeatedly and blindly. It is important to think hard about the next stage of data analysis. Data mining is a very hands-on activity.
8. Believing everything you are told about the data.
9. Believing everything you are told about your own data mining analysis.
10. Measuring your results differently from the way your sponsor measures them.

SECTION 4.7 REVIEW QUESTIONS

1. What are the most common myths about data mining?
2. What do you think are the reasons for these myths about data mining?
3. What are the most common data mining mistakes? How can they be minimized and/or eliminated?

Chapter Highlights

- Data mining is the process of discovering new knowledge from databases.
- Data mining can use simple flat files as data sources or it can be performed on data in data warehouses.
- There are many alternative names and definitions for data mining.
- Data mining is at the intersection of many disciplines, including statistics, artificial intelligence, and mathematical modeling.
- Companies use data mining to better understand their customers and optimize their operations.
- Data mining applications can be found in virtually every area of business and government, including health care, finance, marketing, and homeland security.
- Three broad categories of data mining tasks are prediction (classification or regression), clustering, and association.

- Similar to other information systems initiatives, a data mining project must follow a systematic project management process to be successful.
- Several data mining processes have been proposed: CRISP-DM, SEMMA, KDD, and so on.
- CRISP-DM provides a systematic and orderly way to conduct data mining projects.
- The earlier steps in data mining projects (i.e., understanding the domain and the relevant data) consume most of the total project time (often more than 80% of the total time).
- Data preprocessing is essential to any successful data mining study. Good data lead to good information; good information leads to good decisions.
- Data preprocessing includes four main steps: data consolidation, data cleaning, data transformation, and data reduction.
- Classification methods learn from previous examples containing inputs and the resulting class

- labels, and once properly trained they are able to classify future cases.
- Clustering partitions pattern records into natural segments or clusters. Each segment's members share similar characteristics.
- Data mining can be hypothesis driven or discovery driven. Hypothesis-driven data mining begins with a proposition by the user. Discovery-driven data mining is a more open-ended expedition.
- A number of different algorithms are commonly used for classification. Commercial implementations include ID3, C4.5, C5, CART, and SPRINT.
- Decision trees partition data by branching along different attributes so that each leaf node has all the patterns of one class.
- The Gini index and information gain (entropy) are two popular ways to determine branching choices in a decision tree.
- The Gini index measures the purity of a sample. If everything in a sample belongs to one class, the Gini index value is zero.
- Several assessment techniques can measure the prediction accuracy of classification models, including simple split, k-fold cross-validation, bootstrapping, and area under the ROC curve.

- Cluster algorithms are used when the data records do not have predefined class identifiers (i.e., it is not known to what class a particular record belongs).
- Cluster algorithms compute measures of similarity in order to group similar cases into clusters.
- The most commonly used similarity measure in cluster analysis is a distance measure.
- The most commonly used clustering algorithms are k-means and self-organizing maps.
- Association rule mining is used to discover two or more items (or events or concepts) that go together.
- Association rule mining is commonly referred to as market-basket analysis.
- The most commonly used association algorithm is Apriori, whereby frequent itemsets are identified through a bottom-up approach.
- Association rules are assessed based on their support and confidence measures.
- Many commercial and free data mining tools are available.
- The most popular commercial data mining tools are SPSS PASW and SAS Enterprise Miner.
- The most popular free data mining tools are Weka and RapidMiner.

Key Terms

adaptive resonance theory	data mining	Kohonen's self-organizing feature map	ratio data
algorithm	decision trees	learning algorithm	regression
Apriori algorithm	dendrites	link analysis	result (outcome) variable
area under the ROC curve	discovery-driven data mining	machine learning	SAS Enterprise Miner
artificial neural network (ANN)	distance measure	Microsoft Enterprise Consortium	SEMMA
associations	entropy	multi-layered perceptron (MLP)	sensitivity analysis
axons	fuzzy logic	neural computing	sequence mining
backpropagation	genetic algorithm	neural network	sigmoid function
bootstrapping	Gini index	neurons	simple split
business analyst	heuristics	nominal data	SPSS PASW Modeler
categorical data	hidden layer	numeric data	summation function
chromosome	hypothesis-driven data mining	ordinal data	supervised learning
classification	information gain	pattern recognition	support
clustering	interval data	prediction	support vector machines (SVM)
confidence	k-fold cross-validation	processing elements (PE)	synapse
connection weight	knowledge discovery in databases (KDD)	RapidMiner	transformation function
CRISP-DM			unsupervised learning
			Weka

Questions for Discussion

1. Define data mining. Why there are many names and definitions for data mining?
2. What are the main reasons for the recent popularity of data mining?
3. Discuss what an organization should consider before making a decision to purchase data mining software.
4. Distinguish data mining from other analytical tools and techniques.
5. Discuss the main data mining methods. What are the fundamental differences among them?
6. What are the main data mining application areas? Discuss the commonalities of these areas that make them a prospect for data mining studies.
7. Why do we need a standardized data mining process? What are the most commonly used data mining processes?
8. Discuss the differences between the two most commonly used data mining process.
9. Are data mining processes mere sequential set of activities?
10. Why do we need data preprocessing? What are the main tasks and relevant techniques used in data preprocessing?
11. Discuss the reasoning behind the assessment of classification models.
12. What is the main difference between classification and clustering? Explain using concrete examples.
13. Moving beyond the chapter discussion, where else can association be used?
14. What should an organization consider before making a decision to purchase data mining software?
15. What is ANN? How does it compare to biological neural networks?

Exercises

Teradata University and Other Hands-on Exercises

1. Visit **teradatastudentnetwork.com**. Identify cases about data mining. Describe recent developments in the field.
2. Go to **teradatastudentnetwork.com** or a URL provided by your instructor. Locate Web seminars related to data mining. In particular, watch the Web seminar given by C. Imhoff and T. Zouqes. Then answer the following questions:
   a. What are some of the interesting applications of data mining?
   b. What types of payoffs and costs can organizations expect from data mining initiatives?
3. For this exercise, your goal is to build a model to identify inputs or predictors that differentiate risky customers from others (based on patterns pertaining to previous customers) and then use those inputs to predict new risky customers. This sample case is typical for this domain.

    The sample data to be used in this exercise are in Online File W4.1 in the file **CreditRisk.xlsx**. The dataset has 425 cases and 15 variables pertaining to past and current customers who have borrowed from a bank for various reasons. The dataset contains customer-related information such as financial standing, reason for the loan, employment, demographic information, and the outcome or dependent variable for credit standing, classifying each case as good or bad, based on the institution's past experience.

    Take 400 of the cases as training cases and set aside the other 25 for testing. Build a decision tree model to learn the characteristics of the problem. Test its performance on the other 25 cases. Report on your model's learning and testing performance. Prepare a report that identifies the decision tree model and training parameters, as well as the resulting performance on the test set. Use any decision tree software.

    (This exercise is courtesy of StatSoft, Inc., based on a German dataset from **ftp.ics.uci.edu/pub/machine-learning-databases/statlog/german** renamed CreditRisk and altered.)

4. For this exercise, you will replicate (on a smaller scale) the box-office prediction modeling explained in the opening vignette. Download the training dataset from Online File W4.2, **MovieTrain.xlsx**, which has 184 records and is in Microsoft Excel format. Use the data description given in the opening vignette to understand the domain and the problem you are trying to solve. Pick and choose your independent variables. Develop at least three classification models (e.g., decision tree, logistic regression, and neural networks). Compare the accuracy results using 10-fold cross-validation and percentage split techniques, use confusion matrices, and comment on the outcome. Test the models you have developed on the test set (see Online File W4.3, **MovieTest.xlsx,** 29 records). Analyze the results with different models and come up with the best classification model, supporting it with your results.

Team Assignments and Role-Playing Projects

1. Examine how new data-capture devices such as radio frequency identification (RFID) tags help organizations accurately identify and segment their customers for activities such as targeted marketing. Many of these applications involve data mining. Scan the literature and the Web and then propose five potential new data mining applications of RFID technology. What issues could arise if a country's laws required such tags to be embedded in everyone's body for a national identification system?

2. Interview administrators in your college or executives in your organization to determine how data warehousing, data mining, Online Analytical Processing (OLAP), and visualization BI/DSS tools could assist them in their work. Write a proposal describing your findings. Include cost estimates and benefits in your report.

3. A very good repository of data that have been used to test the performance of many machine-learning algorithms is available at **ics.uci.edu/~mlearn/MLRepository.html**. Some of the datasets are meant to test the limits of current machine-learning algorithms and to compare their performance with new approaches to learning. However, some of the smaller datasets can be useful for exploring the functionality of any data mining software or the software that is available as companion software with this book, such as Statistica DataMiner. Download at least one dataset from this repository (e.g., Credit Screening Databases, Housing Database) and apply decision tree or clustering methods, as appropriate. Prepare a report based on your results. (Some of these exercises may even be proposed as semester-long projects for term papers.)

4. Consider the following dataset, which includes three attributes and a classification for admission decisions into an MBA program:

GMAT	GPA	Quantitative GMAT Score (percentile)	Decision
650	2.75	35	No
580	3.50	70	No
600	3.50	75	Yes
450	2.95	80	No
700	3.25	90	Yes
590	3.50	80	Yes
400	3.85	45	No
640	3.50	75	Yes
540	3.00	60	?
690	2.85	80	?
490	4.00	65	?

a. Using the data shown, develop your own manual expert rules for decision making.
b. Use the Gini index to build a decision tree. You can use manual calculations or a spreadsheet to perform the basic calculations.
c. Use an automated decision tree software program to build a tree for the same data.

5. The purpose of this exercise is to develop a model to predict forest cover type using a number of cartographic measures. The given dataset (Online File W4.1) includes four wilderness areas found in the Roosevelt National Forest of northern Colorado. A total of 12 cartographic measures were utilized as independent variables; seven major forest cover types were used as dependent variables. The table on page 184 provides a short description of these independent and dependent variables:

This is an excellent example for a multiclass classification problem. The dataset is rather large (with 581,012 unique instances) and feature rich. As you will see, the data are also raw and skewed (unbalanced for different cover types). As a model builder, you are to make necessary decisions to preprocess the data and build the best possible predictor. Use your favorite tool to build the models and document the details of your actions and experiences in a written report. Use screenshots within your report to illustrate important and interesting findings. You are expected to discuss and justify any decision that you make along the way.

Name		Description
Number		**Independent Variables**
1	Elevation	Elevation in meters
2	Aspect	Aspect in degrees azimuth
3	Slope	Slope in degrees
4	Horizontal_Distance_To_Hydrology	Horizontal distance to nearest surface-water features
5	Vertical_Distance_To_Hydrology	Vertical distance to nearest surface-water features
6	Horizontal_Distance_To_Roadways	Horizontal distance to nearest roadway
7	Hillshade_9 AM	Hill shade index at 9 A.M., summer solstice
8	Hillshade_Noon	Hill shade index at noon, summer solstice
9	Hillshade_3 PM	Hill shade index at 3 P.M., summer solstice
10	Horizontal_Distance_To_Fire_Points	Horizontal distance to nearest wildfire ignition points
11	Wilderness_Area (4 binary variables)	Wilderness area designation
12	Soil_Type (40 binary variables)	Soil type designation
Number		**Dependent Variable**
1	Cover_Type (7 unique types)	Forest cover type designation

*More details about the dataset (variables and observations) can be found in the online file.

The reuse of this dataset is unlimited with retention of copyright notice for Jock A. Blackard and Colorado State University.

Internet Exercises

1. Visit the AI Exploratorium at **cs.ualberta.ca/~aixplore/**. Click the Decision Tree link. Read the narrative on basketball game statistics. Examine the data and then build a decision tree. Report your impressions of the accuracy of this decision tree. Also, explore the effects of different algorithms.

2. Survey some data mining tools and vendors. Start with **fairisaac.com** and **egain.com**. Consult **dmreview.com** and identify some data mining products and service providers that are not mentioned in this chapter.

3. Find recent cases of successful data mining applications. Visit the Web sites of some data mining vendors and look for cases or success stories. Prepare a report summarizing five new case studies.

4. Go to vendor Web sites (especially those of SAS, SPSS, Cognos, Teradata, StatSoft, and Fair Isaac) and look at success stories for BI (OLAP and data mining) tools. What do the various success stories have in common? How do they differ?

5. Go to **statsoft.com**. Download at least three white papers on applications. Which of these applications may have used the data/text/Web mining techniques discussed in this chapter?

6. Go to **sas.com**. Download at least three white papers on applications. Which of these applications may have used the data/text/Web mining techniques discussed in this chapter?

7. Go to **spss.com**. Download at least three white papers on applications. Which of these applications may have used the data/text/Web mining techniques discussed in this chapter?

8. Go to **nd.com**. Download at least three case studies and/or customer success stories about neural network application. What do the various success stories have in common? How do they differ?

9. Go to **teradata.com**. Download at least three white papers on applications. Which of these applications may have used the data/text/Web mining techniques discussed in this chapter?

10. Go to **fairisaac.com**. Download at least three white papers on applications. Which of these applications may have used the data/text/Web mining techniques discussed in this chapter?

11. Go to **salfordsystems.com**. Download at least three white papers on applications. Which of these applications may have used the data/text/Web mining techniques discussed in this chapter?

12. Go to **rulequest.com**. Download at least three white papers on applications. Which of these applications may have used the data/text/Web mining techniques discussed in this chapter?

13. Go to kdnuggets.com. Explore the sections on applications as well as software. Find names of at least three additional packages for data mining and text mining.

End of Chapter Application Case

Data Mining Helps Develop Custom-Tailored Product Portfolios for Telecommunication Companies

Background

The consulting group argonauten 360° helps businesses build and improve successful strategies for customer relationship management (CRM). The company uses Relevanz-Marketing to create value by facilitating dialog with relevant customers. Its clients include, among many others, BMW, Allianz, Deutsche Bank, Gerling, and Coca-Cola.

The Problem

As a leading consulting company to the telecommunications industry (as well as others), argonauten 360° applies effective advanced analytic technologies for client scoring, clustering, and life-time-value computations as a routine part of its daily work. The requirements for flexible and powerful analytic tools are demanding, because each project typically presents a new and specific set of circumstances, data scenarios, obstacles, and analytic challenges. Therefore, the existing toolset needed to be augmented with effective, cutting-edge, yet flexible, data mining capabilities. Another critical consideration was for the solution to yield quick return on investment. The solution had to be easy to apply, with a fast learning curve, so that analysts could quickly take ownership of even the most advanced analytic procedures.

The Solution

The company needed a unified, easy-to-use set of analytical tools with a wide range of modeling capabilities and straightforward deployment options. Having to learn different tools for different modeling tasks has significantly hindered the efficiency and effectiveness of the company's consultants, causing the company to lean toward a unified solution environment with capabilities ranging from data access on any medium (e.g., databases, online data repositories, text documents, XML files) to deployment of sophisticated data mining solutions on wide range of BI systems.

After 12 months of evaluating a wide range of data mining tools, the company chose Statistica Data Miner (by StatSoft, Inc.) because (according to company executives) it provided the ideal combination of features to satisfy almost every analyst's needs and requirements with user-friendly interfaces.

An Example of an Innovative Project

In Europe, so-called "call-by-call" services are very popular with cell phone users as well as with regular phone users. Such plans have no (or very low) charges for basic service, but bill for the actual airtime that is used. It is a very competitive business, and the success of the call-by-call telecommunications provider depends greatly on attractive per-minute calling rates. Rankings of those rates are widely published, and the key is to be ranked somewhere in the top five lowest cost providers while maintaining the best possible margins. Because of the competitive environment created by this situation, popular wisdom holds that "there is virtually no price-elasticity in this market (to allow providers to charge even the smallest extra margin without losing customers); and even if such price-elasticity existed, it certainly could not be predicted." However, the argonauten 360° consultants analyzed the available data with Statistica's data mining tool and proved that popular wisdom is wrong! Indeed, their successful analyses won argonauten 360° the business of a leading provider of call-by-call services.

The Analysis

The analysis was based on data describing minute-by-minute phone traffic. Specifically, the sale of minutes of airtime over a 1-year period was analyzed. To obtain the best possible discrimination, 20 ensembles of different types of models were developed for estimation purposes. Each model employed a regression-type mathematical representation function for predicting the long-term trends; individual models were then combined at a higher level meta-model. All specific time intervals (time "zones") were carefully modeled, identifying each zone with particular price-sensitivity and competitive pressures.

Results after Two Months

Prior to the application of the models derived via data mining, heuristic "expert-opinions" were used to forecast the expected volume of minutes (of airtime) for the following 2 months. By using Statistica Data Miner, the accuracy of these prognoses improved significantly, while the error rate was cut in half. Given the enormous volume of minute-to-minute calling traffic (airtime), this was deemed to be a dramatically pleasing result, thus providing clear proof for the efficacy and potential benefits of advanced analytic strategies when applied to problems of this type.

Implementing the Solution at the Customer Site

The call-by-call service provider now uses this solution for predicting and simulating optimal cellular (airtime) rates. The system was installed by argonauten 360° as a complete turnkey ("push-of-the-button") solution. Using this solution, the call-by-call service provider can now predict with much greater accuracy the demand (for airtime) in a highly price-sensitive and competitive market and offer the "correct" rates, thus enjoying a key competitive advantage.

In the second phase, this system will be further improved with a "dashboard-like" system that automatically compares predictions with observed data. This system will ensure that, when necessary, argonauten 360° can update the estimates of model parameters to adjust to the dynamic marketplace. Hence, without acquiring any analytic know-how, the call-by-call service provider now has access to a reliable implementation of a sophisticated demand-forecasting and rate-simulation system—something heretofore considered impossible. This is an excellent example of a successful application of data mining technologies to gain competitive advantage in a highly competitive business environment.

QUESTIONS FOR END OF CHAPTER APPLICATION CASE

1. Why do you think that consulting companies are more likely to use data mining tools and techniques? What specific value proposition do they offer?
2. Why was it important for argonauten 360° to employ a comprehensive tool that has all modeling capabilities?
3. What was the problem that argonauten 360° helped solve for a call-by-call service provider?
4. Can you think of other problems for telecommunication companies that are likely to be solved with data mining?

Source: StatSoft, "The German Consulting Company argonauten 360° Uses Statistica Data Miner to Develop Effective Product Portfolios Custom-Tailored to Their Customers," **statsoft.com/company/success_stories/pdf/argonauten360.pdf** (accessed on May 25, 2009).

References

Bhandari, I., E. Colet, J. Parker, Z. Pines, R. Pratap, and K. Ramanujam. (1997). "Advanced Scout: Data Mining and Knowledge Discovery in NBA Data." *Data Mining and Knowledge Discovery,* Vol. 1, No. 1, pp. 121–125.

Bolton, R. J. (2002, January). "Statistical Fraud Detection: A Review." *Statistical Science,* Vol. 17, No. 3, p. 235.

Chan, P. K., W. Phan, A. Prodromidis, and S. Stolfo. (1999). "Distributed Data Mining in Credit Card Fraud Detection." *IEEE Intelligent Systems,* Vol. 14, No. 6, pp. 67–74.

CRISP-DM. (2009). "Cross-Industry Standard Process for Data Mining (CRISP-DM)." **crisp-dm.org** (accessed January 2010).

Davenport, T. H. (2006, January). "Competing on Analytics." *Harvard Business Review.*

Delen, D. (2009). "Analysis of Cancer Data: A Data Mining Approach." *Expert Systems,* Vol. 26, No. 1, pp. 100–112.

Delen, D., R. Sharda, and P. Kumar. (2007). "Movie Forecast Guru: A Web-based DSS for Hollywood Managers." *Decision Support Systems,* Vol. 43, No. 4, pp. 1151–1170.

Delen, D., G. Walker, and A. Kadam. (2005). "Predicting Breast Cancer Survivability: A Comparison of Three Data Mining Methods." *Artificial Intelligence in Medicine,* Vol. 34, No. 2, pp. 113–127.

Dunham, M. (2003). *Data Mining: Introductory and Advanced Topics.* Upper Saddle River, NJ: Prentice Hall.

Fayyad, U., G. Piatetsky-Shapiro, and P. Smyth. (1996). "From Knowledge Discovery in Databases." *AI Magazine,* Vol. 17, No. 3, pp. 37–54.

Gillespie, G. (2004, November). "Data Mining: Solving Care, Cost Capers." *Health Data Management,* **findarticles.com/p/articles/mi_km2925/is_200411/ai_n8622737** (accessed May 2009); and "Highmark Enhances Patient Care, Keeps Medical Costs Down with SAS." **sas.com/success/highmark.html** (accessed April 2006).

Hastie, T., R. Tibshirani, and J. Friedman. (2009). *The Elements of Statistical Learning: Data Mining, Inference, and Prediction,* 2nd ed. New York: Springer.

Haykin, S. S. (2009). *Neural Networks and Learning Machines,* 3rd ed. Upper Saddle River, NJ: Prentice Hall.

Kohonen, T. (1982). "Self-organized Formation of Topologically Correct Feature Maps." *Biological Cybernetics,* Vol. 43, No. 1, pp. 59–69.

Liebowitz, J. "New Trends in Intelligent Systems." Presentation made at University of Granada, **docto-si.ugr.es/seminario2006/presentaciones/jay.ppt** (accessed May 2009).

Nemati, H. R., and C. D. Barko. (2001). "Issues in Organizational Data Mining: A Survey of Current Practices." *Journal of Data Warehousing,* Vol. 6, No. 1, pp. 25–36.

Nischwitz, R., M. Goldsmith, M. Lees, P. Rogers, and L. MacLeod. "Developing Functional Malt Specifications for Improved Brewing Performance." The Regional Institute Ltd., regional.org.au/au/abts/1999/nischwitz.htm (accessed December 2009).

Quinlan, J. R. (1986). "Induction of Decision Trees." *Machine Learning,* Vol. 1, pp. 81–106.

Salford Systems. "The Duke/NCR Teradata Churn Modeling Tournament." **salford-systems.com/churn.php** (accessed April 20, 2009).

SEMMA. (2009). "SAS's Data Mining Process: Sample, Explore, Modify, Model, Assess." **sas.com/offices/europe/uk/technologies/analytics/datamining/miner/semma.html** (accessed August 2009).

Sharda, R., and D. Delen. (2006). "Predicting Box-office Success of Motion Pictures with Neural Networks." *Expert Systems with Applications,* Vol. 30, pp. 243–254.

Shultz, R. (2004, December 7). "Live from NCDM: Tales of Database Buffoonery." **directmag.com/news/ncdm-12-07-04/index.html** (accessed April 2009).

Skalak, D. (2001). "Data Mining Blunders Exposed!" *DB2 Magazine,* Vol. 6, No. 2, pp. 10–13.

StatSoft. (2006). "Data Mining Techniques." **statsoft.com/ textbook/stdatmin.html** (accessed August 2006).

Thongkam, J., G. Xu, Y. Zhang, and F. Huang. (2009, in press). "Toward Breast Cancer Survivability Prediction Models Through Improving Training Space." *Expert Systems with Applications.*

Tseng, W. S., H. Nguyen, J. Liebowitz, and W. Agresti. (2005, January)."Distractions and Motor Vehicle Accidents: Data Mining Application on Fatality Analysis Reporting System (FARS) Data Files." *Industrial Management & Data Systems,* Vol. 105, No. 9, pp. 1188–1205.

Wilson, C. I., and L. Threapleton. (2003, May 17–22). "Application of Artificial Intelligence for Predicting Beer Flavours from Chemical Analysis." *Proceedings of the 29th European Brewery Congress,* Dublin, Ireland,

neurosolutions.com/resources/apps/beer.html (accessed January 2010).

Wilson, R., and R. Sharda. (1994). "Bankruptcy Prediction Using Neural Networks." *Decision Support Systems,* Vol. 11, pp. 545–557.

Yu, W., D. N. Jutla, and S. C. Sivakumar. (2005). "A Churn-Strategy Alignment Model for Managers in Mobile Telecom." *Proceedings of the Communication Networks and Services Research Conference,* IEEE Publications, pp. 48–53.

Zaima, A. (2003). "The Five Myths of Data Mining." *What Works: Best Practices in Business Intelligence and Data Warehousing,* Vol. 15, Chatsworth, CA: Data Warehousing Institute, pp. 42–43.

Zdanowic, J. S. (2004, May). "Detecting Money Laundering and Terrorist Financing via Data Mining." *Communications of the ACM,* Vol. 47, No. 5, p. 53

Text and Web Mining

LEARNING OBJECTIVES

- Describe text mining and understand the need for text mining
- Differentiate between text mining and data mining
- Understand the different application areas for text mining
- Know the process of carrying out a text mining project

- Understand the different methods to introduce structure to text-based data
- Describe Web mining, its objectives, and its benefits
- Understand the three different branches of Web mining
- Understand Web content mining, Web structure mining, and Web log mining

This chapter provides a rather comprehensive overview of text mining and Web mining as they relate to business intelligence (BI) and decision support systems. Both Web mining and text mining are essentially the derivatives of data mining. Because text data and Web traffic data are increasing in volume in an order of magnitude more than the data in structured databases, it is important to know some of the techniques used to process large amounts of unstructured data.

OPENING VIGNETTE: Mining Text for Security and Counterterrorism

Imagine that you are a decision maker in a hostage situation at an American embassy. You are trying to understand, "Who is in charge of the terrorists?" "What is the reason behind this terrorist attack?" and "Is their group likely to attack other embassies?" Even though you have access to all kinds of information sources, you are hardly ever in a position to exploit such vast amounts of information effectively and efficiently for better decision making. How can computers help this process, which relies on accurate and timely intelligence in the midst of a crisis? The Genoa[1] project, part of DARPA's (Defense Advanced Research Projects Agency) total information awareness program, seeks to provide advanced tools and techniques to rapidly analyze information related to a current situation to support better decision making. Specifically, Genoa provides knowledge discovery tools to better "mine" relevant information sources for discovery of patterns in the form of actionable information (i.e., relevant knowledge nuggets).

One of the challenges Genoa faced was to make it easy for the end user to take the knowledge discovered by the analytics tools and embed it in a concise and useful form in an intelligence product. MITRE, a nonprofit innovative research organization chartered to work in the public interest (**mitre.org**), has been tasked with developing text mining–based software system to address this challenge. This system would allow the user to select various text mining tools and, with a few mouse clicks, assemble them to create a complex filter that fulfills whatever knowledge discovery function is currently needed. Here, a filter is a tool that takes input information and turns it into a more abstract and useful representation. Filters can also weed out irrelevant parts of the input information.

For example, in response to the crisis situation discussed earlier, an analyst might use text mining tools to discover important nuggets of information in a large collection of news sources. This use of text mining tools can be illustrated by looking at TopCat, a system developed by MITRE that identifies different topics in a collection of documents and displays the key "players" for each topic. TopCat uses association rule mining technology to identify relationships among people, organizations, locations, and events (shown with P, O, L, and E, respectively, in Figure 5.1). Grouping these relationships creates topic clusters such as the three shown in Figure 5.1, which are built from 6 months of global news from several print, radio, and video sources—over 60,000 news stories in all.

This tool enables an analyst to discover, say, an association between people involved in a bombing incident, such as "McVeigh and Nichols belong to a common organization!" which gives a starting point for further analysis. This, in turn, can lead to new knowledge that can be leveraged in the **analytical model** to help predict whether a particular terrorist organization is likely to strike elsewhere in the next few days. Similarly, the third topic reveals the important players in an election in Cambodia. This discovered information can be leveraged to help predict whether the situation in Cambodia is going to explode into a crisis that may potentially affect U.S. interests in that region.

Now, suppose the user wants to know more about the people in the last topic (the election in Cambodia). Instead of reading thousands of words of text from a number of articles on the topic, the analyst can compose a topic-detection filter with a biographical

---

[1]The Genoa project was started in 1997 and converted into Genoa II in 2003. The parent program, Total Information Awareness, was transitioned into a program called Topsail in 2003. Both programs were highly criticized as being government-led spying programs that invaded privacy and human rights.

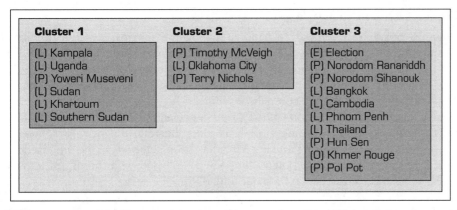

FIGURE 5.1   Topics Derived from Clustering 60,000 News Stories.   *Source:* Mitre Corporation, **www.mitre.org** (accessed May 20, 2009).

summarization filter (like the ones included in TopCat) that gathers facts about key persons from the topic's articles. The result of such a composition would produce a short, to-the-point summary of the topic.

The summarization filter, developed with DARPA funding, identifies and aggregates descriptions of people from a collection of documents by means of an efficient syntactic analysis, the use of a thesaurus, and some simple natural language–processing techniques. It also extracts from these documents salient sentences related to these people by weighting sentences based on the presence of the names of people as well as the location and proximity of terms in a document, their frequency, and their correlations with other terms in the document collection.

The summarization filter in TopCat can also perform a similar function for MITRE's Broadcast News Navigator, which applies this capability to continuously collected broadcast news in order to extract named entities and keywords and to identify the interesting transcripts and sentences that contain them. The summarization filter includes a parameter to specify the target length or the reduction rate, allowing summaries of different lengths to be generated. For example, allowing a longer summary would mean that facts about other people (e.g., Pol Pot) would also appear in the summary.

This example illustrates how mining a text collection using contemporary knowledge discovery tools such as the TopCat summarization filter can reveal important associations at varying levels of detail. The component-based approach employed in implementing TopCat allowed these filters to be easily integrated into intelligence products such as automated intelligence reporting and briefing tools and dashboards. These summarization filters can be connected to a specific region on a Web page of a *briefing book*, which can be shared across a community of collaborating analysts. When a document or a folder of documents is dropped onto a region connected to a filter, the filter processes the textual data, and the information in the form of a textual summary or graphical visualization appears in that region.

QUESTIONS FOR THE OPENING VIGNETTE

1. How can text mining be used in a crisis situation?

2. What is Genoa project? What is the motivation behind projects like Genoa?

3. What is TopCat? What does TopCat do?

4. What is a summarization filter?

5. Comment on the future of text mining tools for counterterrorism.

WHAT WE CAN LEARN FROM THE VIGNETTE

Text mining tools have been part of national intelligence initiatives such as the information awareness program for decades. In this vignette, DARPA and MITRE teamed up to develop capabilities to automatically filter text-based information sources to generate actionable information in a timely manner. They followed component-based architectures so that parts and pieces of this complex system can be revised, used, and reused independent of the rest of information system. Using association, classification, and clustering analysis, these text-based document analysis tools illustrate the power of knowledge extraction from volumes of news articles. What has been achieved in the intelligence field is a good indicator of what can potentially be accomplished with the use of knowledge discovery tools and techniques in the near future.

Source: MITRE Corporation, **mitre.org** (accessed on May 20, 2009); J. Mena, *Investigative Data Mining for Security and Criminal Detection,* Elsevier Science. Burlington, MA, 2003.

5.1 TEXT MINING CONCEPTS AND DEFINITIONS

The information age that we are living in is characterized by the rapid growth in the amount of data and information collected, stored, and made available in electronic media. A vast majority of business data are stored in text documents that are virtually unstructured. According to a study by Merrill Lynch and Gartner, 85 to 90 percent of all corporate data are captured and stored in some sort of unstructured form (McKnight, 2005). The same study also stated that this unstructured data are doubling in size every 18 months. Because knowledge is power in today's business world, and knowledge is derived from data and information, businesses that effectively and efficiently tap into their text data sources will have the necessary knowledge to make better decisions, leading to a competitive advantage over those businesses that lag behind. This is where the need for text mining fits into the big picture of today's businesses.

Text mining (also known as *text data mining* or *knowledge discovery in textual databases*) is the semiautomated process of extracting patterns (useful information and knowledge) from large amounts of unstructured data sources. Remember that data mining is the process of identifying valid, novel, potentially useful, and ultimately understandable patterns in data stored in structured databases, where the data are organized in records structured by categorical, ordinal, or continuous variables. Text mining is the same as data mining in that it has the same purpose and uses the same processes; but with text mining, the input to the process is a collection of unstructured (or less structured) data files such as Word documents, PDF files, text excerpts, XML files, and so on. In essence, text mining can be thought of as a process (with two main steps) that starts with imposing structure to the text-based data sources followed by extracting relevant information and knowledge from this structured text-based data using data mining techniques and tools.

The benefits of text mining are obvious in the areas where very large amounts of textual data are being generated, such as law (court orders), academic research (research articles), finance (quarterly reports), medicine (discharge summaries), biology (molecular interactions), technology (patent files), and marketing (customer comments). For example, the free-form text-based interactions with customers in the form of complaints (or praises) and warranty claims can be used to objectively identify product and service characteristics that are deemed to be less than perfect and can be used as input to better product development and service allocations. Likewise, market outreach programs and focus groups generating large amounts of data. By not restricting product or service feedback to a codified form, customers can present, in their own words, what they think about a company's products and services. Another area where the automated processing of unstructured text has had a lot of impact is in electronic communications and e-mail. Text mining not only can be used to classify and filter junk e-mail, but it can also be used to automatically prioritize e-mail based on importance level as well as to generate automatic responses (Weng and Liu, 2004). Following are among the most popular application areas of text mining:

- *Information extraction.* Identification of key phrases and relationships within text by looking for predefined sequences in text via pattern matching.
- *Topic tracking.* Based on a user profile and documents that a user views, text mining can predict other documents of interest to the user.
- *Summarization.* Summarizing a document to save time on the part of the reader.
- *Categorization.* Identifying the main themes of a document and then placing the document into a predefined set of categories based on those themes.
- *Clustering.* Grouping similar documents without having a predefined set of categories.
- *Concept linking.* Connects related documents by identifying their shared concepts and, by doing so, helps users find information that they perhaps would not have found using traditional search methods.
- *Question answering.* Finding the best answer to a given question through knowledge-driven pattern matching.

See Technology Insight 5.1 for explanations of some of the terms and concepts used in text mining. Application Case 5.1 describes the use of text mining in patent analysis.

TECHNOLOGY INSIGHT 5.1   Text Mining Lingo

The following list describes some commonly used text mining terms:

- *Unstructured data (versus structured data).* Structured data have a predetermined format. They are usually organized into records with simple data values (categorical, ordinal, and continuous variables) and stored in databases. In contrast, unstructured data do not have a predetermined format and are stored in the form of textual documents. In essence, the structured data are for the computers to process while the unstructured data are for humans to process and understand.
- *Corpus.* In linguistics, a **corpus** (plural *corpora*) is a large and structured set of texts (now usually stored and processed electronically) prepared for the purpose of conducting knowledge discovery.
- *Terms.* A *term* is a single word or multiword phrase extracted directly from the corpus of a specific domain by means of natural language processing (NLP) methods.
- *Concepts.* *Concepts* are features generated from a collection of documents by means of manual, statistical, rule-based, or hybrid categorization methodology. Compared to terms, concepts are the result of higher level abstraction.
- *Stemming.* The process of reducing inflected words to their stem (or base or root) form. For instance, *stemmer, stemming, stemmed* are all based on the root *stem*.
- *Stop words.* Stop words (or *noise words*) are words that are filtered out prior to or after processing of natural language data (i.e., text). Even though there is no universally accepted list of stop words, most natural language processing tools use a list that includes articles (*a, am, the, of,* etc.), auxiliary verbs (*is, are, was, were,* etc.), and context-specific words that are deemed not to have differentiating value.

- *Synonyms and polysemes.* Synonyms are syntactically different words (i.e., spelled differently) with identical or at least similar meanings (e.g., *movie, film,* and *motion picture*). In contrast, **polysemes**, which are also called *homonyms*, are syntactically identical words (i.e., spelled exactly the same) with different meanings (e.g., *bow* can mean "to bend forward," "the front of the ship," "the weapon that shoots arrows," or "a kind of tied ribbon").
- *Tokenizing.* A *token* is a categorized block of text in a sentence. The block of text corresponding to the token is categorized according to the function it performs. This assignment of meaning to blocks of text is known as **tokenizing**. A token can look like anything; it just needs to be a useful part of the structured text.
- *Term dictionary.* A collection of terms specific to a narrow field that can be used to restrict the extracted terms within a corpus.
- *Word frequency.* The number of times a word is found in a specific document.
- *Part-of-speech tagging.* The process of marking up the words in a text as corresponding to a particular part of speech (such as nouns, verbs, adjectives, and adverbs) based on a word's definition and the context in which it is used.
- *Morphology.* A branch of the field of linguistics and a part of natural language processing that studies the internal structure of words (patterns of word formation within a language or across languages).
- *Term-by-document matrix (occurrence matrix or term–document matrix).* A common representation schema of the frequency-based relationship between the terms and documents in tabular format where terms are listed in rows, documents are listed in columns, and the frequency between the terms and documents is listed in cells as integer values.
- *Singular-value decomposition (latent semantic indexing).* A dimensionality reduction method used to transform the term-by-document matrix to a manageable size by generating an intermediate representation of the frequencies using a matrix manipulation method similar to principle component analysis.

Application Case 5.1

Text Mining for Patent Analysis

A patent is a set of exclusive rights granted by a country to an inventor for a limited period of time in exchange for a disclosure of an invention (note that the procedure for granting patents, the requirements placed on the patentee, and the extent of the exclusive rights vary widely from country to country). The disclosure of these inventions is critical to future advancements in science and technology. If carefully analyzed, patent documents can help identify emerging technologies, inspire novel solutions, foster symbiotic partnerships, and enhance overall awareness of business' capabilities and limitations.

Patent analysis is the use of **analytical techniques** to extract valuable knowledge from patent databases. Countries or groups of countries that maintain patent databases (United States, European Union, Japan, etc.) add tens of millions of new patents each year. It is nearly impossible to efficiently process such enormous amounts of semi-structured data (patent documents usually contain partial structured and partially textual data). Patent analysis with semiautomated software tools is one way to ease the processing of these very large databases.

A Representative Example of Patent Analysis

Eastman Kodak employs more than 5,000 scientists, engineers, and technicians around the world. During the twentieth century, these knowledge workers and their predecessors claimed nearly 20,000 patents, putting the company among the top 10 patent holders in the world. Being in the business of constant change, the company knows that success (or mere survival) depends on its ability to apply more than a century's worth knowledge about imaging science and technology to new uses and to secure those new uses with patents.

Appreciating the value of patents, Kodak not only generates new patents but also analyzes those created by others. Using dedicated analysts and state-of-the-art software tools (including specialized text mining tools from ClearForest Corp.), Kodak continuously digs deep into various data sources (patent databases, new release archives, and product announcements) in order to develop a holistic view of the competitive landscape. Proper analysis of patents can bring companies like Kodak a wide range of benefits:

- It enables competitive intelligence. Knowing what competitors are doing can help a company to develop countermeasures.
- It can help the company make critical business decisions, such as what new products, product lines, and/or technologies to get into or what mergers and acquisitions to pursue.
- It can aid in identifying and recruiting the best and brightest new talent, those whose names

appear on the patents that are critical to the company's success.

- It can help the company to identify the unauthorized use of its patents, enabling it to take action to protect its assets.
- It can identify complementary inventions to build symbiotic partnerships or to facilitate mergers and/or acquisitions.
- It prevents competitors from creating similar products, and it can help protect the company from patent infringement lawsuits.

Using patent analysis as a rich source of knowledge and a strategic weapon (both defensive as well as offensive), Kodak not only survives but excels in its market segment defined by innovation and constant change.

Source: P. X. Chiem, "Kodak Turns Knowledge Gained About Patents into Competitive Intelligence," *Knowledge Management,* 2001, pp. 11–12; Y-H. Tsenga, C-J. Linb, and Y-I. Linc, "Text Mining Techniques for Patent Analysis," *Information Processing & Management,* Vol. 43, No. 5, 2007, pp. 1216–1245.

SECTION 5.1 QUESTIONS

1. What is text mining? How does it differ from data mining?

2. Why is the popularity of text mining as a BI tool increasing?

3. What are some of popular application areas of text mining?

5.2 NATURAL LANGUAGE PROCESSING

Some of the early text mining applications used a simplified representation called *bag-of-words* when introducing structure to a collection of text-based documents in order to classify them into two or more predetermined classes or to cluster them into natural groupings. In the bag-of-words model, text, such as a sentence, paragraph, or complete document, is represented as a collection of words, disregarding the grammar or the order in which the words appear. The bag-of-words model is still used in some simple document classification tools. For instance, in spam filtering, an e-mail message can be modeled as an unordered collection of words (a bag-of-words) that is compared against two different predetermined bags. One bag is filled with words found in spam messages, and the other is filled with words found in legitimate e-mails. Although some of the words are likely to be found in both bags, the "spam" bag will contain spam-related words such as *stock, Viagra,* and *buy* much more frequently than the legitimate bag, which will contain more words related to the user's friends or workplace. The level of match between a specific e-mail's bag-of-words and the two bags containing the descriptors determines the membership of the e-mail as either spam or legitimate.

Naturally, we (humans) do not use words without some order or structure. We use words in sentences, which have semantic as well as syntactic structure. Thus, automated techniques (such as text mining) need to look for ways to go beyond the bag-of-words interpretation and incorporate more and more semantic structure into their operations. The current trend in text mining is toward including many of the advanced features that can be obtained using natural language processing.

It has been shown that the bag-of-word method may not produce good-enough information content for text mining tasks (classification, clustering, association, etc.). A good example of this can be found in evidence-based medicine. A critical component of evidence-based medicine is incorporating the best available research findings into the clinical decision-making process, which involves appraisal of the information collected from the printed media for validity and relevance. Several researchers from University of Maryland developed evidence assessment models using a bag-of-words method (Lin and Demner, 2005). They employed popular machine-learning methods along with more than half a million research articles collected from MEDLINE (Medical Literature Analysis and Retrieval System Online). In their models, they represented each abstract as a bag-of-words, where each stemmed term represented a feature. Despite using popular classification methods with proven experimental design methodologies, their prediction results were not much better than simple guessing, which may indicate that the bag-of-words is not generating a good enough representation of the research articles in this domain; hence, more advanced techniques such as natural language processing are needed.

Natural language processing (NLP) is an important component of text mining and is a subfield of artificial intelligence and computational linguistics. It studies the problem of "understanding" the natural human language, with the view of converting depictions of human language (such as textual documents) into more formal representations (in the form of numeric and symbolic data) that are easier for computer programs to manipulate. The goal of NLP is to move beyond syntax-driven text manipulation (which is often called "word counting") to a true understanding and processing of natural language that considers grammatical and semantic constraints as well as the context.

The definition and scope of the word "understanding" is one of the major discussion topics in NLP. Considering that the natural human language is vague and that a true understanding of meaning requires extensive knowledge of a topic (beyond what is in the words, sentences, and paragraphs), will computers ever be able to understand natural language the same way and with the same accuracy that humans do? Probably not! NLP has come a long way from the days of simple word counting, but it has an even longer way to go to really understanding natural human language. The following are just a few of the challenges commonly associated with the implementation of NLP:

- *Part-of-speech tagging.* It is difficult to mark up terms in a text as corresponding to a particular part of speech (such as nouns, verbs, adjectives, and adverbs), because the part of speech depends not only on the definition of the term but also on the context within which it is used.
- *Text segmentation.* Some written languages, such as Chinese, Japanese, and Thai, do not have single-word boundaries. In these instances, the text-parsing task requires the identification of word boundaries, which is often a difficult task. Similar challenges in speech segmentation emerge when analyzing spoken language, because sounds representing successive letters and words blend into each other.
- *Word sense disambiguation.* Many words have more than one meaning. Selecting the meaning that makes the most sense can only be accomplished by taking into account the context within which the word is used.
- *Syntactic ambiguity.* The grammar for natural languages is ambiguous; that is, multiple possible sentence structures often need to be considered. Choosing the most appropriate structure usually requires a fusion of semantic and contextual information.

- *Imperfect or irregular input.* Foreign or regional accents and vocal impediments in speech and typographical or grammatical errors in texts make the processing of the language an even more difficult task.
- *Speech acts.* A sentence can often be considered an action by the speaker. The sentence structure alone may not contain enough information to define this action. For example, "Can you pass the class?" requests a simple yes/no answer, whereas "Can you pass the salt?" is a request for a physical action to be performed.

It is a longstanding dream of artificial intelligence community to have algorithms that are capable of automatically reading and obtaining knowledge from text. By applying a learning algorithm to parsed text, researchers from Stanford University's NLP lab have developed methods that can automatically identify the concepts and relationships between those concepts in the text. By applying a unique procedure to large amounts of text, their algorithms automatically acquire hundreds of thousands of items of world knowledge and use them to produce significantly enhanced repositories for WordNet. WordNet is a laboriously hand-coded database of English words, their definitions, sets of synonyms, and various semantic relations between synonym sets. It is a major resource for NLP applications, but it has proven to be very expensive to build and maintain manually. By automatically inducing knowledge into WordNet, the potential exists to make WordNet an even greater and more comprehensive resource for NLP at a fraction of the cost.

One prominent area where the benefits of NLP are already being harvested is in customer relationship management (CRM). Broadly speaking, the goal of CRM is to maximize customer value by better understanding and effectively responding to their actual and perceived needs. An important area of CRM, where NLP is making a significant impact, is sentiment analysis. **Sentiment analysis** is a technique used to detect favorable and unfavorable opinions toward specific products and services using a large numbers of textual data sources (customer feedback in the form of Web postings). See Application Case 5.2 for an example of the successful application of text mining to CRM.

Application Case 5.2

Text Mining Helps Merck to Better Understand and Serve Its Customers

Merck Sharp & Dohme (MSD) is a global, research-driven pharmaceutical company based in Germany that is dedicated to solving the world's health care needs. Established in 1891, MSD discovers, develops, manufactures, and markets vaccines and medicines to address challenging health care needs.

As one of the world's largest pharmaceutical manufacturers, MSD relies heavily on the input it gets from doctors to better help the patients they serve. The expected outcome is better care for patients who are afflicted with illnesses such as AIDS, osteoporosis, heart failure, migraine headaches, and asthma, among many others.

Realizing the importance of knowledge discovery, many years ago, MSD developed an analytics program that uses data and text mining applications to better leverage its data and information assets. MSD uses text mining technology from SPSS to analyze information it collects from a variety of sources and then uses that information to create effective programs that best address physician and patient needs.

Challenge

Like any other profession, the people working in the health care industry have an array of beliefs and opinions. That's where the challenge comes in for MSD. It must get a firm grasp on what doctors are saying in the field and then pass that information on to its product development teams so they can create

(Continued)

Application Case 5.2   (Continued)

better drugs and effective marketing campaigns for those drugs. Considering the range of MSD's target audience, such a task is anything but simple. On one end of the spectrum are the "pioneer" doctors who are very open to new insights and research results and fairly quickly turn scientific findings into practice. At the other end of the scale are the "conservative personality" doctors who follow traditional practices and want to do everything by the book, spend a lot of time researching treatment options, and base their opinions on the thorough study of specialist articles or exchanges with colleagues. To be successful, MSD had to find the right way to approach all types of doctors. However, first it had to identify the various groups. To do so, MSD needed to use all available information from various sources, including internal data and data from external providers.

Solution

MSD decided to use text mining and quantitative analysis tools from SPSS to get a better understanding of the data collected from the surveys, some of which were conducted at various communications seminars, and then provide that valuable information to the marketing team. Some of the characteristics measured in these surveys included the number of years a doctor had been established and the number of patients the doctor serves, along with questions that led to open-ended textual responses. Once the necessary data were obtained, special analytics were used to gain further insight into the data with regard to their significance and correlation among the wide range of characteristics. MSD also used the collected data for profiling purposes. The analytic tools allowed

MSD to allocate doctors to a number of typologies. By segmenting doctors based on measures introduced by the marketing department, MSD decides which action catalog best characterizes the relevant target groups.

Results

For MSD, text mining—the analysis of unstructured, textual data—is indispensable. The text mining functionality is based on the natural grammatical analysis of text. It does not depend solely on keyword search but analyzes the syntax of language and "understands" the content. By doing so, it discovers indispensable knowledge needed to improve the company's competitive position.

MSD works with the Gesellschaft für Konsumforschung panel (Association for Consumer Research, GfK), which uses the daily "diary" entries of doctors on the panel to learn which pharmaceutical representatives have visited them, what product communications were conveyed, and whether they will include these products in the range of drugs they prescribe in the future. Text mining analyses of the product conversations noted by the doctors reveal speech patterns that accompany various prescribing behaviors. This enables MSD to optimize its products and marketing campaigns and to improve its sales representatives' communication skills. Thanks to SPSS and its text mining tools, MSD knows which properties of and information about its drugs are particularly well understood in conversations with the doctors and when the terms used in its marketing campaigns need to be refined.

Source: SPSS, "Merck Sharp & Dohme," **storieshttp://www.spss.com/success/template_view.cfm?Story_ID = 185** (accessed May 15, 2009).

Sentiment analysis offers enormous opportunities for various applications. For instance, it would provide powerful functionality for competitive analysis, marketing analysis, and detection of unfavorable rumors for risk management. A sentiment analysis approach developed by researchers at IBM seeks to extract sentiments associated with polarities of positive or negative for specific subjects (e.g., products or services) from a collection of documents (Kanayama and Nasukawa, 2006). The main issues in sentiment analysis are to identify how sentiments are expressed in texts and whether the expressions indicate positive (favorable) or negative (unfavorable) opinions toward the subject. In order to improve the accuracy of the sentiment analysis, it is important to properly identify the semantic relationships between the sentiment expressions and the subject. By applying semantic analysis with a syntactic parser and sentiment lexicon, IBM's system achieved high precision (75%–95%, depending on the data) in finding sentiments within Web pages and news articles.

NLP has successfully been applied to a variety of tasks via computer programs to automatically process natural human language that previously could only be done by humans. Following are among the most popular of these tasks:

- ***Information retrieval.*** The science of searching for relevant documents, finding specific information within them, and generating metadata as to their contents.
- ***Information extraction.*** A type of information retrieval whose goal is to automatically extract structured information, such as categorized and contextually and semantically well-defined data from a certain domain, using unstructured machine-readable documents.
- ***Named-entity recognition.*** Also known as *entity identification* and *entity extraction*, this subtask of information extraction seeks to locate and classify atomic elements in text into predefined categories, such as the names of persons, organizations, locations, expressions of times, quantities, monetary values, percentages, and so on.
- ***Question answering.*** The task of automatically answering a question posed in natural language; that is, producing a human-language answer when given a human-language question. To find the answer to a question, the computer program may use either a prestructured database or a collection of natural language documents (a text corpus such as the World Wide Web).
- ***Automatic summarization.*** The creation of a shortened version of a textual document by a computer program that contains the most important points of the original document.
- ***Natural language generation.*** Systems convert information from computer databases into readable human language.
- ***Natural language understanding.*** Systems convert samples of human language into more formal representations that are easier for computer programs to manipulate.
- ***Machine translation.*** The automatic translation of one human language to another.
- ***Foreign language reading.*** A computer program that assists a nonnative language speaker to read a foreign language with correct pronunciation and accents on different parts of the words.
- ***Foreign language writing.*** A computer program that assists a nonnative language user in writing in a foreign language.
- ***Speech recognition.*** Converts spoken words to machine-readable input. Given a sound clip of a person speaking, the system produces a text dictation.
- ***Text-to-speech.*** Also called ***speech synthesis***, a computer program automatically converts normal language text into human speech.
- ***Text proofing.*** A computer program reads a proof copy of a text in order to detect and correct any errors.
- ***Optical character recognition.*** The automatic translation of images of handwritten, typewritten, or printed text (usually captured by a scanner) into machine-editable textual documents.

The success and popularity of text mining depends greatly on advancements in NLP in both generation as well as understanding of human languages. NLP enables the extraction of features from unstructured text so that a wide variety of data mining techniques can be used to extract knowledge (novel and useful patterns and relationships) from it. In that sense, simply put, text mining is a combination of NLP and data mining.

SECTION 5.2 QUESTIONS

1. What is natural language processing?
2. How does NLP relate to text mining?
3. What are some of the benefits and challenges of NLP?
4. What are the most common tasks addressed by NLP?

5.3   TEXT MINING APPLICATIONS

As the amount of unstructured data collected by organizations increases, so does the value proposition and popularity of text mining tools. Many organizations are now realizing the importance of extracting knowledge from their document-based data repositories through the use of text mining tools. Following are only a small subset of the exemplary application categories of text mining.

Marketing Applications

Text mining can be used to increase cross-selling and up-selling by analyzing the unstructured data generated by call centers. Text generated by call-center notes as well as transcriptions of voice conversations with customers can be analyzed by text mining algorithms to extract novel, actionable information about customers' perceptions toward a company's products and services. Additionally, blogs, user reviews of products at independent Web sites, and discussion board postings are a gold mine of customer sentiments. This rich collection of information, once properly analyzed, can be used to increase satisfaction and the overall lifetime value of the customer (Coussement and Van den Poel, 2008).

Text mining has become invaluable for customer relationship management. Companies can use text mining to analyze rich sets of unstructured text data, combined with the relevant structured data extracted from organizational databases, to predict customer perceptions and subsequent purchasing behavior. Coussement and Van den Poel (2009) successfully applied text mining to significantly improve the ability of a model to predict customer churn (i.e., customer attrition) so that those customers identified as most likely to leave a company are accurately identified for retention tactics.

Ghani et al. (2006) used text mining to develop a system capable of inferring implicit and explicit attributes of products to enhance retailers' ability to analyze product databases. Treating products as sets of attribute–value pairs rather than as atomic entities can potentially boost the effectiveness of many business applications, including demand forecasting, assortment optimization, product recommendations, assortment comparison across retailers and manufacturers, and product supplier selection. The proposed system allows a business to represent its products in terms of attributes and attribute values without much manual effort. The system learns these attributes by applying supervised and semisupervised learning techniques to product descriptions found on retailers' Web sites.

Security Applications

One of the largest and most prominent text mining applications in the security domain is probably the highly classified ECHELON surveillance system. As rumor has it, ECHELON is assumed to be capable of identifying the content of telephone calls, faxes, e-mails, and other types of data, intercepting information sent via satellites, public switched telephone networks, and microwave links.

In 2007, EUROPOL developed an integrated system capable of accessing, storing, and analyzing vast amounts of structured and unstructured data sources in order to track transnational organized crime. Called the Overall Analysis System for Intelligence Support, this system aims to integrate the most advanced data and text mining technologies available on today's market. The system has enabled EUROPOL to make significant progress in supporting its law enforcement objectives at the international level (EUROPOL, 2007).

The U.S. Federal Bureau of Investigation (FBI) and the Central Intelligence Agency (CIA), under the direction of the Department for Homeland Security, are jointly developing a supercomputer data and text mining system. The system is expected to create a gigantic data warehouse along with a variety of data and text mining modules to meet the knowledge-discovery needs of federal, state, and local law enforcement agencies. Prior to this project, the FBI and CIA each had its own separate databases, with little or no interconnection.

Another security-related application of text mining is in the area of **deception detection**. Applying text mining to a large set of real-world criminal (person-of-interest) statements, Fuller et al. (2008) developed prediction models to differentiate deceptive statements from truthful ones. Using a rich set of cues extracted from the textual statements, the model predicted the holdout samples with 70 percent accuracy, which is believed to be a significant success considering that the cues are extracted only from textual statements (no verbal or visual cues are present). Furthermore, compared to other deception-detection techniques, such as polygraph, this method is nonintrusive and widely applicable not only to textual data but also (potentially) to transcriptions of voice recordings. A more detailed description of text-based deception detection is provided in Application Case 5.3.

Application Case 5.3

Mining for Lies

Driven by advancements in Web-based information technologies and increasing globalization, computer-mediated communication continues to filter into everyday life, bringing with it new venues for deception. The volume of text-based chat, instant messaging, text messaging, and text generated by online communities of practice is increasing rapidly. Even e-mail continues to grow in use. With the massive growth of text-based communication, the potential for people to deceive others through computer-mediated communication has also grown, and such deception can have disastrous results.

Unfortunately, in general, humans tend to perform poorly at deception-detection tasks. This phenomenon is exacerbated in text-based communications. A large part of the research on deception detection (also known as *credibility assessment*) has

involved face-to-face meetings and interviews. Yet, with the growth of text-based communication, text-based deception-detection techniques are essential.

Techniques for successfully detecting deception—that is, lies—have wide applicability. Law enforcement can use decision support tools and techniques to investigate crimes, conduct security screening in airports, and monitor communications of suspected terrorists. Human resources professionals might use deception detection tools to screen applicants. These tools and techniques also have the potential to screen e-mails to uncover fraud or other wrongdoings committed by corporate officers. Although some people believe that they can readily identify those who are not being truthful, a summary of deception research showed that, on average, people are only 54 percent accurate in making

(Continued)

Application Case 5.3   (Continued)

veracity determinations (Bond and DePaulo, 2006). This figure may actually be worse when humans try to detect deception in text.

Using a combination of text mining and data mining techniques, Fuller et al. (2008) analyzed person-of-interest statements completed by people involved in crimes on military bases. In these statements, suspects and witnesses are required to write their recollection of the event in their own words. Military law enforcement personnel searched archival data for statements that they could conclusively identify as being truthful or deceptive. These decisions were made on the basis of corroborating evidence and case resolution. Once labeled as truthful or deceptive, the law enforcement personnel removed identifying information and gave the statements to the research team. In total, 371 usable statements were received for analysis. The text-based deception detection method used by Fuller et al. (2008) was based on a process

known as *message feature mining*, which relies on elements of data and text mining techniques. A simplified depiction of the process is provided in Figure 5.2.

First, the researchers prepared the data for processing. The original handwritten statements had to be transcribed into a word processing file. Second, features (i.e., cues) were identified. The researchers identified 31 features representing categories or types of language that are relatively independent of the text content and that can be readily analyzed by automated means. For example, first-person pronouns such as *I* or *me* can be identified without analysis of the surrounding text. Table 5.1 lists the categories and an example list of features used in this study.

The features were extracted from the textual statements and input into a flat file for further processing. Using several feature-selection methods along with *10*-fold cross-validation, the researchers

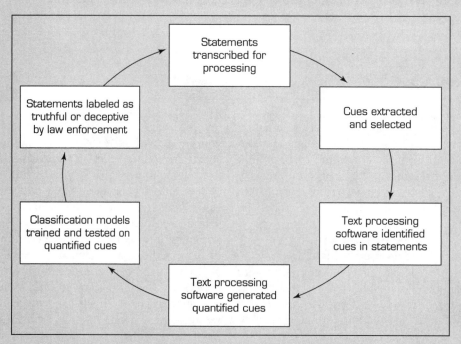

FIGURE 5.2   Text-Based Deception Detection Process.   *Source:* C. M. Fuller, D. Biros, and D. Delen, "Exploration of Feature Selection and Advanced Classification Models for High-Stakes Deception Detection," in *Proceedings of the 41st Annual Hawaii International Conference on System Sciences (HICSS),* January 2008, Big Island, HI, IEEE Press, pp. 80–99.

TABLE 5.1   Categories and Examples of Linguistic Features Used in Deception Detection

Number	Construct (Category)	Example Cues
1	Quantity	Verb count, noun-phrase count, etc.
2	Complexity	Average number of clauses, average sentence length, etc.
3	Uncertainty	Modifiers, modal verbs, etc.
4	Nonimmediacy	Passive voice, objectification, etc.
5	Expressivity	Emotiveness
6	Diversity	Lexical diversity, redundancy, etc.
7	Informality	Typographical error ratio
8	Specificity	Spatiotemporal information, perceptual information, etc.
9	Affect	Positive affect, negative affect, etc.

Source: Based on C. M. Fuller, D. Biros, and D. Delen, "Exploration of Feature Selection and Advanced Classification Models for High-Stakes Deception Detection," in *Proceedings of the 41st Annual Hawaii International Conference on System Sciences (HICSS),* 2008, Big Island, HI, IEEE Press, pp. 80–99; C. F. Bond and B. M. DePaulo, "Accuracy of Deception Judgments," *Personality and Social Psychology Reports,* Vol. 10, No. 3, 2006, pp. 214–234.

compared the prediction accuracy of three popular data mining methods. Their results indicated that neural network models performed the best, with 73.46 percent prediction accuracy on test data samples; decision trees performed second best, with 71.60 percent accuracy; and logistic regression was last, with 65.28 percent accuracy.

The results indicate that automated text-based deception detection has the potential to aid those who must try to detect lies in text and can be successfully applied to real-world data. The accuracy of these techniques exceeded the accuracy of most other deception-detection techniques even though it was limited to textual cues.

Biomedical Applications

Text mining holds great potential for the medical field in general and biomedicine in particular for several reasons. First, the published literature and publication outlets (especially with the advent of the open source journals) in the field are expanding at an exponential rate. Second, compared to most other fields, the medical literature is more standardized and orderly, making it a more "minable" information source. Finally, the terminology used in this literature is relatively constant, having a fairly standardized ontology. What follows are a few exemplary studies where text mining techniques were successfully used in extracting novel patterns from biomedical literature.

Experimental techniques such as DNA microarray analysis, serial analysis of gene expression (SAGE), and mass spectrometry proteomics, among others, are generating large amounts of data related to genes and proteins. As in any other experimental approach, it is necessary to analyze this vast amount of data in the context of previously known information about the biological entities under study. The literature is a particularly valuable source of information for experiment validation and interpretation. Therefore, the development of automated text mining tools to assist in such interpretation is one of the main challenges in current bioinformatics research.

Knowing the location of a protein within a cell can help to elucidate its role in biological processes and to determine its potential as a drug target. Numerous location-prediction systems are described in the literature; some focus on specific organisms, whereas others attempt to analyze a wide range of organisms. Shatkay et al. (2007) proposed a comprehensive system that uses several types of sequence- and text-based features to predict the location of proteins. The main novelty of their system lies in the way in which it selects its text sources and features and integrates them with sequence-based features. They tested the system on previously used datasets and on new datasets devised specifically to test its predictive power. The results showed that their system consistently beat previously reported results.

Chun et al. (2006) described a system that extracts disease–gene relationships from literature accessed via MEDLINE. They constructed a dictionary for disease and gene names from six public databases and extracted relation candidates by dictionary matching. Because dictionary matching produces a large number of false positives, they developed a method of machine learning–based named entity recognition (NER) to filter out false recognitions of disease/gene names. They found that the success of relation extraction is heavily dependent on the performance of NER filtering and that the filtering improved the precision of relation extraction by 26.7 percent at the cost of a small reduction in recall.

Figure 5.3 shows a simplified depiction of a multilevel text analysis process for discovering gene–protein relationships (or protein–protein interactions) in the biomedical literature (Nakov et al., 2005). As can be seen in this simplified example that uses a simple sentence from biomedical text, first (at the bottom three levels) the text is tokenized using part-of-speech tagging and shallow-parsing. The tokenized terms

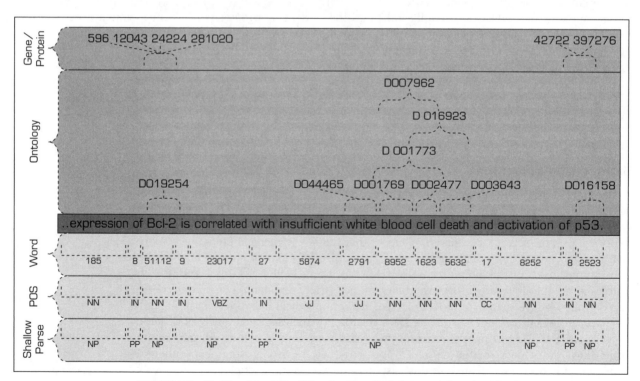

FIGURE 5.3 **Multilevel Analysis of Text for Gene/Protein Interaction Identification.** *Source:* P. Nakov, A. Schwartz, B. Wolf, and M.A. Hearst, "Supporting Annotation Layers for Natural Language Processing." *Proceedings of the Association for Computational Linguistics (ACL)*, interactive poster and demonstration sessions, 2005, Ann Arbor, MI, pp. 65–68.

(words) are then matched (and interpreted) against the hierarchical representation of the domain ontology to derive the gene–protein relationship. Application of this method (and/or some variation of it) to the biomedical literature offers great potential to decode the complexities in the Human Genome Project.

Academic Applications

The issue of text mining is of great importance to publishers who hold large databases of information requiring indexing for better retrieval. This is particularly true in scientific disciplines, in which highly specific information is often contained within written text. Initiatives have been launched, such as *Nature*'s proposal for an Open Text Mining Interface and the National Institutes of Health's common Journal Publishing Document Type Definition (DTD), that would provide semantic cues to machines to answer specific queries contained within text without removing publisher barriers to public access.

Academic institutions have also launched text mining initiatives. For example, the National Centre for Text Mining, a collaborative effort between the Universities of Manchester and Liverpool, provides customized tools, research facilities, and advice on text mining to the academic community. With an initial focus on text mining in the biological and biomedical sciences, research has since expanded into the social sciences. In the United States, the School of Information at University of California, Berkeley, is developing a program called BioText to assist bioscience researchers in text mining and analysis.

As described in this section, text mining has a wide variety of applications in a number of different disciplines. See Application Case 5.4 for an example of how the aviation industry is using text mining of air incident reports to increase safety.

Application Case 5.4

Flying Through Text

Text mining has proven to be a valuable tool in extracting organizational knowledge from written documents stored in digitized form. Analysts are using text mining software to focus on key problem areas through pattern identification. For example, companies in the airline industry can apply text mining to incident reports to increase the quality of organizational knowledge. They can study mechanical, organizational, and behavioral problems in a timely manner through the use of text mining.

Airlines operate with a thorough and systematic analysis of operations. An incident report is prepared whenever an event occurs that might lead to a problem. Text mining techniques can be used to automatically identify key issues from the masses of incident reports. The huge databases that airlines maintain have limited human interpretation, and

the terminology appears different to a computer than to a human.

Aer Lingus (**aerlingus.com**) examined incident reports generated from January 1998 through December 2003 to find possible patterns and correlations. Aer Lingus used Megaputer's PolyAnalyst (**megaputer.com**), a comprehensive data and text mining software. Its goal was to develop a process that investigators could regularly use to identify patterns and associations with regard to incident type, location, time, and other details.

The most frequently occurring terms were identified in the incident reports. PolyAnalyst carries a lexicon of terms that is not complete but that provides a valuable starting point for text analysis. It can also generate a list of key terms (or their semantic equivalents) occurring in the data. A report called a frequent-terms report is created,

(Continued)

Application Case 5.4   (Continued)

which contains the terms identified and their frequency. The objective is to identify interesting clusters. A narrative summary includes a set of terms that divides the narrative descriptions into meaningful groups. For example, the key term *spillage* can be associated with four other key terms: *food, fuel, chemical,* and *toilet.* From the key terms, *food* is semantically related to *coffee, tea,* and *drink.* Thus, *food* becomes the category node, and the different food products reported as spilled are matched to *food.*

Text mining of airline incident reports can identify underlying root causes that may lead to safety improvements. Text mining can also be used with a large set of incident reports data to validate predetermined theories and common sense knowledge as well as harvesting and adding new patterns to the knowledge base.

Sources: J. Froelich, S. Ananyan, and D. L Olson, "Business Intelligence Through Text Mining," *Business Intelligence Journal,* Vol. 10, No. 1, 2005, pp. 43–50.

SECTION 5.3 QUESTIONS

1. List and briefly discuss some of the text mining applications in marketing.
2. How can text mining be used in security and counterterrorism?
3. What are some promising text mining applications in biomedicine?

5.4   TEXT MINING PROCESS

In order to be successful, text mining studies should follow a sound methodology based on best practices. A standardized process model is needed similar to CRISP-DM, which is the industry standard for data mining projects. Even though most parts of CRISP-DM are also applicable to text mining projects, a specific process model for text mining would include much more elaborate data preprocessing activities. Figure 5.4 depicts a high-level context diagram of a typical text mining process (Delen and Crossland, 2008). This context diagram presents the scope of the process, emphasizing its interfaces with the larger environment. In essence, it draws boundaries around the specific process to explicitly identify what is included (and excluded) from the text mining process.

As the context diagram indicates, the input (inward connection to the left edge of the box) into the text-based knowledge discovery process is the unstructured as well as structured data collected, stored, and made available to the process. The output (outward extension from the right edge of the box) of the process is the context-specific knowledge that can be used for decision making. The controls, also called the *constraints* (inward connection to the top edge of the box), of the process include software and hardware limitations, privacy issues, and the difficulties related to processing of the text that is presented in the form of natural language. The mechanisms (inward connection to the bottom edge of the box) of the process include proper techniques, software tools, and domain expertise. The primary purpose of text mining (within the context of knowledge discovery) is to process unstructured (textual) data (along with structured data, if relevant to the problem being addressed and available) to extract meaningful and actionable patterns for better decision making.

At a very high level, the text mining process can be broken down into three consecutive tasks, each of which has specific inputs to generate certain outputs (see Figure 5.5). If, for some reason, the output of a task is not that which is expected, a backward redirection to the previous task execution is necessary.

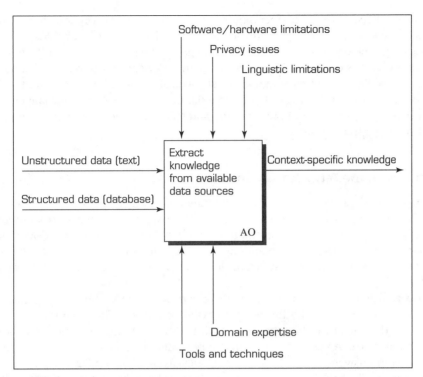

FIGURE 5.4 Context Diagram for the Text Mining Process.

Task 1: Establish the Corpus

The main purpose of the first task activity is to collect all of the documents related to the context (domain of interest) being studied. This collection may include textual documents, XML files, e-mails, Web pages, and short notes. In addition to the readily available textual data, voice recordings may also be transcribed using speech-recognition algorithms and made a part of the text collection.

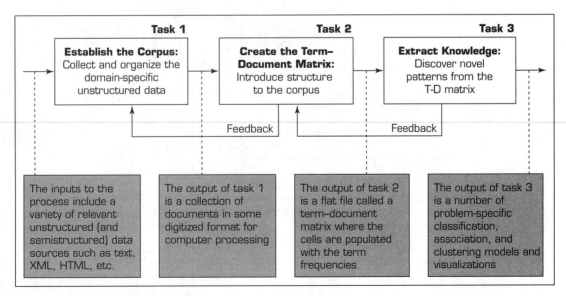

FIGURE 5.5 The Three-Step Text Mining Process.

Once collected, the text documents are transformed and organized in a manner such that they are all in the same representational form (e.g., ASCII text files) for computer processing. The organization of the documents can be as simple as a collection of digitized text excerpts stored in a file folder, or it can be a list of links to a collection of Web pages in a specific domain. Many commercially available text mining software tools could accept these as input and convert them into a flat file for processing. Alternatively, the flat file can be prepared outside the text mining software and then presented as the input to the text mining application.

Task 2: Create the Term–Document Matrix

In this task, the digitized and organized documents (the corpus) are used to create the **term–document matrix (TDM)**. In the TDM, rows represent the documents and columns represent the terms. The relationships between the terms and documents are characterized by indices (i.e., a relational measure that can be as simple as the number of occurrences of the term in respective documents). Figure 5.6 is a typical example of a TDM.

The goal is to convert the list of organized documents (the corpus) into a TDM where the cells are filled with the most appropriate indices. The assumption is that the essence of a document can be represented with a list and frequency of the terms used in that document. However, are all terms important when characterizing documents? Obviously, the answer is "no." Some terms, such as articles, auxiliary verbs, and terms used in almost all of the documents in the corpus, have no differentiating power and therefore should be excluded from the indexing process. This list of terms, commonly called *stop terms* or *stop words,* is specific to the domain of study and should be identified by the domain experts. On the other hand, one might choose a set of predetermined terms under which the documents are to be indexed (this list of terms is conveniently

Documents \ Terms	Investment Risk	Project Management	Software Engineering	Development	SAP	⋮
Document 1	1			1		
Document 2		1				
Document 3			3		1	
Document 4		1				
Document 5			2	1		
Document 6	1			1		
. . .						

FIGURE 5.6   A Simple Term–Document Matrix.

called *include terms* or *dictionary*). Additionally, synonyms (pairs of terms that are to be treated the same) and specific phrases (e.g., "Eiffel Tower") can also be provided so that the index entries are more accurate.

Another filtration that should take place to accurately create the indices is *stemming*, which refers to the reduction of words to their roots so that, for example, different grammatical forms or declinations of a verb are identified and indexed as the same word. For example, stemming will ensure that *modeling* and *modeled* will be recognized as the word *model*.

The first generation of the TDM includes all of the unique terms identified in the corpus (as its columns), excluding the ones in the stop terms list; all of the documents (as its rows); and the occurrence count of each term for each document (as its cell values). If, as is commonly the case, the corpus includes a rather large number of documents, then there is a very good chance that the TDM will have a very large number of terms. Processing such a large matrix might be time consuming and, more important, might lead to extraction of inaccurate patterns. At this point, one has to decide the following: (1) What is the best representation of the indices? and (2) How can we reduce the dimensionality of this matrix to a manageable size?

Representing the Indices Once the input documents are indexed and the initial word frequencies (by document) computed, a number of additional transformations can be performed to summarize and aggregate the extracted information. The raw term frequencies generally reflect on how salient or important a word is in each document. Specifically, words that occur with greater frequency in a document are better descriptors of the contents of that document. However, it is not reasonable to assume that the word counts themselves are proportional to their importance as descriptors of the documents. For example, if a word occurs one time in document *A* but three times in document *B*, then it is not necessarily reasonable to conclude that this word is three times as important a descriptor of document *B* as compared to document *A*. In order to have a more consistent TDM for further analysis, these raw indices need to be normalized. As opposed to showing the actual frequency counts, the numerical representation between terms and documents can be normalized using a number of alternative methods. The following are few of the most commonly used normalization methods (StatSoft, 2009):

- **Log frequencies.** The raw frequencies can be transformed using the log function. This transformation would "dampen" the raw frequencies and how they affect the results of subsequent analysis.

$$f(wf) = 1 + \log(wf) \quad \text{for} \quad wf > 0$$

In the formula, *wf* is the raw word (or term) frequency and $f(wf)$ is the result of the log transformation. This transformation is applied to all of the raw frequencies in the TDM where the frequency is greater than zero.

- **Binary frequencies.** Likewise, an even simpler transformation can be used to enumerate whether a term is used in a document.

$$f(wf) = 1 \quad \text{for} \quad wf > 0$$

The resulting TDM matrix will contain only 1s and 0s to indicate the presence or absence of the respective words. Again, this transformation will dampen the effect of the raw frequency counts on subsequent computations and analyses.

- **Inverse document frequencies.** Another issue that one may want to consider more carefully and reflect in the indices used in further analyses is the relative document frequencies (*df*) of different terms. For example, a term such as *guess* may occur frequently in all documents, whereas another term, such as *software,* may appear only a few times. The reason is that one might make *guesses* in various contexts, regardless of the specific topic, whereas *software* is a more semantically focused term that is only likely to occur in documents that deal with computer software. A common and very useful transformation that reflects both the specificity of words (document frequencies) as well as the overall frequencies of their occurrences (term frequencies) is the so-called **inverse document frequency** (Manning and Schutze, 2009). This transformation for the ith word and jth document can be written as:

$$idf(i, j) = \begin{cases} 0 & \text{if } wf_{ij} = 0 \\ (1 + \log(wf_{ij}))\log \dfrac{N}{df_i} & \text{if } wf_{ij} \geq 1 \end{cases}$$

In this formula, N is the total number of documents, and dfi is the document frequency for the ith word (the number of documents that include this word). Hence, it can be seen that this formula includes both the dampening of the simple-word frequencies via the log function (described above) and a weighting factor that evaluates to 0 if the word occurs in all documents [i.e., $\log(N/N = 1) = 0$], and to the maximum value when a word only occurs in a single document [i.e., $\log(N/1) = \log(N)$]. It can easily be seen how this transformation will create indices that reflect both the relative frequencies of occurrences of words, as well as their semantic specificities over the documents included in the analysis. This is the most commonly used transformation in the field.

REDUCING THE DIMENSIONALITY OF THE MATRIX Because the TDM is often very large and rather sparse (most of the cells filled with zeros), another important question is, "How do we reduce the dimensionality of this matrix to a manageable size?" Several options are available for managing the matrix size:

- A domain expert goes through the list of terms and eliminates those that do not make much sense for the context of the study (this is a manual, labor-intensive process).
- Eliminate terms with very few occurrences in very few documents.
- Transform the matrix using singular value decomposition (SVD).

Singular value decomposition (SVD), which is closely related to principal components analysis, reduces the overall dimensionality of the input matrix (number of input documents by number of extracted terms) to a lower dimensional space, where each consecutive dimension represents the largest degree of variability (between words and documents) possible (Manning and Schutze, 2009). Ideally, the analyst might identify the two or three most salient dimensions that account for most of the variability (differences) between the words and documents, thus identifying the latent semantic space that organizes the words and documents in the analysis. Once such dimensions are identified, the underlying "meaning" of what is contained (discussed or described) in the documents is extracted. Specifically, assume that matrix A represents an $m \times n$ term occurrence matrix where m is the number of input documents and n is the number of terms selected for analysis. The SVD computes the $m \times r$ orthogonal matrix U, $n \times r$ orthogonal matrix V, and $r \times r$ matrix D, so that $A = UDV'$ and r is the number of eigenvalues of $A'A$.

Task 3: Extract the Knowledge

Using the well-structured TDM, and potentially augmented with other structured data elements, novel patterns are extracted in the context of the specific problem being addressed. The main categories of knowledge extraction methods are classification, clustering, association, and trend analysis. A short description of these methods follows.

CLASSIFICATION Arguably the most common knowledge discovery topic in analyzing complex data sources is the **classification** (or categorization) of certain objects. The task is to classify a given data instance into a predetermined set of categories (or classes). As it applies to the domain of text mining, the task is known as *text categorization,* where for a given set of categories (subjects, topics, or concepts) and a collection of text documents, the goal is to find the correct topic (subject or concept) for each document using models developed with a training data set that included both the documents and actual document categories. Today, automated text classification is applied in a variety of contexts, including automatic or semi-automatic (interactive) indexing of text, spam filtering, Web page categorization under hierarchical catalogs, automatic generation of metadata, detection of genre, and many others.

The two main approaches to text classification are knowledge engineering and machine learning (Feldman and Sanger, 2007). With the knowledge-engineering approach, an expert's knowledge about the categories is encoded into the system either declaratively or in the form of procedural classification rules. With the machine-learning approach, a general inductive process builds a classifier by learning from a set of reclassified examples. As the number of documents increases at an exponential rate and as knowledge experts become harder to come by, the popularity trend between the two is shifting toward the machine-learning approach.

CLUSTERING **Clustering** is an unsupervised process whereby objects are classified into "natural" groups called *clusters*. Compared to categorization, where a collection of preclassified training examples is used to develop a model based on the descriptive features of the classes in order to classify a new unlabeled example, in clustering the problem is to group an unlabelled collection of objects (e.g., documents, customer comments, Web pages) into meaningful clusters without any prior knowledge.

Clustering is useful in a wide range of applications, from document retrieval to enabling better Web content searches. In fact, one of the prominent applications of clustering is the analysis and navigation of very large text collections, such as Web pages. The basic underlying assumption is that relevant documents tend to be more similar to each other than to irrelevant ones. If this assumption holds, the clustering of documents based on the similarity of their content improves search effectiveness (Feldman and Sanger, 2007):

- *Improved search recall.* Clustering, because it is based on overall similarity as opposed to the presence of a single term, can improve the recall of a query-based search in such a way that when a query matches a document, its whole cluster is returned.
- *Improved search precision.* Clustering can also improve search precision. As the number of documents in a collection grows, it becomes difficult to browse through the list of matched documents. Clustering can help by grouping the documents into a number of much smaller groups of related documents, ordering them by relevance, and returning only the documents from the most relevant group (or groups).

  The two most popular clustering methods are scatter/gather clustering and query-specific clustering:
- *Scatter/gather clustering.* This document-browsing method uses clustering to enhance the efficiency of human browsing of documents when a specific search query cannot be formulated. In a sense, the method dynamically generates a table of contents for the collection and adapts and modifies it in response to the user selection.
- *Query-specific clustering.* This method employs a hierarchical clustering approach where the most relevant documents to the posed query appear in small tight clusters that are nested in larger clusters containing less similar documents, creating a spectrum of relevance levels among the documents. This method performs consistently well for document collections of realistically large sizes.

ASSOCIATION A formal definition and detailed description of **association** was provided in the chapter on data mining (Chapter 4). The main idea in generating association rules (or solving market-basket problems) is to identify the frequent sets that go together.

In text mining, associations specifically refer to the direct relationships between concepts (terms) or sets of concepts. The concept set association rule $A \Rightarrow C$, relating two frequent concept sets A and C, can be quantified by the two basic measures of support and confidence. In this case, confidence is the percentage of documents that include all the concepts in C within the same subset of those documents that include all the concepts in A. Support is the percentage (or number) of documents that include all the concepts in A and C. For instance, in a document collection, the concept "Software Implementation Failure" may appear most often in association with "Enterprise Resource Planning" and "Customer Relationship Management" with significant support (4%) and confidence (55%), meaning that 4 percent of the documents had all three concepts represented together in the same document and of the documents that included "Software Implementation Failure," 55 percent of them also included "Enterprise Resource Planning" and "Customer Relationship Management."

Text mining with association rules was used to analyze published literature (news and academic articles posted on the Web) to chart the outbreak and progress of bird flu (Mahgoub et al., 2008). The idea was to automatically identify the association among the geographic areas, spreading across species, and countermeasures (treatments).

TREND ANALYSIS Recent methods of trend analysis in text mining have been based on the notion that the various types of concept distributions are functions of document collections; that is, different collections lead to different concept distributions for the same set of concepts. It is therefore possible to compare two distributions that are otherwise identical except that they are from different subcollections. One notable direction of this type of analyses is having two collections from the same source (such as from the same set of academic journals) but from different points in time. Delen and Crossland (2008) applied **trend analysis** to a large number of academic articles (published in the three highest rated academic journals) to identify the evolution of key concepts in the field of information systems.

As described in this section, a number of methods are available for text mining. Application Case 5.5 describes the use of a number of different techniques in analyzing a large set of literature.

Application Case 5.5

Research Literature Survey with Text Mining

Researchers conducting searches and reviews of relevant literature face an increasingly complex and voluminous task. In extending the body of relevant knowledge, it has always been important to work hard to gather, organize, analyze, and assimilate existing information from the literature, particularly from one's home discipline. With the increasing abundance of potentially significant research being reported in related fields, and even in what are traditionally deemed to be nonrelated fields of study, the researcher's task is ever more daunting, if a thorough job is desired.

In new streams of research, the researcher's task may be even more tedious and complex. Trying to ferret out relevant work that others have reported may be difficult, at best, and perhaps even near impossible if traditional, largely manual reviews of published literature are required. Even with a legion of dedicated graduate students or helpful colleagues, trying to cover all potentially relevant published work is problematic.

Many scholarly conferences take place every year. In addition to extending the body of knowledge of the current focus of a conference, organizers often desire to offer additional mini-tracks and workshops. In many cases, these additional events are intended to introduce the attendees to significant streams of research in related fields of study and to try to identify the "next big thing" in terms of research interests and focus. Identifying reasonable candidate topics for such mini-tracks and workshops is often subjective rather than derived objectively from the existing and emerging research.

In a recent study, Delen and Crossland (2008) proposed a method to greatly assist and enhance the efforts of the researchers by enabling a semiautomated analysis of large volumes of published literature through the application of text mining. Using standard digital libraries and online publication search engines, the authors downloaded and collected all of the available articles for the three major journals in the field of management information systems: *MIS Quarterly* (MISQ), *Information Systems Research* (ISR), and the *Journal of Management Information Systems* (JMIS). In order to maintain the same time interval for all three journals (for potential comparative longitudinal studies), the journal with the most recent starting date for its digital publication availability was used as the start time for this study (i.e., JMIS articles have been digitally available since 1994). For each article, they extracted the title, abstract, author list, published keywords, volume, issue number, and year of publication. They then loaded all of the article data into a simple database file. Also included in the combined dataset was a field that designated the journal type of each article for likely discriminatory analysis. Editorial notes, research notes, and executive overviews were omitted from the collection. Table 5.2 shows how the data were presented in a tabular format.

In the analysis phase, Delen and Crossland chose to use only the abstract of an article as the source of information extraction. They chose not to include the keywords listed with the publications for two main reasons: (1) Under normal circumstances, the abstract would already include the listed keywords, and therefore, inclusion of the listed keywords for the analysis would mean repeating the same information and potentially giving them unmerited weight; and (2) The listed keywords may be terms that authors would like their article to be associated with (as opposed to what is really contained in the article), therefore potentially introducing unquantifiable bias to the analysis of the content.

The first exploratory study was to look at the longitudinal perspective of the three journals (i.e., evolution of research topics over time). In order to conduct a longitudinal study, they divided the 12-year period (from 1994 to 2005) into four 3-year periods for each of the three journals. This framework led to 12 text mining experiments with 12 mutually exclusive datasets. At this point, for each of the 12 datasets, they used text mining to extract the most descriptive terms from these collections of articles represented by their abstracts. The results were tabulated and examined for time-varying changes in the terms published in these three journals.

As a second exploration, using the complete dataset (including all three journals and all four periods), they conducted a clustering analysis. Clustering is arguably the most commonly used text mining technique. Clustering was used in this study to identify the natural groupings of the articles (by putting them into separate clusters) and then to list the most descriptive terms that characterized those clusters. They used singular value decomposition to reduce the dimensionality of the term-by-document matrix and then an expectation-maximization algorithm to create the clusters. They conducted several experiments to identify the *optimal* number of clusters, which turned out to be nine. After the construction of the nine clusters, they analyzed the content of those clusters from two perspectives: (1) representation of the journal type (see Figure 5.7) and (2) representation of time. The idea was to explore the potential differences and/or commonalities

(*Continued*)

Application Case 5.5 (Continued)

TABLE 5.2 Tabular Representation of the Fields Included in the Combined Dataset

Journal	Year	Author(s)	Title	Vol/No	Pages	Keywords	Abstract
MISQ	2005	A. Malhotra, S. Gossain, and O. A. El Sawy	Absorptive capacity configurations in supply chains: Gearing for partner-enabled market knowledge creation	29/1	145–187	knowledge management supply chain absorptive capacity interorganizational information systems configuration approaches	The need for continual value innovation is driving supply chains to evolve from a pure transactional focus to leveraging interorganizational partnerships for sharing
ISR	1999	D. Robey and M. C. Boudtreau	Accounting for the contradictory organizational consequences of information technology: theoretical directions and methodological implications		165–185	organizational transformation impacts of technology organization theory research methodology intraorganizational power electronic communication mis implementation culture systems	Although much contemporary thought considers advanced information technologies as either determinants or enablers of radical organizational change, empirical studies have revealed inconsistent findings to support the deterministic logic implicit in such arguments. This paper reviews the contradictory . . .
JMIS	2001	R. Aron and E. K. Clemons	Achieving the optimal balance between investment in quality and investment in self-promotion for information products		65–88	information products internet advertising product positioning signaling signaling games	When producers of goods (or services) are confronted by a situation in which their offerings no longer perfectly match consumer preferences, they must determine the extent to which the advertised features of . . .

among the three journals and potential changes in the emphasis on those clusters; that is, to answer questions such as "Are there clusters that represent different research themes specific to a single journal?" and "Is there a time-varying characterization of those clusters?" They discovered and discussed several interesting patterns using tabular and graphical representation of their findings (for further information, see Delen and Crossland, 2008).

Source: D. Delen and M. Crossland, "Seeding the Survey and Analysis of Research Literature with Text Mining," *Expert Systems with Applications,* Vol. 34, No. 3, 2008, pp. 1707–1720.

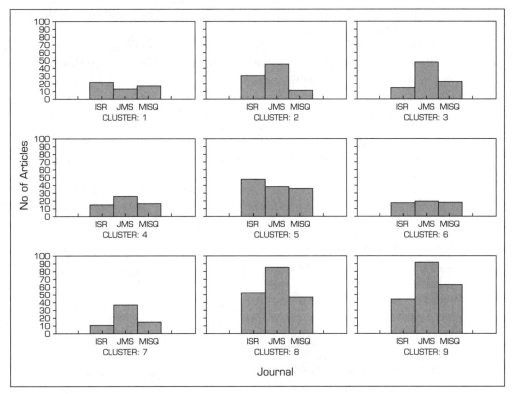

FIGURE 5.7   **Distribution of the Number of Articles for the Three Journals over the Nine Clusters.**
Source: D. Delen and M. Crossland, "Seeding the Survey and Analysis of Research Literature with Text Mining," *Expert Systems with Applications* Vol. 34, No. 3, 2008, pp. 1707–1720.

SECTION 5.4 QUESTIONS

1. What are the main steps in the text mining process?
2. What is the reason for normalizing word frequencies? What are the common methods for normalizing word frequencies?
3. What is singular value decomposition? How is it used in text mining?
4. What are the main knowledge extraction methods from corpus?

5.5   TEXT MINING TOOLS

As the value of text mining is being realized by more and more organizations, the number of software tools offered by software companies and nonprofits is also increasing. Following are some of the popular text mining tools, which we classify as commercial software tools and free software tools.

Commercial Software Tools

The following are some of the most popular software tools used for text mining. Note that many companies offer demonstration versions of their products on their Web sites.

1. ClearForest offers text analysis and visualization tools (**clearforest.com**).
2. IBM Intelligent Miner Data Mining Suite, now fully integrated into IBM's InfoSphere Warehouse software, includes data and text mining tools (**ibm.com**).

3. Megaputer Text Analyst offers semantic analysis of free-form text, summarization, clustering, navigation, and natural language retrieval with search dynamic refocusing (**megaputer.com**).
4. SAS Text Miner provides a rich suite of text processing and analysis tools (**sas.com**).
5. SPSS Text Mining for Clementine extracts key concepts, sentiments, and relationships from call-center notes, blogs, e-mails, and other unstructured data and converts them to a structured format for predictive modeling (**spss.com**).
6. The Statistica Text Mining engine provides easy-to-use text mining functionally with exceptional visualization capabilities (**statsoft.com**).
7. VantagePoint provides a variety of interactive graphical views and analysis tools with powerful capabilities to discover knowledge from text databases (**vpvp.com**).
8. The WordStat analysis module from Provalis Research analyzes textual information such as responses to open-ended questions and interviews (**provalisresearch.com**).

Free Software Tools

Free software tools, some of which are open source, are available from a number of non-profit organizations:

1. GATE is a leading open source toolkit for text mining. It has a free open source framework (or SDK) and graphical development environment (**gate.ac.uk**).
2. RapidMiner has a community edition of its software that includes text mining modules (**rapid-i.com**).
3. LingPipe is a suite of Java libraries for the linguistic analysis of human language (**alias-i.com/lingpipe**).
4. S-EM (Spy-EM) is a text classification system that learns from positive and unlabeled examples (**cs.uic.edu/~liub/S-EM/S-EM-download.html**).
5. Vivisimo/Clusty is a Web search and text-clustering engine (**clusty.com**).

SECTION 5.5 QUESTIONS

1. What are some of the most popular text mining software tools?
2. Why do you think most of the text mining tools are offered by statistics companies?
3. What do you think are the pros and cons of choosing a free text mining tool over a commercial tool?

5.6 WEB MINING OVERVIEW

The World Wide Web (or shortly Web) serves as an enormous repository of data and information on virtually everything one can conceive. The Web is perhaps the world's largest data and text repository, and the amount of information on the Web is growing rapidly every day. A lot of interesting information can be found online: whose homepage is linked to which other pages, how many people have links to a specific Web page, and how a particular site is organized. In addition, each visitor to a Web site, each search on a **search engine**, each click on a link, and each transaction on an e-commerce site creates additional data. Although unstructured textual data in the form of Web pages coded in HTML or XML are the dominant content of the Web, the Web infrastructure also contains hyperlink information (connections to other Web pages) and usage information (logs of visitors' interactions with Web sites), all of which provide rich data for knowledge discovery. Analysis of this information can help us make better use of Web sites and also aid us in enhancing relationships and value to the visitors of our own Web sites.

However, according to Han and Kamber (2006), the Web also poses great challenges for effective and efficient knowledge discovery:

- ***The Web is too big for effective data mining.***   The Web is so large and growing so rapidly that it is difficult to even quantify its size. Because of the sheer size of the Web, it is not feasible to set up a data warehouse to replicate, store, and integrate all of the data on the Web, making data collection and integration a challenge.
- ***The Web is too complex.***   The complexity of a Web page is far greater than a page in a traditional text document collection. Web pages lack a unified structure. They contain far more authoring style and content variation than any set of books, articles, or other traditional text-based documents.
- ***The Web is too dynamic.***   The Web is a highly dynamic information source. Not only does the Web grow rapidly, but its content is constantly being updated. Blogs, news stories, stock market results, weather reports, sports scores, prices, company advertisements, and numerous other types of information are updated regularly on the Web.
- ***The Web is not specific to a domain.***   The Web serves a broad diversity of communities and connects billions of workstations. Web users have very different backgrounds, interests, and usage purposes. Most users may not have good knowledge of the structure of the information network and may not be aware of the heavy cost of a particular search that they perform.
- ***The Web has everything.***   Only a small portion of the information on the Web is truly relevant or useful to someone (or some task). It is said that 99 percent of the information on the Web is useless to 99 percent of Web users. Although this may not seem obvious, it is true that a particular person is generally interested in only a tiny portion of the Web, whereas the rest of the Web contains information that is uninteresting to the user and may swamp desired results. Finding the portion of the Web that is truly relevant to a person and the task being performed is a prominent issue in Web-related research.

These challenges have prompted many research efforts to enhance the effectiveness and efficiency of discovering and using data assets on the Web. A number of index-based Web search engines constantly search the Web and index Web pages under certain keywords. Using these search engines, an experienced user may be able to locate documents by providing a set of tightly constrained keywords or phrases. However, a simple keyword-based search engine suffers from several deficiencies. First, a topic of any breadth can easily contain hundreds or thousands of documents. This can lead to a large number of document entries returned by the search engine, many of which are marginally relevant to the topic. Second, many documents that are highly relevant to a topic may not contain the exact keywords defining them. Compared to keyword-based Web search, Web mining is a prominent (and more challenging) approach that can be used to substantially enhance the power of Web search engines because Web mining can identify authoritative Web pages, classify Web documents, and resolve many ambiguities and subtleties raised in keyword-based Web search engines.

Web mining (or Web data mining) is the process of discovering intrinsic relationships (i.e., interesting and useful information) from Web data, which are expressed in the form of textual, linkage, or usage information. The term *Web mining* was first used by Etzioni (1996); today, many conferences, journals, and books focus on Web data

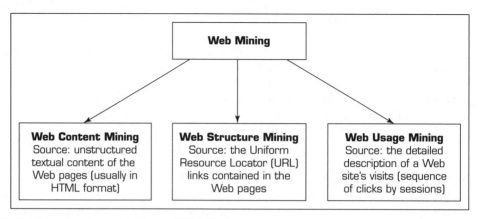

FIGURE 5.8 The Three Main Areas of Web Mining.

mining. It is a continually evolving area of technology and business practice. Figure 5.8 presents the three main areas of Web mining: Web content, Web structure, and Web usage mining.

SECTION 5.6 QUESTIONS

1. What are some of the main challenges the Web poses for knowledge discovery?

2. What is Web mining? How does it differ from regular data mining?

3. What are the three main areas of Web mining?

5.7 WEB CONTENT MINING AND WEB STRUCTURE MINING

Web content mining refers to the extraction of useful information from Web pages. The documents may be extracted in some machine-readable format so that automated techniques can generate some information about the Web pages. **Web crawlers** are used to read through the content of a Web site automatically. The information gathered may include document characteristics similar to what is used in text mining, but it may include additional concepts such as the document hierarchy. Web content mining can also be used to enhance the results produced by search engines. For example, Turetken and Sharda (2004) described a visualization system that takes the results of a search from a search engine such as Google, reads the top 100 documents, clusters those documents by processing them using IBM's Intelligent Text Miner, and then presents the results in a graphical format.

In addition to text, Web pages also contain hyperlinks pointing one page to another. Hyperlinks contain a significant amount of hidden human annotation that can potentially help to automatically infer the notion of *authority*. When a Web page developer includes a link pointing to another Web page, this can be regarded as the developer's endorsement of the other page. The collective endorsement of a given page by different developers on the Web may indicate the importance of the page and may naturally lead to the discovery of authoritative Web pages (Miller, 2005). Therefore, the vast amount of Web linkage information provides a rich collection of information about the relevance, quality, and structure of the Web's contents, and thus is a rich source for Web mining.

A search on the Web to obtain information on a specific topic usually returns a few relevant, high-quality Web pages and a larger number of unusable Web pages. Use of an index based on authoritative pages (or some measure of it) will improve the search results and ranking of relevant pages. The idea of authority (or **authoritative pages**) stems from earlier information retrieval work using citations among journal articles to evaluate the impact of research papers (Miller, 2005). Though that was the origination of the idea, there are significant differences between the citations in research articles and hyperlinks on Web pages. First, not every hyperlink represents an endorsement (some links are created for navigation purposes and some are for paid advertisement). While this is true, if the majority of the hyperlinks are of endorsement type, then the collective opinion will still prevail. Second, for commercial and competitive interests, one authority will rarely have its Web page point to rival authorities in the same domain. For example, Microsoft may prefer not to include links on its Web pages to Apple's Web sites, because this may be regarded as endorsement of its competitor's authority. Third, authoritative pages are seldom particularly descriptive. For example, the main Web page of Yahoo! may not contain the explicit self-description that it is in fact a Web search engine.

The structure of Web hyperlinks has led to another important category of Web pages called a **hub**. A hub is one or more Web pages that provide a collection of links to authoritative pages. Hub pages may not be prominent and only a few links may point to them; however, they provide link to a collection of prominent sites on a specific topic of interest. A hub could be a list of recommended links on an individual's homepage, recommended reference sites on a course Web page, or a professionally assembled resource list on a specific topic. Hub pages play the role of implicitly conferring the authorities on a narrow field. In essence, a close symbiotic relationship exists between good hubs and authoritative pages; a good hub is good because it points to many good authorities, and a good authority is good because it is being pointed to by many good hubs. Such relationship between hubs and authorities makes it possible to automatically retrieve high-quality content from the Web.

The most popular publicly known and referenced algorithm used to calculate hubs and authorities is **hyperlink-induced topic search (HITS)**. It was originally developed by Kleinberg (1999) and has since been improved on by many researchers. HITS is a link-analysis algorithm that rates Web pages using the hyperlink information contained within them. In the context of Web search, the HITS algorithm collects a base document set for a specific query. It then recursively calculates the hub and authority values for each document. To gather the base document set, a root set that matches the query is fetched from a search engine. For each document retrieved, a set of documents that points to the original document and another set of documents that is pointed to by the original document are added to the set as the original document's neighborhood. A recursive process of document identification and link analysis continues until the hub and authority values converge. These values are then used to index and prioritize the document collection generated for a specific query.

Web structure mining is the process of extracting useful information from the links embedded in Web documents. It is used to identify authoritative pages and hubs, which are the cornerstones of the contemporary page-rank algorithms that are central to popular search engines such as Google and Yahoo! Just as links going to a Web page may indicate a site's popularity (or authority), links within the Web page (or the compete Web site) may indicate the depth of coverage of a specific topic. Analysis of links is very important in understanding the interrelationships among large numbers of Web pages, leading to a better understanding of a specific Web community, clan, or clique. Application Case 5.6 describes a project that used both Web content mining and Web structure mining to better understand how U.S. extremist groups are connected.

Application Case 5.6

Caught in a Web

We normally search for answers to our problems outside of our immediate environment. Often, however, the trouble stems from within. In taking action against global terrorism, domestic extremist groups often go unnoticed. However, domestic extremists pose a significant threat to U.S. security because of the information they possess, as well as their increasing ability, through the use of Internet, to reach out to extremist groups around the world.

Keeping tabs on the content available on the Internet is difficult. Researchers and authorities need superior tools to analyze and monitor the activities of extremist groups. Researchers at the University of Arizona, with support from the Department of Homeland Security and other agencies, have developed a Web mining methodology to find and analyze Web sites operated by domestic extremists in order to learn about these groups through their use of the Internet. Extremist groups use the Internet to communicate, to access private messages, and to raise money online.

The research methodology begins by gathering a superior-quality collection of relevant extremist and terrorist Web sites. Hyperlink analysis is performed, which leads to other extremist and terrorist Web sites. The interconnectedness with other Web sites is crucial in estimating the similarity of the objectives of various groups. The next step is content analysis, which further codifies these Web sites based on various attributes such as communications, fund-raising, and ideology sharing, to name a few.

Based on link analysis and content analysis, researchers have identified 97 Web sites of U.S. extremist and hate groups. Oftentimes, the links between these communities do not necessarily represent any cooperation between them. However, finding numerous links between common interest groups helps in clustering the communities under a common banner. Further research using data mining to automate the process has a global aim, with the goal of identifying links between international hate and extremist groups and their U.S. counterparts.

Sources: Based on Y. Zhou, E. Reid, J. Qin, H. Chen, and G. Lai, "U.S. Domestic Extremist Groups on the Web: Link and Content Analysis," *IEEE Intelligent Systems*, Vol. 20, No. 5, September/October 2005, pp. 44–51.

SECTION 5.7 QUESTIONS

1. What is Web content mining? How does it differ from text mining?
2. Define Web structure mining, and differentiate it from Web content mining.
3. What are the main goals of Web structure mining?
4. What are hubs and authorities? What is the HITS algorithm?

5.8 WEB USAGE MINING

Web usage mining is the extraction of useful information from data generated through Web page visits and transactions. Masand et al. (2002) state that at least three types of data are generated through Web page visits:

1. Automatically generated data stored in server access logs, referrer logs, agent logs, and client-side cookies
2. User profiles
3. Metadata, such as page attributes, content attributes, and usage data

Analysis of the information collected by Web servers can help us better understand user behavior. Analysis of this data is often called **clickstream analysis**. By using the data and text mining techniques, a company might be able to discern interesting patterns from

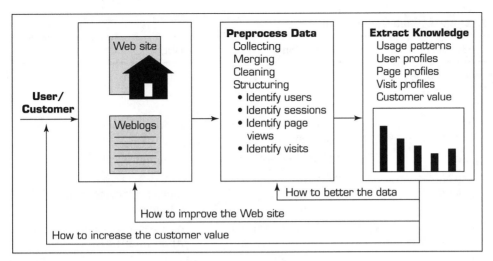

FIGURE 5.9   **Extraction of Knowledge from Web Usage Data.**

the clickstreams. For example, it might learn that 60 percent of visitors who searched for "hotels in Maui" had searched earlier for "airfares to Maui." Such information could be useful in determining where to place online advertisements. Clickstream analysis might also be useful for knowing *when* visitors access a site. For example, if a company knew that 70 percent of software downloads from its Web site occurred between 7 P.M. and 11 P.M., it could plan for better customer support and network bandwidth during those hours. Figure 5.9 shows the process of extracting knowledge from **clickstream data** and how the generated knowledge is used to improve the process, improve the Web site, and most importantly increase the customer value. Nasraoui (2006) listed the following applications of Web mining:

1. Determine the lifetime value of clients.
2. Design cross-marketing strategies across products.
3. Evaluate promotional campaigns.
4. Target electronic ads and coupons at user groups based on user access patterns.
5. Predict user behavior based on previously learned rules and users' profiles.
6. Present dynamic information to users based on their interests and profiles.

   Amazon.com provides a good example of how Web usage history can be leveraged dynamically. A registered user who revisits Amazon.com is greeted by name. This is a simple task that involves recognizing the user by reading a cookie (i.e., a small text file written by a Web site on the visitor's computer). Amazon.com also presents the user with a choice of products in a personalized store, based on previous purchases and an association analysis of similar users. It also makes special "Gold Box" offers that are good for a short amount of time. All these recommendations involve a detailed analysis of the visitor as well as the user's peer group developed through the use of clustering, sequence pattern discovery, association, and other data and text mining techniques.
   Table 5.3 lists some of the more popular Web mining products.

SECTION 5.8 QUESTIONS

1. Define Web usage mining.
2. In an e-commerce environment, what are the potential applications of Web usage mining?

TABLE 5.3   Web Usage Mining Software

Product Name	Description	URL
Angoss Knowledge WebMiner	Combines ANGOSS KnowledgeSTUDIO and clickstream analysis	**angoss.com**
ClickTracks	Visitor patterns can be shown on Web site	**clicktracks.com**
LiveStats from DeepMetrix	Real-time log analysis, live demo on site	**deepmetrix.com**
Megaputer WebAnalyst	Data and text mining capabilities	**megaputer.com/products/ wm.php3**
MicroStrategy Web Traffic Analysis Module	Traffic highlights, content analysis, and Web visitor analysis reports	**microstrategy.com/Solutions/ Applications/WTAM**
SAS Web Analytics	Analyzes Web site traffic	**sas.com/solutions/webanalytics/**
SPSS Web Mining for Clementine	Extraction of Web events	**spss.com/web_mining_for_ clementine**
WebTrends	Data mining of Web traffic information.	**webtrends.com**
XML Miner	A system and class library for mining data and text expressed in XML, using fuzzy logic expert system rules	**scientio.com**

3. What is a clickstream? Why is it important in Web usage mining?

4. What types of information do Web servers collect when users visit a Web page and engage in an interactive activity?

5. Identify value-added features developed by major e-commerce sites that may be based on Web usage mining.

5.9   WEB MINING SUCCESS STORIES

Ask.com (**ask.com**) is a well-known search engine. Ask.com believes that a fundamental component of its success lies in its ability to consistently provide better search results. However, determining the quality of search results is impossible to measure accurately using strictly quantitative measures such as click-through rate, abandonment, and search frequency; additional quantitative and qualitative measures are required. By regularly surveying its audience, Ask.com uses a mix of qualitative and quantitative measures as the basis of key performance indicators, such as "Percentage of Users Saying They Found What They Were Looking For," "Percentage of Users Likely to Use the Site Again," and "Rated Usefulness of Search Results," in addition to open-ended custom questions evaluating the user experience. By integrating quantitative and qualitative data, Ask.com was able to validate the move to its "Ask 3D" design, despite the fact that, in testing, purely quantitative measures showed no difference in performance between the old and new designs.

Scholastic.com (**scholastic.com**) is an online bookstore specializing in educational books for children. It discovered that some visitors failed to make a purchase. The critical questions were "What went wrong?" "Why didn't these visitors make a purchase?" and, ultimately, "How can we win these customers back?" Further analysis of the data showed that part of the reason was that the site didn't carry the titles they were looking for. For example, shoppers were seeking backlist titles they read decades ago and assumed Scholastic would still have them. In this case, the company leveraged Voice of Customer data to identify specific titles people sought that were out of print. This Web-based data quantified the amount of unmet market demand and its impact on future purchase behavior. Scholastic began carrying older titles on its Web site and implemented a feature that allowed the customer to sign up to receive an e-mail when an out-of-print book became available. Of the e-mails sent, about 35 percent of recipients purchased the book.

St. John Health System is a health care system with 8 hospitals, 125 medical locations, and over 3,000 physicians. Its CRM database has over 1.1 million patients. St. John's Web site tracks satisfaction data along with transactions, such as online registration for health assessments and scheduling of physician visits, to determine how many new patients the Web site is responsible for driving into the health system. St. John has seen a 15 percent increase in new patients and a return on investment of four-to-one on funds spent on improving Web site satisfaction, despite a highly competitive health care market and a declining consumer population. This success has turned the heads of the whole organization, which now embraces online customer satisfaction as a key performance indicator with multifaceted value. St. John uses data from the Web site to monitor the success of advertising programs that drive people to the Web site, to prioritize and fund cross-departmental projects that address satisfaction improvement, and to keep the voice of the customer at the center of corporate business decisions.

Forward-thinking companies like Ask.com, Scholastic, and St. John Health System are actively using Web mining systems to answer critically important questions of "Who?" "Why?" and "How?" As documented, the benefit of integrating these systems effectively and efficiently can be significant, in terms of both incremental financial growth and increasing customer loyalty and satisfaction.

Given the continual shift of advertising dollars, resources, and, most important, customers into the online channel, the belief is that executives who aggressively pursue a more holistic view of their customers using Web mining techniques will have a substantial advantage over those who continue to base their analyses on intuitions, gut feelings, and wild guesses. Application Case 5.7 presents a detailed view of Web optimization efforts.

Application Case 5.7
Web Site Optimization Ecosystem

It seems that just about everything on the Web can be measured—every click can be recorded, every view can be captured, and every visit can be analyzed—all in an effort to continually and automatically optimize the online experience. Unfortunately, the notion of "infinite measurability" and "automatic optimization" in the online channel is far more complex than most realize. The assumption that any single application of Web mining techniques will provide the necessary range of insights required to understand Web site visitor behavior is deceptive and potentially risky. Ideally, a holistic view to customer experience is

needed that can only be captured using both quantitative and qualitative data. Forward-thinking companies, like the ones discussed in this section (i.e., **Ask.com**, **Scholastic.com**, and St. John Health System), have already taken steps toward capturing and analyzing a holistic view of the customer experience, which has led to significant gains, in terms of both incremental financial growth and increasing customer loyalty and satisfaction.

According to Peterson (2008), the inputs for Web site optimization efforts can be classified along two axes describing the nature of the data and how

(Continued)

Application Case 5.7   (Continued)

that data can be used. On one axis are data and information; data being primarily quantitative and information being primarily qualitative. On the other axis are measures and actions; measures being reports, analysis, and recommendations all designed to drive actions, the actual changes being made in the ongoing process of site and marketing optimization. Each quadrant created by these dimensions leverages different technologies and creates different outputs, but much like a biological ecosystem, each technological niche interacts with the others to support the entire online environment (see Figure 5.10).

Most believe that the Web site optimization ecosystem is defined by the ability to log, parse, and report on the clickstream behavior of site visitors. The underlying technology of this ability is generally referred to as **Web analytics**. Although Web analytics tools provide invaluable insights, understanding visitor behavior is as much a function of qualitatively

determining interests and intent as it is quantifying clicks from page to page. Fortunately there are two other classes of applications designed to provide a more qualitative view of online visitor behavior designed to report on the overall user experience and report direct feedback given by visitors and customers: **customer experience management (CEM)** and **Voice of Customer (VOC)**:

- Web analytics applications focus on "where and when" questions by aggregating, mining, and visualizing large volumes of data, by reporting on online marketing and visitor acquisition efforts, by summarizing page-level visitor interaction data, and by summarizing visitor flow through defined multistep processes.
- Voice of Customer applications focus on "who and how" questions by gathering and reporting direct feedback from site visitors, by

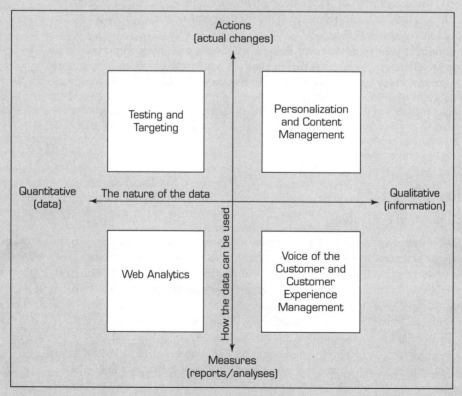

FIGURE 5.10   Two-Dimensional View of the Inputs for Web Site Optimization.   *Source:* E. T. Peterson, The Voice of Customer: Qualitative Data as a Critical Input to Web Site Optimization (2008), **www.foreseeresults.com/ Form_Epeterson_ WebAnalytics.html** (accessed on May 22, 2009).

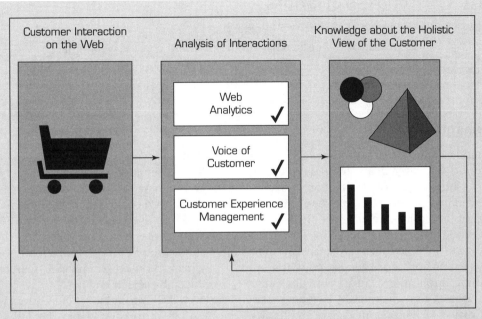

FIGURE 5.11   **A Process View to Web Site Optimization Ecosystem.**

benchmarking against other sites and offline channels, and by supporting predictive modeling of future visitor behavior.

- Customer experience management applications focus on "what and why" questions by detecting Web application issues and problems, by tracking and resolving business process and usability obstacles, by reporting on-site performance and availability, by enabling real-time alerting and monitoring, and by supporting deep-diagnosis of observed visitor behavior.

All three applications are needed to have a complete view of the visitor behavior where each application plays a distinct and valuable role. Web analytics, CEM, and VOC applications form the foundation of the Web site optimization ecosystem that supports the online business's ability to positively influence desired outcomes (a pictorial representation of this process view of the Web site optimization ecosystem is given in Figure 5.11). These similar-yet-distinct applications each contribute to site operator's ability to recognize, react, and respond to the ongoing challenges faced by every Web site owner. Fundamental to the optimization process is measurement, gathering data and

information that can then be transformed into tangible analysis and recommendations for improvement using Web mining tools and techniques. When used properly, these applications allow for convergent validation—combining different sets of data collected for the same audience to provide a richer and deeper understanding of audience behavior. The convergent validation model—one where multiple sources of data describing the same population are integrated to increase the depth and richness of the resulting analysis—forms the framework of the Web site optimization ecosystem. On one side of the spectrum are the primarily qualitative inputs from VOC applications; on the other side are the primarily quantitative inputs from CEM bridging the gap by supporting key elements of data discovery. When properly implemented, all three systems sample data from the same audience. The combination of these data—either through data integration projects or simply via the process of conducting good analysis—supports far more actionable insights than any of the ecosystem members individually.

Source: Based on E. T. Peterson, "The Voice of Customer: Qualitative Data as a Critical Input to Web Site Optimization," 2008, **foreseeresults.com/Form_Epeterson_WebAnalytics. html** (accessed on May 22, 2009).

SECTION 5.9 QUESTIONS

1. Why do we need Web mining?

2. In your own words, what are the pros and cons of Web mining?

3. What are the common characteristics of Web mining success stories?

Chapter Highlights

- Text mining is the discovery of knowledge from unstructured (mostly text based) data sources. Given that a great deal of information is in text form, text mining is one of the fastest growing branches of the business intelligence field.
- Companies use text mining and Web mining to better understand their customers by analyzing their feedbacks left on Web forms, blogs, and **wikis**.
- Text mining applications are in virtually every area of business and government, including marketing, finance, health care, medicine, and homeland security.
- Text mining uses natural language processing to induce structure into the text collection and then uses data mining algorithms such as classification, clustering, association, and sequence discovery to extract knowledge from it.
- Successful application of text mining requires a structured methodology similar to the CRISP-DM methodology in data mining.
- Text mining is closely related to information extraction, natural language processing, and document summarization.
- Text mining entails creating numeric indices from unstructured text and then applying data mining algorithms to these indices.
- Web mining can be defined as the discovery and analysis of interesting and useful information from the Web, about the Web, and usually using Web-based tools.
- Web mining can be viewed as consisting of three areas: Web content mining, Web structure mining, and Web usage mining.
- Web content mining refers to the automatic extraction of useful information from Web pages. It may be used to enhance search results produced by search engines.
- Web structure mining refers to generating interesting information from the links included in Web pages. This is used in Google's page-rank algorithm to order the display of pages, for example.
- Web structure mining can also be used to identify the members of a specific community and perhaps even the roles of the members in the community.
- Web usage mining refers to developing useful information through analysis of Web server logs, user profiles, and transaction information.
- Web usage mining can assist in better CRM, personalization, site navigation modifications, and improved business models.
- Text and Web mining are emerging as critical components of the next generation of business intelligence tools in enabling organizations to compete successfully.

Key Terms

analytical model	deception detection	sentiment analysis	trend analysis
analytical techniques	hub	sequence discovery	unstructured data
association	hyperlink-induced topic	singular value	Voice of Customer
authoritative pages	search (HITS)	decomposition (SVD)	(VOC)
classification	inverse document	speech synthesis	Web analytics
clickstream analysis	frequency	stemming	Web content mining
clickstream data	natural language	stop words	Web crawler
clustering	processing (NLP)	term–document matrix	Web mining
corpus	part-of-speech tagging	(TDM)	Web structure mining
customer experience	polysemes	text mining	Web usage mining
management (CEM)	search engine	tokenizing	wiki

Questions for Discussion

1. Explain the relationship among data mining, text mining, and Web mining.
2. What should an organization consider before making a decision to purchase text mining and/or Web mining software?
3. Discuss the differences and commonalities between text mining and Web mining.
4. In your own words, define text mining and discuss its most popular applications.
5. Discuss the similarities and differences between the data mining process (e.g., CRIPS-DM) and the three-step, high-level, text mining process explained in this chapter.
6. What does it mean to induce structure into the text-based data? Discuss the alternative ways of inducing structure into text-based data.
7. What is the role of natural language processing in text mining? Discuss the capabilities and limitations of NLP in the context of text mining.
8. List and discuss three prominent application areas for text mining. What is the common theme among the three application areas you chose?
9. Discuss the relationship between Web mining and Web analytics.
10. What are the three main areas of Web mining? Discuss the differences and commonalities among these three areas.
11. What is Web content mining? How does it differ from text mining? Discuss and justify your answers with concrete examples.
12. What is Web structure mining? What are authoritative pages and hubs? How do they relate to Web structure mining?
13. Discuss the expected benefits of Web structure mining. Provide examples from real-world applications that you are familiar with.
14. What is Web usage mining? Draw a picture of the Web usage mining process and explain/discuss the major steps in the process.
15. Provide two exemplary business applications of Web usage mining; discuss their usage and business value.

Exercises

Teradata University and Other Hands-on Exercises

1. Visit **teradatastudentnetwork.com**. Identify cases about text and Web mining. Describe recent developments in the field. If you cannot find enough cases at Teradata University network Web site, broaden your search to other Web-based resources.
2. Go to **teradatastudentnetwork.com**, or locate white papers, Web seminars, and other materials related to text mining and/or Web mining. Synthesize your findings into a short written report.
3. Browse the Web and your library's digital databases to identify articles that make the natural linkage between text/Web mining and contemporary business intelligence systems.

Team Assignments and Role-Playing Projects

1. Examine how textual data can be captured automatically using Web-based technologies. Once captured, what are the potential patterns that you can extract from these unstructured data sources?
2. Interview administrators in your college or executives in your organization to determine how text mining and Web mining could assist them in their work. Write a proposal describing your findings. Include a preliminary cost/benefits analysis in your report.
3. Go to your library's online resources. Learn how to download attributes of a collection of literature (journal articles) in a specific topic. Download and process the data using a methodology similar to the one explained in Application Case 5.5.

Internet Exercises

1. Survey some text mining tools and vendors. Start with **ClearForest.com** and **Megaputer.com**. Also consult with **dmreview.com** and identify some text mining products and service providers that are not mentioned in this chapter.
2. Find recent cases of successful text mining Web mining applications. Try text and Web mining software vendors and consultancy firms and look for cases or success stories. Prepare a report summarizing five new case studies.
3. Go to **statsoft.com**. Select Downloads and download at least three white papers on applications. Which of these applications may have used the data/text/Web mining techniques discussed in this chapter?
4. Go to **sas.com**. Download at least three white papers on applications. Which of these applications may have used the data/text/Web mining techniques discussed in this chapter?
5. Go to **spss.com**. Download at least three white papers on applications. Which of these applications may have used the data/text/Web mining techniques discussed in this chapter?

6. Go to **teradata.com**. Download at least three white papers on applications. Which of these applications may have used the data/text/Web mining techniques discussed in this chapter?

7. Go to **fairisaac.com**. Download at least three white papers on applications. Which of these applications may have used the data/text/Web mining techniques discussed in this chapter?

8. Go to **salfordsystems.com**. Download at least three white papers on applications. Which of these applications may have used the data/text/Web mining techniques discussed in this chapter?

9. Go to **kdnuggets.com**. Explore the sections on applications as well as software. Find names of at least three additional packages for data mining and text mining.

End of Chapter Application Case

HP and Text Mining

Hewlett-Packard Company (HP), founded in 1939 by William R. Hewlett and David Packard, is headquartered in Palo Alto, California. The company provides products, technologies, solutions, and services to individuals, small- and medium-sized businesses, and large enterprises on a global basis. HP also offers management software solutions that enable enterprise customers to manage their IT infrastructure, operations, applications, IT services, and business processes, as well as carrier-grade platforms for various applications. Some of HP's popular product categories are commercial and consumer personal computers, workstations, handheld computing devices, inkjet printers, laser printers, digital entertainment systems, calculators and related accessories, software and services, digital photography and entertainment, graphics, imaging and printer supplies for printer hardware, printing supplies, scanning devices, and network infrastructure products, including Ethernet switch products. Retailers form the distribution channel of the company. The company also sells through distribution partners, original equipment manufacturers, and systems integrators.

Text Mining

Customers of HP communicate with the company through millions of e-mails. Structured data analysis is effective in finding out parameters such as from whom, when, where, and how the messages originated. A wealth of information would be available if mining techniques could find out why these e-mails were sent. One of the common interaction points between the customer and the company is the call center. HP is impressed by the business insights that could be culled from communications such as word documents, e-mails, and other sources. The combination of the structured and unstructured data can create a tremendous potential for companies to find valuable business insights.

System

The standard tools that HP previously used could not report useful information from customer-related communications. Now, HP used SAS Institute's Text Miner to uncover analytical insights from customer-related data in call center applications and then standardized those insights. HP implemented Text Miner to combine structured data and text data to produce a hybrid structured/unstructured data set that is stored in a Microsoft SQL Server database with an Analysis Services Online Analytic Processing engine. The system, today, encompasses 300,000 text documents and is roughly 50 gigabytes in size, covering an 18-month period and 3 call centers.

HP implemented Executive Viewer, a Web-based tool developed by Temtec (**temtec.com**) that enables HP to augment the OLAP cubes with predictive modeling, loyalty scores, and customer differentiations created by SAS Enterprise Miner.

Process

Various concepts, such as products used, call frequency, and common customer issues, are used to aggregate text data; the result is consolidated into probabilistic text clusters. This consolidated cluster is then combined with the structured data from third-party providers. HP can now combine and analyze structured data such as revenue with customer desires, attitudes, and needs.

Text analysis is challenging due to dimensionality and data dispersal. Different customer databases contain different structured information that could be integrated without much difficulty. The challenge lies in combining the structured data with unstructured data from text. SAS Text Miner uses a technique called singular value decomposition. Text mining software includes a prebuilt dictionary of words and synonym lists; it is an overwhelming task for the organization to customize the text information generated in its business environments. Text data are available at various sources that are outside the realms of traditional data warehousing. Some of the largest challenges that SAS Text Miner faces are customer activity at the HP Web site as well as finding insights into the businesses of HP's customers.

In addition to the major application of text mining, SAS Text Miner could be used proactively on customer Web sites to generate insights into the customer needs that HP could satisfy. The tool could also be used to analyze multiple suppliers/vendors with various numbers and descriptions in text.

Results

SAS Text Miner was successfully able to develop standard data definitions and product classification models with more than 80 percent accuracy. The system is now being used to support HP in contributing to the top line through improved cross-selling, targeted marketing, customer retention, and better anticipation of customer needs. The information generated from structured/unstructured data now supports multiple business users in various departments.

QUESTIONS FOR END OF CHAPTER APPLICATION CASE

1. What is the practical application of text mining?
2. How do you think text mining techniques could be used in other businesses?
3. What were HP's challenges in text mining? How were they overcome?
4. In what other areas, in your opinion, can HP use text mining?

Sources: Based on M. Hammond, "BI Case Study: What's in a Word? For Hewlett-Packard, It's Customer Insight," *Business Intelligence Journal,* Vol. 9, No. 3, Summer 2004, pp. 48–51; and B. Beal, "Text Mining: A Golden Opportunity for HP," *SearchCRM.com,* June 6, 2005, **searchdatamanagement.techtarget.com/originalContent/ 0,289142,sid91_gci1136611,00.html** (accessed November 2008).

References

Beal, B. (2005, June 6). "Text Mining: A Golden Opportunity for HP." *SearchCRM.com,* **searchdatamanagement. techtarget.com/originalContent/0,289142,sid91_ gci1136611,00.html** (accessed November 2008).

Bond, C. F., and B. M. DePaulo. (2006). "Accuracy of Deception Judgments." *Personality and Social Psychology Reports,* Vol. 10, No. 3, pp. 214–234.

Chiem, P. X. (2001). "Kodak Turns Knowledge Gained About Patents into Competitive Intelligence." *Knowledge Management,* pp. 11–12

Chun, H. W., Y. Tsuruoka, J. D. Kim, R. Shiba, N. Nagata, and T. Hishiki. (2006). "Extraction of Gene-Disease Relations from Medline Using Domain Dictionaries and Machine Learning." *Proceedings of the 11th Pacific Symposium on Biocomputing,* pp. 4–15.

Coussement, K., and D. Van Den Poel. (2009). "Improving Customer Attrition Prediction by Integrating Emotions from Client/Company Interaction Emails and Evaluating Multiple Classifiers." *Expert Systems with Applications,* Vol. 36, No. 3, pp. 6127–6134.

Coussement, K., and D. Van Den Poel. (2008). "Improving Customer Complaint Management by Automatic Email Classification Using Linguistic Style Features as Predictors." *Decision Support Systems,* Vol. 44, No. 4, pp. 870–882.

Delen, D., and M. Crossland. (2008). "Seeding the Survey and Analysis of Research Literature with Text Mining." *Expert Systems with Applications,* Vol. 34, No. 3, pp. 1707–1720.

Etzioni, O. (1996). "The World Wide Web: Quagmire or Gold Mine?" *Communications of the ACM,* Vol. 39, No. 11, pp. 65–68.

EUROPOL. (2007). "EUROPOL Work Program for the 2007." **statewatch.org/news/2006/apr/europol-work- programme-2007.pdf** (accessed October 2008).

Feldman, R., and J. Sanger. (2007). *The Text Mining Handbook: Advanced Approaches in Analyzing Unstructured Data.* Boston, MA: ABS Ventures.

Froelich, J., S. Ananyan, and D. L Olson. (2005). "Business Intelligence Through Text Mining." *Business Intelligence Journal,* Vol. 10, No. 1, pp. 43–50.

Fuller, C. M., D. Biros, and D. Delen. (2008). "Exploration of Feature Selection and Advanced Classification Models for High-Stakes Deception Detection." *Proceedings of the 41st Annual Hawaii International Conference on System Sciences (HICSS),* Big Island, HI: IEEE Press, pp. 80–99.

Ghani, R., K. Probst, Y. Liu, M. Krema, and A. Fano. (2006) "Text Mining for Product Attribute Extraction." *SIGKDD Explorations,* Vol. 8, No. 1, pp. 41–48.

Hammond, M. (Summer 2004). "BI Case Study: What's in a Word? For Hewlett-Packard, It's Customer Insight." *Business Intelligence Journal,* Vol. 9, No. 3, pp. 48–51

Han, J., and M. Kamber. (2006). *Data Mining: Concepts and Techniques,* 2nd ed. San Francisco, CA: Morgan Kaufmann.

Kanayama, H., and T. Nasukawa. (2006). "Fully Automatic Lexicon Expanding for Domain-Oriented Sentiment Analysis, EMNLP: Empirical Methods in Natural Language Processing." **trl.ibm.com/projects/textmining/takmi/ sentiment_analysis_e.htm**.

Kleinberg, J. (1999). "Authoritative Sources in a Hyperlinked Environment." *Journal of the ACM,* Vol. 46, No. 5, pp. 604–632.

Lin, J., and D. Demner-Fushman. (2005). "'Bag of Words' Is Not Enough for Strength of Evidence Classification." *AMIA Annual Symposium Proceedings,* pp. 1031–1032. **pubmedcentral.nih.gov/articlerender.fcgi?artid= 1560897**.

Mahgoub, H., D. Rösner, N. Ismail, and F. Torkey. (2008). "A Text Mining Technique Using Association Rules Extraction." *International Journal of Computational Intelligence,* Vol. 4, No. 1, pp. 21–28.

Manning, C. D., and H. Schutze (2009). *Foundations of Statistical Natural Language Processing (Second Edition).* Cambridge, MA: MIT Press.

Masand, B. M., M. Spiliopoulou, J. Srivastava, and O. R. Zaïane. (2002). "Web Mining for Usage Patterns and Profiles." *SIGKDD Explorations,* Vol. 4, No. 2, pp. 125–132.

McKnight, W. (2005, January 1). "Text Data Mining in Business Intelligence." *Information Management Magazine.* **information-management.com/issues/20050101/1016487-1.html** (accessed May 22, 2009).

Mena, J. (2003). *Investigative Data Mining for Security and Criminal Detection.* Burlington, MA: Elsevier Science.

Miller, T. W. (2005). *Data and Text Mining: A Business Applications Approach.* Upper Saddle River, NJ: Prentice Hall.

MITRE Corporation. **mitre.org** (accessed on May 20, 2009).

Nasraoui, O., M. Spiliopoulou, J. Srivastava, B. Mobasher, and B. Masand. (2006). "WebKDD 2006: Web Mining and Web Usage Analysis Post-Workshop Report." *ACM SIGKDD Explorations Newsletter,* Vol. 8, No. 2, pp. 84–89.

Nakov, P., A. Schwartz, B. Wolf, and M. A. Hearst. (2005). "Supporting Annotation Layers for Natural Language Processing." *Proceedings of the ACL,* interactive poster and demonstration sessions, Ann Arbor, MI. Association for Computational Linguistics, pp. 65–68.

Peterson, E. T. (2008). "The Voice of Customer: Qualitative Data as a Critical Input to Web Site Optimization." **foreseeresults.com/Form_Epeterson_WebAnalytics.html** (accessed May 22, 2009).

Shatkay, H., A. Höglund, S. Brady, T. Blum, P. Dönnes, and O. Kohlbacher. (2007). "SherLoc: High-Accuracy Prediction of Protein Subcellular Localization by Integrating Text and Protein Sequence Data." *Bioinformatics,* Vol. 23, No. 11, pp. 1410–1417.

SPSS. "Merck Sharp & Dohme." **storieshttp://www.spss.com/success/template_view.cfm?Story_ID=185** (accessed May 15, 2009).

StatSoft. (2009). *STATISTICA Data and Text Miner User Manual.* Tulsa, OK: StatSoft, Inc.

Tsenga, Y-H., C-J. Linb, and Y-I. Linc. (2007). "Text Mining Techniques for Patent Analysis." *Information Processing & Management,* Vol. 43, No. 5, pp. 1216–1245.

Turetken, O., and R. Sharda. (2004). "Development of a Fisheye-based Information Search Processing Aid (FISPA) for Managing Information Overload in the Web Environment." *Decision Support Systems,* Vol. 37, No. 3, pp. 415–434.

Weng, S. S., and C. K. Liu. (2004) "Using Text Classification and Multiple Concepts to Answer E-mails." *Expert Systems with Applications,* Vol. 26, No. 4, pp. 529–543.

Zhou, Y., E. Reid, J. Qin, H. Chen, and G. Lai. (2005). "U.S. Domestic Extremist Groups on the Web: Link and Content Analysis." *IEEE Intelligent Systems,* Vol. 20, No. 5, pp. 44–51.

6

Business Intelligence Implementation: Integration and Emerging Trends

LEARNING OBJECTIVES

- Describe the major business intelligence (BI) implementation issues

- List some critical success factors of BI implementation

- Describe the importance and issues in integrating BI technologies and applications

- Understand the needs for connecting BI system with other information systems and describe how it is done

- Define on-demand BI and its advantages and limitations

- List and describe representative privacy, major legal and ethical issues of BI implementation

- Understand Web 2.0 and its characteristics as related to BI and decision support

- Understand social networking concepts, selected applications, and their relationship to BI

- Describe how virtual world technologies can change the use of BI applications

- Describe the integration of social software in BI applications

- Know how Radio Frequency IDentification (RFID) data analysis can help improve supply chain management (SCM) and other operations

- Describe how massive data acquisition techniques can enable reality mining

INTRODUCTION

This chapter covers the major issues of business intelligence (BI) implementation and also introduces some emerging technologies that are likely to impact the development and use of business intelligence applications. Several other interesting technologies are also emerging, but we have focused on those that have already been realized and on some others that are about to impact BI. We introduce these emerging technologies, explore their current applications, and conclude with their relationship to BI. We discuss four major implementation issues: integration, connecting to databases and to other information systems, on-demand BI, and legal, privacy and ethical issues that may affect BI implementation. We close the chapter with a case that illustrates an innovative use of

Radio Frequency IDentification (RFID), BI, and decision support. This chapter contains the following sections:

OPENING VIGNETTE: BI Eastern Mountain Sports Increases Collaboration and Productivity

Eastern Mountain Sports (EMS) (**ems.com**) is a medium-size specialty retailer (annual sales $200 million in 2009) that sells goods in more than 80 physical stores through mail-order catalogs and online. Sports business is done in a very competitive environment. The company needs to make decisions regarding product development, marketing, production, and sales continuously. Good decisions require input and collaboration from employees, customers, and suppliers. During the past few years, the company implemented a BI system that includes business performance management and dashboards. The BI system collects raw data from multiple sources, processes them into data, and conducts analyses that include comparing performance to operational metrics in order to assess the health of the business (see Figure 6.1).

Here is how the system works. Point-of-sale information and other relevant data, which are available on an IBM mainframe computer, are loaded into a Microsoft SQL server and into a data mart. The data are then analyzed with Information Builders' WebFOCUS 7.12 platform. The results are presented via a series of dashboards that users can view by using their Web browsers. This allows users to access a unified, high-level view of key performance indicators (KPIs), such as sales, inventory, and margin levels, and then drill down to granular details that analyze specific transactions.

Despite the cutting edge technology, the system was not performing too well mainly due to insufficient data access, communication, and collaboration among all participants.

THE SOLUTION: INTEGRATING BI WITH SOCIAL SOFTWARE

The company created a multifunctional employee workbench called *E-Basecamp*. E-Basecamp contains all information relevant to corporate goals integrated with productivity tools (e.g., Excel) and role-based content customized to each individual user. The system facilitates collaboration among internal and external stakeholders. EMS is using 20 operation metrics (e.g., inventory levels and turns). These metrics also cover e-tailing,

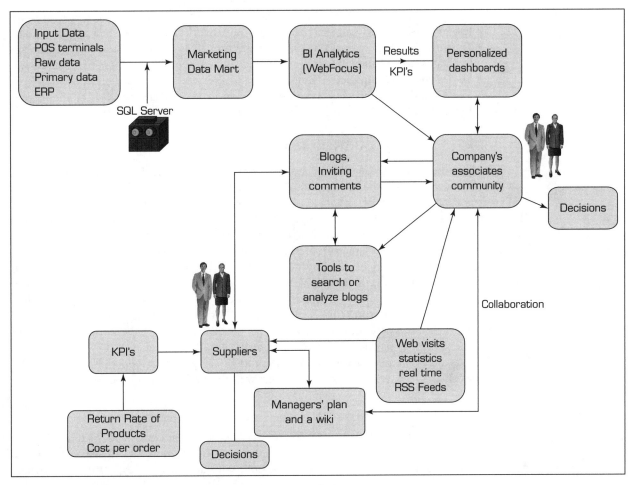

FIGURE 6.1 **Collaborative Decision Making at Eastern Mountain Sports.**

e-marketing where marketing managers monitor Web traffic and conversion rates on an hourly basis. The dashboard shows deviations from targets by means of a color code. Then, EMS added the following set of social software tools.

- **RSS feeds.** RSS feeds (Section 6.7) are embedded into the dashboards to drive more focused inquiries. These feeds are the basis for information sharing and online conversations. For example, by showing which items are selling better than the others, users can collectively analyze the transaction characteristics and selling behaviors that produce the high sales. The knowledge acquired then cascades throughout the organization. For instance, one manager observed an upward spike in footwear sales at store X. An investigation revealed that store X employees had perfected a multistep sales technique that included recommending (both online and in stores) special socks, designed for specific uses along with an inner sole. The information was disseminated using the RSS feed. As a result, sales of footwear increased 57 percent in a year.
- **Wikis.** Wikis are used to encourage collaborative interaction throughout the company. Dashboard users are encouraged to post hypotheses or requests for help and then invite commentary and suggestions, almost like a notepad alongside the dashboard.
- **Blogs.** Blogs were created around specific data or a key metric. The blogs are used to post information and invite comment. Tools are then used to archive, search, and categorize blogs for easy reference. For example, store managers post an inquiry or

explanation regarding sale deviations (from targets). Keeping comments on blogs lets readers observe patterns they might have overlooked using data analysis alone.

- **Twitter.** In 2009, microblogging became prevalent using Twitter. The technology facilitates communication and collaboration and speeding up business processes.
- **Social network service.** Employees and business partners were encouraged to join LinkedIn. Major uses were participation in forums and the use of the answer function. This tool encourages external communication and collaboration.

GOING TO BUSINESS PARTNERS EXTERNALLY

Suppliers are connected to the BI system by blogs, wikis, and RSS feeds. For example, suppliers can monitor the return rate of a product on the dashboard and then invite store managers to provide explanations and suggestions on how to reduce the return rate using wikis or blogs. Assuming that proper security has been installed, suppliers can get data about how well their products sell in almost real time and can prepare better production plans. Also, Twitter and LinkedIn are used extensively with the business partner.

The objective is to build a tighter bond with business partners. For instance, by attaching a blog to suppliers' dashboards, the suppliers can view current sales information and post comments to the blogs. Product managers use a wiki to post challenges for the next season (such as a proposed percentage increase in sales) and then ask vendors to suggest innovative ways to achieve these goals. Several of the customers and other business partners subscribe to the RSS feeds.

Blogs are also embedded into the EMS product lifecycle management (PLM) tool. This allows vendors to have virtual conversations with the product development managers.

RESULTS

The major impact of the BI/social software integration is that conversations take place on blogs, wikis, and forums where all interested parties can participate. This speeds up flow of information and increases participation. Both sales and profit margin are on a constant increase.

QUESTIONS FOR THE OPENING VIGNETTE

1. What was the original BI system used for?
2. Why was it beneficial to integrate it with social software?
3. Differentiate between internal and external integrations in this case and their contributions to EMS.
4. What are the benefits of the integration to suppliers?

WHAT WE CAN LEARN FROM THIS VIGNETTE

By integration of BI and social software, EMS was successful in bolstering communication and collaboration both among its own managers and with its suppliers. Such an integration is referred to as collaborative decision making (CDM; Section 6.10). Social software is based on new computing paradigm known as Web 2.0 (Sections 6.7–6.10). Social software tools facilitate internal and external communication and collaboration. This integration is one example of what can be done by integrating BI with other information technologies (Sections 6.2 and 6.3). Integration is one of the major issues encountered during BI implementation (Section 6.2). Section 6.5 discusses issues of legality, privacy, and ethics of BI practices. We list some trends and emerging technologies in Section 6.6, which are then described in the remainder of the chapter. Web 2.0 (Section 6.7), social networks (Sections 6.8 and 6.10), and virtual worlds (Section 6.9) are some of the cutting-edge technologies related to BI. Other emerging topics that conclude this book are on-demand BI (Section 6.4), use of RFID (Section 6.11), and reality mining (Section 6.12).

Sources: Based on Neville, J., "EMS: Adventures in X-treme Web 2.0," *Optimize*, Vol. 6, No. 1, January 2007, p. 33, (accessed Jan. 2010) and from **ems.com** (accessed January 2010).

6.1 IMPLEMENTING BI: AN OVERVIEW

Implementing BI systems can be very complex. In addition to typical issues in information system implementation, such as conducting appropriate cost–benefit analysis with intangible variables to justify the system and dealing with resistance to change, there are some complex issues related to integration, security, scalability of the system, and handling the construction of a data warehouse, analytics, and dashboards.

BI Implementations Factors

A large number of factors may influence BI implementation. These factors are technological, administrative, behavioral, and so on. Many of these are generic to most information systems and have been researched extensively in the information systems literature. According to Asif (2009), the following are the major factors that affect the decision-making process of BI implementation.

1. Reporting and Analysis Tools
   a. Features and functionality
   b. Scalability and deployability
   c. Usability and manageability
   d. Ability to customize applications
2. Database
   a. Scalability and performance
   b. Manageability and availability
   c. Security and customization
   d. Ability to write back
3. Extraction, Transformation, and Load (ETL) Tools
   a. Ability to read any source
   b. Efficiency and productivity
   c. Cross platform support
4. Costs Involved
   a. Hardware costs (actual or opportunity)
   b. Costs of software (ETL, database, applications, and front end)
   c. Internal development costs
   d. External developments costs
   e. Internal training
   f. Ongoing maintenance
5. Benefits
   a. Time savings and operational efficiencies
   b. Lower cost of operations
   c. Improved customer service and satisfaction
   d. Improved operational and strategic decision making
   e. Improved employee communications and satisfaction
   f. Improved knowledge sharing

These factors need to be analyzed both quantitatively and qualitatively.

CRITICAL SUCCESS FACTORS OF BUSINESS INTELLIGENCE IMPLEMENTATION   Although there could be many factors that could affect the implementation process of a BI system, a report from Vodapalli (2009) as cited on Wikipedia (**http://en.wikipedia.org/wiki/ Business_intelligence**, accessed January 2010) shows that the following are the critical success factors for a business intelligence implementation.

   a. Business driven methodology and project management
   b. Clear vision and planning
   c. Committed management support and sponsorship
   d. Data management and quality issues
   e. Mapping the solutions to the user requirements
   f. Performance considerations of the BI system
   g. Robust and extensible framework

Managerial Issues Related to BI Implementation

Many managerial issues are related to BI implementation. Illustrative topics are:

   1. *System development and the need for integration.*   Developing an effective BI application is complex. For this reason, most BI vendors offer highly integrated collections of applications, including connection to enterprise resource planning (ERP) and customer relationship management (CRM; see Section 6.3). Notable are Oracle, Business Objects, MicroStrategy, IBM, and Microsoft. Most BI vendors provide for application integration, usually Web enabled.

   2. *Cost–benefit issues and justification.*   Some BI solutions discussed in this book are very expensive and are justifiable only in large corporations. Smaller organizations can make the solutions cost effective if they leverage existing databases rather than create new ones. One solution is on-demand BI. Nevertheless a careful cost–benefit analysis must be undertaken before any commitment to BI is made.

   3. *Legal issues and privacy.*   BI analysis may suggest that a company send electronic or printed catalogs or promotions to only one age group or one gender. A man sued Victoria's Secret (a brand of Limitedbrands) because his female neighbor received a mail order catalog with deeply discounted items and he received only the regular catalog (the discount was actually given for volume purchasing). Settling discrimination charges can be very expensive. Some data mining may result in the invasion of individual privacy.

   What will companies do to protect individuals? What can individuals do to protect their privacy? These issues have to be kept in mind as BI solutions are implemented. More on this issue in Section 6.5.

   4. *BI and BPM today and tomorrow.*   The quality and timeliness of business information for an organization is not the choice between profit and loss—it may be a question of survival. No enterprise can deny the inevitable benefits of BI and BPM. Recent industry analyst reports show that in the coming years, millions of people will use BPM dashboards and business analytics (BA) every day. Enterprises are getting more value from BI by extending information to many types of employees, maximizing the use of existing data assets. Visualization tools including dashboards are used by producers, retailers, government, and special agencies. Industry-specific analytical tools will flood the market to support analysis and informed decision making from top level to user level. BI takes advantage of existing IT technologies to help companies leverage their IT investments and use their legacy and real-time data. Thus a planned, careful, proactive approach to BI implementation is becoming a competitive necessity.

5. ***Cost justification; intangible benefits.*** While enterprise systems provide tangible benefits, it is difficult to quantify their intangible benefits. In a down-turned economy with high energy costs, mortgage crises, and political unrest, IT investments must be economically justified.

6. ***Documenting and securing support systems.*** Many employees develop their own decision support or BI modules to increase their productivity and the quality of their work. It is advisable to have an inventory of these ad hoc systems and make certain that appropriate documentation and security measures exist, so that if the employee is away or leaves the organization, the productivity tool remains. Taking appropriate security measures is a must. End users who build their own BI applications are not professional systems builders. For this reason, there could be problems with **data integrity** and the security of the systems developed.

7. ***Ethical issues.*** BI and predictive analytics can lead to serious ethical issues such as privacy and accountability. In addition, mistakes can cause harm to others as well as the company. For example, a company developed a decision support system (DSS) to help people compute the financial implications of early retirement. However, the DSS developer did not include the tax implications, which resulted in incorrect retirement decisions. Another important ethical issue is human judgment, which is frequently a key factor in decision making. Human judgment may be subjective or corrupt, and therefore, it may lead to unethical decision making. Companies should provide an ethical code for system builders. Also, the possibility of automating managers' jobs may lead to massive layoffs. There are ethical issues related to the implementation of expert systems and other intelligent systems. The actions performed by an expert system can be unethical, or even illegal. For example, the expert system may advise you to do something that will hurt someone or will invade the privacy of certain individuals. An example is the behavior of **robots** and the possibility that the robots will not behave the way that they were programmed to. There have been many industrial accidents caused by robots that resulted in injuries and even deaths. The issue is, Should an organization employ productivity-saving devices that are not 100 percent safe? Another ethical issue is the use of knowledge extracted from people. The issue here is, Should a company compensate an employee when knowledge that he or she contributed is used by others? This issue is related to the motivation issue. It is also related to privacy. Should people be informed as to who contributed certain knowledge? A final ethical issue that needs to be addressed is that of dehumanization and the feeling that a machine can be "smarter" than some people. People may have different attitudes toward smart machines, which may be reflected in the manner in which they will work together.

8. ***BI Project failures.*** There have been many cases of failures of all types of BI projects. There are multiple reasons for such failures, ranging from human factors to software glitches. Here are some examples:

 a. Failure to recognize BI projects as enterprise-wide business initiatives and that they differ from typical stand-alone solutions.
 b. Lack of business sponsors with the ability to insure funding
 c. Lack of cooperation by business representatives from the functional areas
 d. Lack of qualified and available staff
 e. No appreciation of the negative impact of "dirty data" on business profitability
 f. Too much reliance on vendors

SECTION 6.1 REVIEW QUESTIONS

1. What are the major types of BI implementation influencing factors?

2. List some factors related to tools and databases.

3. List some of the managerial issues.

4. What are some of the critical success factors in BI projects?

6.2 BI AND INTEGRATION IMPLEMENTATION

Integrating information systems is widely practiced in enterprises, increasing the efficiency and/or effectiveness of the tasks supported. Implementing BI almost always requires one or several integration steps. However, integration is not simple, as described in this section and the following section.

Types of Integration

Computer-based systems can be integrated so that the constituent parts of the system function as one entity, as opposed to each being used separately. Integration can be at the development level or at the application system level (known as *application integration*, our main area of interest). Integration has been considered a top issue of importance for years (Spangler, 2005). There are several types of integration: integration of data, applications, methods, and processes. Integration can also be viewed from two other characteristics: functional and physical.

Functional integration implies that different applications are provided as a single system. For example, working with e-mail, using a spreadsheet, communicating with external databases, creating graphical representations, and storing and manipulating data can all be accomplished at the same workstation. Similarly, working with a business analytics tool and a dashboard is done from one interface, with one menu, resulting in one output.

Physical integration refers to packaging the hardware, software, and communication features required to accomplish functional integration. The discussion in this chapter deals primarily with functional-application integration, which can be done in two ways:

- Integration of two or more decision-support applications, creating a unified application
- Integration of one or more BI tools with other information systems such as blogs, **knowledge management**, databases, or a financial system.

Integration can occur within a company (*internal integration*) or between systems of different companies (*external integration*).

Why Integrate?

There are several major objectives for BI software integration:

- ***Implementing BI.*** For BI systems to operate, they usually need to be connected to data sources, utilities, other applications, and so on. Such connections must be accomplished effectively and efficiently.
- ***Increasing the capabilities of the BI applications.*** Several BI development tools may complement each other. Each tool performs the subtasks at which it is the best. For example, BA can be used to recommend an optimal resource-allocation plan, and an attached dashboard can provide the control system that will alert management to deviations from the plan. The opening vignette demonstrated how social software made the BI system working better.

- *Enabling real-time decision support.* By having tight integration, it is possible to support decision making in a real-time environment. An example is a transportation system that uses wireless communication and Web services to foster data flow.
- *Enabling more powerful applications.* An example is using intelligent systems to provide real-time capabilities.
- *Facilitating system development.* Tighter integration allows faster application development and communication among system components.
- *Enhancing support activities.* Several support activities can improve the operations of BI applications. For example, blogs, Twitter, wikis, and RSS feeds provide communication and collaboration support as shown in the opening vignette.

BI integration may also result in enhanced capabilities that are not possible otherwise. For strategies for successful integration, see Morgenthal (2005).

Levels of BI Integration

Functional integration, discussed previously, can be considered at two different levels: across different BI and within BI. Integration of BI at these levels is appropriate for systems that can be used to solve repetitive and/or sequential decision problems. BI can also be used to facilitate integration by assisting in the transformation of the outputs of one system as inputs to another system. Combining several analytics, each addressing a specific portion of a complex decision problem, is an example of integration across BI. For example, a BA model for supporting marketing-campaign decisions can be combined with a production-planning supply chain improvement model, with certain outputs of the first system as the inputs to the second system.

The second level of integration refers to the integration of several appropriate BI technologies in building a specific complex BI system, especially to take advantage of the strengths of the specific technologies.

Embedded Intelligent Systems

Over the past few years we have seen an increased number of systems that include embedded intelligent components for conducting analysis. In such systems, the intelligent part (e.g., an intelligent agent) is nontransparent to the user, and it may even work in real-time environment. The automated decision systems (ADS) are of this type.

There is an increasing trend to embed intelligent systems in large or complex BI systems, as in the following examples:

- Computer telephony integration at "intelligent" call centers to select and assign a human agent for handling a specific customer call in real time
- Real-time decision making built around online transaction processing (OLTP) systems, such as in collaborative planning, forecasting, and replenishment in supply chain management (SCM), and real-time scheduling decision support
- Support of strategic management planning and analysis, with built-in intelligent agents
- Intelligent agents for process enhancements and management to support collaborative decision-making

SECTION 6.2 REVIEW QUESTIONS

1. List several types of integration.
2. Describe the need for BI integration.
3. List the levels of integration.
4. Describe integration of BI with non-BI systems.
5. Define embedded intelligent systems and describe their benefits.

6.3 CONNECTING BI SYSTEMS TO DATABASES AND OTHER ENTERPRISE SYSTEMS

BI applications, especially large ones, need to be connected to other information systems. The major integration areas discussed in this section are connecting to databases and to back-end systems.

Connecting to Databases

Virtually every BI application requires database or data warehouse (or data mart) access. For example, when BI analyzes customer orders, the products' description, inventory count, and order information are likely to be found in the data warehouse. A BI application can be connected to a database in a variety of ways. Today, most of these connections are accomplished via a *multitiered application architecture* like the one shown in Figure 6.2. This architecture has four tiers:

1. A Web browser where data and information are presented to and data are collected from the end users.
2. A Web server that delivers Web pages, collects the data sent by the end users, and passes data to and from the application server.
3. An application server that executes business rules (e.g., user authorization), formulates database queries based on the data passed by the Web server, sends the queries to the back-end database (or data warehouse or mart), manipulates and formats the data resulting from the query, and sends the formatted response to the Web server.
4. A database (data warehouse or mart) server in which the data are stored and managed and users' requests are processed.

Integrating BI Applications and Back-End Systems

Several technologies can be used to integrate a BI application directly with a back-end application. This is the case, for example, where there is only one data mart (e.g., marketing), but connections are needed to an inventory or other back-end application or databases. Many of the commercial BI suites have built-in integration capabilities. If a company wants to build its own database interface, a couple of options are available. First, all the Web scripting languages (e.g., PHP, JSP, Active Server Pages [ASP]) have commands that simplify the process. Specifically, these scripting languages enable a programmer to build

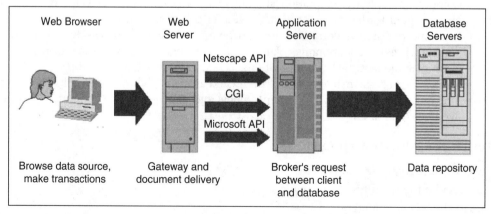

FIGURE 6.2 Multitiered Application Architecture.

Web pages that can issue queries to a back-end database (i.e., relational) and process the database's response to the query. Second, a number of specialized application servers are available that simplify the task of integrating a BI application with one or more back-end databases. Among these specialized servers, BEA Inc.'s WebLogic Server (**bea.com**) is a market leader (now part of Oracle).

In addition to connecting to back-end databases, many BI applications also require integration with a variety of other systems—ERP, CRM, knowledge management, supply chain management, electronic data interchange, and other applications, both inside and outside the company. Such integration can be handled with a class of software called *enterprise application integration (EAI)*. This software focuses on the integration of large systems. TIBCO (**tibco.com**), webMethods (**softwareag.com**), and WebSphere InterChange Server (from IBM) are examples of companies that have offerings in the EAI arena.

Sometimes, the integration requires redesign of processes. For example, Sterngold Corp. (**sterngold.com**) needed to integrate its ordering system with the back office (i.e., order fulfillment, inventory, accounting, payment). The integration required a study of existing processes and redesign of the processes that needed to be altered.

An important integration for large BI systems is the one with ERP.

INTEGRATING BI AND ERP FOR IMPROVED DECISION SUPPORT For many years, ERP platforms had only transaction-processing capabilities and some basic capabilities, including simple reporting, simple analysis and item classification by profitability, turnover, and customer satisfaction. Sophisticated reporting and analysis came from stand-alone BI system. However, companies have recognized that people execute processes better if they can perform an analysis or access business intelligence in real time in the context of the application they are working on. Therefore, ERP vendors have been building business analytics into their platforms so that users don't have to switch. This may result in a significant improvement in the quality of decision making. For example, at the moment a salesman takes an order, BI provides all the information needed to decide if and how much credit to be offered to the customer.

The ERP/BI combinations are most commonly applied to financial decisions; however, companies are starting to apply them to marketing, HR, and various areas of manufacturing.

High-level analysis requires bringing together data from a variety of systems, including supply chain management (SCM), manufacturing execution systems, customer relationship management (CRM) and product lifecycle management (PLM). By planning, forecasting, and simulating scenarios, better decision making is possible.

However, tight integration between various systems still requires a major investment of time. Full integration could take months or even years, and depending on the size of the organization, the complexity of its operations and the quality of its data can be tricky. System builders need to set up dashboards, make sure that the syntax and semantics of the data work together, and check that the data are clean and consistent between the different applications.

Note that furthermore, BI/ERP integration may not be a project with a finite timeline since it is ever expanding. Users may want to optimize the system or make additional data types available to more users.

Middleware

To access a data warehouse, users who need to conduct an analysis, find information, or perform data visualization use software known as *middleware*.

Companies and organizations are now building enterprise-wide BI by integrating previously independent applications together with new developments. BI applications also must be connected to items such as the partners' systems or to public exchanges. BI users need to interact with Internet and intranet applications through a variety of devices, whose characteristics and performance figures span an increasingly wide range. In all such situations, applications use communication protocols and intermediate software that reside on top of the operating systems to perform the following functions:

- Hiding distribution (i.e., the fact that an application is usually made up of many interconnected parts running in distributed locations)
- Hiding the heterogeneity of the various hardware components, operating systems, and communication protocols
- Providing uniform, standard, high-level interfaces to the application developers and integrators so that applications can be easily composed, reused, ported, and made to interoperate
- Supplying a set of common services to perform various general-purpose functions to avoid duplicating efforts and to facilitate collaboration between applications

The intermediate software layers have the generic name of *middleware*. **Middleware** essentially provides a separate program to be the interface between diverse client and server systems. Its main function is to mediate interaction between the parts of an application or between applications. (For more information, see **middleware.objectweb.org** and **en.wikipedia.org/wiki/middleware**.)

IBM is the leading provider of middleware software. It offers a number of on-demand solutions for communication, government, retail, banking, financial markets, and many other industries. IBM Middleware (**ibm.com/middleware**) helps automate systems, integrate operations, connect people, and develop software. Oracle is another company that provides middleware software and services.

Oracle Fusion Middleware (OFM, also known as Fusion Middleware) consists of a portfolio of software products from Oracle Corporation. OFM spans multiple services: J2EE and developer tools, integration services, business intelligence, collaboration, and content management. OFM depends on open standards such as BPEL, SOAP, XML, and JMS.

Oracle Fusion Middleware provides software for the development, deployment, and management of service-oriented architecture (SOA). It includes what Oracle calls "hot-pluggable" architecture, which allows users to make better use of existing applications and systems from other software vendors such as IBM, Microsoft, and SAP AG. For details, see **en.wikipedia/oracle-fusion-middleware**.

SECTION 6.3 REVIEW QUESTIONS

1. Describe the basic elements of a multitiered application architecture.
2. List the ways in which a Management Support System (MSS) application can be connected to back-end databases and other transaction-processing systems.
3. What are the benefits of BI/ERP integration?
4. Define middleware and describe its attributes.

6.4 ON-DEMAND BI

BI initiatives are somewhat capital intensive, as can be inferred from the discussion above. As of now, BI has become more affordable, even for small and medium enterprises due to availability of on-demand BI services. We introduce key concepts related to on-demand BI in this section.

The Limitations of Traditional BI

BI solutions may initially have a negative return on investment (ROI). Reasons include high implementation fees, per-user license fees, maintenance and consulting fees, extensive hidden costs that accumulate over the life of the BI project, and the inability to deliver on the initial program goals and objectives. Also, traditional in-house BI vendors have seldom been able to deliver a unified reporting and analysis solution that allows executives to respond in real time to changing conditions. In addition, the BI solutions remain prohibitively expensive, and they have had long implementation periods—typically 18 months or longer—requiring extensive allocation of valuable IT resources over the life of the project. Finally, open-ended contracts leave businesses unclear about when the implementation period will end.

The On-demand Alternative

Therefore, companies, especially small to medium-sized enterprises (SMEs) are turning to the on-demand BI model as a cost-effective alternative to overly complex and expensive analytic reporting solutions. On-demand computing, also known as **utility computing** or software as a service (SaaS), is described below.

Software as a service (SaaS) is a model of deployment whereby a software or other computer resources are made available when needed. It is like electricity or water. You use them when needed and pay only for what you use. Thus, the concept is also referred to as utility computing. So the users do not need to own any hardware, software, and other facilities, nor to maintain them. Delivery is done by a provider who licenses an application to customers for use as a service on demand. SaaS software vendors may host the application on their own Web servers or download the application to the consumer device, disabling it after use or after the on-demand contract expires. The on-demand function may be handled internally to share licenses within a firm or by a third-party **application service provider (ASP)** sharing licenses among many firms. All the users need is an Internet access and a browser. Payment is made on an actual-use basis or through a fixed subscription fee (for a given number of users).

KEY CHARACTERISTICS AND BENEFITS Characteristics and benefits of SaaS include:

- Ability to handle fluctuating demand, even at peak time (a requirement of any adaptive enterprise)
- Reduced investment in server hardware or shift of server use
- Network-based access to, and management of, commercially available software
- Activities managed from central locations rather than at each customer's site, enabling customers to access applications remotely via the Web
- Application delivery typically closer to a one-to-many model (single instance, multi-tenant architecture) than to a one-to-one model, including architecture, pricing, partnering, and management characteristics
- Centralized feature updating, which obviates the need for end users to download patches and upgrades
- Frequent integration into a larger network of communicating software, either as part of a mashup or as a plug-in to a platform
- Fees are lower initially than traditional software license fees, but are also recurring, and therefore viewed as more predictable as a service, much like maintenance fees for licensed software.

- The total cost, in the long run, may be higher or lower or even the same as in purchasing software or paying license fees. However, in the short run, it is much lower to use SaaS.
- More feature requests from users since there is frequently no marginal cost for requesting new features
- Faster releases of new features since the entire community of users benefits from new functionality
- The embodiment of recognized best practices since the community of users drives a software publisher to support the best practice.
- The development of SaaS applications may use various types of software components and frameworks. These tools can reduce the time to market and the cost of converting a traditional on-premise software product or building and deploying a new SaaS solution.
- Much like any other software, software as a service can also take advantage of Service Oriented Architecture to enable software applications to communicate with each other. Each software service can also act as a service requester, incorporating data and functionality from other services. Enterprise Resource Planning (ERP) software providers leverage SOA in building their SaaS offerings; an example is SAP Business ByDesign from SAP AG.

On-demand BI gives SMEs exactly what they are asking for in today's fast-paced competitive markets: an easy-to-use, quick-to-deploy, and reasonably priced solution. The on-demand model offers a low-risk opportunity for enterprises to utilize BI without drowning in the overheads of a large, expensive, and risky project. As more SMEs experience positive ROI and success using an on-demand BI model, it can be expected that even large corporations will adopt the model. An example of such an application is provided in Application Case 6.1.

Application Case 6.1
Retailer Employs On-Demand BI

Casual Male Retail Group is a specialty retailer of big and tall men's apparel with 520 retail outlets and e-commerce operations and close to $500 million in sales in 2009. The company was using a legacy on-premise reporting application for its catalog operations. But the reporting features built into the system were extremely poor, with little visibility into the business. For example, information managers did not know in real time what they were selling and for what profit, with certain styles by size.

The company used traditional BI that provided unacceptable reports (which lacked features such as exception reporting). Users went to the printer for hundreds of page printouts. Interestingly, the old system contained all the needed information. However, the user just didn't have an intuitive and easy way to get at the catalog business's sales and inventory trends in real time. The situation changed when Casual Male began using an on-demand BI tool from the vendor Oco, which takes all of Casual Male's data, builds and maintains a data warehouse for its offsite, and creates "responsive," real-time reporting dashboards that enable users to have information at their fingertips. With the on-demand BI, merchandise planners and buyers have access to easy-to-consume dashboards chock-full of catalog data. This enables users to know exactly what styles are selling at any given time at each store by size. Also, they know how much inventory is available and where there is a shortage.

Sources: Compiled from Wailgum, T., "Business Intelligence and On-Demand: The Perfect Marriage?" *CIO Magazine*, 2008, at **www.cio.com/article/206551/Business_Intelligence_ and_On_Demand_The_Perfect_Marriage_** (accessed 2010), **advice.cio.com/thomas_wailgum/dont_make_ business_ intelligence_suck_for_users** (accessed 2010), and **Casualmale.com** (accessed 2010).

THE LIMITATIONS OF ON-DEMAND BI   The following are some major limitations of on-demand BI:

1. Integration of vendors' software with company's software may be difficult.
2. The vendor can go out of business, leaving the company without a service.
3. It is difficult or even impossible to modify hosted software for better fit with the users' needs.
4. Upgrading may become a problem.
5. You may relinquish strategic data to strangers.

SECTION 6.4 REVIEW QUESTIONS

1. What is on-demand BI?
2. What are its major benefits?
3. What are the limitations of on-demand systems?

6.5 ISSUES OF LEGALITY, PRIVACY, AND ETHICS

Several important legal, privacy, and ethical issues are related to BI implementation. Here we provide only representative examples and some sources.

Legal Issues

The introduction of BI and especially of automated recommendations may compound a host of legal issues already relevant to computer systems. For example, questions concerning liability for the actions of advice provided by intelligent machines are just beginning to be considered. Another example of an issue is the use of computerized analysis as a form of unfair competition in business (e.g., in the 1990s, there was a well-known dispute over the practices of airline reservation system using computerized pricing).

In addition to resolving disputes about the unexpected and possibly damaging results of some BI systems, other complex issues may surface. For example, who is liable if an enterprise finds itself bankrupt as a result of using the advice of an intelligent BI analysis? Will the enterprise itself be held responsible for not testing the BI system adequately before entrusting it with sensitive data? Will auditing and accounting firms share the liability for failing to apply adequate auditing tests? Will the software developers of systems be jointly liable? Consider the following specific issues:

- What is the value of an expert opinion in court when the expertise is encoded in a BI analytical system?
- Who is liable for wrong advice (or information) provided by an automated BI? For example, what happens if a manager accepts an incorrect diagnosis made by a computer and makes decisions that have a negative impact on employees?
- What happens if a manager enters an incorrect judgment value into a BI system and the result is a large damage to people and/or companies?
- Who owns the knowledge in a BI **knowledge base**?
- Can management force manager to use BI systems?

Here are some other issues to consider:

Privacy

Privacy means different things to different people. In general, **privacy** is the right to be left alone and the right to be free from unreasonable personal intrusions. Privacy has long been a legal, ethical, and social issue in many countries. The right to privacy is recognized today in every state of the United States and many other countries, either by statute or by common law. The definition of *privacy* can be interpreted quite broadly. However, the following two rules have been followed fairly closely in past court decisions: (1) The right of privacy is not absolute. Privacy must be balanced against the needs of society. (2) The public's right to know is superior to the individual's right to privacy. These two rules show why it is difficult, in some cases, to determine and enforce privacy regulations. Privacy issues online have their own characteristics and policies. For privacy and security issues in the data warehouse environment, see Elson and LeClerc (2005). One area where privacy may be jeopardized is discussed next.

COLLECTING INFORMATION ABOUT INDIVIDUALS   Implementing BI may require data about individual employees. The complexity of collecting, sorting, filing, and accessing information manually from numerous sources (public and/or companies) was, in many cases, a built-in protection against misuse of private information. It was simply too expensive, cumbersome, and complex to invade a person's privacy. The Internet, in combination with large-scale databases, a data warehouse, and social networks, has created an entirely new dimension of accessing and using personal data. The inherent power in systems that can access vast amounts of data can be used for the good of a company or society. For example, by matching records with the aid of a computer, it is possible to eliminate or reduce fraud, crime, corporate mismanagement, and so on. However, what price must the individual pay in terms of loss of privacy so that the company can better fight fraud? Private information about employees may aid in better decision making, but the employees' privacy may be affected. Similar issues are related to information about customers.

THE WEB AND INFORMATION COLLECTION   The Internet offers a number of opportunities to collect private information about individuals. Here are some of the ways it can be done:

- By reading an individual's social network profile and postings
- By looking up an individual's name and identity in an Internet directory
- By reading an individual's e-mails, blogs, or discussion boards postings
- By wiretapping employees' wireline and wireless communication
- By conducting surveillance on employees
- By asking an individual to complete Web site registration
- By recording an individual's actions as he or she navigates the Web with a browser, using cookies or spyware

Single-sign-on facilities that let a user access various services from a provider are beginning to raise some of the same concerns as cookies. Internet services (such as Google, Yahoo!, and MSN) let consumers permanently enter a profile of information along with a password and use this information and password repeatedly to access services at multiple sites. Critics say that such services create the same opportunities as cookies to invade an individual's privacy.

The use of data warehousing and mining technologies in BI analysis as well as in the administration and enforcement of corporate laws and regulations may increase peoples' concern regarding privacy of information. These fears, generated by the perceived abilities of data mining and business analytics, will have to be addressed at the outset of almost any BI development effort.

MOBILE USER PRIVACY   Many users are unaware of the private information being tracked through mobile personal digital assistant (PDA) or cell phone use. For example, Sense Networks' models are built using data from cell phone companies that track each phone as it moves from one cell tower to another, from GPS-enabled devices that transmit users'

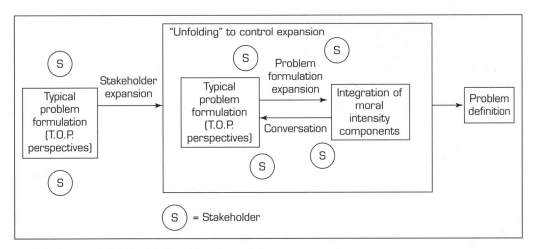

FIGURE 6.3 A Model of Ethical Problem Formulation.

locations, and from PDAs transmitting information at Wi-Fi hotspots. Such data can be used in BI analysis, for example. Sense Networks claims that the company is extremely careful and protective of users' privacy.

Ethics in Decision Making and Support

Several ethical issues are related to BI and computerized decision support. A comprehensive overview of ethics in problem formulation and decision making is provided by Chae et al. (2005), who suggested the model of ethical problem formulation that is shown in Figure 6.3.

Representative ethical issues that could be of interest in BI implementations include the following:

- Electronic surveillance
- Ethics in BI design
- Invasion of individuals' privacy
- Use of proprietary databases
- Use of intellectual property such as knowledge and expertise
- Accuracy of data, information, and knowledge
- Accessibility to information
- Use of corporate computers for non-work-related purposes
- How much decision making to delegate to computers

Personal values constitute a major factor in the issue of ethical BI and decision making. The study of ethical issues in BI is complex because of its **multidimensionality** (Chae et al., 2005). Therefore, it makes sense to develop frameworks to describe ethics processes and systems. Mason et al. (1995) explained how technology and innovation expand the size of the domain of ethics and discuss a model for ethical reasoning that involves four fundamental focusing questions: Who is the agent? What action was actually taken or is being contemplated? What are the results or consequences of the act? Is the result fair and just for all stakeholders? They also described a hierarchy of ethical reasoning in which each ethical judgment or action is based on rules and codes of ethics, which are based on principles, which in turn are grounded in ethical theory. For more on ethics in decision making, see Murali (2004).

NON-WORK-RELATED USE OF THE INTERNET Employees are tempted to use e-mail, e-commerce sites, and so on for non-work-related purposes. In some companies, this use is tremendously out of proportion with the work-related uses (Anandarajan, 2002). The problem has several dimensions. For example, e-mail can be used to harass other employees. This poses a legal threat to a company. It can also be used to conduct illegal gambling activity (e.g., betting on results of a football game). Some employees may use corporate e-mail to advertise or even conduct their own businesses. Last but not least is the time employees waste surfing non-work-related Web sites during working hours and interacting in social networks.

SECTION 6.5 REVIEW QUESTIONS

1. List some legal issues of BI.
2. Describe privacy concerns in BI.
3. Explain privacy concerns on the Web.
4. List ethical issues in BI.
5. Relate BI to privacy.

6.6 EMERGING TOPICS IN BI: AN OVERVIEW

BI is becoming a major area of application where companies are investing considerable resources and hope to reap major benefits including competitive advantage. Therefore, both BI vendors and implementing companies are continuously attempting to apply cutting-edge technologies. Although it is a challenge to predict which future areas will impact BI or will be impacted by BI, the following topics are discussed in this chapter:

- Web 2.0 revolution as it related to BI (Section 6.7)
- Online social networks (Section 6.8)
- Virtual worlds as related to BI (Section 6.9)
- Integration social networking and BI (Section 6.10)
- RFID and BI (Section 6.11)
- Reality Mining (Section 6.12)

The Future of Business Intelligence

Gartner Inc. predicted (Gartner, 2009) these developments in the BI market:

- By 2012, business units will control at least 40 percent of the total budget for business intelligence.
- By 2010, 20 percent of organizations will have an industry-specific analytic applications delivered via software as a service as a standard component of their business intelligence portfolio.
- In 2009, collaborative decision making will emerge as a new product category that combines social software with business intelligence platform capabilities.
- By 2012, one-third of analytic application applied to business processes will be delivered through coarse-grained application mashups.
- Because of lack of information, processes, and tools, through 2012, more than 35 percent of the top 5,000 global companies will regularly fail to make insightful decisions about significant changes in their business and markets.

6.7 THE WEB 2.0 REVOLUTION

Web 2.0 is the popular term for describing advanced Web technologies and applications, including blogs, wikis, RSS, mashups, user-generated content, and social networks. A major objective of Web 2.0 is to enhance creativity, information sharing, and collaboration. One of the most significant differences between Web 2.0 and the traditional Web is the greater collaboration among Internet users and other users, content providers, and enterprises. As an umbrella term for an emerging core of technologies, trends, and principles, Web 2.0 is not only changing what is on the Web but also how it works. Web 2.0 concepts have led to the evolution of Web-based **virtual communities** and their hosting services, such as social networking sites, video-sharing sites, and more. Many believe that companies that understand these new applications and technologies—and apply the capabilities early on—stand to greatly improve internal business processes and marketing. Among the biggest advantages is better collaboration with customers, partners, and suppliers, as well as among internal users.

Representative Characteristics of Web 2.0

The following are representative characteristics of the Web 2.0 environment:

- The ability to tap into the collective intelligence of users. The more users contribute, the more popular and valuable a Web 2.0 site becomes.
- Data are made available in new or never-intended ways. Web 2.0 data can be remixed or "mashed up," often through Web service interfaces, much the way a dance-club DJ mixes music.
- Web 2.0 relies on user-generated and user-controlled content and data.
- Lightweight programming techniques and tools let nearly anyone act as a Web site developer.
- The virtual elimination of software-upgrade cycles makes everything a *perpetual beta* or work in progress and allows rapid prototyping, using the Web as an application development platform.
- Users can access applications entirely through a browser.
- An architecture of participation and *digital democracy* encourages users to add value to the application as they use it.
- A major emphasis is on social networking, social computing, and social software.
- Innovative support is provided for information sharing and collaboration. Rapid and continuous creation of new business models is evidenced in Web 2.0 applications.

Other important features of Web 2.0 are its dynamic content, rich user experience, metadata, scalability, open-source basis, and freedom (net neutrality). Most Web 2.0 applications have a rich, interactive, user-friendly interface based on Ajax (Asynchronous JavaScript and XML) or a similar framework. Ajax is an effective and efficient Web development technique for creating interactive Web applications. The intent is to make Web pages feel more responsive by exchanging small amounts of data with the server behind the scenes so that the entire Web page does not have to be reloaded each time the user makes a change. This is meant to increase the Web page's **interactivity**, loading speed, and usability.

Web 2.0 Companies and New Business Models

A major characteristic of Web 2.0 is the global spreading of innovative Web sites and start-up companies. As soon as a successful idea is deployed as a Web site in one country, other sites appear around the globe. This section presents some of these sites. For example, approximately 120 companies specialize in providing Twitter-like services in dozens of countries. An excellent source for material on Web 2.0 is Search CIO's *Executive Guide: Web 2.0* (see **searchcio.techtarget.com/general/0,295582,sid19_gci1244339,00.html#glossary**).

A new business model that has emerged from Web 2.0 is the accumulation of the "power of the crowd." The potential of such a business model is unlimited. For example, Wikia (**wikia.com**) is working on community-developed Web searches. If they can create a successful one, Google will have a challenger.

Many companies provide the technology for Web 2.0, and dozens of firms have emerged as providers of infrastructure and services to social networking. A large number of start-ups appeared during 2005–2008. For a guide to the 25 hottest Web 2.0 companies and the powerful trends that are driving them, see **money.cnn.com/magazines/ business2/business2_archive/2007/03/01/8401042/index.htm**.

SECTION 6.7 REVIEW QUESTIONS

1. Define Web 2.0.

2. List the major characteristics of Web 2.0.

3. What new business model has emerged from Web 2.0?

6.8 ONLINE SOCIAL NETWORKING: BASICS AND EXAMPLES

Social networking is built on the idea that there is structure to how people know each other and interact. The basic premise is that social networking gives people the power to share, making the world more open and connected. Although social networking is usually practiced in social networks such as MySpace and Facebook, aspects of it are also found in Wikipedia and YouTube.

We first define *social networks* and then look at some of the services they provide and their capabilities.

A Definition and Basic Information

A *social network* is a place where people create their own space, or homepage, on which they write blogs (Web logs); post pictures, videos, or music; share ideas; and link to other Web locations they find interesting. In addition, members of social networks can tag the content they create and post it with key words they choose themselves, which makes the content searchable. The mass adoption of social networking Web sites points to an evolution in human social interaction.

THE SIZE OF SOCIAL NETWORK SITES Social network sites are growing rapidly, with some having over 100 million members. The typical annual growth of a successful site is 40 to 50 percent in the first few years and 15 to 25 percent thereafter. For a list of the major sites, including user counts, see **en.wikipedia.org/wiki/List_of_social_ networking_websites**.

SOCIAL NETWORK ANALYSIS SOFTWARE **Social network analysis software** is used to identify, represent, analyze, visualize, or simulate network nodes (e.g., agents, organizations, or knowledge) and edges (relationships) from various types of input data (relational and nonrelational), including mathematical models of social networks. Various input and output file formats exist.

Network analysis tools enable researchers to investigate representations of networks of different forms and different sizes, from small (e.g., families, project teams) to very large. Visual representations of social networks are popular and important to understand network data and to convey the results of the analysis.

Some of the representative tools that enable such presentations are:

- Business-oriented social network tools such as InFlow and NetMiner
- Social Networks Visualizer, or SocNetV, which is a Linux-based open-source package

For details, see **en.wikipedia.org/wiki/Social_network_analysis_software**.
Social networking is strongly related to mobile devices and networks.

Mobile Social Networking

Mobile social networking refers to social networking where members converse and connect with one another using cell phones or other mobile devices. The current trend for social networking Web sites such as MySpace and Facebook is to offer mobile services. Some social networking sites offer mobile-only services (e.g., Brightkite and Fon11).

There are two basic types of mobile social networks. The first type is companies that partner with wireless carriers to distribute their communities via the default start pages on cell phone browsers. For example, users can access MySpace via AT&T's wireless network. The second type is companies that do not have such carrier relationships (also known as "off deck") and rely on other methods to attract users. Examples of this second type include MocoSpace (**mocospace.com**) and Mobikade (**mkade.com**).

Windows Live Spaces Mobile can be viewed on mobile devices with limited screen size and slow data connections. It allows users to browse and add photos, blog entries, and comments directly from their mobile devices. However, it has also introduced several other features to improve the user experience with handheld devices.

For more information on Windows Live Spaces Mobile, see **mobile.spaces.live .com** and **en.wikipedia.org/wiki/Windows_Live_Spaces_Mobiles.**

Mobile social networking is much more popular in Japan, South Korea, and China than it is in the West, generally due to better mobile networks and data pricing (flat rates are widespread in Japan). The explosion of mobile Web 2.0 services and companies means that many social networks can be based from cell phones and other portable devices, extending the reach of such networks to the millions of people who lack regular or easy access to computers.

With the current software that is available, interactions within mobile social networks are not limited to exchanging simple text messages on a one-to-one basis. In many cases, they are evolving toward the sophisticated interactions of Internet virtual communities.

MOBILE ENTERPRISE NETWORKS Several companies have developed (or fully sponsor) mobile-based social networks. For example, in 2007, Coca-Cola created a social network that could be accessed only by cell phones in an attempt to lure young people to its sodas and other products.

MOBILE COMMUNITY ACTIVITIES In many mobile social networks, users can use their mobile devices to create their profiles, make friends, participate in chat rooms, create chat rooms, hold private conversations, and share photos, videos, and blogs. Some companies provide wireless services that allow their customers to build their own mobile community and brand it (e.g., Sonopia at **sonopia.com**).

Mobile video sharing, which is sometimes combined with photo sharing, is a new technological and social trend. Mobile video-sharing portals are becoming popular (e.g., see **myubo.com** and **myzenplanet.com**). Many social networking sites are offering mobile features. For example, MySpace has partnership agreements with a number of U.S. wireless providers to support its MySpace Mobile service. Similarly, Facebook is available in both the United States and Canada via a number of wireless carriers. Bebo has joined forces with O2 Wireless in the United Kingdom and Ireland. This phenomenon is just the next step in the race to establish access to social networking sites across multiple mediums. Some argue that these deals do more to sell mobile phones than to promote the social networking sites; however, the social networks are more than happy to collect the residual attention.

Major Social Network Services: Facebook and Orkut

Now that you are familiar with social network services, let's take a closer look at some of the most popular ones.

FACEBOOK: THE NETWORK EFFECT   Facebook (**facebook.com**), which was launched in 2004 by former Harvard student Mark Zuckerberg, is the second-largest social network service in the world, with more than 200 million active users worldwide as of April 2009. When Zuckerberg first created Facebook, he had very strong social ambitions and wanted to help people connect to others on the Web.

A primary reason why Facebook has expanded so rapidly is the network effect—more users means more value. As more users become involved in the social space, more people are available to connect with. Initially, Facebook was an online social space for college and high school students that automatically connected students to other students at the same school. However, Facebook realized that it could only keep college and university users for 4 years. In 2006, Facebook opened its doors to anyone aged 13 or older with a valid e-mail address. Expanding to a global audience has enabled Facebook to compete directly with MySpace.

Today, Facebook has a number of applications that support photos, groups, events, marketplaces, posted items, and notes. Facebook also has an application called "People You May Know," which helps users connect with people they might know. More applications are being added constantly. A special feature on Facebook is the News Feed, which enables users to track the activities of friends in their social circles. For example, when a user changes his or her profile, the updates are broadcast to others who subscribe to the feed. Users can also develop their own applications or use any of the millions of Facebook applications that have been developed by other users.

ORKUT: EXPLORING THE VERY NATURE OF SOCIAL NETWORKING SITES   Orkut (**orkut .com**) was the brainchild of a Turkish Google programmer of the same name. Orkut was to be Google's homegrown answer to MySpace and Facebook. Orkut follows a format similar to that of other major social networking sites; a homepage where users can display every facet of their personal life they desire using various multimedia applications.

A major highlight of Orkut is the individual power afforded to those who create their own groups and forums, which are called "communities." Who can join and how posts are edited and controlled lie solely in the hands of the creator of each community. Moderating an Orkut community is comparable to moderating one's own Web site, given the authority the creator possesses with regard to design and control of content. Orkut users gain substantial experience with Web 2.0 tools, creating an enormous wave of online proficiency, which is sure to contribute to the development of the online environment.

Orkut recognizes that it is the users who dictate the content of their chosen social networking site. Given this, Orkut has adapted in a number of interesting ways. First, it is adding more languages, expanding the Hindi, Bengali, Marathi, Tamil, and Telugu sites, which expands the popularity of the site and improves user control over the site. Second, Orkut greets its users on their national and religious holidays with fun features. For example, it wished Indian users a Happy Diwali (**en.wikipedia.org/wiki/Diwali**) by providing a feature that allows users to redesign their personal sites with Diwali-themed colors and decorations.

Implications of Business and Enterprise Social Networks

Although advertising and sales are the major electronic commerce activities in public social networks, there are emerging possibilities for commercial activities in business-oriented networks such as LinkedIn and in enterprise social networks.

Recognizing the opportunities, many software vendors are developing Web tools and applications to support enterprise social networking. For example, IBM Lotus is encouraging its 5,000-plus solution providers who are working with Notes/Domino,

Sametime, and other Lotus software to add Lotus Connections to their product lineups, building applications based on social networking technology.

Representative areas and examples of enterprise social networking follow.

FINDING AND RECRUITING WORKERS Most of the public social networks, especially the business-oriented ones, facilitate recruiting and job finding (Hoover, 2007). For example, recruiting is a major activity at LinkedIn and was the driver for the site's development. To be competitive, companies must look at the global market for talent, and they can use global social networking sites to find it. Large companies are using their in-house social networks to find in-house talent for vacant positions. Application Case 6.2 illustrates one such application that combines BI and social networking.

Application Case 6.2

Using Intelligent Software and Social Networking to Improve Recruiting Processes

The Internet has made advertising and applying for jobs online a much simpler process. However, sometimes with simplicity comes complexity. The challenge now for some large companies is how to cost-effectively manage the online recruiting process, because online ads are attracting large numbers of applicants. For example, Infosys now receives in excess of 1 million job applications each year to fill about 9,000 positions. It might sound like a good problem to have too many applicants, but companies are finding that there is often a poor match between the skills and attributes they require and the many hundreds of applications received. Thus, despite attracting a lot of applicants, they often still suffer from a shortage of good applications. Furthermore, how can a company be sure it is accessing and attracting the very best talent in a particular field? Some interesting new developments are changing the way companies may address these issues.

Trovix (a **Monster.com** company) offers a service to companies based on its award-winning HR software, which uses embedded intelligence to help manage the entire recruitment process. Trovix argues that its tools Trovix Recruit and Trovix Intelligent Search can emulate human decision makers and assess a candidate's amount, depth, relevance, and recency of work experience, education, and the like. The software presents in rank order the best candidates to fit an advertised position. Other features enable tracking of applicants, reporting, and communications. A number of institutions are using this service, including Stanford University, which needs to fill thousands of positions each year.

Trend Micro adopted Trovix and was able to screen 700 applicants and list the top 10 in about 20 minutes. The accuracy is probably no better than manual processing, but the software can screen applicants in a much shorter period of time.

A slightly more personal approach is available through some of the social networking sites, which offer support for companies to locate the best talent for a particular position. Sites such as Jobster (**jobster.com**) and LinkedIn (**linkedin.com**) rely more on a networking approach. Jobs posted on Jobster, for example, are linked to other job sites, to blogs, to user groups, to university alumni sites, and so on. People who are part of the social network are encouraged to recommend others who might be suited to a particular job, irrespective of whether they are actively seeking new work. In this way, a company looking to recruit the best talent has its job advertised much more widely and may benefit from word-of-mouth recommendations and referrals. For example, LinkedIn offers prospective employers a network of more than 8 million people across 130 industries, meaning much larger exposure for job vacancies and a much larger talent pool to seek referrals from. Sites such as Jobster can also track where applicants come from, helping companies adopt better recruitment strategies and thus achieve better returns from their investments in seeking the best staff.

Sources: Based on J. McKay, "Where Did Jobs Go? Look in Bangalore," *Gazette.com*, March 21, 2004, **post-gazette.com/pg/04081/288539.stm** (accessed July 2009) and "Trovix Makes Good at Stanford University: Premier Educational Institution Turns to Intelligent Search Provider for Recruiting Top Talent," March 8, 2006, **trovix.com/about/press/050806.jsp** (accessed July 2009).

MANAGEMENT ACTIVITIES AND SUPPORT Applications in this category are related to supporting managerial decision making based on analysis of data collected in social networks. Some typical examples include identifying key performers, locating experts and finding paths to access them, soliciting ideas and possible solutions to complex problems, and finding and analyzing candidates for management succession planning. For example, Deloitte Touche Tohmatsu set up a social network to assist its human resources managers in downsizing and regrouping teams. Hoover's has established a social network that uses Visible Path's technology to identify target business users for relationship building and to reach specific users. The Advances in Social Network Analysis and Mining conference on the use of data mining in social networks (July 2009 in Athens, Greece) has been dedicated to this topic.

TRAINING Several companies use enterprise social networking, and virtual worlds in particular, for training purposes. For example, Cisco is trying to use its virtual campus in Second Life for product training and executive briefings. IBM runs management and customer interaction training sessions in Second Life too.

KNOWLEDGE MANAGEMENT AND EXPERT LOCATION Applications in this category include activities such as knowledge discovery, creation, maintenance, sharing, transfer, and dissemination. An elaborate discussion on the role of discussion forums, blogs, and wikis for conversational knowledge management can be found in Wagner and Bolloju (2005). Other examples of these applications include expert discovery and mapping communities of expertise.

Consider the following examples of social networking for knowledge management and expert location:

- Innocentive (**innocentive.com**), a social network with over 150,000 participating scientists, specializes in solving science-related problems (for cash rewards).
- Northwestern Mutual Life created an internal social network where over 7,000 financial representatives share captured knowledge (using **Awareness.com** blogging software).
- Caterpillar created a knowledge network system for its employees, and it even markets the software to other companies.

Companies also are creating *retiree corporate social networks* to keep retirees connected with each other and with the organization. These people possess huge amounts of knowledge that can be tapped for productivity increases and **problem solving** (e.g., Alumni Connect from SelectMinds). With 64 million people retiring within the next few years (per the Conference Board), preserving their knowledge is critical.

ENHANCING COLLABORATION Collaboration in social networking is done both internally, among employees from different units working in **virtual teams** for example, and externally, when working with suppliers, customers, and other business partners. Collaboration is done mostly in forums and other types of groups and by using wikis and blogs. For details on collaboration in social networks, see Coleman and Levine (2008).

USING BLOGS AND WIKIS WITHIN THE ENTERPRISE The use of these tools is expanding rapidly. Jefferies (2008) reports on a study that 71 percent of the best-in-class companies use blogs and 64 percent use wikis for the following applications:

- Project collaboration and communication (63%)
- Process and procedure document (63%)
- FAQs (61%)

- E-learning and training (46%)
- Forums for new ideas (41%)
- Corporate-specific dynamic glossary and terminology (38%)
- Collaboration with customers (24%)

The term *Web 2.0* was coined by O'Reilly Media in 2004 to refer to a supposed second generation of Internet-based services that let people generate and control content using tools such as wikis, blogs, social networks, and folksonomies (O'Reilly, 2005). Recognizing the potential of Web 2.0, researchers at the MIT Center for Digital Business (Brynjolfsson and McAfee, 2007) and Harvard Business School (McAfee, 2006; and Cross et al., 2005) extended the Web 2.0 concept into *Enterprise 2.0* (the use of Web 2.0 within the enterprise), asserting that the Web 2.0 tools create a collaborative platform that reflects the way knowledge work is really and naturally done. These tools have the potential to enhance communication and collaboration and aid in virtual team decision-making processes (Turban et al., 2009).

SECTION 6.8 REVIEW QUESTIONS

1. Define social network.
2. List some major social network sites.
3. Describe the global nature of social networks.
4. Describe mobile social networking.
5. Identify Facebook's major strategic issues (e.g., look at the marketing efforts at **insidefacebook.com** and at **facebook.com**).
6. Much of Facebook's early success was due to the close affiliation of its members' networks. How does Facebook expand into new markets without losing what originally made the site popular and alienating existing users?

6.9 VIRTUAL WORLDS

Virtual worlds have existed for a long time in various forms, including stereoscopes, Cinerama, simulators, computer games, and head-mounted displays. For our purposes, **virtual worlds** are defined as artificial worlds created by computer systems in which the user has the impression of being immersed. The intention is to achieve a feeling of telepresence and participation from a distance. Current popular virtual worlds include Second Life (**secondlife.com**), Google Lively (**lively.com**), and EverQuest (**everquest.com**). A good overview of the technologies, applications, and social and organization issues of virtual worlds can be found at Wikipedia (**en.wikipedia.org/wiki/Virtual_world**). In these virtual worlds, trees move with the wind, water flows down a stream, birds chirp in the trees, and trucks roar in the street. Users create digital characters called *avatars* that interact, walk, and talk with other computer-generated individuals in computer-generated landscapes. Some even run global businesses.

Real-world institutions ranging from universities and businesses to governmental organizations are increasingly incorporating virtual worlds into their strategic marketing initiatives. Virtual worlds are becoming an important channel for reaching a wider consumer base, as well as for "seeing" the customers and interacting with them in a way that was not possible a few years ago. Concepts such as virtual currencies often allow participants to buy or sell virtual goods or services such as attire or training. Virtual worlds provide rich and enhanced modes of advertising that can be immersive or absorptive, active or passive. The advertising can include audio and video in addition to text, enhancing product knowledge and customers' purchase intentions. Although studies on the use of online avatars in marketing are few, some evidence suggests that avatars and virtual representations may positively influence trust and online purchasing intention, because they simulate experiences customers have in real stores (Stuart, 2007) However, not all real-world attributes can be experienced virtually, because not all of the human senses, such as "taste," can be digitized and presented on a computer monitor (Tsz-Wai et al., 2007).

Second Life can be an effective business tool. Managers can exploit Second Life today for real-world decision support. According to John Brandon, in a *Computerworld* article (2007) on the top business sites in Second Life:

> What makes the IBM presence even more interesting, though, is what takes place behind closed doors. Regular 'brainstorming' meetings with clients have produced interesting ideas, such as a grocer that would sell items in Second Life and have them delivered to homes, and a fuel company that would hold regular training sessions for employees—which would not be open to the public.

The use of Second Life for decision support needs to be carefully planned. Professor Dan Power wrote a column some time back on the advantages and disadvantages of virtual worlds for decision support. See Technology Insight 6.1 for excerpts from that column.

Although virtual worlds are becoming interesting tools for businesses and consumers, some short-term technical and practical considerations have kept them from gaining widespread acceptance. For example, participation in most of these virtual environments requires downloading of a "plug-in." However, many businesses and government organizations prohibit any kind of software downloads on employees' computers. This limits the use of these services to a select few employees, typically those in IT.

Despite a few limitations, consumer applications of virtual worlds are growing at a fast pace. One of the coauthors of this book (Sharda) has been involved in virtual world applications for trade shows. *Trade show* is only one of numerous terms describing a temporary market event, held at some intervals, where a large number of potential buyers (attendees) and sellers (exhibitors) interact for the purpose of learning about new goods and services. Trade shows such as book shows, technology shows, and human resource shows (career fairs) are held worldwide throughout the year.

TECHNOLOGY INSIGHT 6.1   Second Life as a Decision Support Tool

Major advantages of using Second Life for decision support:

1. ***Easy access and low cost.***   The client is a free download, and people can participate without paying a membership fee. The client is still evolving, and the new voice client is in testing by the community, so the software may need to be downloaded every few weeks with updates.
2. ***Experienced and dedicated designer/builders.***   A quick visit to Second Life showcases the possibilities and the wonders that are still to come. Second Life has few restrictions and provides broad and flexible content authoring experiences for developers. The quantity of available objects, textures, and scripts to reuse is impressive, and designers are available to create custom avatars, buildings, and products. If you can make a rough sketch, a good builder can create a prototype quickly. If supplied with the floor plans and dimensions, a builder can replicate your factory or, given enough time, replicate an entire city.
3. ***Tools and venues for communications-driven decision support.***   Tools include streaming video, streaming voice, PowerPoint, agenda and meeting management tools, chat recorders, and even name tags for avatars.

4. ***A large, dedicated user base.*** It doesn't cost much to "hire" people/avatars to work for you in Second Life. The pay is in Linden dollars, and you can easily hire employees from more than 50 countries. Companies like Manpower are in Second Life and can help sort out employment issues. Second Life is an easy way for a company to "go global." Also, many of the users have great computing skills.

5. ***Impression management and creativity enhancement.*** Avatars look like whatever the user wants. Anonymity has some advantages for certain types of decision support. Second Life breaks down barriers to creative thinking and frees the imagination. Some people are reluctant to use videoconferencing because of concerns about how they will appear; with Second Life, users can consciously manage the impressions they create during meetings, events, and activities.

6. ***Time compression.*** A day in Second Life is 4 hours long. People connect quickly and teleport from venue to venue. Second Life operates around the clock. The 7/24/365 nature of Second Life can speed up activities and change users' time perceptions.

7. ***Easy data integration from real life using RSS feeds.*** The possibilities for integrating data from various Web sources into Second Life are expanding rapidly.

8. ***Encourages active participation and experiential learning.*** People experience Second Life, and those experiences impact real life. A Second Life meeting can be both enjoyable and memorable. A walk through a virtual factory can help people understand what it will be like when built.

Major disadvantages of using Second Life for decision support:

1. ***Learning time and training costs.*** Company executives are generally unfamiliar with Second Life, and the learning curve is at least 8 hours to gain a basic comfort level. A good coach can make the learning process much easier for a "newbie" manager.

2. ***Distractions are numerous.*** Second Life is a big virtual space with a lot going on, from shopping to sex, from sunning at the beach to skiing, from dancing under the stars at the Romantic Starlight Ballroom to a live music performance at the Second Life synagogue. Some of the distractions are very pleasant, but they create the possibility that employees will be playing when they should be working. Also, companies will need disclaimers, and HR will need to review policies on sexual harassment.

3. ***Pranksters and spam are common.*** All sorts of crazy people are floating around Second Life with too much time to waste. Many of them devise pranks and engage in nasty activities, from defacing buildings to harassing worshippers at a synagogue or conference attendees. Security of many types is an issue.

4. ***Technology problems persist.*** Some technology problems include slow responses, lags in resizing objects, the need to empty cache memory following crashes (which do happen), and frequent software updates.

5. ***Chat is a very slow communication tool.*** The new voice client will speed up interaction of people in Second Life, but chat will still have a use, especially with the automatic translators for multilanguage communication. Voice interaction will be invaluable for Second Life meetings.

6. ***Resistance to use.*** Second Life is not like anything most executives have experienced, and there will be resistance to using this technology. It is easy to view Second Life as a game and to overlook the real-world, decision-support possibilities.

7. ***Addiction.*** Some people have become addicted to using Second Life and spend hours on the system, becoming sleep deprived and neglecting real-life activities. Company HR personnel will need to monitor the behavior and attitudes of employees who are heavy users of tools like Second Life.

Source: D. Power, "What Are the Advantages and Disadvantages of Using Second Life for Decision Support?" *DSS News,* Vol. 8, No. 15, July 29, 2007, **dssresources.com/newsletters/195.php** (accessed July 2009).

Physical trade shows allow face-to-face interactions, the richest form of communication. Disadvantages of traditional trade shows include restricted geographic reach, limited operating hours, high cost of participation, and the need to get maximum exposure through the strategic location of exhibition stands. To gain more value from trade-show participation, many show participants now use technologies such as virtual worlds to gain more visibility. Some information technology tools mimic the specific activities of trade shows. For example, it is common today to use Webinars, presentations, lectures, or seminars that are transmitted over the Web (Good, 2005). These tools typically offer a one-way communication from presenter to audience, but can be interactive, with the ability to give, receive, and discuss information between the presenter and the audience. However, Webinars typically do not deliver the content, stakeholder information, and lead data available to an exhibitor at a traditional trade show.

Virtual world technology may be useful in replicating a trade-show participation experience by organizing virtual events that can extend the reach of the event to include many more attendees and perhaps even more exhibitors. A virtual trade show is held in cyberspace and may be viewed as an extension of the physical exhibition or in lieu of a physical event. It replicates many of the information exchange, communication, and community-gathering aspects of a physical event. Its structure often includes a virtual exhibit hall, which users enter by permission and with specific capabilities, to view virtual trade-show displays or to build virtual booths to exhibit information, just as they would at a trade fair in a convention center. The virtual trade show may have other components such as a virtual Web conference, a collection of Web seminars, or other educational presentations. Visitors fill out an online registration form to create an online badge before entering the virtual exhibit hall to visit various booths. The virtual booths often look like real-world, trade-show booths, with desks and displays that users can relate to easily. Virtual trade shows can serve as international trade shows, business matchmakers, procurement fairs, and product launches. The experience also translates well for other applications such as virtual job fairs, virtual benefits fairs, online employee networks, distributor fairs, and venture capital fairs. This recognition of the synergies between virtual worlds and trade shows has been employed by some virtual trade-show companies. One of these is **iTradeFair.com**. An example virtual booth is shown in Figure 6.4.

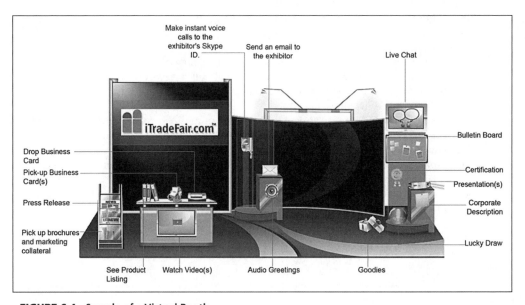

FIGURE 6.4   Sample of a Virtual Booth.

The trade fair participant goes to a specific virtual trade-show homepage. The participant first visits a virtual exhibit floor. On the virtual exhibit floor, the participant can select a virtual booth and gather information or engage in live interaction and information dissemination. Technologies enable communication through features such as chat, Web callback, fax, and e-mail. Special speakers or guests can communicate through video-streamed keynote Webcasts. Attendees can also interact with each other through a chat room. Although this enables the event attendees to exchange information in a same-time, different-place mode, it is not as media rich as the avatar visibility experience through Second Life.

One of the main reasons for exhibitors to participate in trade fairs is to acquire new leads and contacts. In a virtual show, exhibitors can receive attendee leads in real time. A generic attendee report (similar to traditional show attendee lists) containing every registered attendee is available to all exhibitors through the event producer. Exhibitors can also access detailed traffic reports of all attendees who visit their virtual booth. Attendees visiting the booth can drop a business card. A record of all attendees who drop off their digital business card is available. The report includes all attendees' names, titles, and relevant contact information and whether the attendee has requested additional information on any products and services, the company in general, or employment opportunities. A comprehensive "Booth Footprints Report" is available on all registered attendees who view an exhibitor's virtual booth. This report provides insight into what is of interest to each specific visitor. For obvious privacy and security purposes, all reports are under controlled access. But such reports provide a wealth of information to the trade-show producers and exhibitors and can be analyzed through business intelligence technologies.

As described in this section, virtual worlds provide an opportunity to offer decision support capabilities in a novel way. In the next few years, we will see a further expansion of immersive decision-support capabilities. In addition, such environments (e.g., **iTradeFair.com**'s virtual trade shows) generate massive amounts of data about users' activities and participation in online activities. These massive datasets can be analyzed through BI technologies to better understand customer behavior and customize products/services or the technology environments. Sections 6.11 and 6.12 describe other technologies that enable large-scale data collection and the possibilities of the analysis of such massive datasets.

SECTION 6.9 REVIEW QUESTIONS

1. What is a virtual world?
2. What are the advantages and disadvantages of providing decision support through virtual worlds?
3. What activities of a physical trade show can be experienced in a virtual event? Which ones cannot be replicated?
4. What type of data analysis might you perform on data about users in a specific virtual world setting (e.g., a company island in Second Life, a virtual trade-show booth)?

6.10 SOCIAL NETWORKS AND BI: COLLABORATIVE DECISION MAKING

The opening case demonstrated how blogs, wikis, and RSS supplement BI. The system described showed the potential benefits of using social software and BI. In fact, this combination can be extremely useful. And indeed, one of the major IT consulting companies, Gartner Inc., predicts that such integration can provide a significant opportunity for BI initiatives by typing information directly to decision making in the enterprise. They refer to such combinations as collaborative decision making.

The Rise of Collaborative decision making

In a major report, Gartner Inc.'s researchers (Schlegel et al., 2009) describe that a new style of decision support, **collaborative decision making (CDM)**, which combines social software and BI, is emerging, and it may dramatically improve the quality of decision making by directly linking the information contained in BI systems with collaborative input gleaned through the use of social software.

The key findings of this report are:

- CDM is a category of decision-support system for nonroutine, complex decisions that require iterative human interactions.
- Ad hoc tagging regarding value, relevance, credibility, and decision context can substantially enrich both the decision process and the content that contributes to the decisions.
- Tying BI to decisions and outcomes that can be measured will enable organizations to better demonstrate the business value of BI.

Despite unprecedented information availability, the past decade suffered from several imperfect decisions made in both the public and the private sectors. It is not enough to provide voluminous access to information and expect good decisions to be made as a result. Numerous social, cultural, and educational factors influence how well individuals and organizations are able to improve their decision-making ability, and need to be included in the analysis. CDM can rectify the deficiency in decision making by adding these missing factors.

Collaboration in Virtual Teams' Decision Making

Restrictions on travel because of the difficult economy force many companies to find a new way to work, collaborate, and make decisions. Gartner Inc. researchers believe that the information technology market responds to the need of collaboration in virtual teams by creating systems that foster a CDM process using social software. The business application of social software techniques pioneered by consumer-driven social networks services, such as Facebook and Myspace, is well under way. Organizations already use collaborative social software to keep informed about where colleagues are and what they are doing and thinking, and to mobilize them for urgent meetings to address problems. Designing collaborative environments that enable decision makers to discuss an issue, brainstorm options, evaluate their pros and cons, and agree on a course of action is a natural evolution of the above trend. Adding social software elements (such as tagging, recommendations, ratings, and contextual information) enriches the collaborative environment, making it (and the results derived from it) more useful.

CDM enables BI systems to tie information modeled in BI systems directly to the decision made in the collaborative environment. BI systems have traditionally been overtly disconnected from the business process. As a result, it is sometimes difficult to see the business value of BI, even in the most insightful reports and analyses. In addition, decision making has been considered an unstructured process that is not repeatable, so there is a lack of tools that facilitate the work of the decision makers. Figure 6.5 shows how CDM tools support the decision-making process.

HOW CDM WORKS Combining BI with collaboration and social software provides a direct way to show the value of BI because the analytical insights and measures are linked to business decisions and framed in the social context. For example, in making

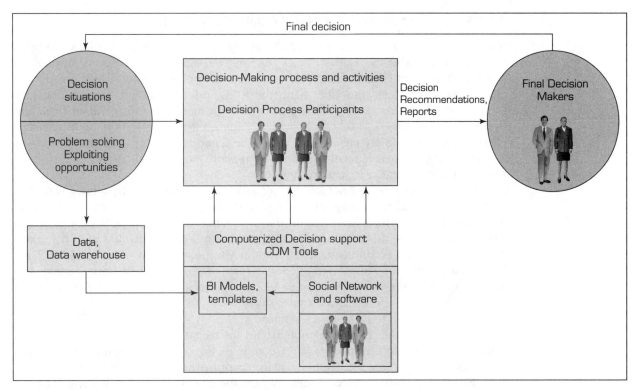

FIGURE 6.5 The Framework for Collaborative Decision Making.

an investment decision, users can rate their assumptions about future revenue, expense, or interest rate and compare the results of those predictions with a key performance indicator (KPI) that measures sales and profit. The BI platform could then update the prediction model with actual interim results on the appropriate KPIs, helping the users (participants in the KPI) exceed a critical threshold, requiring a rethinking of a decision. Today, collaboration on decisions that are more strategic in nature than ever before—decisions that may transform the business—involves nonroutine activities such as **brainstorming** discovering, innovating, creating and leading teams, learning, and relating. The outcome of manual processes of such decision can easily be lost or become part of corporate folklore in the form of anecdotes, with no formal process for decision audit, assessment, and closed-loop learning. Clearly, this is an area in need of an information system to facilitate this manual process, and CDM can be an ideal mechanism.

SECTION 6.10 REVIEW QUESTIONS

1. What is the logic of combining BI and social networks?
2. Why is it referred to as collaborative decision making?
3. What can you learn from the Figure 6.5?
4. What are the major benefits of CDM?
5. What are the specific contributions to collaboration of social networks?
6. Explain how CDM works.

6.11 RFID AND NEW BI APPLICATION OPPORTUNITIES[1]

With a June 2003 mandate that its top 100 suppliers place RFID tags on pallets and cases shipped to stores in the Dallas, Texas, region, Wal-Mart jump-started a 50-year-old technology that, until the mandate, had found limited (but successful) use in a variety of niche areas. Since that announcement, the RFID industry has blossomed. The U.S. Department of Defense soon followed with its own mandate; Target, Albertson's, and Best Buy, among others, quickly followed suit. Initial efforts focused on the largest suppliers in the retail supply chain (e.g., Procter & Gamble, Gillette, Kraft) but have now spread to include smaller retail suppliers—Wal-Mart's next 200 largest suppliers began shipping tagged products in January 2006.

RFID is a generic technology that refers to the use of radio frequency waves to identify objects. Fundamentally, RFID is one example of a family of automatic identification technologies, which also include the ubiquitous bar codes and magnetic strips. Since the mid-1970s, the retail supply chain (and many other areas) has used bar codes as the primary form of automatic identification. The potential advantages of RFID have prompted many companies (led by large retailers such as Wal-Mart, Target, and Albertson's) to aggressively pursue this technology as a way to improve their supply chain and thus reduce costs and increase sales.

How does RFID work? In its simplest form, an RFID system consists of a tag (attached to the product to be identified), an interrogator (i.e., reader), one or more antennae attached to the reader, and a computer (to control the reader and capture the data). At present, the retail supply chain has primarily been interested in using passive RFID tags. *Passive tags* receive energy from the electromagnetic field created by the interrogator (e.g., a reader) and backscatter information only when it is requested. The passive tag will remain energized only while it is within the interrogator's magnetic field.

In contrast, *active tags* have a battery on board to energize them. Because active tags have their own power source, they don't need a reader to energize them; instead they can initiate the data transmission process on their own. On the positive side, active tags have a longer read range, better accuracy, more complex rewritable information storage, and richer processing capabilities (Moradpour and Bhuptani, 2005). On the negative side, due to the battery, active tags have a limited lifespan, are larger in size than passive tags, and are more expensive. Currently, most retail applications are designed and operated with passive tags. Active tags are most frequently found in defense or military systems, yet they also appear in technologies such as EZ Pass, where tags are linked to a prepaid account, enabling drivers to pay tolls by driving past a reader rather than stopping to pay at a tollbooth (U.S. Department of Commerce, 2005).

The most commonly used data representation for RFID technology is the Electronic Product Code (EPC), which is viewed by many in the industry as the next generation of the Universal Product Code (UPC) (most often represented by a bar code). Like the UPC, the EPC consists of a series of numbers that identifies product types and manufacturers across the supply chain. The EPC code also includes an extra set of digits to uniquely identify items.

Currently, most RFID tags contain 96 bits of data in the form of serialized global trade identification numbers (SGTIN) for identifying cases or serialized shipping container codes (SSCC) for identifying pallets (although SGTINs can also be used to identify pallets). The complete guide to tag data standards can be found on EPCglobal's Web site

---

[1]This section is adapted from our own research conducted in collaboration with Dr. Bill Hardgrave of the University of Arkansas and director of the RFID Research Center.

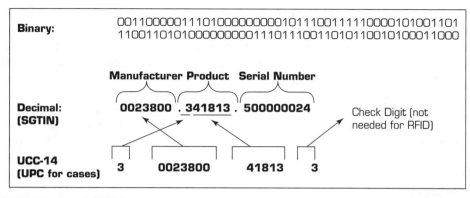

FIGURE 6.6 Sample RFID Tag Data.

(**epcglobalinc.org**). EPCglobal, Inc. is a subscriber-driven organization of industry leaders and organizations focused on creating global standards for the EPC to support the use of RFID.

As illustrated in Figure 6.6, tag data, in their purest form, are a series of binary digits. This set of binary digits can then be converted to the SGTIN decimal equivalent. As shown, an SGTIN is essentially a UPC (UCC-14, for shipping-container identification) with a serial number. The serial number is the most important difference between the 14-digit UPC used today and the SGTIN contained on an RFID tag. With UPCs, companies can identify the product family to which a case belongs (e.g., 8-pack Charmin tissue), but they cannot distinguish one case from another. With an SGTIN, each case is uniquely identified. This provides visibility at the case level rather than the product-family level.

One of the applications of the massive amounts of data that are generated by RFID is in supply chain management (Delen et al., 2007). Most suppliers put a tag on a product as it leaves their facility. As a product moves from the supplier to the retail distribution center (DC) and then on to the retail outlet, it may pass through a number of RFID-read locations. Readers capture and record the case's tag data as the product passes through these points. As product is delivered to the distribution center, read portals (created by stationary readers and antennae on each side of the delivery door) capture the pallet and case data. As a representative example, Table 6.1 traces the actual

TABLE 6.1 Sample RFID Data

Location	EPC	Date/Time	Reader
DC 123	0023800.341813.500000024	08-04-05 23:15	Inbound
DC 123	0023800.341813.500000024	08-09-05 7:54	Conveyor
DC 123	0023800.341813.500000024	08-09-05 8:23	Outbound
ST 987	0023800.341813.500000024	08-09-05 20:31	Inbound
ST 987	0023800.341813.500000024	08-09-05 20:54	Sales floor
ST 987	0023800.341813.500000024	08-10-05 1:10	Sales floor
ST 987	0023800.341813.500000024	08-10-05 1:12	Backroom
ST 987	0023800.341813.500000024	08-11-05 15:01	Sales floor
ST 987	0023800.341813.500000024	08-11-05 15:47	Sales floor
ST 987	0023800.341813.500000024	08-11-05 15:49	Box crusher

movements of a single case of product (SGTIN: 0023800.341813.500000024) from its arrival at the distribution center to its end of life at the box crusher. This particular case of product arrived at distribution center 123 on August 4, was put on the conveyor system on August 9, and departed shortly thereafter. (For readability, only one read per portal per event is shown; duplicate reads at a single portal were removed.) It arrived at store 987 about 12 hours after leaving the DC, went almost immediately to the sales floor, returned from the sales floor about 5 hours later, and was put in the backroom where it stayed until the following day, where it once again went to the sales floor, returned about 45 minutes later, and then went to the box crusher for ultimate disposal. This product mostly follows the prescribed route but veers off course toward the end as it goes out the sales floor and back again on two separate occasions.

What can the snippet of data from Table 6.1 tell us (as one simple instance of RFID data)? If we examine closely, the data offer up several insights.

First, knowing the dates/times of movement is important for ensuring such things as freshness of the product, tracking recalls, or getting products to the stores in a timely manner (especially for time-sensitive products). For example, consider the situation faced by companies offering promotions on their products. Advertising (local and national) is generally launched to promote the products, and the fate of the product is determined in the first few days after the promotion begins. If the product is not on the shelf in a timely manner, sales may suffer. Gillette has used RFID to determine whether stores have stocked their shelves with particular items for a particular promotion. It found that in those stores that used RFID to move a product from the backroom to the shelf before a promotion started, sales were 48 percent higher than those that did not move the product in a timely manner (Evans, 2005). RFID provided the data and the insight needed.

Second, the data provide insight into the backroom process of moving freight to the sales floor. In the example provided in Table 6.1, we see that the product moved to the sales floor twice. Perhaps the first time it was taken out, it did not fit on the shelf and was returned to the backroom. The second time it went out, it fit on the shelf. This "unnecessary case cycle" raises several questions. Moving the product out to the sales floor and back unnecessarily wastes precious human resources, and the more times a product is handled, the higher the chances are that it will be damaged. Also, why did the product make two trips to the sales floor? If the product was not needed until August 11 (the day it fit on the shelf), why was it delivered to the store on August 10? This could signal a problem with the forecasting and replenishment system. Or, perhaps a worker placed a manual order for the product when it wasn't needed. If so, why was the manual order placed? It could be that the product was in the backroom but was not visible or easy to find. Rather than taking the time to look for it, the worker manually ordered the product. While the product was in transit, another worker found the product in the backroom and stocked the shelf. When the manually ordered product arrived, it would not fit on the shelf and an unnecessary trip (for the manually ordered product) was created. How can RFID help in this situation? When a worker attempts to place a manual order, the system can check to see if a case currently exists in the backroom (as determined by a backroom read). If a case exists, the system could help the worker find the case by using a handheld or portable RFID reader.

Third, it provides a precise indication of how long it took the product to move through the supply chain and the exact time between each of the key read points—on a case-by-case basis! This type of insight has never before been possible. Lead times are generally estimated based upon the movement of large quantities of product families through the system. Also, visibility at the store level was not possible before RFID. This visibility requires developing the appropriate measures to be able to determine the distribution center performance. Delen et al. (2007) proposed several performance measures to capture this visibility.

RFID can also be used by companies to improve either the efficiency or effectiveness of various existing processes by incremental process change. For example, early evidence suggested that RFID can reduce the amount of time to receive product at a warehouse (Katz, 2006). Instead of scanning each case of product individually with a barcode scanner, RFID-tagged product can be read automatically at a receiving-door portal. Gillette reported a reduction in pallet-receiving time at its distribution center from 20 to 5 seconds due to RFID and its tag-at-source strategy (Katz, 2006). The process of receiving was not drastically changed (i.e., forklifts unloaded the product as before). The only change was eliminating the need to manually scan the product. Thus, the process became more efficient. Processes can also be made more effective. For example, Wal-Mart found a 26 percent reduction in out-of-stocks by using RFID data to generate better lists of products to be replenished (Hardgrave et al., 2006). The shelf replenishment process was not changed but improved by the use of RFID. Wal-Mart has also reduced the number of unnecessary manual orders by 10 percent, thus making the ordering and forecasting system more effective (Sullivan, 2005). RFID is also being used in receiving to reduce the number of errors, which improves inventory accuracy, ultimately leading to better forecasting and replenishment.

RFID data have been used in many other related applications. For example, perishable goods present some of the biggest challenges for supply chain management due to the high number of variants with different perishability characteristics, requirements to account for the flow of goods in some supply chains, and large volumes of goods handled over long distances. Although food represents a major portion of the perishables portfolio, many other products, including fresh-cut flowers, pharmaceuticals, cosmetics, and auto parts among others, require strict environmental controls to retain their quality. Due to the extremely large volumes of goods handled, the likelihood for problems increases (Sahin et al., 2007). The elimination of even a small percentage of spoilage, for example, adds up to a significant improvement to the supply chain. Therefore, the optimal management of the perishables supply chain is of paramount importance to businesses in this market segment.

The success of today's highly volatile perishables supply chains depends on the level (and the timeliness) of product visibility. Visibility should provide answers to the questions of "Where is my product?" and "What is the condition of my product?" Already, several companies have begun experimenting with RFID for perishables. Consider the following examples:

- Samworth Brothers Distribution (UK; sandwiches, pastries, etc.) has implemented real-time temperature monitoring in its trucks (Swedberg, 2006a).
- Fresh Express uses RFID to look at flow-through of the product coupled with expiration dates (Intel, 2007).
- Starbucks uses temperature tracking for food-preparation products going to retail outlets (Swedberg, 2006b).
- Sysco uses RFID to check load conditions without opening doors (Collins, 2005).
- A regional restaurant chain (700 restaurants) uses RFID-based temperature monitoring to determine conditions of beef patties, eggs, onions, and so on (Banker, 2005).
- TNT uses RFID to monitor temperature profiles of products moving from Singapore to Bangkok (Bacheldor, 2006).

The End of Chapter Application Case includes a very interesting emerging application that includes an innovative use of RFID and BI. The overall lesson is that

RFID technology generates massive amounts of data that can be analyzed to achieve great insights into a company's environment, a major purpose for the very existence of BI and decision support. The following section illustrates another emerging opportunity for BI arising from massive data being collected.

SECTION 6.11 REVIEW QUESTIONS

1. What is RFID?
2. What kinds of data are read/recorded through RFID?
3. What can a company learn by reading RFID at a distribution center?
4. Search online for applications of RFID in health care, entertainment, and sports.

6.12 REALITY MINING

Just as RFID generates major data streams ripe for further analysis through business intelligence that can assist in decision making, another massive data source is emerging, along with the technologies, to make sense of the data. Indeed, a new name has been given to this type of data mining—**reality mining**. Eagle and Pentland (2006) appear to have been the first to use this term. Alex (Sandy) Pentland of MIT and Tony Jebara of Columbia University have a company called Sense Networks (**sensenetworks.com**) that focuses on the development of reality-mining applications. The material in this section is adapted and included with permission from Sense Networks.

Many devices in use by consumers and businesspeople are constantly sending out their location information. Cars, buses, taxis, mobile phones, cameras, and personal navigation devices all transmit their locations, thanks to network-connected positioning technologies such as GPS, Wi-Fi, and cell tower triangulation. Millions of consumers and businesses use location-enabled devices for finding nearby services, locating friends and family, navigating, tracking of assets and pets, dispatching, and engaging in sports, games, and hobbies. This surge in location-enabled services has resulted in a massive database of historical and real-time streaming location information. It is, of course, scattered and by itself not very useful. Reality mining builds on the idea that these datasets could provide remarkable real-time insight into aggregate human activity trends.

By analyzing and learning from these large-scale patterns of movement, it is possible to identify distinct classes of behaviors in specific contexts, called "tribes" (Eagle and Pentland, 2006). Macrosense is an application platform developed by Sense Networks that takes the data being generated by all of these mobile devices and, after spatial and time-based cleaning, applies proprietary clustering algorithms to these massive datasets to classify the incoming data streams as belonging to different types of customers, clients, and so on. This approach allows a business to better understand its customer patterns and also to make more informed decisions about promotions, pricing, and so on.

Sense Networks is now adapting this general technology to help consumers find people with similar interests. This application is called Citysense. Figure 6.7 includes a map of an area of San Francisco. It is best seen in color at **sensenetworks.com/ citysense.php**, but even the black-and-white image shows that it is possible to learn where people are going at this particular time. Each dot represents the presence of people and animates to show patterns of how people group and move around the city over time. Sense Networks' core analytical platform, Macrosense, is also able to analyze the aggregate information shown in Citysense to cluster users and identify tribes. Macrosense is able to identify which tribes are where by sampling the distribution of

FIGURE 6.7 CitySense Example View of San Francisco.

tribes at any given place and time, making it possible to infer what it means when a user is there at that place and time. For example, rock clubs and hip-hop clubs each retain distinct tribal distributions. When a user is out at night, Macrosense learns their preferred tribe distribution from time spent in these places. Sense Networks says that in future releases of Citysense, tribes will be included, and when users visit other cities, they will be able to see hotspots recommended on the basis of this distribution and combined with overall activity information.

Users who go to rock clubs will see rock club hotspots, users who frequent hip-hop clubs will see hip-hop hotspots, and those who go to both will see both. The question "Where is everybody like me right now?" is thus answered for these users—even in a city they have never visited before. Simulating the real world via the use of tribes makes it possible to provide personalized services to each user without collecting personally identifiable information.

By applying algorithms that reduce the dimensionality of location data, reality mining can characterize places according to the activity and movement between them. From massive amounts of high-dimensional location data, these algorithms uncover trends, meaning, and relationships to eventually produce human understandable representations. It then becomes possible to use such data to automatically make intelligent predictions and find important matches and similarities between places and people. Loecher et al. (2009) provided some details of their algorithms. Essentially, activity information as recorded through cell phone data is used to study the behavioral links between places in the real world. This also takes into account the time of the day, because one group of people may go to the one location for work in the morning; however, an entirely different group of people may frequent the same location at night because of a nightclub nearby. Due to the temporal sensitivity of the number and type of people frequenting a place (which can be far more dynamic than a static Web page on the Internet), the raw data describing places in the real world require a staggering number of dimensions.

According to the material provided by Sense Networks, it attributes 487,500 dimensions to every place in a city. The dimensions are based on the movement of people in and out of that place over time and the places those people visit before and afterwards. Their "Minimum Volume Embedding" algorithms reduce the dimensionality of location and temporal data to two dimensions while retaining over 90 percent of the information. This allows for visualizations of data that allow humans to better understand key dimensions to extract key relationships in the flow of people in a city, such as the flow of those shopping, commuting to and from work, or socializing. In addition, they also employ historical data combined with demographic, weather, and other variables. Once a broad understanding of the spatial behaviors in a city is available, companies can leverage the continuously updating clusters to better understand their own customers from sparse location data, discover trends in aggregate consumer behavior for correlation with financial indicators, and predict demand for services and places.

One key concern in employing these technologies is the loss of privacy. If someone can track the movement of a cell phone, the privacy of that customer is a big issue. But Sense Networks claims that it only needs to gather aggregate flow information, not individually identifiable information, to be able to place someone in a tribe.

See the Sense Networks Web site (**sensenetworks.com**) for the latest developments in this area. The technology is evolving fast. Baker (2009) and a recent story in *Economist* (2009) highlighted some of the possible applications of reality mining for business government. For example, a British company called Path Intelligence (**pathintelligence.com**) has developed a system called FootPath that ascertains how people move within a city or even within a store. All of this is done by automatically tracking movement without any cameras recording the movement visually. Such analysis can help determine the best layout for products or even public transportation options. The automated data collection enabled through capture of cell phone and Wi-Fi hotspot access points presents an interesting new dimension in nonintrusive market research data collection and, of course, microanalysis of such massive datasets.

SECTION 6.12 REVIEW QUESTIONS

1. Define reality mining.
2. What types of data are used in reality mining?
3. Briefly describe how the data are used to create profiles of users.
4. What other applications can you imagine if you were able to access cell phone location data? Do a search on location-enabled services.

Key Terms

application service
   provider (ASP)
brainstorming
collaborative decision
   making (CDM)
data integrity
functional integration
interactivity

knowledge base
knowledge management
middleware
mobile social
   networking
multidimensionality
physical integration
privacy

problem solving
reality mining
RFID
robot
social network analysis
   software
software as a service
   (SaaS)

utility
   computing
virtual
   community
virtual team
virtual worlds
Web 2.0

Questions for Discussion

1. Some say that on-demand BI will be the dominating model of delivery of BI. Discuss.
2. Discuss the benefits and limitations of collaborative decision making in virtual teams.
3. Distinguish between physical and functional integrations in implementing a large BI project for marketing decision support.
4. Discuss the value of embedded intelligence in BI applications. Will intelligent BI be able to replace humans? Discuss.
5. Discuss why it is so important to connect databases and back-end systems to BI.
6. What are the potential benefits and challenges of using RFID in supply chain management?
7. Given that RFID data streams are large but only include basic tracking information, how would you derive useful information from these streams? You may want to read Delen et al. (2007).

8. What are the benefits and issues of using virtual worlds for decision support?
9. If you had an opportunity to participate in a virtual career fair, what factors would motivate and inhibit your participation?
10. "Location-tracking-based profiling (reality mining) is powerful but also poses privacy threats." Comment.
11. What are the major characteristics of Web 2.0? What are some of the advantages of Web 2.0 applications?
12. Discuss the use of virtual communities to do business on the Internet.
13. How can wikis be used to facilitate knowledge management?
14. Discuss the relationship between mobile devices and social networking.

Exercises

Internet Exercises

1. Real-time decision support by BI application is cited as a major benefit. Surf the Internet to identify examples and benefits. Visit Teradata University Network, (TUN), and **information-management.com**.
2. Find some blogs dedicated to BI implementation and identify some of the current issues they discuss.
3. Enter three BI vendors (e.g., Cognus IBM company, Business objects, a SAP company, Oracle) and find their activities in the on-demand BI. Write a report.
4. Enter **Oracle.com**. Find what it offers in middleware for BI and check the status of its fusion project.
5. Enter the *RFID Journal* Web site (**rfidjournal.com**). List at least two applications related to supply chain management and two applications in one of the following areas: health care, education, entertainment, and law enforcement.
6. Enter **blog.itradefair.com**. What are some of the interesting applications of virtual trade fairs?
7. Enter **youtube.com**. Search for videos on cloud computing. Watch at least two. Summarize your findings.

8. Enter **sensenetworks.com**. Review the Citysense application and media reports about it. Write a report on what you learned.
9. Enter the Web site of a social network service (e.g., **myspace.com** or **facebook.com**). Build a home page. Add a chat room and a message board to your site using the free tools provided. Describe the other capabilities available. Make at least five new friends.
10. Enter **pandora.com**. Find out how you can create and share music with friends. Why is this a Web 2.0 application?
11. Enter **smartmobs.com**. Go to blogroll. Find three blogs related to Web 2.0 and summarize their major features.
12. Enter **mashable.com** and review the latest news regarding social networks and network strategy. Write a report.
13. Access Hof's "My Virtual Life" (2008) at **businessweek. com/print/magazine/content/06_18/b3982001.htm? chang=g1** and meet the seven residents in the slide show. Prepare a table that shows the manner in which

they make money, the required skills, and the reason they do it in Second Life.

14. Identify two virtual worlds (other than Second Life).

15. Enter **secondlife.com** and find any islands that relate to BI and decision support. Write a report on what they offer.

16. Enter **yedda.com** and explore its approach to knowledge sharing.

Group Assignment

1. Investigate the status of on-demand BI by visiting vendors (e.g. Cognus, IBM, Oracle) and using search engines (bing, google, yahoo), and also visit forums (e.g., TSN, **aspnews.com**, **utilitycomputing.ccom/forum**). Identify major concerns and achievements, and prepare a report and class presentation.

2. Prepare a list of examples of situations in which social software can support BI application. Provide references and companies' names.

3. Item-level RFID tagging will be useful to retail stores as well as to customers. Stores already use RFID to track inventory more accurately. Customers could use RFID to locate items more easily, possibly even using a within-store GPS to find an item. However, RFID does have some potential privacy issues. Form two groups. One group will argue for RFID adoption and the other group will argue against it.

4. Search the Web for "virtual trade shows." Form two teams arguing for and against the use of virtual worlds in business applications.

5. Location-tracking-based clustering provides the potential for personalized services but challenges for privacy. Divide the class in two parts to argue for and against applications such as Citysense.

6. Each group is assigned to a social network that features business activities (e.g., LinkedIn, Xing, Facebook, Second Life). Each group will then register with **hellotxt.com** to find out what is going on in the site with regard to recent business activities. Write a report and make a class presentation.

7. With Hello TXT, log on to the site and enter your text message into the dashboard. Then select the sites you want to update with your new status message, and Hello TXT does the rest, reaching out to your various pages to add your new status message. It is a great centralized way to keep all your various profiles as up-to-date as possible, and it is designed to update your LinkedIn status by answering the question "What are you working on?"

8. As a group, sign in to **secondlife.com** and create an avatar. Each group member is assigned to explore a certain business area (e.g., virtual real estate, educational activities, diplomatic island). Make sure the avatar interacts with other people's avatars. Write a report.

9. Enter **facebook.com** and **myspace.com** and find out how 10 well-known corporations use the sites to conduct commercial activities. Also, compare the functionalities of the two sites.

10. Several hospitals are introducing or considering the introduction of an intelligent bedside assistant that provides physicians and staff with a patient's medical record database for diagnosis and prognosis. The system supplies any information required from the patient's medical records, makes diagnoses based on symptoms, and prescribes medications and other treatments. The system includes an expert system as well as a DSS. The system is intended to eliminate some human error and improve patient care. You are a hospital administrator and are very excited about the benefits for the patients. However, when you called a staff meeting, the following questions were raised: What if the system malfunctions? What if there is an undetected error in the program or the rules? The system, once implemented, takes full responsibility for patient care because physicians rely on it. A loss of data or an error in the program may lead to disaster. For example, suppose there is a bug in the database program, and, as a result, a critical piece of information is missing from the patient's record. A physician who relies on the system could prescribe a drug on the basis of incomplete data. The consequence of this mistake could be life threatening. Another possibility is that some of the rules in the knowledge base might not be accurate for all patients. Would you implement such a system? Why or why not?

11. Read Chae et al. (2005). Summarize all the ethical issues described there and then find examples in each area.

12. Divide the class into two sections: those who believe that BI will replace business analysts, and those who oppose the idea. Conduct a debate.

13. Identify ethical issues related to managerial decision making. Search the Internet, join chat rooms, and read articles from the Internet. Prepare a report on your findings.

14. Investigate the American Bar Association's Technology Resource Center (**abanet.org/tech/ltrc/techethics.html**) and **nolo.com**. What are the major legal and societal concerns and advances addressed there? How are they being dealt with?

15. Explore several sites related to health care (e.g., **WebMD.com**, **who.int**). Find issues related to MSS and privacy. Write a report on how these sites improve health care.

16. Go to **computerworld.com** and find five legal issues related to BI and MSS.

End of Chapter Application Case

Coca-Cola's RFID-Based Dispenser Serves a New Type of Business Intelligence

Coca-Cola, the soft-drink giant based in Atlanta, Georgia, wanted to develop a way to increase sales and find a cheaper way to test new products. During the summer of 2009, the company installed new self-serve soft-drink dispensers with RFID technology in selected fast-food restaurants in California, Georgia, and Utah, and plans to eventually distribute the dispensers nationwide. The new dispensers, called Freestyle, hold up to 30 flavor cartridges, which enable customers to create 100 different drinks, including sodas, juices, teas, and flavored waters. Each beverage requires only a few drops of flavoring. Customers use the dispensers by choosing a brand and flavoring options on the dispenser's LCD panel, which runs on the Windows CE operating system.

The RFID technology will allow Coca-Cola to test new drink flavors and concepts, observe what flavors and combinations customers are choosing, identify regional preferences, and keep track of the amounts they are drinking. By being able to use the flavors in multiple combinations through the dispensers, the company can see what new combinations are most popular and then produce them for other markets. This process saves Coca-Cola money. Previously, it would bottle new products and send them out to various markets. Sometimes, the products were canceled after only a year or two because they did not gain in popularity.

The RFID technology will also help individual restaurants keep track of when it is time to order new cartridges, thus increasing inventory accuracy, and determine what flavors are most popular so that they know which ones to stock. Individual restaurants are able to view reports concerning beverage consumption created from the data collected from the RFID system and reorder products by using an e-business portal developed by Coca-Cola. The technology even allows them to see what beverages are most popular at different times of the day.

The RFID technology in this case works by a RFID chip being placed on each flavor cartridge and an RFID reader being located in the dispenser. Each night, the information recorded is sent to Coca-Cola's SAP data warehouse system at its Atlanta headquarters via a private Verizon wireless network. Microsoft System Center Configuration Manager for Mobile Devices runs at the Coca-Cola headquarters and controls the dispensers through the wireless network. Additionally, Coca-Cola can use the wireless network to send instructions for new mix combinations to the dispensers and to shut down recalled cartridges instantly nationwide.

This short case illustrates the potential of new technologies when innovative uses are developed by creative minds. Most of the technologies described in this chapter are nascent and have yet to see widespread adoption. Therein lies the opportunity to create the next "killer" application. For example, use of RFID is beginning to grow, with each company exploring its use in supply chains, retail stores, manufacturing, or service operations. This case illustrates that with the right combination of ideas, networking, and applications, it is possible to develop creative technologies that have the potential to impact a company's operations in multiple ways.

QUESTIONS FOR END OF CHAPTER APPLICATION CASE

1. What is the benefit of RFID for reducing inventory in this case?
2. How would a restaurant benefit from having RFID-enabled syrup cartridges?
3. What benefit would a customer derive from the new dispenser?
4. What issues might impact the widespread acceptance of this dispenser?

Source: Adapted from M. H. Weier, "Coke's RFID-Based Dispensers Redefine Business Intelligence," *Information Week,* June 6, 2009, **informationweek.com/story/showArticle.jhtml?articleID=21 7701971** (accessed July 2009).

References

Anandarajan, M. (2002, January). "Internet Abuse in the Workplace." *Communications of the ACM.*

Asif, S. (2009). " An Overview of Business Intelligence (**www.inforica.com/in/download/bipresentation .pdf**)". Inforica Inc.,

Bacheldor, B. (2006, October). "TNT Uses RFID to Track Temperatures of Sensitive Goods." *RFID Journal.* Available at **www.rfidjournal.com/article/articleview/2726/1/1/**

Baker, S. (2009, February 26). "Mapping a New, Mobile Internet." *BusinessWeek.* **businessweek.com/magazine/ content/09_10/b4122042889229.htm** (accessed July 2009).

Banker, S. (2005, September). "Achieving Operational Excellence in the Cold Chain." *ARC Brief.* **sensitech. com/PDFs/coldchain_info/achieving_xcellence_CC. pdf** (accessed September 2009).

Brandon, J. (2007, May 2). "The Top Eight Corporate Sites in Second Life." *Computerworld,* **computerworld.com/s/ article/9018238/The_top_eight_corporate_sites_in_ Second_Life** (accessed July 2009).

Brynjolfsson, E., and A. P. McAfee. (2007, Spring). "Beyond Enterprise." *MIT Sloan Management Review,* pp. 50–55.

Chae, B., D.B. Paradice, J.F. Courtney, and C.J. Cagle. (2005, August). "Incorporating An Ethical Perspective into Problem Formulation." *Decision Support Systems,* Vol. 40.

Coleman, D., and S. Levine. (2008). *Collaboration 2.0.* Cupertino, CA: Happy About Info.

Collins, J. (2005, June 13). "Sysco Gets Fresh with RFID." *RFID Journal.* Available at **www.rfidjournal.com/ article/articleview/1652/**

Cross, R., J. Liedtka, and L. Weiss. (2005, March). "A Practical Guide to Social Networks." *Harvard Business Review.* Available at **ftp://ftp.cba.uri.edu/Classes/Beauvais/ MBA540/Readings/Cross_et_al.pdf**

Delen, D., B. Hardgrave, and R. Sharda. (2007, September/ October). "RFID for Better Supply-Chain Management Through Enhanced Information Visibility." *Production and Operations Management,* Vol. 16, No. 5, pp. 613–624.

Eagle, N., and A. Pentland. (2006). "Reality Mining: Sensing Complex Social Systems." *Personal and Ubiquitous Computing.* Vol. 10, No. 4, pp. 255–268.

Economist. (2009, June 4). "Sensors and Sensitivity." **economist.com/sciencetechnology/tq/displayStory .cfm?story_id=13725679** (accessed July 2009).

Elson, R.J. and R. LeClerc. (2005, Summer). "Security and Privacy Concerns in the Data Warehouse Environment." *Business Intelligence Journal.* Available at **http://findarticles.com/ p/articles/mi_qa5525/is_200507/ai_n21377336/**

Evans, B. (2005). "Business Technology: Implementing RFID Is a Risk Worth Taking/" *InformationWeek's RFID Insights.* **informationweek.com/news/mobility/RFID/show Article.jhtml?articleID=164302282** (accessed July 2009).

Gartner. (2009, January 15). "Gartner Reveals Five Business Intelligence Predictions for 2009 and Beyond." **gartner. com/it/page.jsp?id=856714** (accessed January 2010).

Good, R. (2005). "What is Web Conferencing?" **masternewmedia.org/reports/webconferencing/ guide/what_is_web_conferencing.htm** (accessed July 2009).

Hardgrave, B. C., M. Waller, and R. Miller. (2006). "RFID Impact on Out of Stocks? A Sales Velocity Analysis." White paper, RFID Research Center, Information Technology Research Institute, Sam M. Walton College of Business, University of Arkansas. **itrc.uark.edu** (accessed July 2009).

Intel. (2007). "Early RFID Adopters Seize the Initiative." White paper. **www.intel.com/cd/00/00/33/74/337466_337466 .pdf** (accessed September 2009).

Jefferies, A. (2008, October 30). "Sales 2.0: Getting Social about Selling." *CRM Buyer.* Available at **www.crmbuyer.com/ story/64968.html?wlc=1270580493**

Katz, J. (2006, February). "Reaching the ROI on RFID." *IndustryWeek.* **industryweek.com/ReadArticle.aspx? ArticleID=11346** (accessed July 2009).

Loecher, M., D. Rosenberg, and T. Jebara. (2009). "Citysense: Multiscale Space Time Clustering of GPS Points and Trajectories." *Joint Statistical Meeting 2009.*

Mason, R.O., F.M. Mason, and M.J. Culnan. (1995). *Ethics of Information Management* Thousand Oaks, CA: Sage.

McAfee, A. P. (2006). "Enterprise 2.0: The Dawn of Emergent Collaboration." *MIT Sloan Management Review,* Vol. 47, No. 3, pp. 21–29.

McKay, J. (2004, March 21). "Where Did Jobs Go? Look in Bangalore." **Gazette.com. post-gazette.com/pg/04081/ 288539.stm** (accessed July 2009).

Moradpour, S., and M. Bhuptani. (2005). "RFID Field Guide: Deploying Radio Frequency Identification Systems." New York: Sun Microsystems Press.

Morgenthal, J.P. (October, 2005). "Strategies for Successful Integration." *Optimize,* Vol. 48, pp. 87.

Murali, D. (2004, December 2). "Ethical Dilemmas in Decision Making."*Business Line.*

Neville J. (2007, January), "EMS: Adventures in X-treme Web 2.0" *Optimize.* Vol. 6, No. 1, p. 33.

O'Reilly, T. (2005, September 30). "What is Web 2.0?" **O'Reillynet.com oreilly.com/web2/archive/what-is- web-20.html** (accessed July 2009).

Power, D. J. (2007, July 29). "What Are the Advantages and Disadvantages of Using Second Life for Decision Support?" *DSS News,* Vol. 8, No. 15, **dssresources.com/faq/index. php?action=artikel&id=138** (accessed Jan. 2010).

Sahin, E., M. Z. Babaï, Y. Dallery, and R. Vaillant. (2007). "Ensuring Supply Chain Safety Through Time Temperature Integrators." *The International Journal of Logistics Management.* Vol. 18, No. 1, pp. 102–124.

Schlegel, K., R. L. Sallam, T. Austin, and C. Rozwell. (2009). "The Rise of Collaborative Decision making." *Special Research Note G00164718, April 9* **mediaproducts. gartner.com/ Microsoft/vol16/article8/article8.html** (accessed Jan 2010 – registration required).

Spangler, T. (2005, May), "Top Projects in 2005." *Baseline,* Issue 44, pp. 6–10.

Stuart, B. (2007). "Virtual Worlds as a Medium for Advertising." *SIGMIS Database,* Vol. 38, No. 4, pp. 45–55.

Sullivan, L. (2005, October). "Wal-Mart RFID Trial Shows 16% Reduction in Product Stock-Outs." *Information Week* **informationweek.com/story/showArticle.jhtml? articleID=172301246** (accessed Jan 2010).

Swedberg, C. (2006a, October). "Samworth Keeps Cool with RFID." **RFID Journal. rfidjournal.com/article/article- view/2733/** (accessed September 2009).

Swedberg, C. (2006b, December). "Starbucks Keeps Fresh with RFID." *RFID Journal.* **rfidjournal.com/article/ articleview/2890/** (accessed September 2009).

Tsz-Wai, L., P. Gabriele, and I. Blake. (2007). "Marketing Strategies in Virtual Worlds." *SIGMIS Database,* Vol. 38, No. 4, pp. 77–80.

Turban, E., A. P. J. Wu, and T.-P. Liang. (2009). "The Potential Role of Web 2.0 Tools in Virtual Teams Decision Making and Negotiation: An Exploratory Study." Working paper National Sun Yat-sen University, Kaohsiung, Taiwan.

U.S. Department of Commerce. (2005). "Radio Frequency Identification: Opportunities and Challenges in Implementation." Department of Commerce, pp. 1–38.

Vodapalli, N. K. (2009). "Critical Success Factors of BI Implementation". IT University of Copenhagen. **mit.itu. dk/ucs/pb/download/BI%20Thesis%20Report-New. pdf?file_id=871821.**

Wagner, C., and N. Bolloju. (2005). "Supporting Knowledge Management in Organizations with Conversational Technologies: Discussion Forums, Weblogs, and Wikis." *Journal of Database Management*, Vol. 16, No. 2.

Wailgum, T., (March 27, 2008). Business Intelligence and On-Demand: The Perfect Marriage? *CIO Magazine*. Available at **www.cio.com/article/206551/Business_Intelligence_ and_On_Demand_The_Perfect_Marriage_**

Weier, M. H. (2009, June 6). "Coke's RFID-Based Dispensers Redefine Business Intelligence," *Information Week.* **informationweek.com/story/showArticle. jhtml?articleID=217701971** (accessed July 2009).

GLOSSARY

active data warehousing *See* real-time data warehousing.

ad hoc query A query that cannot be determined prior to the moment the query is issued.

adaptive resonance theory An unsupervised learning method created by Stephen Grossberg. ART is a neural network architecture that is aimed at being brainlike in unsupervised mode.

algorithm A step-by-step search in which improvement is made at every step until the best solution is found.

analytical models Mathematical models into which data are loaded for analysis.

analytical techniques Methods that use mathematical formulas to derive an optimal solution directly or to predict a certain result, mainly in solving structured problems.

analytics The science of analysis.

application service provider (ASP) A software vendor that offers leased software applications to organizations.

Apriori algorithm The most commonly used algorithm to discover association rules by recursively identifying frequent itemsets.

area under the ROC curve A graphical assessment technique for binary classification models where the true positive rate is plotted on the Y-axis and false positive rate is plotted on the X-axis.

artificial intelligence The subfield of computer science concerned with symbolic reasoning and problem solving.

artificial neural network (ANN) Computer technology that attempts to build computers that operate like a human brain. The machines possess simultaneous memory storage and work with ambiguous information. Sometimes called, simply, a *neural network. See* neural computing.

association A category of data mining algorithm that establishes relationships about items that occur together in a given record.

authoritative pages Web pages that are identified as particularly popular based on links by other Web pages and directories.

automated decision support A rule-based system that provides a solution to a repetitive managerial problem. Also known as *enterprise decision management (EDM)*.

automated decision system (ADS) A business-rule-based system that uses intelligence to recommend solutions to repetitive decisions (such as pricing).

axon An outgoing connection (i.e., terminal) from a biological neuron.

backpropagation The best-known learning algorithm in neural computing where the learning is done by comparing computed outputs to desired outputs of training cases.

balanced scorecard (BSC) A performance measurement and management methodology that helps translate an organization's financial, customer, internal process, and learning and growth objectives and targets into a set of actionable initiatives.

best practices The best methods for solving problems in an organization. These are often stored in the knowledge repository of a knowledge management system.

BI governance The process of prioritizing BI projects.

bootstrapping A sampling technique where a fixed number of instances from the original data are sampled (with replacement) for training and the rest of the dataset is used for testing.

brainstorming The process by which people generate ideas, usually supported by software (e.g., developing alternative solutions to a problem). Also known as *idea generation.*

business analyst An individual whose job is to analyze business processes and the support they receive (or need) from information technology.

business analytics The application of models directly to business data. Business analytics involve using DSS tools, especially models, in assisting decision makers. It is essentially OLAP/DSS. *See* business intelligence (BI).

business intelligence (BI) A conceptual framework for decision support. It combines architecture, databases (or data warehouses), analytical tools, and applications.

business performance management (BPM) An advanced performance measurement and analysis approach that embraces planning and strategy. *See* corporate performance management (CPM).

categorical data Data that represent the labels of multiple classes used to divide a variable into specific groups.

chromosome A candidate solution for a genetic algorithm.

classification Supervised induction used to analyze the historical data stored in a database and to automatically generate a model that can predict future behavior.

clickstream analysis The analysis of data that occur in the Web environment.

clickstream data Data that provide a trail of the user's activities and show the user's browsing patterns (e.g., which sites are visited, which pages, how long).

cloud computing Information technology infrastructure (hardware, software, applications, and platform) that is available as a service, usually as virtualized resources.

clustering Partitioning a database into segments in which the members of a segment share similar qualities.

collaborative decision making (CDM) A new style of decision support that integrates BI and social software.

complexity A measure of how difficult a problem is in terms of its formulation for optimization, its required optimization effort, or its stochastic nature.

confidence In association rules, the conditional probability of finding the RHS of the rule present in a list of transactions where the LHS of the rule exists.

connection weight The weight associated with each link in a neural network model. Neural networks learning algorithms assess connection weights.

corporate performance management (CPM) An advanced performance measurement and analysis approach that embraces planning and strategy. *See* business performance management.

corporate portal A gateway for entering a corporate Web site. A corporate portal enables communication, collaboration, and access to company information.

corpus In linguistics, a large and structured set of texts (usually stored and processed electronically) prepared for the purpose of conducting knowledge discovery.

CRISP-DM A cross-industry standardized process of conducting data mining projects, which is a sequence of six steps that starts with a good understanding of the business and the need for the data mining project (i.e., the application domain) and ends with the deployment of the solution that satisfied the specific business need.

critical success factors (CSFs) Key factors that delineate the things that an organization must excel at to be successful in its market space.

cube A subset of highly interrelated data that is organized to allow users to combine any attributes in a cube (e.g., stores, products, customers, suppliers) with any metrics in the cube (e.g., sales, profit, units, age) to create various two-dimensional views, or *slices*, that can be displayed on a computer screen.

customer experience management (CEM) Applications designed to report on the overall user experience by detecting Web application issues and problems, by tracking and resolving business process and usability obstacles, by reporting on-site performance and availability, by enabling real-time alerting and monitoring, and by supporting deep diagnosis of observed visitor behavior.

dashboard A visual presentation of critical data for executives to view. It allows executives to see hot spots in seconds and explore the situation.

data Raw facts that are meaningless by themselves (e.g., names, numbers).

data cube A two-dimensional, three-dimensional, or higher-dimensional object in which each dimension of the data represents a measure of interest.

data integration Integration that comprises three major processes: data access, data federation, and change capture. When these three processes are correctly implemented, data can be accessed and made accessible to an array of ETL, analysis tools, and data warehousing environments.

data integrity A part of data quality where the accuracy of the data (as a whole) is maintained during any operation (such as transfer, storage, or retrieval).

data mart A departmental data warehouse that stores only relevant data.

data mining A process that uses statistical, mathematical, artificial intelligence, and machine-learning techniques to extract and identify useful information and subsequent knowledge from large databases.

data quality The holistic quality of data, including their accuracy, precision, completeness, and relevance.

data visualization A graphical, animation, or video presentation of data and the results of data analysis.

data warehouse (DW) A physical repository where relational data are specially organized to provide enterprise-wide, cleansed data in a standardized format.

data warehouse administrator (DWA) A person responsible for the administration and management of a data warehouse.

database A collection of files that is viewed as a single storage concept. The data are then available to a wide range of users.

database management system (DBMS) Software for establishing, updating, and querying (e.g., managing) a database.

deception detection A way of identifying deception (intentionally propagating beliefs that are not true) in voice, text, and/or body language of humans.

decision making The action of selecting among alternatives.

decision support systems (DSS) A conceptual framework for a process of supporting managerial decision making, usually by modeling problems and employing quantitative models for solution analysis.

decision tree A graphical presentation of a sequence of interrelated decisions to be made under assumed risk. This technique classifies specific entities into particular classes based upon the features of the entities; a root followed by internal nodes, each node (including root) is labeled with a question, and arcs associated with each node cover all possible responses.

dendrite The part of a biological neuron that provides inputs to the cell.

dependent data mart A subset that is created directly from a data warehouse.

diagnostic control system A cybernetic system, meaning that it has inputs, a process for transforming the inputs into outputs, a standard or benchmark against which to compare the outputs, and a feedback channel to allow information on variances between the outputs and the standard to be communicated and acted upon.

dimension table A table that addresses *how* data will be analyzed.

dimensional modeling   A retrieval-based system that supports high-volume query access.

discovery-driven data mining   A form of data mining that finds patterns, associations, and relationships among data in order to uncover facts that were previously unknown or not even contemplated by an organization.

distance measure   A method used to calculate the closeness between pairs of items in most cluster analysis methods. Popular distance measures include Euclidian distance (the ordinary distance between two points that one would measure with a ruler) and Manhattan distance (also called the rectilinear distance, or taxicab distance, between two points).

DMAIC   A closed-loop business improvement model that includes the following steps: defining, measuring, analyzing, improving, and controlling a process.

drill down   The investigation of information in detail (e.g., finding not only total sales but also sales by region, by product, or by salesperson). Finding the detailed sources.

enterprise application integration (EAI)   A technology that provides a vehicle for pushing data from source systems into a data warehouse.

enterprise data warehouse (EDW)   An organizational-level data warehouse developed for analytical purposes.

enterprise decision management   *See* automated decision support (ADS).

enterprise information integration (EII)   An evolving tool space that promises real-time data integration from a variety of sources, such as relational databases, Web services, and multidimensional databases.

entropy   A metric that measures the extent of uncertainty or randomness in a data set. If all the data in a subset belong to just one class, then there is no uncertainty or randomness in that data set, and therefore the entropy is zero.

expert   A human being who has developed a high level of proficiency in making judgments in a specific, usually narrow, domain.

extraction   The process of capturing data from several sources, synthesizing them, summarizing them, determining which of them are relevant, and organizing them, resulting in their effective integration.

extraction, transformation, and load (ETL)   A data warehousing process that consists of extraction (i.e., reading data from a database), transformation (i.e., converting the extracted data from its previous form into the form in which it needs to be so that it can be placed into a data warehouse or simply another database), and load (i.e., putting the data into the data warehouse).

forecasting   Predicting the future.

functional integration   The provision of different support functions as a single system through a single, consistent interface.

fuzzy logic   A logically consistent way of reasoning that can cope with uncertain or partial information. Fuzzy logic is characteristic of human thinking and expert systems.

genetic algorithm   A software program that learns in an evolutionary manner, similar to the way biological systems evolve.

geographical information system (GIS)   An information system capable of integrating, editing, analyzing, sharing, and displaying geographically referenced information.

Gini index   A metric that is used in economics to measure the diversity of the population. The same concept can be used to determine the purity of a specific class as a result of a decision to branch along a particular attribute/variable.

global positioning systems (GPS)   Wireless devices that use satellites to enable users to detect the position on earth of items (e.g., cars or people) the devices are attached to, with reasonable precision.

grain   A definition of the highest level of detail that is supported in a data warehouse.

graphical user interface (GUI)   An interactive, user-friendly interface in which, by using icons and similar objects, the user can control communication with a computer.

heuristics   Informal, judgmental knowledge of an application area that constitutes the rules of good judgment in the field. Heuristics also encompasses the knowledge of how to solve problems efficiently and effectively, how to plan steps in solving a complex problem, how to improve performance, and so forth.

hidden layer   The middle layer of an artificial neural network that has three or more layers.

hub   One or more Web pages that provide a collection of links to authoritative pages.

hyperlink-induced topic search (HITS)   The most popular, publicly known and referenced algorithm in Web mining, which is used to discover hubs and authorities.

hypothesis-driven data mining   A form of data mining that begins with a proposition by the user, who then seeks to validate the truthfulness of the proposition.

independent data mart   A small data warehouse designed for a strategic business unit or a department.

information overload   An excessive amount of information being provided, making processing and absorbing tasks very difficult for the individual.

information   Data organized in a meaningful way.

information gain   The splitting mechanism used in ID3 (a popular decision-tree algorithm).

intelligence   A degree of reasoning and learned behavior, usually task or problem solving oriented.

intelligent agent   An expert or knowledge-based system embedded in computer-based information systems (or their components) to make them smarter.

interactivity A characteristic of software agents that allows them to interact (communicate and/or collaborate) with each other without having to rely on human intervention.

interval data Variables that can be measured on interval scales.

inverse document frequency A common and very useful transformation of indices in a term-by-document matrix that reflects both the specificity of words (document frequencies) as well as the overall frequencies of their occurrences (term frequencies).

key performance indicator (KPI) Measure of performance against a strategic objective and goal.

k-fold cross-validation A popular accuracy assessment technique for prediction models where the complete dataset is randomly split into k mutually exclusive subsets of approximately equal size. The classification model is trained and tested k times. Each time it is trained on all but one fold and then tested on the remaining single fold. The cross-validation estimate of the overall accuracy of a model is calculated by simply averaging the k individual accuracy measures.

knowledge Understanding, awareness, or familiarity acquired through education or experience; anything that has been learned, perceived, discovered, inferred, or understood; the ability to use information. In a knowledge management system, knowledge is information in action.

knowledge base A collection of facts, rules, and procedures organized into schemas. A knowledge base is the assembly of all the information and knowledge about a specific field of interest.

knowledge discovery in databases (KDD) A machine-learning process that performs rule induction or a related procedure to establish knowledge from large databases.

knowledge management The active management of the expertise in an organization. It involves collecting, categorizing, and disseminating knowledge.

Kohonen's self-organizing feature map A type of neural network model for machine learning.

Lean Manufacturing Production methodology focused on the elimination of waste or non-value-added features in a process.

learning A process of self-improvement where the new knowledge is obtained through a process by using what is already known.

learning algorithm The training procedure used by an artificial neural network.

link analysis The linkage among many objects of interest is discovered automatically, such as the link between Web pages and referential relationships among groups of academic publication authors.

machine learning The process by which a computer learns from experience (e.g., using programs that can learn from historical cases).

management science The application of a scientific approach and mathematical models to the analysis and solution of managerial decision situations (e.g., problems, opportunities). Also known as *operations research* (OR).

metadata Data about data. In a data warehouse, metadata describe the contents of a data warehouse and the manner of its use.

Microsoft Enterprise Consortium Worldwide source for access to Microsoft's SQL Server 2008 software suite for academic purposes—teaching and research.

middleware Software that links application modules from different computer languages and platforms.

mobile social networking Members converse and connect with one another using cell phones or other mobile devices.

multidimensional analysis A modeling method that involves data analysis in several dimensions.

multidimensional database A database in which the data are organized specifically to support easy and quick multidimensional analysis.

multidimensional OLAP (MOLAP) OLAP implemented via a specialized multidimensional database (or data store) that summarizes transactions into multidimensional views ahead of time.

multidimensionality The ability to organize, present, and analyze data by several dimensions, such as sales by region, by product, by salesperson, and by time (four dimensions).

multi-layered perceptron (MLP) Layered structure of artificial neural network where several hidden layers can be placed between the input and output layers.

natural language processing (NLP) Using a natural language processor to interface with a computer-based system.

neural computing An experimental computer design aimed at building intelligent computers that operate in a manner modeled on the functioning of the human brain. *See* artificial neural network (ANN).

neural network *See* artificial neural network (ANN).

neuron A cell (i.e., processing element) of a biological or artificial neural network.

nominal data A type of data that contains measurements of simple codes assigned to objects as labels, which are not measurements. For example, the variable *marital status* can be generally categorized as (1) single, (2) married, and (3) divorced.

numeric data A type of data that represents the numeric values of specific variables. Examples of numerically valued variables include age, number of children, total household income (in U.S. dollars), travel distance (in miles), and temperature (in Fahrenheit degrees).

Online Analytical Processing (OLAP) An information system that enables the user, while at a PC, to query the system, conduct an analysis, and so on. The result is generated in seconds.

sequence discovery   The identification of associations over time.

sequence mining   A pattern discovery method where relationships among the things are examined in terms of their order of occurrence to identify associations over time.

sigmoid function   An S-shaped transfer function in the range of 0 to 1.

simple split   Data is partitioned into two mutually exclusive subsets called a *training set* and a *test set* (or *holdout set*). It is common to designate two-thirds of the data as the training set and the remaining one-third as the test set.

singular value decomposition (SVD)   Closely related to principal components analysis, it reduces the overall dimensionality of the input matrix (number of input documents by number of extracted terms) to a lower dimensional space, where each consecutive dimension represents the largest degree of variability (between words and documents).

Six Sigma   A performance management methodology aimed at reducing the number of defects in a business process to as close to zero defects per million opportunities (DPMO) as possible.

snowflake schema   A logical arrangement of tables in a multidimensional database in such a way that the entity relationship diagram resembles a snowflake in shape.

social network analysis (SNA)   The mapping and measuring of relationships and information flows among people, groups, organizations, computers, and other information- or knowledge-processing entities. The nodes in the network are the people and groups, whereas the links show relationships or flows between the nodes. SNAs provide both visual and mathematical analyses of relationships.

software agent   A piece of autonomous software that persists to accomplish the task it is designed for (by its owner).

Software as a Service (SaaS)   Software that is rented instead of sold.

speech (voice) recognition   An area of artificial intelligence research that attempts to allow computers to recognize words or phrases of human speech.

speech synthesis   The technology by which computers convert text to voice (i.e., speak).

SPSS PASW Modeler   A very popular, commercially available, comprehensive data, text, and Web mining software suite developed by SPSS (formerly Clementine).

star schema   Most commonly used and simplest style of dimensional modeling.

stemming   A process of reducing words to their respective root forms in order to better represent them in a text-mining project.

stop words   Words that are filtered out prior to or after processing of natural language data (i.e., text).

story   A case with rich information and episodes. Lessons may be derived from this kind of case in a case base.

strategic goal   A quantification of an objective for a designated period of time.

strategic objective   A broad statement or general course of action that prescribes targeted directions for an organization.

strategic theme   A collection of related strategic objectives, used to simplify the construction of a strategic map.

strategic vision   A picture or mental image of what the organization should look like in the future.

strategy map   A visual display that delineates the relationships among the key organizational objectives for all four balanced scorecard perspectives.

SQL (Structured Query Language)   A data definition and management language for relational databases. SQL front-ends most relational DBMS.

summation function   A mechanism to add all the inputs coming into a particular neuron.

supervised learning   A method of training artificial neural networks in which sample cases are shown to the network as input, and the weights are adjusted to minimize the error in the outputs.

support   The measure of how often products and/or services appear together in the same transaction; that is, the proportion of transactions in the dataset that contain all of the products and/or services mentioned in a specific rule.

support vector machines (SVM)   A family of generalized linear models, which achieve a classification or regression decision based on the value of the linear combination of input features.

synapse   The connection (where the weights are) between processing elements in a neural network.

system architecture   The logical and physical design of a system.

term–document matrix (TDM)   A frequency matrix created from digitized and organized documents (the corpus) where the columns represent the terms and rows represent the individual documents.

text mining   The application of data mining to nonstructured or less structured text files. It entails the generation of meaningful numeric indices from the unstructured text and then processing those indices using various data-mining algorithms.

tokenizing   Categorizing a block of text (token) according to the function it performs.

transformation (transfer) function   In a neural network, the function that sums and transforms inputs before a neuron fires. It shows the relationship between the internal activation level and the output of a neuron.

trend analysis   The collecting of information and attempting to spot a pattern, or *trend*, in the information.

unstructured data   Data that do not have a predetermined format and are stored in the form of textual documents.

Online Transaction Processing (OLTP) Transaction system that is primarily responsible for capturing and storing data related to day-to-day business functions.

oper mart An operational data mart. An oper mart is a small-scale data mart typically used by a single department or functional area in an organization.

operational data store (ODS) A type of database often used as an interim area for a data warehouse, especially for customer information files.

optimization The process of identifying the best possible solution to a problem.

ordinal data Data that contain codes assigned to objects or events as labels that also represent the rank order among them. For example, the variable *credit score* can be generally categorized as (1) low, (2) medium, and (3) high.

parallel processing An advanced computer processing technique that allows a computer to perform multiple processes at once, in parallel.

part-of-speech tagging The process of marking up the words in a text as corresponding to a particular part of speech (such as nouns, verbs, adjectives, adverbs, etc.) based on a word's definition and context of its use.

pattern recognition A technique of matching an external pattern to a pattern stored in a computer's memory (i.e., the process of classifying data into predetermined categories). Pattern recognition is used in inference engines, image processing, neural computing, and speech recognition.

performance measurement systems Systematic methods of setting business goals together with periodic feedback reports that indicate progress against goals.

physical integration The seamless integration of several systems into one functioning system.

polysemes Words also called *homonyms*; they are syntactically identical words (i.e., spelled exactly the same) with different meanings (e.g., *bow* can mean "to bend forward," "the front of the ship," "the weapon that shoots arrows," or "a kind of tied ribbon").

prediction The act of telling about the future.

predictive analysis Use of tools that help determine the probable future outcome for an event or the likelihood of a situation occurring. These tools also identify relationships and patterns.

predictive analytics A business analytical approach toward forecasting (e.g., demand, problems, opportunities) that is used instead of simply reporting data as they occur.

privacy In general, the right to be left alone and the right to be free of unreasonable personal intrusions. Information privacy is the right to determine when, and to what extent, information about oneself can be communicated to others.

problem solving A process in which one starts from an initial state and proceeds to search through a problem space to identify a desired goal.

processing element (PE) A neuron in a neural network.

prototyping In system development, a strategy in which a scaled-down system or portion of a system is constructed in a short time, tested, and improved in several iterations.

RapidMiner A popular, open-source, free-of-charge data mining software suite that employs a graphically enhanced user interface, a rather large number of algorithms, and a variety of data visualization features.

ratio data Continuous data where both differences and ratios are interpretable. The distinguishing feature of a ratio scale is the possession of a nonarbitrary zero value.

real-time data warehousing (RDW) The process of loading and providing data via a data warehouse as they become available.

reality mining Data mining of location-based data.

regression A data mining method for real-world prediction problems where the predicted values (i.e., the output variable or dependent variable) are numeric (e.g., predicting the temperature for tomorrow as 68°F).

relational database A database whose records are organized into tables that can be processed by either relational algebra or relational calculus.

Relational OLAP (ROLAP) The implementation of an OLAP database on top of an existing relational database.

result (outcome) variable A variable that expresses the result of a decision (e.g., one concerning profit), usually one of the goals of a decision-making problem.

RFID A generic technology that refers to the use of radio frequency waves to identify objects.

risk A probabilistic or stochastic decision situation.

robot A machine that has the capability of performing manual functions without human intervention.

SAS Enterprise Miner A comprehensive, and commercial data mining software tool developed by SAS Institute.

scenario A statement of assumptions and configurations concerning the operating environment of a particular system at a particular time.

scorecard A visual display that is used to chart progress against strategic and tactical goals and targets.

search engine A program that finds and lists Web sites or pages (designated by URLs) that match some user-selected criteria.

SEMMA An alternative process for data mining projects proposed by the SAS Institute. The acronym "SEMMA" stands for "sample, explore, modify, model, and assess."

sensitivity analysis A study of the effect of a change in one or more input variables on a proposed solution.

sentiment analysis The technique used to detect favorable and unfavorable opinions toward specific products and services using a large numbers of textual data sources (customer feedback in the form of Web postings).

sequence discovery The identification of associations over time.

sequence mining A pattern discovery method where relationships among the things are examined in terms of their order of occurrence to identify associations over time.

sigmoid function An S-shaped transfer function in the range of 0 to 1.

simple split Data is partitioned into two mutually exclusive subsets called a *training set* and a *test set* (or *holdout set*). It is common to designate two-thirds of the data as the training set and the remaining one-third as the test set.

singular value decomposition (SVD) Closely related to principal components analysis, it reduces the overall dimensionality of the input matrix (number of input documents by number of extracted terms) to a lower dimensional space, where each consecutive dimension represents the largest degree of variability (between words and documents).

Six Sigma A performance management methodology aimed at reducing the number of defects in a business process to as close to zero defects per million opportunities (DPMO) as possible.

snowflake schema A logical arrangement of tables in a multidimensional database in such a way that the entity relationship diagram resembles a snowflake in shape.

social network analysis (SNA) The mapping and measuring of relationships and information flows among people, groups, organizations, computers, and other information- or knowledge-processing entities. The nodes in the network are the people and groups, whereas the links show relationships or flows between the nodes. SNAs provide both visual and mathematical analyses of relationships.

software agent A piece of autonomous software that persists to accomplish the task it is designed for (by its owner).

Software as a Service (SaaS) Software that is rented instead of sold.

speech (voice) recognition An area of artificial intelligence research that attempts to allow computers to recognize words or phrases of human speech.

speech synthesis The technology by which computers convert text to voice (i.e., speak).

SPSS PASW Modeler A very popular, commercially available, comprehensive data, text, and Web mining software suite developed by SPSS (formerly Clementine).

star schema Most commonly used and simplest style of dimensional modeling.

stemming A process of reducing words to their respective root forms in order to better represent them in a text-mining project.

stop words Words that are filtered out prior to or after processing of natural language data (i.e., text).

story A case with rich information and episodes. Lessons may be derived from this kind of case in a case base.

strategic goal A quantification of an objective for a designated period of time.

strategic objective A broad statement or general course of action that prescribes targeted directions for an organization.

strategic theme A collection of related strategic objectives, used to simplify the construction of a strategic map.

strategic vision A picture or mental image of what the organization should look like in the future.

strategy map A visual display that delineates the relationships among the key organizational objectives for all four balanced scorecard perspectives.

SQL (Structured Query Language) A data definition and management language for relational databases. SQL frontends most relational DBMS.

summation function A mechanism to add all the inputs coming into a particular neuron.

supervised learning A method of training artificial neural networks in which sample cases are shown to the network as input, and the weights are adjusted to minimize the error in the outputs.

support The measure of how often products and/or services appear together in the same transaction; that is, the proportion of transactions in the dataset that contain all of the products and/or services mentioned in a specific rule.

support vector machines (SVM) A family of generalized linear models, which achieve a classification or regression decision based on the value of the linear combination of input features.

synapse The connection (where the weights are) between processing elements in a neural network.

system architecture The logical and physical design of a system.

term–document matrix (TDM) A frequency matrix created from digitized and organized documents (the corpus) where the columns represent the terms and rows represent the individual documents.

text mining The application of data mining to nonstructured or less structured text files. It entails the generation of meaningful numeric indices from the unstructured text and then processing those indices using various data-mining algorithms.

tokenizing Categorizing a block of text (token) according to the function it performs.

transformation (transfer) function In a neural network, the function that sums and transforms inputs before a neuron fires. It shows the relationship between the internal activation level and the output of a neuron.

trend analysis The collecting of information and attempting to spot a pattern, or *trend*, in the information.

unstructured data Data that do not have a predetermined format and are stored in the form of textual documents.

Online Transaction Processing (OLTP) Transaction system that is primarily responsible for capturing and storing data related to day-to-day business functions.

oper mart An operational data mart. An oper mart is a small-scale data mart typically used by a single department or functional area in an organization.

operational data store (ODS) A type of database often used as an interim area for a data warehouse, especially for customer information files.

optimization The process of identifying the best possible solution to a problem.

ordinal data Data that contain codes assigned to objects or events as labels that also represent the rank order among them. For example, the variable *credit score* can be generally categorized as (1) low, (2) medium, and (3) high.

parallel processing An advanced computer processing technique that allows a computer to perform multiple processes at once, in parallel.

part-of-speech tagging The process of marking up the words in a text as corresponding to a particular part of speech (such as nouns, verbs, adjectives, adverbs, etc.) based on a word's definition and context of its use.

pattern recognition A technique of matching an external pattern to a pattern stored in a computer's memory (i.e., the process of classifying data into predetermined categories). Pattern recognition is used in inference engines, image processing, neural computing, and speech recognition.

performance measurement systems Systematic methods of setting business goals together with periodic feedback reports that indicate progress against goals.

physical integration The seamless integration of several systems into one functioning system.

polysemes Words also called *homonyms*; they are syntactically identical words (i.e., spelled exactly the same) with different meanings (e.g., *bow* can mean "to bend forward," "the front of the ship," "the weapon that shoots arrows," or "a kind of tied ribbon").

prediction The act of telling about the future.

predictive analysis Use of tools that help determine the probable future outcome for an event or the likelihood of a situation occurring. These tools also identify relationships and patterns.

predictive analytics A business analytical approach toward forecasting (e.g., demand, problems, opportunities) that is used instead of simply reporting data as they occur.

privacy In general, the right to be left alone and the right to be free of unreasonable personal intrusions. Information privacy is the right to determine when, and to what extent, information about oneself can be communicated to others.

problem solving A process in which one starts from an initial state and proceeds to search through a problem space to identify a desired goal.

processing element (PE) A neuron in a neural network.

prototyping In system development, a strategy in which a scaled-down system or portion of a system is constructed in a short time, tested, and improved in several iterations.

RapidMiner A popular, open-source, free-of-charge data mining software suite that employs a graphically enhanced user interface, a rather large number of algorithms, and a variety of data visualization features.

ratio data Continuous data where both differences and ratios are interpretable. The distinguishing feature of a ratio scale is the possession of a nonarbitrary zero value.

real-time data warehousing (RDW) The process of loading and providing data via a data warehouse as they become available.

reality mining Data mining of location-based data.

regression A data mining method for real-world prediction problems where the predicted values (i.e., the output variable or dependent variable) are numeric (e.g., predicting the temperature for tomorrow as 68°F).

relational database A database whose records are organized into tables that can be processed by either relational algebra or relational calculus.

Relational OLAP (ROLAP) The implementation of an OLAP database on top of an existing relational database.

result (outcome) variable A variable that expresses the result of a decision (e.g., one concerning profit), usually one of the goals of a decision-making problem.

RFID A generic technology that refers to the use of radio frequency waves to identify objects.

risk A probabilistic or stochastic decision situation.

robot A machine that has the capability of performing manual functions without human intervention.

SAS Enterprise Miner A comprehensive, and commercial data mining software tool developed by SAS Institute.

scenario A statement of assumptions and configurations concerning the operating environment of a particular system at a particular time.

scorecard A visual display that is used to chart progress against strategic and tactical goals and targets.

search engine A program that finds and lists Web sites or pages (designated by URLs) that match some user-selected criteria.

SEMMA An alternative process for data mining projects proposed by the SAS Institute. The acronym "SEMMA" stands for "sample, explore, modify, model, and assess."

sensitivity analysis A study of the effect of a change in one or more input variables on a proposed solution.

sentiment analysis The technique used to detect favorable and unfavorable opinions toward specific products and services using a large numbers of textual data sources (customer feedback in the form of Web postings).

unsupervised learning   A method of training artificial neural networks in which only input stimuli are shown to the network, which is self-organizing.

user interface   The component of a computer system that allows bidirectional communication between the system and its user.

utility (on-demand) computing   Unlimited computing power and storage capacity that, like electricity, water, and telephone services, can be obtained on demand, used, and reallocated for any application and that are billed on a pay-per-use basis.

virtual (Internet) community   A group of people with similar interests who interact with one another using the Internet.

virtual team   A team whose members are in different places while in a meeting together.

virtual worlds   Artificial worlds created by computer systems in which the user has the impression of being immersed.

Voice of Customer (VOC)   Applications that focus on "who and how" questions by gathering and reporting direct feedback from site visitors, by benchmarking against other sites and offline channels, and by supporting predictive modeling of future visitor behavior.

Web 2.0   The popular term for advanced Internet technology and applications, including blogs, wikis, RSS, and social bookmarking. One of the most significant differences between Web 2.0 and the traditional World Wide Web is greater collaboration among Internet users and other users, content providers, and enterprises.

Web analytics   The application of business analytics activities to Web-based processes, including e-commerce.

Web content mining   The extraction of useful information from Web pages.

Web crawler   An application used to read through the content of a Web site automatically.

Web mining   The discovery and analysis of interesting and useful information from the Web, about the Web, and usually through Web-based tools.

Web service   An architecture that enables assembly of distributed applications from software services and ties them together.

Web structure mining   The development of useful information from the links included in Web documents.

Web usage mining   The extraction of useful information from the data being generated through Web page visits, transactions, and so on.

Weka   A popular, free-of-charge, open-source suite of machine-learning software written in Java, developed at the University of Waikato.

wiki   A piece of server software available in a Web site that allows users to freely create and edit Web page content, using any Web browser.

INDEX

Note: Page numbers followed by t or f refer to tables or figures. Those followed by an A or T refer to Applications Cases or Technology Insights boxes respectively.

A

Academic applications, 205
Access modeling, 54t, 63, 67f
AccessNS, 5
Access to data sources, 45
Accuracy metrics for classification
    models, 159t
Active, concept of, 67f, 69t
  active data warehousing (ADW), 30,
    65, 66A
  corporate information factory, 41f, 44, 69
  compared, 69t
  decision evolution, 67f
  definitions, 65
  real-time realities, 65, 68T
  teradata EDW, 67f
  traditional data warehouse compared, 69t
Active Server Pages (ASP), 240
Active tags, 262
Activity-based costing (ABC), 114
Acxiom, 13
  PersonicX, 13
Ad hoc or on-demand reports, 9, 18,
  59T, 67f
Ad hoc queries, 12, 26, 85
  and analysis, 67f
Advanced analytics, 72
Advanced business analytics, 72
Advanced Scout, 147
Advances in Social Network Analysis and
  Mining conference, 254
Aer Lingus, 205–206A
Agglomerative classes, 166
Airline industry and text mining, 205–206A
AJAX (Asynchronous JavaScript and
  XML), 249
Adkaike Information Criterion, 165
Albertson's, 262
Alerting, 5, 12, 225
Alert systems, 9f, 15, 62, 77A
Algorithms, 166, 168–169
  Apriory, 145, 154, 168, 169f
  backpropagation learning, 171f
  CART/SPRINT, 133f, 163, 174, 175t, 177f
  Genetic, 162
  K-means, 166, 166f
  Minimum Volume Embedding
    algorithms, 268
Allied Signal, 106
All-in-one software packages, 21
Alumni Connect, 254
Amazon.com, 135 , 221
Ambeo, 70T
Analysis, 40, 134, 212. *See also* specific types
Analysis Services, 228A
Analytical applications, 13t
Analytical decision making, 97, 135
Analytical processing, 32. *See also* Online
  Analytical processing (OLAP)

Analytic application, activities available, 13t,
  72, 248
Analytic processing, 17–18
Angoss Software, 174, 177f, 222t
Application service provider (ASP), 243
Application tier, of BPM system, 240, 240f
Apollo Management, 84
Apriory algorithm, 154, 168, 169f
Area under the ROC curve method, 161, 161f
Architecture
  best selection, 43–45
  of BI, 10, 10f
  factors affecting selection, 44t
  independent data marts, 41f
  open-source frameworks,
  warehousing architecture, 38–45, 38f, 39f,
    41–42, 41f, 43f
  web-based, 39f
  See also specific types
Arkansas, state of, 176
Artificial intelligence, 9. *See also* Neural
  networks
Artificial neural network (ANN). *See* Neural
  networks
Ascential, 20
Ash Institute for Democratic Governance
  and Innovation (JFK School of
  Government), 126
Ask.com, 222
ASP model, 71
Association rule, 167
Associations, 141, 144–145, 166–168
  defined, 212
  neural network, 174
  rule learning, 144
  rule mining, 166–168
  text mining, 212
Assumption checklist, 94A
AT&T, 34A, 65, 251
Authority, 218
Automated decision systems (ADS), 14–15
  event-driven alerts, 15
  framework, 15f
  intelligent price setting example, 14–15A
Automatic content personalization,
  224f, 233f
Automatic summarization, 199
Axons, 169
Axson, David, 96

B

BA. *See* Business analytics
Back-end systems, 240–240
Bag-of-words, 195–196
Balance, in BSC, 99
Balanced scorecard (BSC), 103 –104, 104f
  aligning strategies and actions, 104–106
  definition and functions, 103–104

  integration with Six Sigma, 111
  as methodology, 12, 103 –104, 104f, 105
  for performance measurement, 103 –104,
    104f
  Six Sigma compared, 111t
Banking, 146
Bayesian classifiers, 162
Bayesian Information Criterion, 165
BEA, 241
Bebo, 251
Benchmarks, 98
Best Buys, 262
Bethune, Gordon, 77
BI. *See* Business intelligence
BI Competency Center (BICC), 19
Binary frequencies, 209
Biomedical applications, 203–205
  gene/protein interactions identification,
    204f
BioText, 205
Briefing book, 191A
Blogs, 233–234
Bloomberg, Mayor, 126
Blue Cross and Blue Shield, 163–164A
Bootstrapping method, 161
BPM Standards Group, 85
Branch, 162
Brobst, Stephen, 68T
Brokerage and securities trading, 146
BSC. *See* Balanced scorecard
Budget-centric planning, 90
Budgeting, and financial planning,
  90–91, 114
BPM applications, 112–114
Business activity monitoring (BAM), 34
  benefits, 20
  described, 20
  enterprise data warehouse (EDWW)
    and, 34
  real-time BI, 20
  vendors, 20
Business analytics (BA), 1–11
  advanced applications, 10, 72
  data mining, 136–137A
  defined, 10
  essentials, 16f
  input data for, 126, 173A
  reports and queries, 10
  success and usability, 18, 235, 236
  tools and techniques, 10–11
  using the Web, 218f, 220–221
  why projects fail, 95
Business cycles, time compressed, 12
Business environment
  changes and computerized decision
    support, 6–8
  complexity for organizations, 6–7
  major factors, 7t
  organizational responses, 7–8
  understanding, 149